Hawaii

with Kids

Open Road *is* Travel!

Praise for Rachel Christmas Derrick's *Hawaii Guide*

Recommended by *Conde Nast Traveler,* the first edition of *Hawaii Guide* was named one of the three best American and Canadian guidebooks by the Lowell Thomas Travel Journalism Awards. The judges noted: "The author's conversational writing style and obvious knowledge of Hawaii lead the reader effortlessly and enjoyably from one island to the next. . . . [Her] willingness to express her personal reaction to restaurants, hotels, and sightseeing attractions enhances the book's readability and lifts it out of the sterility found in many others of this genre."

About the Author

Rachel Christmas Derrick has spent many years poking around the Hawaiian Islands (even "forbidden" Niihau), evaluating everything from familiar attractions to lesser known wonders. The author of Open Road Publishing's award-winning *Hawaii Guide*, she now turns her sights on the special vacation needs and interests of families with children. Her extensive travels with her husband and their young daughter and son have convinced her that Hawaii is among the best places in the world to take kids.

Derrick's articles about Hawaii and elsewhere have been published in *The New York Times, The New York Daily News, The New York Post, The Washington Post, The Boston Globe, Los Angeles Times, Islands, Travel & Leisure, Essence, Modern Bride*, and *Newsweek*, among many others. In addition to Hawaii, assignments have sent her to Bora Bora, Moorea, Australia, England, Wales, Brazil, Costa Rica, Mexico, Bermuda, The Bahamas, and throughout the Caribbean.

Open Road *is* Travel!

Open Road Publishing has guide books to exciting, fun destinations on four continents. As veteran travelers, our goal is to bring you the best travel guides available anywhere!

No small task, but here's what we offer:

• All Open Road travel guides are written by authors with a distinct, opinionated point of view – not some sterile committee or team of writers. Our authors are experts in the areas covered and are polished writers.

• Our guides are geared to people who want to make their own travel choices. We'll show you how to discover the real destination – not just see some place from a tour bus window.

• We're strong on the basics, but we also provide terrific choices for those looking to get off the beaten path and experience the country or city – not just see it or pass through it.

• We give you the best, but we also tell you about the worst and what to avoid. Nobody should waste their time and money on their hard-earned vacation because of bad or inadequate travel advice.

• Our guides assume nothing. We tell you everything you need to know to have the trip of a lifetime – presented in a fun, literate, no-nonsense style.

• And, above all, we welcome your input, ideas, and suggestions to help us put out the best travel guides possible.

෩

Hawaii

with Kids

Open Road *is* Travel!

Rachel Christmas Derrick

Open Road Publishing

Open Road Publishing

We offer travel guides to American and foreign locales. Our books tell it like it is, often with an opinionated edge, and our experienced authors always give you all the information you need to have the trip of a lifetime. Write for your free catalog of all our titles:

Open Road Publishing
P.O. Box 284, Cold Spring Harbor, NY 11724
E-mail: Jopenroad@aol.com

ISBN 1-59360-030-5
Library of Congress Control Number: 2004111066

Acknowledgments

A multitude of thanks goes to my research assistants, especially my husband Karlton, our daughter, Shamsa, and our son, Khari. You all know that I could not have written this book without you! I am also grateful to the tireless efforts of MaryAnne Howland, John Robert Howland, and June Christmas. Scores of other people, including many at the Hawaii visitors bureaus, made invaluable contributions to this book, helping with everything from information gathering to fact-checking, and I truly appreciate your assistance.

Contents

SIDEBARS

∾

SIDEBARS

᷈ꧥ

Hawaii

with Kids

1. INTRODUCTION

We introduced our daughter to Hawaii when she was just four months old. OK, so now at age seven she doesn't remember the first time she saw a whale—when it suddenly emerged only a few yards from our boat during a whale-watching trip off Maui. But she loves hearing the story of how she locked eyes with the humpback as the crew excitedly explained that the whale had caught them completely by surprise and that they hadn't meant to break conservation rules by getting so close. With its dramatic wildlife and many other captivating attractions, Hawaii offers constant adventures (and perpetual tales) for children—and adults—of all ages.

However, these islands lure visiting *ohana* (families) with much more. Family ties are a big deal in Hawaii, and it shows. On weekends, beaches and public parks are full of multigenerational local ohana picnicking, singing to slack-key guitars and ukuleles, or just "talking story." Elaborate traditional luau celebrating babies' first birthdays rival wedding receptions. But in Hawaii, "family" isn't limited by blood. Local *keiki* ("KAY-kee," children) know lots of adults they call "Auntie" and "Uncle," whether they are relatives or not. The upbeat, easygoing atmosphere of these islands is all about embracing everyone, from singles to newlyweds, from toddlers to elderly grandparents.

With family travel among the state's fastest growing trends, it's easier than ever to vacation with the kids. A wide selection of accommodations, restaurants, and activities invites families with children to stay, play, and dine together while allowing parents and children worry-free time apart as well. Almost everywhere you go, it's clear that kids are truly appreciated. So don't be surprised if a giddy child who makes a full speed break across the irresistibly open space of a hotel lobby is met with a sweeping arm catch from a friendly staff member instead of with steely glares.

Phenomenal Family Fun

The 50th state is famous for its amazing coastlines—with sand that ranges in color from white, golden, and black to gray, green, and even red—and its mammoth waves that turn master surfers into local heroes. Snorkeling and scuba diving give thrilling peeks at the Pacific's multi-hued underworld. However, you certainly wouldn't want your kids to think that you flew more than two thousand miles just to get wet. By all means, hit the ocean as often as you can. Even when you think you've found your favorite beach, a short drive or an exhilarating hike will take you to yet another beautiful sandy stretch. But also be sure not to miss Hawaii's other pleasures that seem tailor-made for families with children.

While Oahu, Maui, the Big Island of Hawaii, Kauai, Molokai, and Lanai each has a distinct personality, within each island is a convenient wealth of contrasting vistas and activities as well. Mother Nature offers arid volcanic moonscapes, lush valleys, thundering waterfalls, and soaring cliffs for viewing and exploring. Ride bicycles down a mountainside, kayak along a tranquil river, or get up close and personal with a dolphin.

You can also take a helicopter or submarine ride, visit a science museum, or board an old sugarcane train. For a taste of Hawaiian culture, try the sensuous moves of hula dancing, learn to string a *lei*, or sample *lomi lomi* salmon at an oceanside luau. Step into the past with a visit to a royal palace or the ruins of a *heiau* ("HAY-ow," an ancient temple). Or simply play a game of *konane* ("ko-NAH-nay," Hawaiian checkers) while relaxing on your *lanai* (patio or balcony) and absorbing your gorgeous surroundings.

Lots of adventures in Hawaii have been designed especially with children in mind: The whole family can take surfing lessons, go behind the scenes with a zookeeper, or join an after-dark flashlight tour of an aquarium for a look at nocturnal marine life. On Turtle Independence Day, you can snap photos of your children as they carefully carry baby green sea turtles to the ocean to be released.

You Deserve a Break

Whether you are a couple or a single parent, there may come a time when you need a break from the kids. Send them off on an overnight camping trip on a battleship or sign them up for one of the day camp-like programs that many of the larger hotels and condos offer. This book also includes details for finding good babysitters or popular teen hangouts for the kids so you can sneak off to romantic spots, health spas, exercise facilities, and the golf course.

Sleeping & Eating

Places for families to stay in Hawaii are as diverse as the islands themselves. Bedrooms come in everything from sprawling resorts complete with gourmet restaurants and chocolate-covered macadamia nuts on pillows at night to private beachfront houses, from condos with living rooms and fully-equipped kitchens to no-frills camping cottages. When it's time to dine, plenty of good restaurants win children over with kids' menus, crayons, and patient, engaging waiters.

Fun Facts & Helpful Tips

Look for sidebars with fun facts and helpful tips for both parents and kids. For instance, I offer suggestions for enhancing children's experiences, such as mailing unboxed coconuts instead of postcards to friends at home and keeping daily journals. To give everyone a feel for local culture, I've included plenty of Hawaiian legends and historical tidbits.

Whether you are traveling with squirmy infants, the Are-we-there-yet?-set, self-sufficient teens, or all of the above, *Hawaii with Kids* will help you design a vacation that suits the varied desires of your whole family.

Chapter 2

OVERVIEW

We had run out of snacks and our three-year-old daughter and 18-month old son were not happy. We kept pointing to the umbrella-like monkeypod trees, tubular African tulips, and splashes of magenta bougainvillea outside the car windows, but we gathered from the rising wails that the children weren't falling for our attempt at distraction. Then my husband spotted a roadside fruit stand piled high with papayas and bananas. But no vendor was in sight. Luckily, however, we noticed the sign that invited us simply to take some fruit and leave our money in a box. Double-fisted with fresh, sweet bananas, the kids were suddenly (and thankfully) quiet.

This roadside honor system exemplifies Hawaii's spirit of *aloha*, brought to this Pacific archipelago by Polynesians more than a millennium ago. Often replacing the words "hello" and "good-bye," aloha has come to mean many different things—from trust, tolerance, graciousness, and understanding to friendliness, caring, and love. Above all, it encompasses the ideal of healthy interaction among human beings and between people and their environment. The second most important Hawaiian word visitors young and old should master is *mahalo* (mah-HAH-low), which means "thank you." To really impress residents, try saying *mahalo nui loa* (mah-HAH-low NOO-ee LOW-ah), mean-

Prices & Telephone Numbers

All prices quoted in this book are subject to change without notice. When no telephone area code appears, the number is local, using Hawaii's **808** area code.

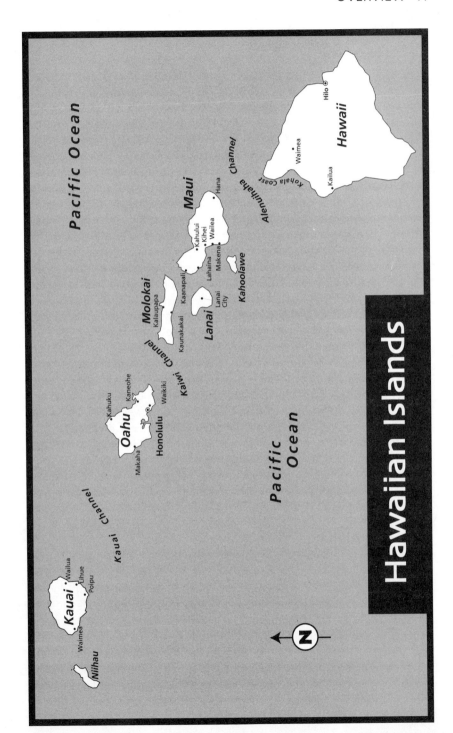

ing "Thank you so much." *To learn more Hawaiian words, see Chapter 7, "Talking Like a Local."*

Collecting Smiles
Sometimes we ask our kids to count the smiles they get each day in Hawaii when they say "aloha" or "mahalo."

Crossroads of Cultures
Hawaii-loa, the Polynesian sailor who legend says discovered these Pacific islands somewhere between 300 and 750 A.D., gave them his name. Today few other places rival the mostly harmonious racial and cultural blending that characterizes the diverse population of this 50th American state. This is one of the reasons that, in a world with countless other gorgeous, beach-fringed islands to choose from, more than four million mainlanders vacation in Hawaii each year.

Some residents of Hawaii proudly announce their multi-cultural heritage. Your chatty tour bus driver might mention that he's Hawaiian-Chinese-Portuguese or if you get into a conversation with your waiter, she might talk about her Filipino-Puerto Rican-Korean ancestry. There is a greater concentration of Japanese and other Asians in Hawaii than anywhere else in the country. This is the only U.S. state where Caucasians are not the majority.

Many residents are quick to make the distinction between being Hawaiian (a descendant of the original brown-skinned inhabitants of the islands) and being from Hawaii (anyone of any race or ethnic group who was born here or has lived here a long time). As exotic as these islands may seem, remind your children to resist the urge to refer to the rest of the country as "the United States" or "America." If you say "the mainland" or "the continental U.S.," you'll avoid annoyed corrections.

Spreading Aloha
While some 130 islands, sandbars, and exposed reefs make up this Pacific state, the main inhabited islands are Oahu (home of Honolulu and Waikiki), Maui, Hawaii (a.k.a. the Big Island), Kauai, Molokai, and Lanai. With its closest neighbor the diminutive Christmas Island chain, about 2,000 miles to the south, Hawaii is the most isolated group of islands on earth. Some 2,400 miles of ocean lie between this U.S. state and North America, the nearest continent. The islands of Hawaii began forming 25 to 40 million years ago when volcanoes gurgled, spouted, and belched their way up through cracks in the ocean floor. In a few short centuries, the spirit of aloha may spread to a new member of the archipelago. About 30 miles off the coast of the Big Island, another island, Loihi, is in gestation.

Which Island Should We Visit?

Which Hawaiian island (or islands) should you choose for your family vacation? I had traveled to Hawaii for many years B.C. (before children) and thought I knew the ropes. Then when my husband and I became parents, we found that vacationing with the younger editions forced us to take in Hawaii at a much more delicious pace. Instead of scurrying around to three or four islands in a single trip, we now spend more time exploring different parts of one.

Here are highlights of the very different main islands, from the busiest to the quietest. The first four—Oahu, Maui, Hawaii, and Kauai—are much more developed and thus draw more visitors than the last two—Molokai and Lanai. Where more than one pronunciation of an island's name is given, the first is the most common and the last is the more correct. The symbol ' (used in authentic Hawaiian) indicates an abrupt pause before the following syllable.

O'ahu (oh-WAH-hoo)

The home of Honolulu, the capital of the state, Oahu is Hawaii's best-known island. It is only the third largest, after Hawaii and Maui, yet the majority of the state's population resides here. **Waikiki Beach**, **Pearl Harbor,** and the **USS Arizona Memorial** are the most popular tourist attractions in the state. Two other stops that are high on most families' lists are the outdoor **Polynesian Cultural Center** (where Hawaiians and people from other Pacific islands demonstrate ancient artistic, musical, and culinary traditions in authentic-looking "villages") and **Sea Life Park** (where whales, dolphins, and other aquatic entertainers put on great shows). Both parents and children can learn all about dolphins and even touch them in **Dolphin Quest** programs at the Kahala Mandarin Oriental hotel. Families also love the **Waikiki Aquarium**, the **Honolulu Zoo**, sprawling **Kapiolani Park**. Whether you want to board a battleship and a **submarine** or climb an extinct volcano and learn to snorkel, you can do it on Oahu.

The North Shore, across the island from Honolulu, is a world away from the highrises, shopping malls, and crowds of Waikiki. On this pastoral northern coast, waves curl at 30 feet during winter months. To the surprise of many who picture only Honolulu and Waikiki when they think of this island, most of mountainous Oahu is carpeted with countryside.

Maui (MOW-ee)

Looking down on Maui from the air, you'll see what appears to be two islands joined by a valley. The West Maui Mountains dominate the smaller northern segment, while towering **Haleakala volcano** rises in the southeastern region. Quiet towns, eucalyptus forests, and wild **rodeos** are found along the cool "upcountry" slopes of Haleakala. Watching the sun rise over its crater, then horseback riding or hiking into it, or riding a mountain bike down the volcano, are favorite activities among families with older children. Younger children love riding the **Sugar Cane Train** and visiting the **Maui Ocean Center**, a sprawling waterfront aquarium.

Kaanapali Beach, a long, gentle crescent backed by highrise hotels and condominiums, is a younger, more low-key version of Waikiki. Other, smaller resort areas offer more tranquil choices. **Historic Lahaina**, the old whaling port, was once the capital of the whole Hawaiian kingdom. Explore the depths in a **submarine** or go **whale watching**. During the winter, Maui is the best island for spotting these humpbacks, either by boat or from shore (so you might want to pack some binoculars). One of Maui's most spectacular drives is along the winding coastal "highway" that leads to isolated **Hana**, a lush, drowsy town tucked away in the southeast. Here you are much more likely to hear people speaking Hawaiian than in the rest of Maui, which is home to many transplants from Southern California and other parts of the mainland.

Hawai'i (hah-WHY-ee, hah-WHY'ee, or hah-VIE'ee)

Commonly referred to as the **Big Island**, Hawaii is so much larger than its siblings that the rest of the chain could fit inside it—with room to spare. Hawaii is the only island where you can see **active volcanoes**, which spout fireworks from time to time. With stark, ebony lava flows stretching for miles, it is also the most unusual-looking member of the family. The sand of beaches comes in white, black, salt and pepper, and even green!

In sharp contrast to its volcanic moonscape, the island boasts rain forests, flower nurseries, and lush valleys. **Rodeos** are held on one of the largest privately owned cattle ranches in the US. The beach-rimmed Kona Kohala Coast, in the west, is treated to the least amount of rainfall in all of inhabited Hawaii. Here at the Mauna Lani Bay Hotel & Bungalows in July, visiting children can help release the once-endangered **green sea turtles** that the hotel raises. **Submarine rides** let you explore the undersea world without getting wet. Mauna Kea volcano is so tall that it is sometimes covered with snow—and experts even ski down its slopes!

Kaua'i (cow-WHY, COW-why, or cow-WAH'ee)

By many accounts the most beautiful Hawaiian island, Kauai is a relative newcomer to tourism. Tiny rural towns are flanked by miles of sugarcane fields and flourishing foliage. The island's jagged mountains, plunging waterfalls, and isolated beaches have played supporting roles in films such as *South Pacific, Jurassic Park,* and *Raiders of the Lost Ark.*

Although Kauai receives more rain than other Hawaiian islands, a visit here is well worth risking a few soggy days. Besides, the lush landscape is almost as stunning when wet. The driest part of the island is around Poipu in the south, where sandy crescents scallop the shore. Unlike most children's programs that don't take kids until age five, the day camp at Poipu's **Hyatt**

Regency Kauai is open to potty-trained children as young as three. Among the island's most impressive natural attractions are massive, arid **Waimea Canyon** and the awesome cliffs of **Na Pali coast**. Families love the tranquility of **kayaking** along the Hanalei River and the exhilaration of **surf kayaking** in the ocean.

Moloka'i (MOLE-oh-kye or mole-oh-KAH'ee)

Mention Molokai to mainlanders, and the first thing many say is, "Oh, you mean where the leper colony is?" Molokai is certainly famous for the victims of Hansen's Disease, whose tragic story you can learn all about. But it is also known for its unspoiled landscape, slow pace, and delightfully small number of tourists. For older children and adults, one of Molokai's most exciting activities is a ride down a 2,000-foot cliff on the back of a mule.

In the verdant eastern region, the road winds heavenward to striking cliff-edge views. At the island's largest hotel, in the arid west, visitors may choose among different "campsites" (where they slumber in fancy bungalows with private baths) or stay in an attractive modern lodge. In January you and your kids can watch local children compete in Hawaiian games during the annual **Makahiki Festival**, a revival of an old peacetime celebration.

Lana'i (lahn-EYE or lah-NAH'ee)

In 1922, Jim Dole bought most of Lanai to start the fields that gave "The Pineapple Island" its nickname. While neat rows of this sweet juicy fruit once blanketed the island, other types of agriculture now grow in its place. After slumbering happily with a single 10-room hotel since the 1940s, Lanai was transformed in a major way by the birth of two luxury hotels, the first in 1990 and the second the following year.

Before then, most visitors were friends of residents, hunters, or hardy travelers looking for unadulterated peace and quiet way off the beaten path. True, the number of hotels tripled. But since the grand total is only three, the island remains almost as undeveloped as before. The beachfront **Manele Bay Hotel** draws families with its children's program focusing on exciting Hawaiian cultural activities. Searching for ancient **petroglyphs** (rock carvings) and eerie **rock formations** continues to be a favorite visitor pastime. Locals are still quick to strike up conversations with vacationers over drinks on the wooden porch of the island's original accommodation, Hotel Lanai. Many residents of Lanai "City," the quiet inland plantation town nestled amid spikey Norfolk pines, welcome the advent of all the non-plantation jobs that larger-scale tourism has brought.

Top 10 Beaches for Kids (and Their Adults)

Many visitors flock to Waikiki Beach on Oahu and Kaanapali on Maui, but residents head to lots of other quieter strands of sand. With calm waters perfect for both adults and kids, here are some family favorites:

1. Napili Beach, *Maui*

This is what you come to Hawaii for—a placid cove frequented by turtles, eels, and reef fish and edged by a stunning curve of talcum studded with palms.

2. Kauna'oa Beach, *Hawaii, the Big Island*

Back in 1965 when Laurance Rockefeller built the first resort along the lava-strewn, desolate-looking Kohala coast, he had his pick of untouched golden beaches—and he chose this still-pristine beauty where summer waves are calm enough for kids.

3. Kailua Beach, *Oahu*

Here the soft white stuff is great for building sand castles, the small shore-break waves attract young boogie boarders, and teenagers come for the volleyball games.

4. Hulopoe Beach, *Lanai*

Spinner dolphins often make their corkscrew leaps out of the water just offshore, and kids love exploring the tidal pools.

5. Hapuna Beach, *Hawaii, the Big Island*

During the summer, the waves along this gorgeous shore are sedate enough for young children, while the churning winter surf draws teen bodysurfers.

6. Baldwin Beach Park, *Maui*

With the West Maui mountains in the background, this is among the island's most beautiful sandy expanses.

7. Dixie Maru Beach, *Molokai*

Although local families stream in on weekends, this tranquil spot is never really crowded, and visiting children easily find local buddies.

8. Poipu Beach Park, *Kauai*

Good for swimming and bodysurfing, as well as palm-shaded picnics, this beach sports a shallow natural pool that seems designed for toddlers and other young children.

9. Hanauma Bay, *Oahu*

Colorful, fish-packed waters make for excellent walk-in snorkeling off this protected crescent where smoking is prohibited.

10. Lydgate Beach Park, *Kauai*

When the kids need a break from the sand, they can hang with local children in the playground.

While all beaches in Hawaii are public, some have chairs, umbrellas, or facilities that are available to hotel guests only.

Hawaiian History in a (Kukui) Nutshell

Without a written language, early Hawaiians preserved much of their history, as we know it today, in their lyrical legends, soothing songs, expressive hula dances, and detailed oral genealogies. After they arrived from Boston, Massachusetts, in 1820, American missionaries developed the first written version of the Hawaiian language. By 1846, Hawaiians were among the most literate people in the world.

Here are a few other highlights of Hawaii's past:

• circa 300-750 A.D.

After traveling some 2,500 miles in 60- to 100-foot double-hulled sailing canoes, Polynesians (probably from the Marquesas, now part of French Polynesia) are the first people to arrive in Hawaii. Carrying whole families along with dogs, pigs, and fowl, their masted vessels also bring plants that will become staples in Hawaii, among them taro, breadfruit, yams, sugarcane, coconuts, and bananas.

Don't You Dare!

To follow the will of the gods, a system of strict *kapu* (taboos) evolved among the early Hawaiian settlers. Adhering to the *kapu* was considered crucial to the well-being of individuals and of the group. Some of these restrictions were geographic, others dietary. For instance, women were not allowed to prepare or cook food, nor were they permitted to eat bananas, coconuts, or pork. Men were prohibited from eating dogmeat. Violating these or any other *kapu*, even unknowingly, would result in severe punishment, often swift death.

• circa 1300

The first settlers are joined by Tahitians, most likely from the island of Raiatea (whose ancient name was Haiviki). Tahitians introduce rituals of human sacrifice, but they also bring sophisticated practices for preserving the environment while maintaining healthy livestock and agriculture.

• 1778

British Captain James Cook, commander of the H.M.S. *Resolution* and the H.M.S. *Discovery*, lands at Kauai. He christens the archipelago the Sandwich Islands after the fourth Earl of Sandwich, his patron.

• 1779

Cook is killed during a dispute with residents over a longboat stolen from one of his ships.

•1810

King Kamehameha I, a.k.a., Kamehameha the Great, a towering 6' 6" tall, becomes Hawaii's most powerful leader after bringing all the islands under his rule.

•1819

After Kamehameha I dies, feisty Kaahumanu, his favorite wife, convinces the new king to do away with Hawaii's longstanding *kapu* (taboos).

•1820

Without the foundation of their ancient cultural traditions, Hawaiians are receptive to the religious teachings of American missionaries, who first arrive at Kealakekua Bay on the Big Island.

•1849

Along with France and Great Britain, the United States recognizes Hawaii as an independent country after Kamehameha III transforms the islands into a constitutional monarchy.

•1852

With Western diseases continuing to kill Hawaiians in huge numbers, foreign workers must be recruited. Chinese indentured laborers are the first to arrive, to work on sugar plantations and as domestics for wealthy Caucasian families. This is the beginning of a dramatic shift in Hawaii's population that will forever alter the racial and ethnic makeup of the islands. For nearly the next 100 years, people from other countries stream into Hawaii to live and work. The Japanese start to come in 1868, and Filipinos, Koreans, Portuguese, Puerto Ricans, Norwegians, and Germans follow.

•1875

Hawaii signs a treaty with the United States that gives the islands a duty-free market for sugar in the U.S.

•1891

Upon his death, King Kalakaua is succeeded by his sister Liliuokalani, who becomes the last Hawaiian monarch.

•1893

Queen Liliuokalani announces that she will draw up a new constitution, one that returns rule of the country to the monarchy and restores the right to vote and to run for office to Hawaiians (not just Caucasians). Declaring her intended actions revolutionary, a small, independent group of Caucasian businessmen (most of whom are Hawaiian-born sons of American missionaries) promptly deposes her.

• 1894

Sanford Dole is named president of what is now called "The Republic of Hawaii." In vain, practically every Hawaiian in the islands, nearly 40,000 people, sign a petition of protest sent to U.S. President Grover Cleveland.

• 1895

After a failed coup attempt by supporters of Liliuokalani, she is imprisoned in Iolani Palace for almost eight months.

• 1898

President William McKinley gives the annexation of Hawaii the green light.

• 1903

Hawaii's pineapple industry takes shape when James Dole, a cousin of Sanford Dole (who was appointed the first governor of the territory of Hawaii in 1901), produces some 2,000 cases of pineapple. This fruit will overtake sugarcane as Hawaii's top crop.

• 1941

Thousands of U.S. servicemen and many civilians die when the Japanese suddenly attack Pearl Harbor on December 7th, causing the US to enter into World War II.

• 1959

Hawaii is granted statehood by Congress. Daniel Inouye becomes the first American of Japanese ancestry to serve in the U.S. House of Representatives and the U.S. Senate gets its first American of Chinese ancestry, Hiram Fong. The first Boeing 707 jets link Hawaii to San Francisco. By the end of the year, tourism is booming on Oahu.

• 1986

John Waihe'e is elected governor, making him the first Hawaiian to lead the islands since the overthrow of the monarchy nearly a century ago.

• 2002

Kilauea Volcano, on the Big Island of Hawaii, marks the twentieth year of its current eruption, the longest in recorded history of any volcano.

Chapter 3

TRAVELING WITH KIDS

As far as family-friendly activities go beyond the beach and pool, Oahu entertains with the greatest number of choices, followed by Maui and the Big Island of Hawaii. However, especially if your main focus is strengthening family bonds and spending some time unwinding together, Kauai, Molokai, and Lanai are also good choices. No matter which island or islands you select, here are some tips on making getting to and from Hawaii, and being there, as pleasant as possible for the whole family.

Think Hawaiian

To get you and your family into the spirit of these Pacific islands, read some of the legends and historical tidbits in Chapter 9, "Hawaiian Tales." In fact, these stories can be good entertainment during your long plane ride, and they make great bedtime reading during your trip.

Make a List

When we started traveling with our children, gone were the days when we could fit everything we needed into suitcases small enough to wheel onto the plane. It's amazing how much paraphernalia such little people require. So it's easy to forget something crucial. Make a check list—and don't forget to check it right before you leave for the airport! This is particularly important for your carry-ons. Sure, you can buy underwear or toothbrushes in Hawaii if you forget to pack them, but you can't buy diapers or pacifiers on the plane.

Don't Fear Flying

Hawaii is some 2,000 miles from the closest land. So unless you take a cruise (which will leave you with little time on terra firma), you're going to spend a lot of time in the air. Here are some tips for coping with air travel:

·When making flight reservations, ask for seats in the bulkhead of the plane. This area is more spacious than other rows.

·Request special meals (such as kids', vegetarian, or seafood) in advance and confirm them the day before your flight.

·If you're taking a baby on your vacation, it's best to bring along a car seat to use on the plane (and in your rental car during your stay). Because many airlines allow children under age two to fly free when sitting in an adult's lap, you may be tempted to forgo purchasing a seat for your infant. However, experts warn that leaving the car seat at home really isn't safe. Turbulence—always unpredictable—can easily injure the little one. You may wonder why you should bother buying a ticket for your child when there are often empty seats where you could put your car seat. The problem is that if the plane is full, you're in trouble.

·Besides, airlines often offer discounts for children age two to eleven.

·If you need to refrigerate baby bottles or if you have other child-related requests in the air, flight attendants are usually quite accommodating.

·To combat boredom, let young children each carry a backpack filled with a couple of their favorite toys, music or taped stories, coloring books, crayons, markers, pads, finger puppets, and books. Silly Putty, decks of cards, pipe cleaners, puzzles (with pieces in zip-lock plastic bags), and miniature magnetic checkers and chess also have served us well. And remember, these diversions are not just for the plane. You can use them throughout your trip.

·Be sure to bring some new items to surprise your kids with during the flight, and during the rest of the trip as well. Reveal these new diversions one at a time, over hours on the plane and over days during your vacation.

·When helping your children select which books to take, suggest a few long chapter books instead of lots of shorter books. This will cut down on weight and bulk.

Suckers

If you're traveling with infants or young kids, don't forget pacifiers, lollipops, or gum for them to suck or chew during take-offs and landings to stave off ear pressure pain.

Car Seats, Strollers, & Other Carriers

As I mention above, experts say a small child is safest on an airplane when strapped into a car seat, and you'll make good use of the seat if you rent a car during your trip. Auto rental agencies in Hawaii do rent car seats. However, despite your toddler-size reservation, you may discover when you get there that only infant seats are left, or that the sole remaining seat is sticky from the spilled juice of the previous occupant.

Once your child is about three years old, using a car seat on an airplane may no longer be practical. Larger legs or the shape of the car seat may mean that the meal tray cannot be folded down flat in front of the child, so everything from crayons to juice goes sliding off. But by law you'll still need the car seat for your rental car in Hawaii. Our solution has been to check our car seats with the rest of our luggage. We found padded car seat covers that enabled us to strap the seats on like backpacks for easy transport.

When our kids were younger, we could not have survived Hawaii without our Baby Bjorn (the all-fabric strap-on carrier that hugs the baby to your chest) and our light-weight, collapsible stroller. You can wheel the stroller all the way to the door of the plane, then check it with a flight attendant, and it will be waiting for you as soon as you deplane. When our son or daughter was not using the stroller in the airport and around Hawaii, it was great for carrying some of our bags.

Many parents also find that taking backpack carriers or durable, light-weight jogging strollers is great for times when little legs tire.

Immortalize Your Trip

Our daughter loves keeping a daily journal, and my earliest memories are of drawing pictures, stapling them into a "book," and dictating the stories to my parents to write. Whether in pictures, words, or both, journals can be a great way of preserving your travels.

Map it Out

Let the kids trace your journeys on maps, whether within a single island or from one to another. You can use a different color marker for each day of your vacation, and your kids can decide on the color code.

Be Prepared for Snack Attacks

If you're visiting islands other than Oahu (which has a convenient island-wide public bus system), you'll probably be spending a good amount of time driving. We like taking a lightweight thermal bag to carry water, juice, and munchies. Along with healthy treats like baby carrots and crackers, we pack local favorites such as taro chips, poi balls, or taro butter mochi (see Chapter

8, "Eating Like a Local"). A thermal bag also comes in handy for picnics at the beach or in the park.

Thirst Quenchers

When I was a kid, my mother used to freeze cans of juice for me to take on class trips. But by lunch time, most of the drink was still as hard as concrete. Other times she would add ice cubes to my juice container, but then I'd have to quench my thirst with a diluted mess. If you stay at an accommodation with a kitchen or at least a refrigerator with a freezer, here's a better trick for keeping beverages nice and cool while you are out and about: Fill half a water bottle with juice, then freeze it. When you're ready to hit the road, fill the other half with juice. (We also do this with water.) This way you can have a sip immediately while the frozen part keeps the rest cold for hours as it slowly melts.

Play Games

Hawaii is full of amazing scenery along long, winding roads. There's nothing worse than having your blissful appreciation of nature's beauty punctured by whines of "When are we gonna get there?" Kids love games—especially if a little friendly competition is involved. To keep our children occupied during long drives, we play Twenty Questions and make up songs. A real winner in our family is seeing who will be the first to spot the next group of horses or cattle in a field. Our kids love shouting "Cows on the left!" or "Horses on the right!"

Try challenging your kids (and yourselves) to learn, and use, a new Hawaiian or Pidgin word each day of your trip. To get you started, see Chapter 7, "Talking Like a Local."

Our children also enjoy playing counting games, with everything from the number of people wearing leis to the number of kids carrying surf boards. Especially in lush areas like Hanalei on Kauai and Hana on Maui, it's not unusual for rain to fall while the sun is still shining. Counting rainbows is another popular pastime in our family. Spotting a rainbow in East Maui, our three-year-old son once exclaimed, "It's so pretty I want to slide down it!"

Find a Good Babysitter

Sure, my husband and I love vacationing with our kids. But there are times when instead of helping our daughter cut her mahi mahi, we'd rather sip mai tais while quietly gazing across a candlelit table at each other, or instead of refereeing shouts of "He's touching me again!" and "She won't give me back my—!" we'd rather take an afternoon "nap" alone in our hotel room. Thank goodness for babysitters!

We've had great experiences with babysitting services in Hawaii. On most islands, you can arrange for a sitter to come to your hotel room, condo, or rental home, or you can have her take your kids outside, such as to the pool or beach. Some sitters bring their own toys to share with children to break the ice, so you may want to ask about this when you make your reservation.

Rates range from about $12-$15 an hour for one child to $15-$20 an hour for three siblings. Each additional sibling, cousin, or friend runs anywhere from $2-$7 an hour. There is usually a three- or four-hour minimum. Surcharges may apply after midnight or on holidays. Hawaii state tax may boost your total by 4.166%. You may also be charged for transportation or parking fees. Payment is generally in cash, but you may be asked for your credit card number to hold your reservation. You can usually find a good babysitter with a day or two's notice, but it's best to make arrangements as far in advance as possible. If you'd like to use the same sitter on more than one occasion, contact a service at least a week in advance. To arrange for a nanny to travel with you to more than one island, try to contact a company at least a month in advance.

Name Calling

In Hawaii it is considered polite for children to address adults such as family friends and babysitters as "Auntie" or "Uncle" so-and-so, instead of using just their first names, especially with older adults.

Here are some of the most reliable babysitting companies, island by island:

Oahu and the Big Island of Hawaii

Sitters Unlimited of Hawaii Tel. 808/674-8440, www.sittershawaii.com. Staffed by teachers, nurses, and other highly qualified caretakers, this company has been around since 1985. Sitters Unlimited carries Commercial General Liability Insurance and is licensed and bonded with the State of Hawaii Department of Commerce & Consumer Affairs. Sitters are trained and experienced in CPR and first aid. They have all been fingerprinted and cleared for TB and criminal records, including child abuse.

Aloha Nannies Tel. 808/394-5434. www.alohanannies.com. Mainly serving Oahu (but with some nannies also available on Maui, the Big Island, and Kauai), this company provides experienced CPR- and first aid-trained babysitters who are licensed and insured, have been tested for TB, and have had their backgrounds checked. Many families that use this service spend a few days with a nanny on Oahu, then take her when they travel to one of the other islands. Having the sitter share a room with the children can not only be cost effective but can allow parents much-needed rest. The cost for traveling with a nanny is about $100 a day, plus food and travel expenses, for up to 10 hours of daily work.

Maui

Happy Kids Maui Tel. 888-669-1991 or 808/667-5437, www.happykidsmaui.com. Serving all areas of Maui, this agency is bonded and insured, and babysitters are trained in CPR and first aid.

The Nanny Connection, Inc. Tel. 808/875-4777 or 808/667-5777, www.thenannyconnection.com. This child care referral service can also hook you up with an experienced babysitter who has been pre-screened and trained in CPR and first aid.

Kauai

Babysitters of Kauai Happy Kidds Tel. 808/632-2252, www.babysittersofkauai.com. All sitters who work for this company are age 20 or older, experienced, non-smokers, and trained in CPR and first aid. Happy Kidds, which serves all parts of Kauai, carries liability insurance.

Molokai

Here babysitters generally do not go to visitor accommodations. Instead, vacationers may take their children to the caregivers' homes. For recommended babysitters on this island, ask at your hotel or contact the **Molokai Visitors Association** Tel. 800/800/6367. Sometimes hotel housekeepers and other staff will agree to stay with your children after hours.

Lanai

If you're staying at the **Manele Bay Hotel**, call the resort to hire a babysitter trained in CPR and first aid. Tel. 808/565-7700. The sitter can play with your children in the children's room (used for the hotel's daily children's program), take them around the property, or entertain them in your hotel room.

Leaving the Kids

To get our kids (and ourselves!) comfortable with a new babysitter, we have her arrive at least a half hour before we need to leave. This way, the kids can get used to her while we are around, and we can leisurely give her any necessary instructions. Whenever possible, we use the same sitter if we want to go out again sans kids.

༂

Sign Up for a Children's Program

Particularly during Easter vacation, the summer, and the Christmas season, many of the larger resorts and some of the middle-sized ones offer supervised children's programs so parents can have a break while kids hang with their peers. There is generally an additional charge for these sessions, which are full- or half-day (morning or afternoon). Most include lunch. Among the activities offered in these "day camps" are lei-making classes, basket-weaving workshops, hikes, athletic competitions, swimming, and sand castle-building contests. Some resorts also offer movies and other entertainment at night. Evening programs may be every night or just one or two evenings a week and some include dinner.

At the **Kona Village Resort** on the Big Island, children rehearse all week for an on-stage hula performance at the Friday night luau. Most hotel programs are for children between the ages of five and twelve. However, the **Hyatt Regency Kauai** takes children as young as three (as long as they are potty trained). Rates for full-day children's programs run from about $25 to $65, including lunch and snacks. Half-day sessions range from about $25 without lunch to $50 with lunch.

Even when accommodations don't have full-fledged "camps," many, including **Hotel Hana-Maui**, offer individual classes, such as in *lauhala* weaving (palm-like leaves), or nature walks. Some, such as the **Kauai Marriott Resort & Beach Club**, have crafts sessions and other special activities for children as young as two if accompanied by an adult. These sessions are generally free to guests.

Turn to the island chapters in the book for details of accommodations that offer these special children's programs and activities. Note that some accommodations join forces for programs, so even if your hotel offers one, it may not be on the premises. Be sure to clarify this before signing up.

Here are a few other questions to ask ahead of time:
·What is the ratio of caretakers/counselors to children?
·How strict is the sign-in and sign-out policy for arrivals and departures?
·Are the children grouped by age?
·Exactly what activities will they engage in and where will they be taken?
·How much time will kids spend at the pool or beach and what kind of expert supervision will be provided?

Avoiding Problems

Remember to specify any food allergies before leaving your child at a hotel camp or with a babysitter. And don't forget to slather your son or daughter (and yourselves) with sunscreen each day before heading outdoors.

Go (Coco)Nuts!

Everyone gets postcards from vacationing friends. But how many people receive unboxed, unwrapped coconuts in their mail boxes? We've tried mailing coconuts to the mainland on several occasions, and it actually works. Your children's friends will get such a kick out of it. Be sure to find fallen coconuts that are brown (not green), with smooth surfaces. There should be a little liquid sloshing around inside. Use a thick, indelible marker to write the name, address, and greeting directly onto the coconut. When you have it weighed at the post office, be sure that the stamps are firmly affixed.

Some stores, in malls and elsewhere, sell coconuts for this purpose, but it is cheaper if you find and mail them yourself. One good place to look is under the coconut palms around the lava fields on the grounds of the Mauna Lani resort on the Big Island. (Be sure to wear sturdy shoes, since the lava can be very rough and sharp.)

·Is lunch or dinner included?
·In case of an emergency, how will staff find you?

Stay Safe

Being on vacation often tempts travelers to relax their safety standards. However, in Hawaii—and anywhere else in the world—you and your children should take the same precautions that you would at home:

·Make sure that your children carry some form of identification, with their names, your names, your cell phone number(s), and the name, location, and telephone number of the accommodation where you are staying. Particularly for when you are at the beach or pool (when they may not have this ID on them), be sure that your children know their full names, your full names, and the names of their hometowns.

·Remind young children to keep you in sight, no matter where they are, and you do the same for them, especially when you are at the beach or pool.

·If young children do get separated from you, they should either ask the closest woman with a child for help or go to the nearest person who works at a hotel, restaurant, or store. Tell them to look for someone behind a desk or counter or wearing a uniform, such as a security guard, police officer, or waiter. Siblings (or friends) should remain together and children should not leave the area where they last saw you until you come to get them.

·Remind older children not to hitch-hike.

·As on the mainland, using marijuana (a.k.a. *pakalolo*) is illegal in Hawaii. Anyone who possesses, smokes, sells or grows it is subject to severe penalties. Possession of cocaine is far more serious. Remind your kids that narcotics officers don't give special treatment to visitors who are "just having a little fun" on their vacation.

·The legal drinking age is 21 in Hawaii.

·No alcohol is permitted in Hawaii's state or national parks.

Chapter 4

PLANNING YOUR TRIP

Especially when you are traveling with kids, the more planning you do before you go, the more enjoyable and hassle-free your vacation will be. Hawaii is full of different things to see and do, even on the four islands that are much less busy than Oahu and Maui. To help you decide which island, or islands, appeal to you and your family, read about the highlights of each island in Chapter 2 and look for the section called "Which Island Should We Visit?"

Then turn to the individual island chapters later in the book for descriptions of the attractions, accommodations, and restaurants that my family, and many families I've spoken to, have enjoyed most. Island chapters also include details to help you choose the area (or areas) you'd like to stay in or visit, as well as tips for getting around. In Hawaii, there's something for children and adults of every age. So there's no reason that everyone in the family should not get to do something that he or she really wants. Remember, the name of the game is compromise. Don't give up that visit to Oahu's Hawaiiana-packed Bishop Museum just because your little one has a puny attention span. Simply make your visit shorter than you otherwise would and take your child to Kapiolani Park afterwards to run around and play. The good thing about Hawaii is that so many of its best attractions are outdoors and wide open spaces are easy to come by.

Following are the nuts and bolts you'll need to help you decide when to go, how to get there, how to get around, and what type of accommodation to choose.

A Family Affair

Let your children help you plan your trip. As you read through this book, give them a few options and let them make some choices about what to do and see. Chapter 9, "Hawaiian Tales," is designed to get kids—and the rest of the family—into the aloha spirit before, during, and after your vacation.

When to Go
Weather

Generally speaking, weather in Hawaii can be divided into two seasons: summer and winter. Summer, which lasts from about May through mid-October, brings daytime temperatures in the mid-80s. This is the drier time of year. When it does rain, showers are usually brief. In the winter season, lasting from about mid-October through April, daytime temperatures hover in the high 60s to low 80s. At night, the mercury can dip as much as ten degrees so you may need light jackets or heavy sweaters at this time.

The high seasons, when some hotel prices are steeper and reservations are more difficult to come by, run from about mid-December into January, parts of March and April (when kids are out of school for Easter vacation and spring break), then again during the summer.

Spring and Fall (May through June and September through mid-October) can be the best times to go, since the islands are less crowded, the weather is driest, and the trade winds are at their most refreshing.

No matter what time of year, higher elevations are much colder than sea level. So if you intend to go to the summit of Haleakala volcano to watch the sun rise, for instance, be prepared with sweaters, jackets, hats, and even gloves.

Special Events

Throughout the year, Hawaii hosts scores of festivals, concerts, rodeos, crafts fairs, parades, street fairs, and other special events that appeal to families with children. For the most up-to-date calendar of events, call 800/GO-HAWAII (800/464-2924) or visit www.gohawaii.com.

Considering vacationing in the fall? You'll be just in time for the annual **Aloha Festivals** (www.alohafestivals.com), a statewide celebration of Hawaiian culture. From hula, local food, and parades to block parties with people dancing in the streets, the whole family can join in.

During the annual **Makahiki festival**, celebated in January on Molokai, visiting children can watch local kids compete in ancient Hawaiian games, from wrestling while standing on one leg to spear hurling.

In February, Maui kicks off the **Chinese New Year** with traditional lion dances down Front Street, Lahaina. Also in February, future marathoners age 12 and younger can join the 1+ mile **Keiki Great Aloha Fun Run & Circus Party** in Oahu. On the Big Island in March and April, the highlight of the week-long **Merrie Monarch Festival** is Hawaii's most prestigious hula competition.

On Oahu in June, music and hula performances accompany the **Kamehameha I decoration ceremony**, in which the king's statue is draped with 13-foot floral leis that have been made at the site throughout the day. Then, marching bands and floral floats fill Honolulu streets during the **King Kamehameha Day parade**.

What to Pack

Keep your suitcases as light as possible. By day, Hawaii is an extremely casual place. You'll spend most of your time in bathing suits, shorts and T-shirts, or sundresses, and sandals or rubber flip-flops (known as *zoris*, their Japanese name, or "slippers"). At night, dress can also be as casual as you want. However, if you're planning to splurge at any of Hawaii's excellent high-end restaurants, men should pack slacks and a couple of collared shirts (maybe a sports jacket as well) and women, a couple of dresses or nice skirts and tops.

Be sure to bring plenty of sun block and insect repellent, although you'll have no problem buying some once you arrive. If you'll be hiking, camping, or visiting high elevations (such as volcanoes), bring a heavy sweater and windbreaker, long pants, gloves, and sturdy walking shoes or sneakers. Strong shoes also come in handy if you're going to be walking across lava (for example, if you plan to search for petroglyphs or hunt for fallen coconuts on the Big Island).

Also see Chapter 3, *Traveling with Kids*, and Health Concerns in Chapter 5, *Basic Information*.

Using Travel Agents & Other Specialists

Before you talk to a travel agent, do some homework. Read through the descriptions of accommodations in this book. Scour newspaper travel sections for ads for money-saving deals. Travel agents should be able to advise you on flights that are discounted depending on the time of year, day of week, and time of day you want to travel. They should also provide inside information on getting the best rates for rental cars. Another source for the lowest available airfare is one of the discount companies such as Tel. 800/FLY-4-LESS.

Package Deals

Before you book a money-saving air-hotel-car rental package deal, remember that these packages are only worth the saving if they take you where you want to go and if you can stay where you want to stay. In some cases, hotels that are part of packages are those that don't sell out easily because they aren't of the best quality, or aren't in the most desirable locations; or, while the hotel may be fabulous, the package rooms may be in the least expensive category (a.k.a. small or view-less). Be sure you are clear about exactly what is included in the price of the package (airport transfers, continental breakfast, snorkeling cruise, etc.).

Many hotels offer family packages, including perks such as half-price additional rooms or "kids eat free" programs. See *Deciding Where to Stay*, below.

Booking Activities

As far as attractions go, it's generally cheaper to shop around for good tour deals once you arrive in Hawaii than to prebook through a travel agent or your hotel activities desk. You can save 20 percent to 40 percent if you go directly to tour agents. Tax will usually be added to the quoted price for cruises, horseback riding, helicopter tours, and other excursions.

Hang Loose

No matter how long or short your vacation, be sure to plan enough down time. Don't schedule an activity for every day of your trip. One day you might wake up dying to climb to the top of Diamond Head crater (yes, it's easy enough for kids), and another day you'll just want to relax. At age seven and five, our kids usually max out at one planned activity per day, with the rest of the time left for the ocean or pool.

Deciding Where to Stay

There is a wonderfully varied array of places to stay in Hawaii, from quiet vacation homes in residential areas to opulent beach resorts. Choices in between these extremes are plentiful. Settings range from oceanfront to mountainside, from lush to arid. Since competition for your presence is so stiff among accommodations here, there are many comfortable, moderately priced hotels and condominiums to choose from.

Many hotels have mini-refrigerators in rooms and coin-operated washers and dryers. Quite a few offer children's programs, but note that not all are on the premises. Along with lots of swimming, games, lei-making, sandcastle building, and other activities, some of these programs give each child a backpack stuffed with goodies such as a visor, T-shirt, and journal. While kids are in these supervised programs, parents can do their own thing. With 99 holes of golf at its four Hawaii properties and children's programs at resorts on Maui and the Big Island, **Prince Resorts Hawaii, Inc.** (Tel. 866-PRINCE-6, Web site: www.princeresortshawaii.com), for example, attracts parents who love teeing off.

Family packages put together by hotels might include tickets to a concert, meals for children under age 12, a family horseback outing, or golf lessons for the kids. For instance **Aston** (Tel. 800/922-7866,www.astonishingkids.com), with hotels and condominiums on Oahu, Maui, the Big Island of Hawaii, and Kauai, offers kids age 11 and younger free admission to top attractions, such as Oahu's Sea Life Park, Maui's Sugar Cane Train, and the Big Island's Parker Ranch museum.

Starwood Hotels (Tel. 888/488-3535, Web site: www.starwood.com) has 13 hotels and resorts on five islands (including Sheratons and Westins). With this collection's Family Value Vacation packages, you get a 50% discount on a second room and children under age 12 eat free at certain restaurants with a paying adult.

On several islands, **Outrigger** hotels and condos (Web site: www.outrigger.com) and the more economical **Ohana** properties (Web site: www.ohanahotels.com) also have lots of family-friendly features. Among the many other resorts with attractive family packages and programs are **Hilton Hawaiian Village** (Tel. 800/445-8667, www.hiltonhawaii.com/hhvrp.html) and **Turtle Bay Resort** (Tel. 808/293-6000, www.turtlebayresort.com), both on Oahu; the **Four Seasons Resort Hualalai** (Tel. 888/340-5662, www.fourseasons.com/hualalai), on the Big Island; and the **Hyatt Regency Kauai** (Tel. 808/742-1234 or 800/233-1234, www.hyatt.com).

Also see Chapter 3, *Traveling with Kids.*

Costs

All prices quoted in this book for accommodations are "rack rates," the published prices for one room, apartment, or cottage for one night. However, especially at the larger properties, major discounts (often in the form of package deals) are usually available. How much you save will depend on the number of nights you stay and the time of year you travel. Generally, children

---

Local Flavor

As soon as you arrive at your accommodation, check local newspapers or call the activities desk or the concierge to find out about local events taking place during your stay. You might turn up a fund-raising luau, a dance or musical performance, a street fair, or a drama production at a neighborhood theater. Many activities geared to families with children are free.

෨

under a certain age (often 12 or 18) stay free in their parents' room if using the existing bedding (usually two double or queen-size beds in a hotel room).

When it's time to pay your hotel bill, you'll find that 11.416% in state taxes has been added.

Top Hotels

Especially outside of Oahu (where Waikiki hotels are close together), most top hotels are in sprawling, beautifully landscaped, oceanfront settings. Particularly on Maui, the Big Island of Hawaii, Kauai, and Lanai, many have open-air lobbies with ponds and flourishing foliage. Some have extensive collections of Hawaiian, Pacific, and Asian art. Many have excellent day camp programs for children.

While hotels in Waikiki may not be as spacious, all top hotels have features including swimming pools; air-conditioned rooms with cable TV, stocked minibars, one or more telephones, clock-radios and lanais (balconies or patios); several restaurants (of far higher quality than you would expect to find in most mainland hotels); room service; daily and nightly entertainment; luau; Hawaiian crafts demonstrations; a full menu of sports; a tour-booking desk; and a highly professional, attentive staff.

Extras often come in the form of fresh flowers; bathrobes and slippers (for use during your stay); bathrooms with double sinks, an array of toiletries, both tubs and shower stalls, and separate rooms for toilets; in-room safes (sometimes for a per-use fee); coffee-makers; refrigerators; and nightly turn-down service with chocolates on your pillows. Internet access, fax machines, and other business-related services are generally available.

Even if you can't afford to spend your whole vacation in a top hotel, consider booking a room in one for a night or two just for the fun of it.

Mid-range Hotels

Often on or near beaches, many of these have a wide array of facilities, activities, and services, including swimming pools, tennis courts, a choice of restaurants, and nightly entertainment. Children's programs may be offered, but they may be at nearby resorts. Especially on Oahu, some of these hotels are frequently packed with tour groups.

Budget Hotels

Some are near beaches and many have swimming pools. Rooms tend to be basic, but comfortable, with no-frills decor. Fans often cool rooms instead of air conditioners. Some of the better budget hotels attract tour groups.

Condominiums

Maui weighs in with the widest selection of condos. However, these home-like units, from studios to multi-bedroom apartments, are plentiful on other islands as well. Families love them because having a kitchen means you don't have to drag the kids to a restaurant for every meal and you can always have snacks and beverages on hand.

While most of these accommodations don't have restaurants or night spots on the premises, many condo complexes are on the beach and the majority come complete with pools, cable TV, and other hotel-style facilities and services, plus washers and dryers. In most cases, these apartments are individually furnished by their owners, so units within a single complex may vary greatly in decor. Also, some may be only partially air-conditioned, with a ceiling fan cooling the bedroom or living room.

At some condos, the front office closes at night and it may be closed or have limited hours on weekends. So be sure to make check-in arrangements in advance if you plan to arrive off-hours. There may not be an activities desk to help you arrange tours or helicopter rides. Some units do not have telephones. A minimum stay of several nights may be required.

Especially outside of Oahu, some condos don't have elevators. So consider the location of your room when you're packing. My husband and I had lots of luggage during one of our month-long stays in Hawaii with our two young children. Lugging our suitcases, stroller, and other kid-related paraphernalia up to our unit, on the third floor, while keeping an eye on our two impatient preschoolers wasn't fun.

Housekeeping service is generally available, but it is not always daily, and it sometimes requires a surcharge. On another trip, we checked into a condo without reading the fine print. The next evening when we returned to our apartment after a long day out and about, we were surprised to discover that the beds were still unmade, the dishes were still in the sink, and our damp towels had not been changed. It turned out that housekeeping service would be provided only once during our weeklong stay (unless we arranged to pay more). We had assumed that because this condo was so upscale that daily cleaning service would be included in the cost of our unit.

Vacation Homes

If you're interested in renting a comfortable, beautifully appointed vacation home or cottage, whether by the beach or in the cool countryside, contact **Hawaii's Best Bed & Breakfasts** (Tel.-800/262-9912 or 808/985-7488, www.bestbnb.com). For the best selection, you'll need to make your rerservations about six months in advance for winter holidays and at least three months in advance the rest of the year.

Housekeeping Cabins

If you're traveling with hearty older children, you might consider a rustic cabin in a state or national park. At some of these inexpensive accommodations for adventurous souls who thrive on gorgeous hiking trails, basic kitchen facilities are on hand, and linens are provided. Try **Waianapanapa State Park**, overlooking a black sand beach, or **Polipoli State Park**, six thousand feet above sea level on a slope of Haleakala volcano, both on Maui (Division of Parks, Tel. 808/984-8109).

Getting to Hawaii
By Air
Hawaii is served by a wide selection of major airlines, so you'll have a lot of flexibility in booking a non-stop or connecting flight. The least expensive fares are often available through the airlines' web sites. Most planes touch down in Honolulu, the capital, on Oahu, though you can also book flights on major carriers to Maui, the Big Island of Hawaii, and Kauai. Many travelers fly into Honolulu, then switch to local inter-island carriers for flights to other islands.

The best time to select your seat is when you make your reservation. You can also reserve special meals at this time, such as children's, vegetarian, kosher, low-salt, seafood, or fruit.

Jet Lag
While most people suffer from jet lag after long flights, there are things you can do to take the edge off it. First, to help you adjust psychologically, set your watch to the time of your destination (Hawaii or home) as you board the plane. Dehydration is a major contributor to the groggy, sapped feeling after hours in the air. During your flight, encourage your children to drink at least a glass of water per hour, and you do the same. Also, avoid alcohol. Eat meals at times that are as close as possible to meal times of your destination (try to nibble a little, even if you're not hungry when served).

Get as much sleep as possible before and during the flight. But you should also encourage your family to do stretching exercises in your seats and take periodic walks up and down the aisle to improve circulation. Younger children love cruising the aisles. One mother once told me that she was sure she had walked to Hawaii, because she was so busy trailing after her two-year-old that she barely had a chance to sit down!

National Airlines
• **Aloha**, Tel. 800/367-5250, www.alohaairlines.com
• **American Airlines**, Tel. 800/433-7300, www.aa.com
• **American Trans Air (ATA)**, Tel. 800/742-9244, www.pleasantholidays.com

- **Continental**, Tel. 800/231-0856, www.continental.com
- **Delta**, Tel. 800/221-1212, www.delta.com
- **Hawaiian**, Tel. 800/367-5320, www.hawaiianair.com
- **Northwest-KLM**, Tel. 800/225-2525, www.nwa.com
- **United**, Tel. 800/241-6522, www.united.com

Inter-island Airlines
- **Aloha**, Tel. 800/367-5250, www.alohaairlines.com
- **Hawaiian**, Tel. 800/367-5320, www.hawaiianair.com
- **Island Air**, Tel. 800/323-3345, www.islandair.com

By Sea
A cruise is another way to visit Hawaii, but you'll spend far more time at sea than on the islands. Some cruise lines offer children's programs as extensive as those at resort hotels. Many ships visit Hawaii on their way to other ports. To spend the greatest amount of time cruising through the Hawaiian Islands, try **Norwegian Cruise Line (**Tel. 800/327-7030, www.ncl.com). For details about the most economical deals, contact **Cruises, Inc.** (800/854-0500 or 800/467-2457, www.cruisesinc.com).

Getting Around Hawaii
Many air-hotel package deals include transportation to and from the airport. On Oahu, shuttle buses run between the airport and Waikiki hotels. Oahu is the only island with an extensive public bus system. On other islands, it's best to rent a car or take a bus or van tour if you plan to see more than your hotel. Taxis are available on all islands, but they can be expensive.

By Bus
Oahu's convenient public bus system is known as TheBus. It may take a little longer than driving for you to get where you're going, but what's the rush? Bus and van tours to the most popular sights are available on all islands. On Maui and the Big Island of Hawaii, some resorts, or parts of resorts, are linked by shuttle buses for their guests.

By Rental Car
We've always been highly satisfied with the service and vehicles of **Budget Rent-A-Car** (Tel. 800/527-0700), which offers some of Hawaii's best auto deals. Another good company is **Dollar** (Tel. 800/367-7006, or, in Hawaii, Tel. 800/342-7398).

In comparing the charges of different car rental companies, make sure that you take into account factors such as the daily versus the weekly rate, the cost of insurance, whether you need to pick up and drop off the car at two different locations, and whether you'll be charged a flat rate for gas or have unlimited mileage. With unlimited mileage, mid-size rental cars begin at about $30 a day, plus insurance, state taxes, and a small daily surcharge. Weekly rates are the most economical. If you're going to be island hopping, you can rent a car ahead of time for all islands through one company.

During the busiest seasons (winter and summer), you'll need to reserve a car well in advance, and you'll find that rates may be somewhat more expensive than during the quieter seasons (spring and fall). Note that some hotels and condominiums include car rental in their rates.

Since you never know when you might get snagged by an irresistible beach while driving, it's a good idea to take your beachwear, sun block, hats, visors, sunglasses, and towels whenever you set out. So as not to cause accidents or annoy residents, pull over into designated overlooks to enjoy scenic spots instead of driving slowly to absorb your surroundings. Always allow extra time to get wherever you're going (especially the airport).

Rental companies prohibit drivers from taking cars, even 4-wheel-drive vehicles, onto unpaved or rugged roads. However, some of Hawaii's most dramatic sights can only be reached by less than smooth roads, so many travelers take the risk of violating their contracts.

The law requires that you always wear seatbelts and that you strap children under age three into car seats (which are available for rent, if you're not planning to bring your own).

Also see Chapter 3, *Traveling with Kids.*

By Taxi

Taxis are plentiful in Honolulu. While cabs are available on other islands, distances can be great, so you could end up spending more than if you rented a car for a day or two. If you'd rather leave the driving to someone else, personalized taxi tours can be arranged.

Wheel Deals?

If you haven't rented a car before arrival, avoid those "$5 a day" and other too-good-to-be-true deals offered by people handing out flyers on the street, especially in Waikiki. Hidden costs or ulterior motives (such as an attempt to rope you into a trip to a less than popular luau or a two-hour visit to a time-share resort with a mandatory tour) can often make these "incredible" deals more expensive than others. Once in Hawaii, it is best to rent a car either at the airport or through your hotel.

‿

Chapter 5

BASIC INFORMATION

Here is some information for you to use while you are in Hawaii—everything from money matters and internet access to health concerns and ocean safety.

Babysitters

See Chapter 3, *Traveling with Kids.*

Business Hours & Holidays

Shopping malls and quite a few stores on main drags remain open in the evenings. Retail stores, especially those in hotels, rarely take Sundays off.

Banking hours are usually from 8:30am to 3 or 3:30pm, Monday through Friday. (However, some banks stay open until 6pm on Thursdays or Fridays.) ATMs are easy to come by. Businesses are generally open from 8am or earlier to 4 or 5pm.

Most post offices open at 8 or 8:30am and close at 4:30pm during the week; on Saturdays, hours are often 8am to noon. The main post office in Honolulu is open from 7:30am to 4:30pm Monday through Friday and 7:30am to noon on Saturdays.

Stores, banks, and most businesses are closed on the main U.S. national holidays. Some may also close on Prince Kuhio Day (March 26), King Kamehameha Day (June 11), and Admission Day (third Friday in August).

Children's Programs

See Chapter 3, *Traveling with Kids,* and hotel descriptions in island chapters.

Health & Medical Concerns

Packing a small first-aid kit is a good idea. Also be sure to bring insect repellent, sun block, and sunglasses for you and the kids. While it's perfectly fine to drink tap water in Hawaii, don't drink from streams or natural pools since they may contain parasites. Fresh vegetables, fruit, and dairy products are also safe.

No matter how dark your skin is, be sure to use a good sun block whenever you're outdoors. Hats and visors will also come in handy. Don't spend your whole first day frying on the beach. Expose your skin to heavy doses of sun gradually, and avoid being in direct sunlight for long stretches between 10am and 2pm, when the rays are strongest. Don't forget that even on hazy days, the sun's powerful ultraviolet light comes through.

However, if you do end up with a burn, stay out of the sun. Take a cool bath and apply a first-aid spray or lotion. Aloe gel is especially soothing. Get medical help right away if your burn is so bad that you feel feverish, nauseated, dizzy, or have chills or a headache.

Hospitals

In an emergency, dial **911**.

If you need a doctor, the staff at your accommodation can help you contact one. Hawaii's largest hospital, **Queen's Medical Center** (1301 Punchbowl Street, Honolulu: emergency Tel. 808/547-4311, main number Tel. 808/538-9011) in Oahu, is one of the country's best medical facilities.

On other islands, contact the following:
- **Maui Memorial Hospital** (in Wailuku, Tel. 808/244-9056)
- **Kona Community Hospital** (in the Big Island's Kailua-Kona area, Highway 11, Kealekekua, Tel. 808/322-9311)
- **Hualalai Urgent Care** (in Kona at the Crossroads on the Big Island, Tel. 808/327-4357)
- **Hilo Hospital** (in Hilo on the Big Island, 1190 Waianuenue Avenue, Tel. 808/974-4700)
- **Wilcox Memorial Hospital** (in Lihue, Kauai, Tel. 808/245-1100)
- **Molokai General Hospital** (Kaunakakai, Tel. 808/553-5331)
- **Lanai Community Hospital** (Lanai City, Tel. 808/565-6411)

Mail. Internet, & Faxes

Most of the larger hotels and some condos in Hawaii have internet access and fax machines available for use by guests.

Some hotels here sell stamps at the same price as in the post office. There doesn't seem to be a great deal of consistency in the length of time mail takes to travel between Hawaii and the mainland; allow anywhere from four days to ten days or more. Express Mail and courier companies, such as Federal

Express, offer two-day service between the continental U.S. and the main islands. However, be forewarned that weekend pick-ups and drop-offs may not be available on islands other than Oahu, so those two days can turn into three or four.

Sending Hawaii Home

Some **lei stands** and many florists will send Hawaiian blossoms to you or your friends on the mainland.

Inspected, boxed **pineapples** can be purchased at the airport or at fruit stands that deliver them to the airport in time for your flight or mail them directly to the mainland. While in Hawaii, eat your fill of guava, passion fruit, mangoes, and avocados. The U.S. Department of Agriculture discourages people from taking or mailing these fruits to the mainland since they can carry fruit flies and other destructive bugs. Visitors are urged to bake, can, dry, stew, or otherwise preserve fresh fruit before sending it to the mainland. Of course, this is only practical if you are staying in a private home or condo with kitchen facilities.

If you're mailing boxes of **macadamia nuts** to the mainland, have them wrapped in plain brown paper instead of writing the addresses directly onto the boxes. Otherwise, those flashy, attractive packages may never reach their destinations!

Money & Banking

While credit cards are widely used in Hawaii, not all establishments accept them and those that do don't necessarily honor all major cards. If you run out of money during your stay, ATMs are available in and outside of banks. You may also be able to cash a personal check, get a cash advance, or arrange for someone at home to wire you money through offices of American Express, Western Union, or your credit card company. Some of the larger hotels have American Express offices on the premises. Traveler's checks are widely accepted. It is best to get at least a portion in small denominations ($10s or $20s) since some places have a limit on the amount they will cash. In case of loss or theft, be sure to keep your traveler's check receipt and a list of serial numbers separate from the checks themselves.

Safety

In an emergency, dial **911** for police, the fire department, or an ambulance.

While Hawaii may have the look and feel of paradise, it is still a part of the real world and crime is no stranger. Whenever you can, take advantage of hotel in-room safes or front desk safety deposit boxes. Carry as few valuables as possible when you go out, and never leave your things unattended—not even in the locked trunk of a parked car. Especially when you're on the beach or in a park, always keep your eye on your possessions—and, of course, on your children! Avoid remote, unpopulated areas after dark.

Before hiking, check with park rangers about impending and recent weather conditions. You might set out on a dry sunny day, but a rainfall the day before might have left trails muddy and slippery.

Beach Safety

Many beaches in Hawaii have no lifeguards. Particularly if you are vacationing with teenagers who might venture off on their own, be sure that they understand that rip currents, jellyfish, and high surf can make some beaches better for sunbathing and picnicking than swimming, at certain times of day or year. Water conditions change with the season, so that calm beach of summer may be treacherous in winter. But remember, some beaches in Hawaii, no matter how beautiful, are *always* dangerously rough, with deceptively strong currents. If signs warn you not to enter the water because of rough conditions, don't!

Never turn your back on the ocean. A huge wave can suddenly appear in what seemed to be calm waters. Never swim alone, and don't let your children do so, even if they are strong swimmers. If you get snagged by a rip current, swim parallel to the shore. Don't swim in the vicinity of surfers, since they can't always spot bathers.

Experts make surfing and body surfing look easy. But you and your children should try these sports only after you've had supervised instruction from someone who is highly skilled. When near coral reefs (which can give nasty cuts), wear protective shoes, such as reef slippers or diving booties. Avoid walking on partially exposed wet boulders—a nearly invisible growth of algae can make them slippery.

You and your kids should always be sure to use sun block, no matter how dark the natural color of your skin. Remember to reapply it frequently, since sweat and sea- or pool water can wash it off.

Shopping

With shops selling everything from kites and children's clothing to fine art and designer threads, Hawaii is a Nirvana for shopping addicts. Oahu, of course, is where you'll find the widest selection of stores, in and outside of malls. Chic boutiques and T-shirt shops line Kalakaua Avenue and other streets in Waikiki. The expansive **DFS Galleria** and the older **Royal Hawaiian Shopping Mall** are centrally located in Waikiki. **ABC discount stores**, one of which seems to be on every corner, sell Kona coffee and macadamia nuts, usually at very appealing prices, along with grocery staples and beach necessities.

Off the main tourist strip, the **Ala Moana Shopping Center** is among the world's largest malls. If you can't find it here, it probably doesn't exist. Also in Honolulu, the **Ward Center** is an attractive, upscale shopping and dining complex. My favorite place to shop on Oahu is **Hale'iwa**, the quiet North Shore former plantation town with weathered wooden buildings dating back to the 1920s and earlier. The clothing, jewelry, and artwork in the many boutiques here are some of the most imaginative I've seen.

For atmosphere, it is difficult to beat Kauai's **Kilohana Plantation**. Bedrooms, hallways, and even bathrooms in this handsome mansion and out buildings have been converted into eye-pleasing (if not always wallet-friendly) boutiques. In Hanalei, on Kauai's northern shore, handmade pottery, jewelry, and paintings by local artists are plentiful. Other good areas for spending money are Lahaina and Kaanapali (**Whalers Village**) on Maui and Kailua-Kona on the Big Island. Many hotels, especially the larger ones, have shops, but you generally pay more for the convenience. Some of the larger condos have mini markets on the premises.

If your accommodation has a kitchen, a refrigerator, or if you just want some picnic fixin's, you'll find the best grocery prices at the big chain stores such as **Safeway**, where you can get a discount card on the spot.

Single Parents

Since "Hawaii" and "honeymoon" are practically synonymous, you'll see plenty of love-struck couples everywhere. But single parents can certainly enjoy the islands just as much as those with mates. It's easy to meet other parents around the pool or on the beach. Sightseeing tours and snorkeling cruises are other good ways to socialize with adults while your children are also having fun.

Want to leave the kids with a sitter so you can have a child-free dinner or hit a night spot? Single mothers should feel perfectly comfortable traveling alone in Hawaii. However, the 50th state is not immune to crime, so women (and men) should take the same precautions they would in any other non-utopia. Don't hitchhike; never turn your back on your belongings; limit (or avoid) alcohol; and don't go into remote areas at night.

Taxes

An 11.416% tax will be added to your hotel bill. This includes a 4.166% state sales tax (which is also added to groceries and all other purchases) and a 7.25% room tax. Various state surcharges, road-use tax, and sales tax are applied to car rental costs.

Telephones

Hawaii's area code is **808**. A local call is one that is made within an island. Calls to other islands or to the mainland are classified as long distance. To dial another island, you need to dial I-808+number. Most hotels add a hefty surcharge to calls made from your room. Note that a fee is often charged for access to a line even when a guest uses a telephone calling card or credit card, and sometimes even when you are calling a toll free number. Phone cards are available at many retail stores.

Time Zone

Hawaiian Standard Time is two hours earlier than the Pacific Standard Time of the continental West Coast and five hours earlier than Eastern Standard Time. So if it's 9am in Hawaii, it's 11am in California, noon in Colorado, 1pm in Illinois, and 2pm in New York. That is, unless Daylight Saving Time (from the last Sunday in April through the last Sunday in October) is in effect on the mainland. In this case, since Hawaii does not observe Daylight Saving Time, the difference in time is increased by an hour.

Tipping

Tipping is 15 percent for waiters and, for tour guides, anywhere from a couple of dollars per visitor to 10% or 15%. For help with your luggage at hotels and airports, plan to give about $1 per bag.

Visitor Information
Hawaii Visitors & Convention Bureau
2270 Kalakaua Avenue, Suite 801
Honolulu, HI 96815
808/923-1811
800/GO-HAWAII (800/464-2924)
www.gohawaii.com

Maui Visitors Bureau
1727 Wili Pa Loop
Wailuku, HI 96793
808/244-3530
800/525-MAUI (800/525-6284)
www.visitmaui.com

Big Island Visitors Bureau (Island of Hawaii)
Kona-Kohala Coast:
King's Shops
250 Waikoloa Beach Drive, suite B-15
Waikoloa
808/886-1655

Hilo:
250 Keawe Street, at Haili Street
808/961-5797
www.bigisland.org

Kona/Kohala Resort Association (Hawaii, the Big Island)
808/886-4915
800/318-3637
www.kkra.org

Kaua'i Visitors Bureau
4334 Rice Street, suite 101
Lihue, HI 96766
808/245-3971
800/262-1400
www.kauaivisitorsbureau.com

Moloka'i Visitor Association
Komoi Professional Building, suite 700
Kaunakakai, Molokai
808/553-3876
808/553-5221
800/800/6367
www.molokai-hawaii.com

Destination Lana'i
730 Lanai Avenue, suite 102
Lanai City, HI 96763
808/565-7600
800/947-4774
www.visitlanai.net

Chapter 6

TALKING LIKE A LOCAL

Since it's phonetic, Hawaiian is not nearly as difficult to pronounce as it appears to the uninitiated. It consists of only seven consonants (*h, k, l, m, n, p, w*), five vowels (*a, e, i, o, u*), and no letter is silent. Each syllable ends with a vowel. The accent is usually on the next to last syllable of a word.

Consonants sound just as they do in English, with the exception of *w*. This letter is pronounced like a *v* when it precedes the last vowel of a word (such as *ewa* or *Kahoolawe*). Vowels sound pretty much like those in Spanish: *a* as in *around*; *e* like the *a* in *day*; *i* like the *ee* in *see*; *o* as in *so*; and *u* as in *sue*. When two or three vowels are together, they each get their own syllable (unless they are part of a diphthong). The double *o* in *Kahoolawe* sounds like "oh-oh" and the double *a* in *Kapaa* sounds like "ah-ah." The four diphthongs are *au*, pronounced *ow*; *ae* and *ai*, both pronounced like the *y* in *sky*; and *ei*, which rhymes with *hay*.

A mark like a backwards apostrophe was once commonly used in many words to signal a sharp pause between syllables. This punctuation is used much less in writing these days and pronunciations have changed accordingly. To purists, however, Hawaii (Hawai'i) will always be "Hah-VY'ee." You'll also hear some people correctly pronounce the names of the islands: "cow-WAH'ee" (Kaua'i), "mole-oh-KAH'ee" (Moloka'i), and "lah-NAH'ee" (Lana'i) instead of "cow-WHY," "MOLE-oh-kye," and "lah-NYE." In this book, I've used this mark only when two letters might otherwise appear to be a diphthong, to indicate the difference between *pau* ("pow"-finished) and *pa'u* ("*pah*-ooo"- a long skirt), for instance.

Most residents today will greet you with "aloha" and say "mahalo" instead of "thank you." Knowing other common Hawaiian words can prevent you from going places you shouldn't, such as into a men's room (many of which are marked *kane*) if you're a *wahine* (woman). You'll often hear terms such as *kamaaina* (longtime island resident), *malihini* (visitor, newcomer, stranger), and *haole* (Caucasian and/or mainlander).

Spend some time in remote, quiet Hana, Maui, if you want to hear people speaking Hawaiian. Otherwise, for the most part, the Hawaiian language is alive mainly on street signs, in place and hotel names, and in a sprinkling of words that pepper English and Pidgin, the local dialect.

So when you don't understand what people are saying, the Hawaiian language will rarely be the reason. Japanese, Korean, Tagalog, Cantonese, and Pidgin are far more widely spoken. Sometimes referred to as "lazy English," Pidgin is used with a real flourish among young Hawaiians and other locals. Originating with the laborers who came to work on Hawaii's plantations, it is a colorful blend of Hawaiian, English, Cantonese, Portuguese and a chop suey of other tongues. Its vocabulary and pronunciation can vary from island to island and even region to region within a single island.

What's the Word?

You'll notice that even though quite a few Hawaiian names are long, in many cases syllables are simply repeated. Take, for example, one of the rainiest places in the world, Mt. Waialeale (why AH-lay AH-lay) on Kauai, or the historic valley on the Big Island of Hawaii called *Pohakuhaku* (poh HAH-koo HAH-koo).

Wrapping your tongue around *humuhumunukunukuapuaa* (a small trigger fish with a shark-sized name) may appear an impossible feat at first. But if you look closely, you'll see that the trick is to sound redundant: HOO-moo HOO-moo NOO-koo NOO-koo AH-poo AH-ah.

When Hawaiian residents speak English, their accent tends to be sing-songy, elevating in pitch at the end of a sentence. Someone who answers your telephone call might ask you to "Hold on, yeh?" A person who gives you directions might end with, "Simple, yeh?" Be sure to spend some time "talking story" (chatting or gossiping) with locals.

Not all communication in Hawaii is either oral or written. When someone raises his palm with the three middle fingers down and the thumb and pinky extended and gives it a couple of quick shakes, this is a greeting or a good natured signal to "hang loose" ("relax" or "cool out").

Children are quick to learn new languages, so why not practice some of the words and phases below? (For names of Hawaiian foods, see Chapter 7, *Eating Like a Local*.)

Hawaiian-Pidgin-English Glossary

aa (AH-ah): the rough kind of lava
ae (eye): yes
aikane (eye-KAH-nay): friend
alii (ah-LEE-ee): Hawaiian chief, royalty, person or people of high rank
aloha (ah-LOW-hah): welcome, hello, good-bye, love, friendship . . .
aole (ah-OH-lay): no
brah (bra) **bro'** (brother): friend
cockaroach: to steal something or take something in an underhanded manner
da kine (dah kyne): thingamajig, whatchamacallit
diamondhead: east toward Diamond Head volcano on Oahu
ewa (AY-va—as in Eva Gabor): west toward Oahu's Ewa Plantation
hale (HAH-lay): house
haole (HOW-lee): Caucasian, mainlander, foreigner
hapa (HAH-pah): half
hapa-haole (HAH-pah HOW-lee): part Caucasian and part Hawaiian; not authentically Hawaiian
hauoli la hanau (how-OH-lee lah hah-NOW): Happy Birthday
hauoli makahiki hou (how-OH-lee mah-kah-HEE-key ho-oo): Happy New Year
heiau (HAY-ee-ow): ancient Hawaiian temple(s)
hono (HO-no): bay
hoolaulea (ho-oh-lau-LAY-ah): gathering, celebration, street party
Howzit?: How goes it? What's happening?
hula (WHO-lah): traditional Hawaiian dance
imu (EE-moo): underground oven still used in luau
kahuna (kah-WHO-nah): Hawaiian priest
kai (kye): ocean
kamaaina (kah-mah-EYE-nah): longtime resident
kane (KAH-nay): man
kapu (kah-POO): taboo, forbidden, off-limits, keep out
kau kau (cow cow): food
keiki (KAY-kee): child
kiawe (key-AH-vay): mesquite tree or wood
koa (KO-ah): an increasingly scarce tree prized for its wood
kokua (ko-KOO-ah): help
lanai (lah-NYE): terrace, balcony, patio, porch
lauhala (lau-HAH-lah): pandanus leaves (used for weaving)
lei (lay): long necklace made of flowers; garland
li' dat (lie dat): like that
li' dis (lie dis): like this

lilikoi (LEEL-lee-koi): passion fruit
lua (LOO-ah): toilet
luau (LOO-ow): feast, celebration
mahalo (mah-HAH-low): thank you
makai (mah-KYE): in the direction of the sea
malihini (MAH-lee-HEE-nee): visitor, newcomer
malo (MAH-low): loincloth once worn by Hawaiian men
mauka (MOW-kah): toward the mountains, inland
mauna (MOW-nah): mountain
mele kalikimaka (MAY-lay kah-LEE-key-MAH-kah): Merry Christmas
muumuu (MOO-moo or MOO-oo-MOO-oo): roomy, full-length dress
ohana (oh-HAH-nah): clan, family
okole (oh-KO-lay): buttocks
pahoehoe (pah-HOY-hoy): smooth or ropy lava
pali (PAH-lee): cliff
paniolo (pah-nee-OH-low): cowboy in Hawaii
pau (pow): finished
pau hana time (pow HAH-nah time): quitting time; when the work day is over
pa'u (PAH-oo): a long skirt once worn by Hawaiian women
puka (POO-kah): hole
pupu (POO-poo): hors d'oeuvres
shaka! (SHAH-kah): All right! Great! Excellent!
talk story: chew the fat, chat, gossip
tutu or **tutu wahine** (too-too wah-HEE-nee): grandmother
ukulele (oo-koo-LAY-lay): small, guitar-like instrument with four strings; literally "leaping flea"
wahine (wah-HEE-nee): woman

Chapter 7

EATING LIKE A LOCAL

The old saying "You are what you eat" couldn't be more true than in Hawaii. The food here is a melange of American, Hawaiian, Japanese, Chinese, Portuguese, Korean, Filipino, European—and so are the people.

A style of cooking known as Hawaiian regional or Pacific Rim cuisine has emerged throughout the Islands, particularly at the more upscale restaurants and resorts. Annual food and wine festivals are held at some of the hotels along the Kona coast on the Big Island of Hawaii and Kapalua on Maui. Incorporating Hawaii's freshest vegetables, fruits, macadamia nuts, seafood, and meat, these dishes are influenced by the Pacific, the East, and the West. They are artistically presented, with special attention to texture, color, sauces, and seasonings. Gone is the heavy, old-fashioned "Polynesian" cuisine in which pineapple seemed to be the common denominator.

Using planting, gathering, digging and cooking utensils made of wood, ancient Hawaiians lived off such staples as breadfruit, sweet potatoes, taro, bananas, and coconuts. They used shells to remove skins from cooked taro and breadfruit and fashioned knives from bamboo, rocks, and sharks' teeth.

Gourds, sometimes painted with intricate geometric designs, were transformed into bowls and drinking cups. Wooden plates were reserved for high ranking individuals. These *alii* also used special bowls to dispose of their leftovers and bones. It was the job of their servants to hide this uneaten food so that no one could use it to cast evil spells on the *alii*.

As in the old days, locals today throw **luau** to celebrate births, birthdays, weddings, and simply being alive. These are quite different from the commercial affairs most tourists are herded off to. At these gatherings of family and friends, someone might spontaneously begin to sing, or play the slack key guitar.

Whether or not you attend a luau, you'll have plenty of chances to sample **pupus** (appetizers), usually a variety of tidbits served on a platter during happy hours. Also be sure to try the trademark dish of modern Hawaii: a **plate lunch** (also called mixed plate, a Bento lunch, or a box lunch). This blend of Japanese, Hawaiian, and Chinese food comes in the form of a meat or fish entree served with two scoops of white rice (which isn't considered rice unless it's moist and sticky), and a scoop of macaroni salad. It's often eaten with chopsticks and is sold in many mom-and-pop fast-food joints.

Also look out for Hawaiian-style curry, which is green and not very hot. Serving these and other local dishes, roadside "BBQ" stands and "drive-ins" border main roads, particularly on Oahu.

Hawaii's Most Popular Foods
From the Sea
Ahi: Hawaiian big-game yellowfin tuna that often turns up grilled, as a "burger" sandwich, baked inside *ti* leaves, or served raw as sashimi or in sushi.

Aku: Skipjack tuna.

A'u: Marlin or broadbill swordfish.

Hapu: Hawaiian sea bass.

Lehi: Orange snapper.

Limu: One of the few ancient Hawaiian culinary traditions that thrives today is the prepared on and consumption of *limu*, commonly known as seaweed. This vegetable is extremely rich in vitamins and minerals. It is served with raw fish as part of sashimi and sushi or cooked in soups and stews. Today, some Hawaiians still collect edible seaweed that has washed ashore, just as their ancestors did. Many varieties of this sea plant are also an important part of the diet in Asian cultures, such as Japan's. The Japanese presence in Hawaii has added to the wealth of traditional Hawaiian seaweed dishes. Most of the seaweed used for sushi in the state is imported from Japan.

Doggy Dinner?
Some ancient Hawaiian culinary traditions have survived, but many have been lost, a few happily so. No one today seems to miss the old practices of eating dogmeat, having separate dining quarters for men and women, and banning women from consuming pork, bananas, coconuts and other "manly" foods.

&

Lomi lomi: Salmon diced with green leaf onions and tomatoes, served cold. Hawaiians created this dish with the salted and smoked salmon introduced by 19th century whalers.

Lomi o'io: With its bones soft enough to chew, raw bonefish is mashed and mixed with *limu*.

Mahi-mahi: A dolphin fish, not a mammal – so it's no relation to Flipper. The texture reminds me of moist pork chops. Perhaps Hawaii's best-known fish, it is especially delicious grilled.

Onaga: Red snapper.

Ono: A game fish also called wahoo. The very appropriate name is the Hawaiian word for "delicious."

Opakapaka: Pink snapper; popular for the first meal of the day.

Poke: Cubed or sliced raw *ahi*, mixed with pounded *limu*, tomatoes, onions, and *kukui nuts*.

Sashimi: A Japanese favorite; paper-thin slices of raw fish.

Sushi: Almost as common as tacos in some mainland cities, this dish is made by rolling vinegared rice, vegetables, and/or raw fish in seaweed or placing raw fish on a lump of sticky rice. It is even served in some McDonald's in Hawaii.

Uku: Gray snapper.

Ulua: Deep-sea pompano.

Luau – The Real McCoy

If you scour local newspapers, listen to radio stations, and ask around, you might be lucky enough to find out about a luau sponsored by a civic organization or other group to raise money for one cause or another. Nothing feels packaged or rigidly programmed at these home-style festive events.

From the Land

Breadfruit: This large, round, starchy vegetable was brought to Hawaii by the early Polynesians. It is served baked, fried, roasted, or boiled. Its mild flavor makes it a good side dish with highly seasoned food. (Also see Taro, below.)

Chicken luau: Cooked with coconut milk and *taro* leaves.

Kalua pig: The centerpiece of any luau; the entire (often deboned) porker is cooked in an *imu* (an earthen oven). The pig is stuffed with fiery hot lava rocks, wrapped in moistened burlap bags and *ti* leaves, surrounded by more hot rocks, and roasted in the pit for several hours, along with breadfruit, yams, fish, and other goodies. The crispy skin is considered the best part by many. At some luau, guests are invited to observe the ceremony involving the removal of the pig from the ground.

Kim chee: Korean pickled and spiced cabbage or other vegetables.

Kula or Maui onions: Some of the sweetest onions around. You may be lucky enough to find them made into breaded rings and served with spicy mustard.

Lau lau: Ground pork and/or fish wrapped in *taro* or *ti* leaves and then steamed or baked.

Macadamia nuts: Perhaps macadamia nuts taste so good because they are so long in the making: It takes about seven years for a tree to grow its first nuts, then about eight more years before it is producing to capacity. They're also hard to get to: 300 pounds of pressure per square inch is needed to crack their shells. However, you won't have to worry about cracking them. They are sold in endless varieties, but shell-covered isn't one of them. You'll find them plain, salted, dipped in chocolate, or dressed in caramel or coconut glaze. You can also sample them in cookies, ice cream, pies, on fish and chicken, and on and on. They are rich and creamy in texture, and far from low in calories. Although they contain no cholesterol, they are usually roasted in coconut oil, a saturated fat.

Manapua: This steamed dough stuffed with pork or black beans originated in China.

Poi: Pounded, fermented *taro* root, cooked and mashed into a sticky paste. Sort of brownish-purple-gray in color, this side dish, served with meat or fish, has a mild, slightly sour or tangy taste. When mainlanders say *poi* tastes like wallpaper paste, Hawaiians remark that they don't know what that means since wallpaper paste isn't eaten in Hawaii. "You keep your sauerkraut and cottage cheese and we'll keep our *poi*," they joke. This dish is eaten with the fingers. Two-finger *poi* is thicker than the three-finger variety, because it takes fewer fingers to spoon up.

Portuguese sausage: Spicy; often eaten with rice for breakfast or used in Portuguese bean soup to add flavor.

Saimin: Noodle soup with dumplings and vegetables topped with sliced pork and/or seafood. Some say it originaced in Japan while others maintain it was inspired by a Chinese dish called *sae mein*.

SPAM: Ask your parents if they remember SPAM, and they'll probably tell you they haven't gone near this canned meat since the days when their mothers used to stick it in their lunch boxes. Well, in Hawaii people eat SPAM with a vengeance. This chopped pork shoulder and ham, in its blue Hormel tin, was introduced to Hawaii during the 1940s, mainly for use by the military. It thus has come to be referred to as **S**outh **P**acific **A**rmy **M**eat, but its name is actually a contraction of "spiced ham." People in Hawaii eat it like a delicacy, putting it in soups, stews, on the side for breakfast, and as the main event for lunch and dinner. As a matter of fact, for several years, Maui hosted an annual summer SPAM cookoff where both professional and novice chefs competed for prizes for the tastiest, most creative recipes using the meat.

Teriyaki beef: A spicy Japanese dish made with soy sauce, sugar, vegetables and strips of meat. Teriyaki chicken and fish are also popular.

Taro: Starchy root from which *poi* is made; also served baked or roasted. When cooked, it looks and tastes something like a potato. Be sure to try highly addictive *taro* chips, sold in grocery stores bagged like potato chips. *Taro* leaves are used to wrap meat or seafood for steaming or boiling. Taro is not only high in calcium, potassium, antioxidants, and vitamin A, but it is also quite versatile. For some delicious recipes from taro pancakes to breadfruit chowder, order a copy of *Taro & Breadfruit (or Potato!)* by Ellane Baker (contact the author at P.O. Box 1007, Kapaa, Hawaii 96746 or taromama@taromama.com).

Ti leaves: Ancient Hawaiians believed that the *ti* plant held a godly power that warded off evil spirits. Food is often wrapped in these leaves for cooking or storage. The genuinely Hawaiian hula skirts are made from *ti* leaves (as opposed to the grass skirts you'll see a lot, which actually originated elsewhere in the Pacific).

Fruit

In our family, we call it nature's candy. Not only can you enjoy fresh, juicy fruit in restaurants or roadside stands, but in many areas, you and the kids can pick quite a bit of it yourself. Coconuts, bananas, and pineapple are delicious in the 50th state. Here's a rundown on some of the other popular natural snacks:

Guavas are best for picking between June and October, when they are softest to the touch and unmarred. They contain five times more Vitamin C than oranges. The most common type of this thin-skinned fruit is the yellow, lemon-sized variety. Another, smaller kind is called the strawberry guava, because of its taste and red color. The yellow, oval **lilikoi** (passion fruit) is ripe during the summer and fall. It grows on vines that drape themselves on bushes and over tree limbs. The vines of the small, round purple passion fruit burst into color with their white and lavender flowers. The vines of the yellow, banana-shaped banana passion fruit bloom with pink blossoms. Lilikoi makes a wonderfully refreshing beverage.

Growing on bushy, towering trees, **mangoes** are a favorite tropical fruit. They are extremely juicy and their meat is slippery when ripe (during the spring and summer). Part of the fun - especially for children - is making a mess while eating them.

Summer is the best time to pluck **papayas** off their skinny trees. Pick them when they are just starting to turn yellow.

High up in lush, shady regions of Hawaii, **mountain apples** are waiting to be sampled. The trees bloom with fluffy red flowers. The small, pear-shaped fruit is red on the outside, with white meat inside. Mountain apples ripen between July and December.

Usually ripe in late May or early June, **Methley plums** (also called Kokee plums) are found throughout Kokee State Park on Kauai.

Be sure to try soft, sweet **lychee** and **poha** (Cape gooseberries). Peel the skin off the **red berries** that grow on coffee trees around November and suck on the two beans in each. The coating has a candylike flavor (but don't try to eat the beans!). Avocados, very popular in salads or pseudo-Japanese sushi, ripen from June to November in their towering trees.

Sweets

Nature's candy (fruit) is just the beginning of satisfying a sweet tooth in Hawaii. Here are some other local favorites:

Haupia: Jiggly coconut pudding cut into squares. People often bring it to luau the way mainlanders might carry a bottle of wine to a friend's house for dinner.

Lilikoi: Also known as passion fruit; it makes a tart pie or is sweetened and turned into a beverage, often mixed with other fruit juices.

Malasadas: From Portugal; sugary balls of fried dough often called "holeless doughnuts."

Manju: Sweet Japanese pastry with black bean paste inside.

Molokai sweet bread: Reflecting the "chop suey" heritage of many locals, this bread, based on a Portuguese recipe, is created in a Japanese bakery on Molokai.

Poi balls: These chewy, sweet, fried balls are appealing to many visitors, whether they like the taste of poi (fermented taro root) or not. Look for them on the Big Island.

Shave ice: Called a snow cone in some parts of the mainland, this refreshing cup of crushed ice is flavored with syrup made from *lilikoi*, pineapple, coconut or other fruit.

Hula pie: You'll find this for dessert at many restaurants, each serving its own variation. The basic ingredients are ice cream on a cookie crust, macadamia nuts, and whipped cream.

Taro butter mochi: Sometimes sold at roadside food stands (such as Hanalei Taro & Juice Co. in Hanalei, Kauai), this scrumptious dessert is a cross between pudding and cake. It is made with taro, butter, sugar, and a hint of coconut milk. It may not be low in calories, but it is high in calcium, potassium, and antioxidants.

Other Snacks

The Original Maui Kitch'n Cook'd Potato Chips, those thick and crunchy wonders, have played a large part in changing the face of potato chips across the mainland. There are other chips with "Maui" in their names, but this brand is the best. If you're on the Big Island, Hilo also produces a version.

Looking like potato chips with purple threads running through them, **taro chips** are also delicious. Other niblets eaten straight from the bag are **dried shrimp**, which can be very salty. They are also used in cooking.

Beverages

Sure, you'll find plenty of rum-based **Mai Tais** and **Blue Hawaiis**, but for my money, nothing is more enjoyable than Hawaii's wonderful fruit juices, especially **guava nectar** (a pink beverage that has a thick, grainy texture something like pear nectar) and **lilikoi** (passion fruit juice). Kids love **POG** (a delicious concoction of Passion, Orange, and Guava juices).

Kona coffee, originating on the Big Island, is renowned for its rich aroma and taste. It is sold in many flavors and blends, both regular and decaf.

Chapter 8

HAWAIIAN TALES

To get your whole family into the aloha spirit, share these legends, tales, and intriguing historical tidbits about Hawaii at bedtime or any time of day, before, during, and after your trip. These stories can help speed the hours spent flying to and from Hawaii, by the way. Younger children may enjoy drawing pictures of their favorite parts.

The Birth of Hawaii

According to ancient legend, Hawaii would not have existed if Papa, the earth mother, and Wakea, the father of the sky and the heavens, had not fallen in love. Their first offspring was the Big Island of Hawaii and their second, Maui. Worn out by the rigors of childbearing, Papa went to Tahiti to recuperate. While she was away, Wakea fell in love with someone else and she gave birth to Molokai and Lanai. Papa got wind of this affair and returned to Hawaii in a jealous rage. However, Wakea soon soothed away her fury. After kissing and making up, they went on to produce Oahu, Kauai, and Niihau (the island off Kauai now inhabited almost exclusively by native Hawaiians and traditionally "forbidden" to outsiders). With their energy nearly spent, Kahoolawe (now arid and uninhabited) was the last island Papa and Wakea could manage.

Scientists, however, have a different version of Hawaii's genesis: A hot spot deep inside the earth was what gave birth to Hawaii, experts say. Somewhere between 25 and 40 million years ago, a long crack opened up in the ocean floor. Molten lava pulsed through, forming water-covered craters. Inch by inch and over millions of years, the part of the earth's crust called the Pacific Plate slowly shifted above the hot spot, resulting in a chain of undersea mountains. They grew taller with each eruption, but it wasn't until a few million years ago that, one by one, they finally broke the ocean's surface in their trek toward the sky.

Wind, rain, and pounding waves carved jagged cliffs and scooped out wide valleys in the young islands. Plants began to sprout from spores that had traveled on the ocean breezes, and later from seeds brought by the tides and migrating birds. One new species appeared on Hawaii about every 40,000 years! When the ancient Polynesians began to settle the islands (somewhere between 300 and 750 A.D.), they brought a variety of fruits and vegetables, including bananas, coconuts, breadfruit, taro, and yams. At first, ancient Hawaiians lived in a world free from biting and stinging insects and poisonous snakes. Until the arrival of European explorers in 1788, they also had no communicable diseases.

Compared to most of the world's land masses, which came into their own about 300 million years ago, the Hawaiian Islands are geologic infants. Kauai is the oldest inhabited island in the chain, and the Big Island of Hawaii is the youngest. As you read these words, not only is a new island forming (Loihi, near the Big Island), but the Big Island itself is still growing. Here, the Kilauea and Mauna Loa volcanoes continue to put on periodic fiery displays that add land mass to the island. Although these are the state's only two active volcanoes, Hawaii also has a trio of dormant volcanoes: the Big Island's Mauna Kea and Hualalai, and Maui's Haleakala.

Don't Mess with the Volcano Goddess

Ancient Hawaiians didn't need snow to go sledding (although they could certainly find the white stuff at the chilly summit of Mauna Kea on the Big Island). Called *holua*, this sport was the highlight of the Makahiki Festival, the annual season of peace. The holua runs were made from piled, packed lava rocks that were cushioned with grass, leaves and mats, then wet with hundreds of gallons of water. Clinging to narrow wooden sleds, competitors zoomed headfirst down the runways. Remnants of several holua runs remain on the Big Island, in Kona.

According to one legend involving a Big Island holua contest, Kahawali, the chief of Puna, in the east, was about to enter a match. Dancers and musicians were keeping the crowd occupied while they waited for the competition to begin. Itching with curiosity about the reason for all the partying, Pele, the volcano goddess, descended from her Kilauea home. She disguised herself as a local chief and demanded that Kahawali race her down the hill instead of the man he'd planned to challenge. Tickled by the boldness of this woman, the chief agreed. But the holua was far more difficult than Pele had expected, and she was soundly beaten by Kahawali.

Shouting that the contest must have been rigged, she insisted on a rematch. Someone must have damaged her borrowed sled, she told him. He agreed to another bout. But then she demanded that they switch sleds so that all would be fair. He dismissed her request, climbed onto his sled, and began whizzing down the slope. An infuriated Pele jumped up and down, waving her fists in the air, sparking a volcanic eruption. Riding the red-hot river of lava, she pursued Kahawali down the hill.

It made no difference to her that the dancers, musicians, and onlookers were being swallowed up by the fiery cascade. Horror swept over the chief as he realized who his competitor really was. Leaving his entire family to the lava flow, he scrambled into his canoe and paddled as fast as his arms would move, fleeing to Maui, Lanai, Molokai, and finally hiding out at the home of his father on Oahu.

Why Leaves are Flat

In the old days, the sky weighed heavily upon the earth, barely leaving breathing room between the ground and the heavens. Plants, with their thick, balloon-like leaves, were forced to push the clouds and the sky up into the stratosphere, inch by inch. The more they shoved, the flatter their leaves became. Eventually, the sky was raised far enough to allow human beings to crawl around from place to place. Then for the price of a drink from a woman's gourd, Maui, the demigod, hoisted the skies up even farther, past the tops of trees, beyond the summits of mountains. Thus, men could finally walk upright on earth.

Exotic Blossoms

The shampoo ginger plant probably came to Hawaii hundreds of years ago, with the early Polynesian immigrants. It produces a bright-red, three-inch bulb. The thick juice of the ripe plant quenched thirst on long journeys. The clear no-suds liquid was, and still is, also used to wash hair, leaving it soft and silky. So if you happen to be hiking with dirty hair, you're in luck!

One of Hawaii's rarest plants is the silversword. Growing on the lunarlike heights of Maui's Haleakala volcano, it resembles a cone-shaped, gray sea anemone. This delicate-to-the-human-touch-yet-hardy-to-the-elements plant thrives where few others can. There are extreme temperature fluctuations at these heights. After a 90-degree day, there might be a snowfall at night. It is against the law to remove or even touch a silversword plant.

And that's not Hawaii's only *kapu* (taboo) flower. The ohia, Hawaii's most common native tree, is noted for its fluffy blood-red blossoms, which are considered sacred to Pele, the volcano goddess. According to Hawaiian legend, Madame Pele will send rainstorms, claps of thunder, or volcanic eruptions if mortals are fool enough to pick one of her flowers.

Sacred Hikes

You may come across hikers with *ti* leaves tied around their ankles or waists. Old-time Hawaiians will explain that a mischievous spirit hides behind bushes and rocks, waiting to trip up innocent passersby. However, since the ti plant is sacred to the god Lono, the spirit will not grab an ankle tied with its leaves.

Family Feuds & Herbal Remedies

Today some families in Hawaii still settle arguments with the *hooponopono* ritual, as ancient Hawaiians once did: After everyone has gotten their concerns off their chests, they all eat the tender leaves of *limu kala*, a variety of seaweed (*kala* means to "forgive"). Herbal medicine is still practiced here and there. People who never went to doctors as children will tell you what they learned from their parents. For example, chewing baby guava leaves relieves motion sickness, guava juice can work better than Pepto Bismol, and tea made from eucalyptus leaves or ginger root sends colds and congestion packing.

Too Much Fun?

In the old days, the Hawaiian Islands themselves served as both a canvas for artistic expression and a playground for happy abandon. Stick-figure drawings were carved into the petrified lava flows that still blanket vast areas. Many of these petroglyph fields remain today, especially on the Big Island of Hawaii. Trees were whittled into totem poll-like *tiki*. The breasts of brightly plumed birds were plucked clean so that their feathers could be used to decorate cloaks and helmets worn by the *alii* (chiefs or aristocracy). Bowls and water containers made from gourds were often etched or painted with elaborate designs.

In the high art of *lauhala*, pandanus leaves were woven into baskets and sleeping mats. Roots, vines, and other fronds used for weaving were frequently dyed black, red, and white to create intricate patterns when braided. Especially among the *alii*, surfing was a favorite sport. People also amused themselves with foot and canoe races, wrestling matches, sliding down hillsides on sleds, and many other games. Singing, dancing the hula, and strumming the ukeke (a Hawaiian stringed instrument not to be confused with the ukulele, a Portuguese import) were also popular pastimes.

When American missionaries began arriving in 1820, they swiftly put an end to all this frivolity. As far as they seemed to be concerned, Hawaiians were simply having too much fun. Where once there had been pride and enjoyment, the missionaries instilled guilt and a sense of shame for the scanty way

Hawaiians dressed, their expressive dances, and their music (which sounded out of tune to Western ears).

After decades of suppression by missionaries, the arts were briefly brought back to life in the late 1800s by King David Kalakaua, who earned himself the nickname "The Merrie Monarch" in the process. Then the 1893 overthrow of the Hawaiian monarchy and the US takeover of the Islands sent this side of Hawaiian culture back underground. It was not until the 1970s that Hawaiian arts began to experience the renaissance that is still apparent today.

Wearing Trees

Ancient Hawaiians created cloth, called *kapa* (or *tapa),* by pounding water-soaked bark. In the old days, *kapa* was decorated with a wide variety of patterns and colors, from black, brown, and red to lavender, blue, and yellow. Men wore *kapa malo* (loin cloths) and women dressed in *kapa pa'u* (long skirts). Capes were used by both sexes, and sandals, blankets, house partitions, even wicks for stone lamps were also made from *kapa.*

Beating out a length of the cloth could take anywhere from several hours to a full day. Women were responsible for creating this cloth, no simple feat. First they had to soak the bark of mulberry trees in the sea for a week. Then they pounded it and soaked it for another seven days. After beating it again until it was thin enough, and allowing it to be dried and bleached by the sun, they painted or stamped designs onto it using woodcuts, ferns, or bamboo to apply dyes made from fruit, roots, leaves, or minerals. As if this weren't enough, they often scented the kapa by blending fragrances into the dyes.

When ancient Hawaiians looked up into the sky and saw fluffy clouds, they knew that what they were really seeing was kapa spread out to dry by the goddess Hina, a renowned kapa maker. To hold the cloth down, she put large stones at the corners. When Hawaiians heard thunder, they were convinced that the weighty stones were being blown away by strong winds. When they saw lightning, they understood that Hina was rolling up her kapa and sunlight was glinting off the moving cloth.

Beginning in the late 18th century, when Westerners introduced Hawaiians to their own more durable woven fabric, the painstaking production of delicate kapa eventually came to an end.

Hula – For Men Only?

With the beating of *ipu* drums in ancient evenings, everyone knew it was time for hula dances to begin. Surprisingly enough, hula was first performed exclusively by men. It was part of a religious ritual and was considered outside the realm of proper female activity. Much of Hawaii's history was passed on through the hand and hip movements of the meaning-laden dances and through the accompanying chants. Known as *kahiko* (kah-*hee*-ko), this often war-like old form of hula was serious business. If dancers lost their concentration and changed a single step or motion, there could be dreadful consequences, since in doing so they would be altering history. *Kahiko* is always accompanied by drums and chanting. In the more fanciful dances, performers would tell humorous tales of the soap opera love lives of the *alii*.

Modern hula, now danced almost exclusively by women, tends to be more graceful and sensual than the ancient style of dance. Called *auana* ("ow-WAH-nah"), this newer version is accompanied by stringed instruments and songs. Smiling a lot (since they no longer have to worry about scrambling historical events by improvising a step), the dancers wear more revealing or form-fitting clothing. The bright green *ti*-leaf skirts worn by some dancers are authentically Hawaiian (if not somewhat skimpier than in the past), but the grass skirts you'll also see actually originated elsewhere in the Pacific.

What? No Game Boy?

In ancient Hawaii, kids found endless ways to amuse themselves. They played *konane*, similar to checkers, with black and white stones, and slid down hillsides on clusters of sturdy, bright green *ti* leaves. They flew kites made from *kapa* (bark cloth) or pandanus leaves, walked on stilts, swung from vines, and played catch with square balls made from woven palm fronds.

A Chinese Circle

The Waikiki Circle Hotel on Oahu, the tall cylindrical building across Kalakaua Avenue from the beach has an intriguing history. It was founded by the first Asian woman to own a hotel in exclusive, central Waikiki. Emma Kwock Chun, who transformed herself from an illiterate immigrant to a millionaire, was born in China in 1892. When she was only 12 years old, her parents sent her to Hawaii to work as a nanny and housekeeper for a Chinese family. At age 16, she was married off by a matchmaker to a 40-year-old shoe cobbler. She began buying property with the money she thriftily saved.

Eventually, she managed to purchase a rooming house for World War II soldiers and she cooked and cleaned for these military men. In 1962, her Circle Hotel opened on the site of the rooming house. Still an inspiration to many, Emma Kwock Chun died in 1975.

Surf's Up

The best-known and most popular ancient Hawaiian sport, surfing was once called "the sport of kings." This was because certain beaches and kinds of boards could only be used by the *alii* (Hawaiian royalty). Boards were once cut from native *koa* or breadfruit trees, then lovingly carved, stained, and preserved with a rubbing down of glistening *kukui* nut oil. American missionaries were aghast that surfing was done in such skimpy clothing, and sometimes even naked, so they banned the sport. But it made a comeback in the early 1900s. Travelers from all over would come to Hawaii to learn at the expert hands of the "beachboys" who helped make Waikiki famous.

One of the best known was Duke Paoa Kahanamoku, a world championship surfer who maneuvered a 114-pound, 16-foot board made of koa wood. In 1915, he went to Australia to introduce the sport to hundreds of amazed onlookers. On Oahu, Waikiki's Kahanamoku Beach and Lagoon is named for this master athlete who was a champion Olympic swimmer as well. When you see the huge statue of Kahanamoku, by the "healing stones" along the beach, you'll wonder how the sign that says "Actual Size" could possibly be true. Whether these words refer to the man or the surfboard he's holding, he had to have been one powerful dude. The feet are longer than my forearms!

Bathing in Gold

An old legend tells of a mysterious and disconcertingly beautiful woman, Kauholokahiki, who was only allowed to bathe in golden waters. A chief on Oahu fell in love with her on sight, married her, then was devastated when she told him about the restrictions of her personal hygiene. He dreaded making the arduous journey to another island to search out yellow waters for his bride. If he failed to find them, he would have to give up the woman he loved. Then when she told him about the golden Waimanalo stream that flowed from the foot of Oahu's Koolau Mountains, he was beside himself with joy.

Lions & Hawaiians

Ancient Hawaiians once settled in Kahana Valley on Oahu. To hear them tell it, the Crouching Lion, the mountain formation on the ridge along the shore, isn't a feline at all, but Kauhi, a god who was chained to the cliff to guard the area. For years he performed his duty faithfully, if less than happily, until one day Hii-aka, the younger sister of the volcano goddess Pele, happened by the sleeping Kauhi. Struck by her beauty, the awakened god struggled to stand. He tried to break free of his chains so that he could go away with the goddess and be finished with his boring job. However, his joints rusty and his strength sapped from moving so little for so many years, he could only manage to rise to the crouching position he maintains to this day.

Cave Tales

According to a legend about one aquatic Waianapanapa grotto, near Hana on Maui, a Hawaiian princess fled from her jealous husband. She made the mistake of hiding on a ledge in a cave that was known to be used by lovers for secret rendezvous. Her frenzied husband ran everywhere searching for his wayward wife. While he was catching his breath by the cave, he caught something else as well: a glimpse of her reflection in the water at the grotto's entrance. Convinced that she must have gone there to meet another man, he flew into a rage, bashing her head against the wall and killing her.

Locals say that it is the princess's blood that, even today, turns the cave pool red every April. Some claim you can still hear the echoes of her terrified shrieks. However, according to others, the water turns crimson from the tiny red shrimp that multiply in the pool in the spring and the "shrieks" are the sound of the wind whooshing in and out of the grotto. Exploration of most of Waianapanapa's caves is best left to divers or extremely strong swimmers. Everyone else can swim off the striking black sand beach.

No Place to Hide

An old legend explains how the meadow facing Kokee Lodge on Kauai came into being. This verdant open expanse once sprouted as many trees as the rest of the area. A trans-island trail to Kalalau Valley cuts through these dense woods. Residing in this forest was a terrifying *akua* (spirit), who got his kicks by hiding behind trees and then roughing up, even sometimes killing, unsuspecting travelers. The people of Kauai begged one of their gods to do away with this cruel spirit. But the evil akua paid no attention to the god's orders to cease and desist. The deity became so infuriated at the spirit's disrespect that the god swooped down and tore up all the trees by their roots. He piled them up, set them ablaze, and decreed that trees would never again grow here and thus akua would have no place to hide.

Don't Peek!

According to early Hawaiians, the Menehune, an elf-like race of creatures, agreed to construct Kauai's stone-enclosed Alakoko fishpond for a young prince and princess. However, they made it clear to all that absolutely no one would be allowed to watch them at work. In just one night, they built the pond. The heavy stones were transported to the stream by passing them from Menehune to Menehune in a line that stretched for 25 miles. When the job was almost done, the royal pair could no longer resist taking a look at the industrious little people. Catching them on their hillside perch, the Menehune turned the two into the twin stone pillars that you can see today on the ridge above the pond.

Did Father Know Best?

A triplet of peaks known as the Three Sisters watches over Kalalau Valley on Kauai. Legend has it that a storm once ripped through a coastal village in Kalalau, sweeping away homes and taro fields. Three goddesses who lived in mountain caves behind the valley felt sorry for the poor mortals below. They turned themselves into human beings and went down to help the villagers. With this divine aid, the results of the storm's vicious handiwork were repaired in just one day. While the villagers rejoiced, grateful for this superhuman assistance, the father of the sisters fumed. How dare his daughters lower themselves by fraternizing with mere mortals! To punish the wayward goddesses, he transformed them into the three pillars of stone that still stand.

Keep Away

While many ancient Hawaiians saw Molokai as a religious sanctuary, others were kept away by frightening tales of island sorcery. The poisonwood gods the island was known for first presented themselves at an *ulu maika* (stone bowling) course at Maunaloa. Among the men betting on the stone discs as they rolled them, Kaneiakama was losing badly. A god appeared to him, advising him to increase his wagers. Grateful when he won, he gave a large portion of his winnings to the god. In a flash, a grove of trees appeared. Becoming their caretaker, Kaneiakama discovered that when the wood was whittled into images, it could have devastating effects on enemies. Molokai was thus able to keep hostile outsiders at bay.

Chapter 9

OAHU WITH KIDS

Honolulu, Waikiki Beach, the extinct Diamond Head volcano, the USS *Arizona* Memorial, Pearl Harbor—these famous attractions are all found an Oahu, one reason that this is the state's most visited island. Popular with families, Oahu is a wonderful place for kids, whether your child wants to go behind the scenes with a zookeeper, get nose to fin with a shark, camp overnight on a battleship, watch a whale perform gravity-defying tricks, step into Hawaii's maritime past, learn to surf with fellow teenagers, play golf, or simply run wild through a sprawling park.

While Oahu is the most populous chunk of the archipelago, it's not the largest. That honor belongs to the island of Hawaii, commonly known as the Big Island (and thus often mistakenly thought to be the main island). Following Maui in size, Oahu is only the third largest.

If you're looking for action, you'll find plenty on Oahu. It would take ages to sample all the excellent restaurants, museums, and after-dark entertainment. You can give your wallet a real workout in the stores and boutiques that hit you from all sides as you walk down Kalakaua Avenue, the main drag in Waikiki, or even as you wander around your hotel. However, to many outsiders who equate Oahu with Waikiki's highrises, crowds, and tacky-to-sophisticated stores and restaurants, it comes as a surprise that most of the island is countryside. Breezes ripple agricultural fields and flowering trees. Jagged red cliffs plunge to royal blue waters edged in frothy white foam. Plump clouds lounge on the tops of rugged, jade-colored mountains.

There is no question that Oahu is the most developed island in the chain. Yet most of the development is contained on the southern coast, where Honolulu, the capital of the state, is located. The vast majority of the island's hotels (most of which are highrises) are clustered here in Waikiki. But this tourist haven is only a small (albeit jam-packed) neighborhood within Honolulu, which in turn takes up only a small portion of the island's 608 square miles.

Name that Hotel

Some hotels and condos in Waikiki have dizzyingly similar names, particularly those that are parts of chains. So be sure you know exactly which one is yours before you try to get a taxi or airport van driver to take you there. Oahu's main chains are Outrigger, Ohana, Aston, Marc, and Sheraton.

Getting Around

Honolulu International Airport, near Pearl Harbor, is *ewa* (west) of downtown Honolulu and Waikiki, where most hotels are located. The 20-minute drive can turn into 45 minutes during rush hours. Especially when rooms are booked as part of fly/stay package deals, complimentary airport shuttle service is often provided to Waikiki hotels, as well as to the few far-flung accommodations elsewhere on the island. Follow airport signs to taxis, shuttle buses, public buses, and rental car desks. Car rental agencies located at or near the airport provide complimentary shuttle service from the baggage claim area to and from their offices. You'll see courtesy phones for contacting them.

However, if you're based in Honolulu, driving a car can be far more trouble than it's worth. Who wants to spend their vacation fighting traffic or grumbling about how much they have to pay for hotel parking? But for the greatest degree of freedom and convenience (especially if you're traveling with young children), you might consider renting wheels for part of your stay for explorations beyond the capital city.

Oahu's convenient public bus system, known as **TheBus**, Tel. 296-1818, Fare: $2 (adults), $1 (age 6 to 18), exact change required, is the least expensive and often the most interesting way to get around the island. While riding with residents going about their business, you can often pick up tips about little-known places to go or things to see and do. These buses can take you to Oahu's major attractions, including beaches all over the island. (Be sure to ask for any necessary transfers, which are free, when you pay your fare.) In about four hours, you can travel practically the entire perimeter of the island, passing some spectacular coastal scenery. To avoid rush hours, travel between 9am and 3pm, or after 6pm. TheBus does not run between 1:30am and 3:30am.

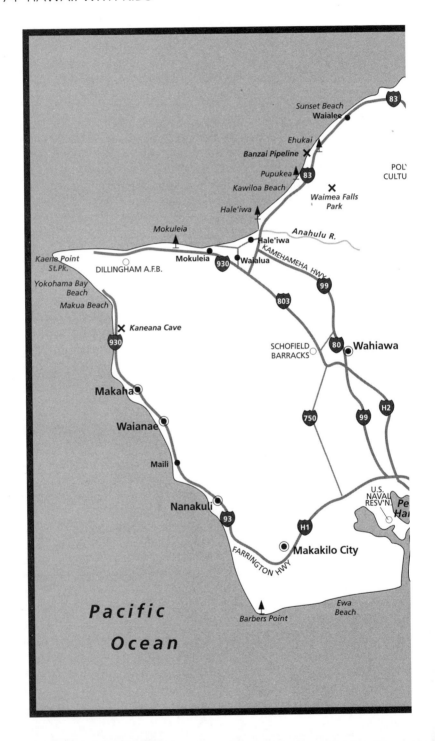

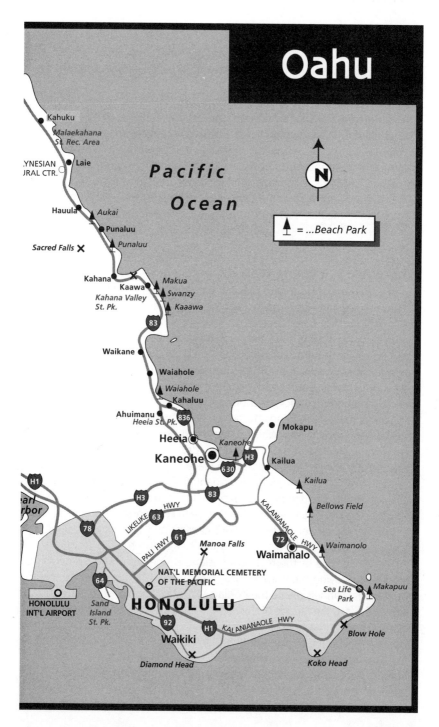

Oahu

Pacific Ocean

N

⬆ = ...Beach Park

Kahuku
Malaekahana St. Rec. Area
.YNESIAN
JRAL CTR. Laie
Hauula *Aukai*
Punaluu
Sacred Falls ✕ *Punaluu*
Kahana
Kaawa *Makua*
Kahana Valley St. Pk. *Swanzy*
Kaaawa
83
Waikane
Waiahole
Waiahole
Kahaluu
Ahuimanu 836
Heeia St. Pk.
Heeia *Kaneohe* Mokapu
Kaneohe H3
630 Kailua
Kailua
H1
83
arl H3
rbor 63 LIKELIKE HWY *Bellows Field*
78 PALI HWY KALANIANAOLE HWY
61 *Manoa Falls* ✕ 72 *Waimanolo*
Waimanalo
64 NAT'L MEMORIAL CEMETERY OF THE PACIFIC
Sea Life Park *Makapuu*
HONOLULU INT'L AIRPORT
Sand Island St. Pk. HONOLULU
92 H1 KALANIANAOLE HWY
Waikiki *Blow Hole*
✕ ✕
Diamond Head *Koko Head*

Local Lingo

If you're planning to drive in Hawaii, you'll have to get used to the local way of giving directions. If someone tells you to "Go Diamond Head," that means to drive east, toward Oahu's Diamond Head volcano. If you are east of Diamond Head, they might send you "Koko Head," toward another easterly landmark. "Ewa" (AY-vah) means to go west on Oahu, toward Ewa Beach (the *w* should make you think "west," even though it's pronounced like *v*). On both Oahu and the other islands, "mauka" (MOW-kah) is Hawaiian for "toward the mountains" (remember that the first syllable sounds like that of "mountain"), while "makai" (mahk-EYE) means "toward the sea."

Where Are We Going Now?

Waikiki (part of Honolulu) may be a mere one and a half square miles in size, but its glitz and glitter get most of the attention given Oahu. By daybreak, the streets are filled with activity as pedestrians stroll by joggers, families munch early breakfasts, and men with metal detectors comb the beach for wayward coins. Hundreds of hotels, restaurants, shops, nightclubs, and bars are packed into Waikiki. ABC Drug Stores (which sell everything from groceries and liquor to clothing and beach gear) are omnipresent—there are sometimes even two on a single block, anchoring it like bookends.

Created by human hands (to rid the once swampy area of mosquitoes), the Ala Wai Canal forms Waikiki's northern and western borders. Luxury condominiums with views of verdant hillsides stand along the shores of this glistening waterway. Canoe races take place on the canal in the evenings. In the east, Waikiki is bounded by Kapahulu Avenue, Kapiolani Park, and Diamond Head, the extinct volcano that has become an unforgettable landmark. Waikiki Beach and the Pacific Ocean command the southern coast. Most of Oahu's dinner and moonlight cruises, and glass-bottom boat trips leave from Kewalo Basin, just beyond the ewa (western) end of Waikiki.

The low profile of the rest of the island is fine with both residents and visitors who, leaving the hordes behind, escape to greater Honolulu and the rural regions. Tunnels pierce the Koolau Mountains between the city and the windward coast, the far side of the island. Along the North Shore, beaches lure master surfers and a handsome old plantation town draws visitors to small shops selling imaginative art, clothing, and crafts.

If you want to take a wonderful drive, one of the most dramatic is from Diamond Head past Makapuu Lookout to Waimanalo, then through the Koolau Mountains along the Pali Highway, to Honolulu. Others are the mountainous Tantalus-Round Top Drive; and the beach-trimmed windward coast and North Shore.

Another scenic drive is to cut across the mountains from Honolulu to the windward coast along Likelike Highway. When you emerge from Wilson Tunnel, a spectacular vista will be laid out before you: Peppered with houses, vibrantly green open spaces sweep to the foot of the mountains and to the water's edge. Banana trees and wild guava border the road. This side of the island is wetter and thus more lush than the leeward coast.

Sights & Adventures
KAPIOLANI PARK, Waikiki.

At the base of Diamond Head, this attractive, spacious park is really the only part of Waikiki frequented by Oahu's residents. Especially on weekends, it churns with people jogging; playing soccer, softball, Frisbee, and tennis (on lighted courts), and flying kites. Our kids love the huge lawns where they can run far and wide while remaining within our view. Local families gather in

Shop 'til You Drop

Along **Kalakaua Avenue**, Waikiki's main thoroughfare, visitors pour in and out of shops such as Tiffany, Gucci, Chanel, and Celine. The centrally located **Royal Hawaiian Shopping Center** takes up a chunk of Kalakaua Avenue. Out front, the **Waikiki Old Town Trolley** departs for tours of Honolulu, but it concentrates on tourist traps.

Other shopping meccas include the crowded, open-air **International Marketplace** and **King's Village**, with its clock tower, both near Kalakaua and Kaiulani. King's Village is tucked behind the twin-towered Hyatt Regency Waikiki and across from the Sheraton Princess Kaiulani Hotel. The cobblestone alleys and the appealing old architecture make this a pleasant place to stop, if only to see a Burger King in a most unlikely building. In addition to the restaurants and shops here, you can watch hula or candle-carving demonstrations, among other activities. For a pleasant diversion, follow the royal path through King's Village to trace the history of Hawaii's royalty described on handcrafted plaques along the way.

Just outside of Waikiki, the upscale **Ward Centre**, on Ala Moana Boulevard in Honolulu, is filled with sophisticated shops and restaurants trimmed in oak, with brass railings, and set off by hand-carved wooden signs, brick walkways, wooden columns, stained-glass light fixtures, and hanging lamps. But my favorite place to shop on Oahu is **Hale'iwa**, the scenic old plantation town on the North Shore, where quirky boutiques and galleries sell all kinds of distinctive jewelry, clothing, and art.

clusters to hear each other strum ukuleles or slack key guitars. Concerts of Hawaiian music as well as jazz, reggae, and European classical draw people with picnic dinners and blankets spread out on the grass.

David Kalakaua, who reigned as Hawaii's king from 1874 to 1891, was inspired to create this park by his visits to the mainland, where he saw large patches of green set aside for public pleasure. He dedicated this verdant spot in 1877, naming it after his queen. In those days, peacocks roamed freely and there were ponds stocked with goldfish. But these ponds were filled in during the 1920s. Horse racing thrived here for a while, until public distaste for the increasingly wild betting put an end to it.

HONOLULU ZOO, Kapiolani Park, 151 Kapahulu Avenue, Waikiki; Tel. 971-7171 or 926-3191, www.honzoosoc.org; open 9am-4:30pm daily (children's zoo closes at 4pm); admission: $6 (age 13 and older); $1 (age 6 to 12), free for children 5 and younger; Family passes: $25 per year (for 2 adults and up to six children age 17 or younger from one household, including admission to the Foster Botanical Garden)

Built in 1914, this zoo has added nearly 1,000 animals to its original half a dozen. And it offers much more than just sights, sounds, and, well, smells. Of course, young children can touch and feed dozens of friendly animals at the petting zoo. But what makes this zoo special are the many other interactive experiences for kids. The "Keiki Zookeeper" program, for instance, lets children age 6 to 10 go behind the scenes to help zookeepers with their daily animal care. "Ohana Adventures" is a chance for parents and children (age 5 and older) to create snacks or toys for the animals. If you're on Oahu during a full moon (with kids age 5 or older), consider taking a "Twilight Tour" of the zoo.

The day camp invites kids (age 5 to 11) to spend a week, a day, or part of a day learning all about caring for zoo animals, the importance of conservation, and how endangered wildlife can be saved, plus a chance to take part in animal games and art projects. Families can even spend the night at the zoo during the "Snooze at the Zoo" camp outs that include storytelling, campfire songs, pizza, walking tours, a special peek at nocturnal creatures, and breakfast; pitch your tent or curl up in your sleeping bags under the stars.

On Wednesday nights during the summer, The Wildest Show in Town, Tel. 526-6610, presents a free conert series at the zoo.

WAIKIKI AQUARIUM, Kapiolani Park, 2777 Kalakaua Avenue, on the Diamond Head (east) end of Waikiki Beach, Waikiki; Tel. 923-9741, www.waquarium.org; open 9am-5pm daily (last entry: 4:30pm); admission: $8 (adults), $4 (age 13 to 17), free for children age 12 and younger.

At the Waikiki Aquarium, which dates back to 1904, children age 5 and older, accompanied by an adult, can take an after dark flashlight tour of the exhibits to learn about the nocturnal habits of all kinds of marine life. They can also explore shoreline, reef, and tide pool habitats by day to learn about reef conservation from naturalists, or design and build their own shark model for "Shark Olympics" races.

Children age 8 to 14 (who can swim and are comfortable using a mask and snorkel) can take a weeklong marine biology class here, including in-the-water and in-the-lab study. The aquarium even offers programs for children age 1 to 3 (accompanied by adults) including weekly sessions in crafts, movement, and music related to various types of sea life. If all you want to do is take an audio wand tour of the exhibits of seals, giant clams, sharks, sea turtles, lobsters, crocodiles, and fish, that's fine too.

Beware of Freebies

Timeshare booths around Waikiki offer big discounts, even free-bies, on most major attractions. The catch is that you have to attend a two-hour sales presentation first. If you have time to spare, a little patience, and a lot of sales resistance (if you don't intend to buy any property), you could end up with a couple of free tickets for a cruise or other excursion.

ATLANTIS SUBMARINE, Tel. 973-9811, 800/548-6262; rates: $70 (adults) or $43 (children age 2 to 12); minimum height: 36".

I recommend taking this plunge on Oahu only if you're not going to Maui or the Big Island, where the submarine visits natural coral reefs. Here when your 48- or 64-passenger sub descends about 100 feet, what you'll see is fish swarming around a sunken naval tanker and an artificially created reef. Still dying to stay dry while you visit the depths? Note that although the submarine ride takes only about 45 minutes, you'll need to allow some two hours for this excusion, including time on the catamaran shuttle that departs from the Hilton Hawaiian Village dock in Waikiki.

DOLPHIN QUEST OAHU, Kahala Mandarin Oriental, Hawaii, 5000 Kahala Avenue, Honolulu, HI 96816, Kahala (just east of Waikiki), Tel. 808/739-8918 or 800/248-3316, www.dolphinquest.org. Sessions begin at $125 for 30 minutes.

In programs designed for children as young as five as well as adults, participants learn all about dolphins and interact with them—by touching, feeding, and playing games—in shallow water. Stingrays, Hawaiian green turtles, and tropical reef fish are also part of the fun. While some animal lovers complain that keeping dolphins in captivity is harmful to them, others say that these mammals are well cared for and that the educational benefits of these programs are immense.

ALOHA TOWER, Pier 9, Honolulu Harbor, at the harbor end of Fort Street mall, next to the Maritime Center, Honolulu.

Built in 1921, 184-foot Aloha Tower overlooks the water and **Aloha Tower Marketplace**. This l0-story tower, a short walk from the Maritime Center, was once the tallest building in Hawaii. Built in 1926, it was turned over to the military for use during World War II. From the top floor observation deck, you can take in the view of Honolulu Harbor, the city's forest of buildings, and the coast. The Marketplace offers a variety of outdoor vendors, shops, and restaurants.

During the 1820s, in the old whaling days, more than 50 ships a year anchored off Honolulu, bringing many foreigners who decided to settle in this Pacific city. A century later, great numbers of tourists began to pour off ships here, welcomed by crowds of people selling leis and the music of the Royal Hawaiian Band.

HAWAII MARITIME CENTER, Pier 7, Honolulu Harbor, near the foot of Punchbowl Street, next to Aloha Tower; Tel. 536-6373; open 8:30am-5pm daily; admission $7.50 (adults), $4.50 (age 6-17), including the use of a portable cassette for listening to the taped guided tour.

During the late 1800s, King Kalakaua, a.k.a. the Merrie Monarch, sponsored surfing meets and canoe races, reviving these Hawaiian pastimes. His boathouse was also the site of parties and performances that resuscitated hula and Hawaiian music, which had been driven underground by disapproving American missionaries who had arrived during the 1820s. The king and his friends spent so much time here that he installed Hawaii's first telephone line, between the boathouse and Iolani Palace.

So when the Hawaii Maritime Center opened in 1988 near the place where the boathouse once stood, it did so on November 16th, King Kalakaua's birthday. And the highlight of the center is the Kalakaua Boathouse Museum, which resembles the original two-story building. Displays and videos celebrate Polynesian and Western maritime contributions, as well as the monarch's love of the Hawaiian arts. Exhibits include everything from shark tooth tools and an intricately woven Hawaiian red and yellow feather cape to rotund iron caldrons first used to melt whale blubber, then later for boiling sugar or making *okolehao* (*ti* plant liquor). Look for the huge humpback whale skeleton.

Admission to the maritime center includes an opportunity to board the *Falls of Clyde*, an 1878 four-masted, square-rigged ship docked at the pier. Two replicas of ancient Hawaiian **double-hulled sailing canoes** are also docked here—when they aren't off on voyages, that is. Made the traditional way, the *Hawaiiloa* is carved from tree trunks, while the *Hokulea* was fashioned from fiberglass. Both canoes have traveled through the Pacific using only ancient navigational techniques.

BISHOP MUSEUM AND PLANETARIUM, 1525 Bernice Street, Honolulu, about 3 miles from Waikiki; Tel. 847-3511 or (planetarium) 848-4136, www.bishopmuseum.org; open 9am-5pm, daily; admission: $15 (adults), $12 (children 6-17).

Named in honor of Bernice Pauahi Bishop, the granddaughter of Kamehameha the Great, this museum houses a fabulous collection of Hawaiiana and often has exhibits specifically geared to families with children. When Charles Bishop met Princess Pauahi after he came to Hawaii from New York in 1846, she was engaged to Lot Kamehameha, who was next in line to take over Hawaii's throne. But her plans soon changed. The princess and her foreign husband went on to open Hawaii's first bank, and he became a noted politician and entrepreneur as well as a generous philanthropist.

Extremely proud of her culture, Bernice Bishop—the last direct descendant of King Kamehameha I—loved collecting Hawaiian arts and antiques. So it was only fitting that, as a memorial to her after her 1884 death, Charles Bishop founded this museum in 1889. As the years passed, the collection snowballed and now encompasses items from many Polynesian cultures. The museum also serves as a center for research in anthropology and the islands' natural history.

The two main galleries, demonstration and performance hall, Science Center, and planetarium are set on ten acres. The fascinating show at the planetarium vividly and visually explains how the ancient Polynesians sailed to Hawaii in canoes about 1,000 years ago.

A huge whale skeleton hangs from the ceiling in the main hall of the museum. Displays include an old-fashioned grass *hale* (house); *kapa* (cloth made from pounded bark); a Hawaiian throne; elaborate royal feathered capes and headdresses; crowns worn by King Kalakaua and Queen Kapiolani; and paintings of members of the Hawaiian monarchy. Human teeth (of dead enemies) are artfully inlaid into wooden waste bowls.

During the summer, the Bishop Museum hosts an evening concert series.

PUNCHBOWL, 2177 Puowaina Drive, Honolulu; Tel. 532-3720; open daily 8am-6:30pm, near the Bishop Museum.

With its commanding views of the city way below, scenic Punchbowl is officially called the National Memorial Cemetery of the Pacific.. The military and their families lie beneath the headstones lying flat on the manicured lawns decorated with small clusters of flowers. High up winding roads, this peaceful locale has a lookout with a wraparound view of the mountains; Diamond Head, which seems to rise out of Honolulu's tall buildings; the avant-garde State Capitol; the Ala Moana Shopping area; and the Pacific Ocean. As tranquil and attractive as the grounds are, don't get any ideas about picnicking here as we once did. When we tried, we were promptly informed that no food is allowed on the premises.

FOSTER BOTANIC GARDENS, 180 North Vineyard Boulevard, near the Bishop Museum; Tel. 522-7066 or 522-7064; open daily 9am-4pm; admission $5 (adults), $1 (age 6-12).

During the summer these blossoming gardens provide a serene setting for children's story times (call for details). Any time of year, paths wend their ways through nine acres and thousands of species of tropical flowers, trees, and other plants, including ferns, orchids, multi-colored bromeliads, ginger, vanilla plants, pineapple, guava and banana trees. Birds call back and forth to each other throughout the grounds. Ninety-minute tours are conducted every afternoon, but you're also welcome to explore on your own. Ask about the hikes on Oahu and other islands led by the Friends of Foster Botanic Gardens.

Next to the garden, you can sit in the sun on the verandah or spend a few pensive moments inside **Kwan Yin Temple**.

HONOLULU ACADEMY OF ARTS, 900 South Beretania Street, Honolulu; Tel. 532-8701 or 532-8726; open 10am-4:30pm, Tuesday-Saturday, 1-5 pm on Sunday, admission $7 (adults), $4 (seniors and age 13 to 18); open 11am to 5pm on Family Days (the third Sunday of most months), when admission is free.

Monthly Family Day is a great time to visit this venerated academy filled with Asian art, from furniture and bronzes to Japanese prints, along with contemporary and traditional Western works. Not only is admission free on then, but entertainment might include music, dance, or storytelling, along with art projects and treasure hunts (with prizes) through the galleries. Each Family Day has a different theme, such as Talk to the Animals, Unroll Your Imagination, or Hunt for Heroes and Heroines. Spend some time relaxing in one of the sunny courtyards with tiled fountains. You might come upon a class of art students busily sketching by a lily pond in an enclosed garden while birds provide background music.

MISSION HOUSES MUSEUM, 553 South King Street, Honolulu; Tel. 531-0481; open 10am-6pm, Tuesday-Saturday, noon to 5pm on Sunday; admission: $10 (adults), $6 (age 6 to 21).

This museum is made up of restored buildings that were once homes and headquarters of missionaries. On Saturdays and Sundays, during the family program, kids are invited to complete workbooks with their parents, examine the types of toys and games missionary children played with, and try on period clothing.

In 1820, the one wooden house (the others are of coral stone) was sent dismantled, all the way from Boston, and is the oldest home in Hawaii. It just didn't seem right to folks back home to have American missionaries living in grass houses while they did God's work. Adding local wood and old ship timbers to the pre-fab materials, the missionaries constructed a cozy four-bedroom house, now the Islands' oldest remaining wooden structure. As many as three or four families lived in this house at any given time!

Hawaiian chiefs came here, dressed in their new European clothes, to learn to read and write Hawaiian or take singing lessons in European music. Commoners also flocked to the house, for religious services and to get Western medicines to combat the new diseases foreigners had brought to Hawaii, which were devastating to the indigenous population. Missionary books, quilts, furniture and other household items are on display.

The second-oldest house, where the museum entrance is, was built in 1831. The third, dating back to 1841, is where the old hand-operated printing presses are exhibited and demonstrated. The shelves in this building are piled with worn books and illustrations printed in the early 1800s with engraved plates or wood blocks.

The weekend after Thanksgiving, an annual crafts fair takes place on the grounds.

KAWAIAHA'O CHURCH, King Street, across from Mission Houses Museum and near Iolani Palace, Honolulu; Tel. 522-1333, Sunday services: 8am and 10:30am.

The original permanent Protestant church built by the missionaries, Kawaiaha'o Church was made of 14,000 hand-cut coral stones. While the porous coral may appear light in weight, each block would tip a scale at about 1,000 pounds. Designed by famous missionary Hiram Bingham and built between 1837 and 1842, Kawaiaha'o Church has a prominent clock tower. Services are conducted in both English and Hawaiian. Many people wear leis with their muumuus or jackets. Japanese weddings frequently take place here during the week.

Outside, you'll see the tomb of Lunalilo, who became Hawaii's first elected king in 1873. To show how close he felt to his people, he walked barefoot to this church for his swearing in. Although his reign was brief, he was able to restore the vote for Hawaiian commoners and return to them their right to hold elective office. Instead of being buried at the Royal Mausoleum in Nuuanu Valley with the other alii (chiefs), Lunalilo chose to end up here, with the regular folks.

IOLANI PALACE, 364 South King Street (at Richards Street), Honolulu; Tel. 538-1471 (tour information) or 522-0832 (reservations); open 9am-2pm, Tuesday-Saturday; the 45-minute tours begin every 15 minutes; admission $20 (adults), $5 (age 5 to 17); children under 5 are not allowed in the palace; purchase tickets at least 30 minutes prior to tour time.

Dignified Iolani, the United State's only royal palace, sits on a smooth patch of green in the midst of the capital's choking traffic and tall, modern buildings. A fence of gold-tipped spears encloses thriving pandanus, banyan, and flame trees, while a palm-lined promenade leads to the entrance. Its name meaning "bird of heaven," this opulent four-story Victorian palace is Italian Renaissance in style.

Ironically, it was built in 1882 by King Kalakaua, who was revered by

Hawaiians for reviving pride in Hawaiian culture. For example, he is credited with bringing back the hula, traditional music, and songs and poetry written in the Hawaiian tongue. All this had been sent underground by American missionaries. The first leader of any country to sail around the world, Kalakaua borrowed from the architecture that most impressed him during his visits with nearly a dozen heads of state, from Britain to Japan. Apart from its residents, the main Hawaiian presence in the palace was the ubiquitous prized native koa wood.

Moderation was a concept for which this king had little use. On at least one occasion, he threw a banquet for 5,000 guests. He antagonized Honolulu's business community (most of whom were Caucasian descendants of missionaries) by his extravagant spending. Bent on designing a regal mansion Hawaiians could be proud of, he cut no corners when he had elaborate Iolani Palace built.

The high-ceilinged interior is graced with intricately carved balustrades, plaster cornices with detailed designs, chandeliers, candelabras, mirrors with gold leaf frames, and spacious bathtubs lined in copper. The furniture Kalakaua chose was custom made by a Boston firm that had built furniture for the American White House. Amid this splendor, King Kalakaua entertained many notable guests, including Robert Louis Stevenson.

After the king's sudden death in San Francisco in 1891, his sister, Liliuokalani, followed him to the throne. In 1893, she was deposed by a group of mostly foreign, Hawaii-based businessmen who turned Iolani Palace into the seat of their provisional government. In 1895, they convicted Liliuokalani of treason for being part of a widely supported attempt to restore her to power. In a move that could hardly be more humiliating, the queen's accusers held her trial in the Throne Room, where she had once reigned.

Upon entering the palace today, you'll don felt booties so as not to mar the glossy hardwood floors. You can wander into the velvet-draped Throne Room and the upstairs guest bedroom where the queen was imprisoned for nine months as punishment for wanting to continue leading her own country. Today you'll see a seven-foot-long twisted narwhal tusk in the Throne Room topped with a gold ball. Given to Kalakaua by a whaling captain, the tusk served as a *puloulou*—a staff that was infused with *mana* (spiritual power) and thus ensured that the area surrounding the monarch was sacred.

Iolani Palace housed the Territorial Government for more than 50 years and served as the capitol for a while after Hawaii became a state in 1959. Headed by Abigail Kawananakoa, Kalakaua's great-grandniece, a group of volunteers painstakingly restored the palace, locating and bringing back much of the original furniture that had been sold off. A rare early copy of *Legends and Myths of Hawaii*, written by Kalakaua, sits in the king's quarters along with his books in Hawaiian, English, German, and French. (You can pick up a new edition of *Legends* today in bookstores throughout the Islands.) In the entry hall, walls are hung with portraits of Hawaiian royalty, beginning with Kamehameha the Great.

A Haunted Palace

During the 1930s, people on the mainland read newspaper articles about the eerie haunting of Iolani Palace. Hawaii's state legislature actually suspended its work for a while, after a series of mysterious accidents were attributed to angry spirits in the mansion. Even today, some people swear that at night they sometimes see candlelight dancing in the window of the upstairs bedroom where the queen was imprisoned. Others say they hear the tinkling keys of the palace guards who once patrolled the mansion.

CHINATOWN, just off Nimitz Highway, about 16 blocks bordered roughly by North Hotel, River, Beretania, and Nuuanu streets.

One of Honolulu's first neighborhoods, Chinatown got its name during the late 19th century, when Chinese immigrants began moving in. They took jobs as laundry workers, tailors, bakers, and grocers. Today orange ducks hang in restaurant windows. Bakeries and stores selling homemade Chinese candy lure passersby inside. At herbal medicine shops, wooden drawers filled with natural ingredients line walls like library card catalogues. Dried lizard tails sit in jars, and the air is thick with incense, tiger balm, and ginseng. People go in and out of acupuncture offices. The streets are perfumed by fresh flowers from lei stands. Men gather at pool halls, while Chinese, Vietnamese, and Filipino restaurants do a brisk business. Many immigrants have also settled here from Cambodia and Laos.

Especially on Saturday mornings, serious shopping takes place in this neighborhood. At sprawling **Oahu Market**, on King and Kekaulike streets, boxes are heaped with live crabs attempting to claw their way out in slow motion. Counters are covered with whole suckling pigs, glistening fresh fish, chicken feet (for soup), and all kinds of cabbage, seaweed, *ti* leaves, fruit and other vegetables. Built in 1904, the market was about to be sold to developers by its owners in 1984. Not only did the merchants get together to buy it, but

Lingering Leis

Chinatown is a good place to buy leis. If your accommodation has a refrigerator in your room, you're in luck. You can keep leis fresh for several days by placing them in a plastic bag and keeping them cold between wearings.

they also raised thousands more dollars to renovate it. **Maunakea Market**, at Maunakea Street between Hotel and Pauahi, is geared more toward tourists.

HONOLULU THEATRE FOR YOUTH, 2846 Ualena Street, Honolulu, HI 96819-1910, Tel. 808/839-9885, www.htyweb.org.

Producing an entertaining selection of well-known classics and works of local writers (with adult full-time actors), this theater has been around for more than half a century. Each season includes plays for families and children at different age levels, from preschoolers to teens. If you're visiting during December, don't miss *Christmas Talk Story*, which has become an island tradition.

USS ARIZONA MEMORIAL AT PEARL HARBOR, US Naval Reservation, Pearl Harbor, Honolulu; Tel. 422-2771, tours 8am to 3pm, visitor center open until 5pm. Tours are free; however, tickets are required, the wait for the hour and 15 minute tour can exceed two hours, and tickets may be unavailable after noon. No bags of any kind (not even purses, diaper bags, or camera bags) or strollers with pockets are allowed in the visitor center, so you must use a storage facility in the parking lot ($2 per item).

Hawaii's number-one visitor attraction honors the more than 2,000 Navy, Army, and Marine personnel and civilians who died and some 1,000 who were wounded in the December 7, 1941, Japanese attack on Pearl Harbor that thrust the United States into WWII.

Most of the American casualties occurred when the USS *Arizona* was bombed. Only about 150 of the 1,200 or so bodies on board could be recovered from the broken, twisted battleship, so the sunken vessel became an aquatic grave for the remaining dead. Today when survivors of the *Arizona* bombing die, they may have their cremated ashes put in urns and placed by divers on the ship with their comrades. Other Pearl Harbor attack survivors may have their cremated ashes scattered on the harbor.

The white concrete memorial above the ship was built in 1962. It does not touch any part of the sunken wreck. Even after so many decades, the oil still seeps from its tanks and creates a rainbow slick on the surface of the water. These shimmering bands of color, often scattered with leis tossed by visitors, look like abstract art. Across the harbor (which gets its name from the pearl oysters that were found in it), the **Visitor Center** houses a museum, bookstore, and a theater that shows a moving film about the attack.

Elvis Presley fans are proud to note that "The King" gave all of the money he made at his 1961 Pearl Harbor concert to the USS Arizona War Memorial building fund. This was the largest single donation.

Departing from the Visitor Center, you can take one of the free Navy shuttle boats across the harbor to stand on the Memorial (shuttles run from 7:45am to 3pm); excluding the time you'll spend waiting your turn, the tour lasts about an hour and 15 minutes.

If you're driving to Pearl Harbor, it's best to set out as early as possible so you can arrive when the wait for the shuttle boat is shortest. (Even "short" waits can last more than an hour, but at least you can visit the museum and shop during this time.) Other options are to board one of the Pearl Harbor tour boats that depart daily from Kewalo Basin near Waikiki, or to take the **Arizona Memorial shuttle bus**, which leaves from various hotels in Waikiki, Tel. 839-0911, about $8 round trip for the 45- to 60-minute ride each way, or the less expensive public bus, about 90 minutes from Waikiki.

Junior Rangers

When you get to the USS *Arizona* Memorial visitor center, ask about the kids' activity books that lead children on a historical journey. Young children get a kick out of earning the official Junior Ranger Badges and becoming official Junior Rangers.

USS BOWFIN SUBMARINE MUSEUM AND PARK, next to the Pearl Harbor Arizona Memorial Visitor Center, Tel. 423-1341; open daily 8am-4:30pm; admission: $8 (adults), $3 (kids 4-12).

The USS *Bowfin* submarine is a memorial to the 52 subs that were lost during WWII and the more than 3,000 men who died in them. Walk through the cramped vessel to see what life was like for the men.

THE BATTLESHIP MISSOURI, next to the Pearl Harbor Arizona Memorial Visitor Center, Tel. 455-1600 or 423-1341, www.ussmissouri.com; tours 9am to 3:58pm; admission: $16 (adults), $8 (children under age 12), plus additional costs for guided tours.

Stand on Battleship Row, where World War II began, and visit areas of this impressive battleship that have been preserved just as they were more than 60 years ago. A one-hour guided introductory tour will show you the layout of the ship while you learn about *Missouri*'s systems and weapons and hear about the ship's history. The Explorer's Tour takes you into once-restricted areas, including the crew's galley, Chef's mess, brig, machine shop, laundry room, post office, barbershop, and "Broadway," the corridor that runs a third of the length of the ship.

Ask about the special program that hosts youth for overnight camping aboard the ship.

HAWAIIAN WATERS ADVENTURE PARK, 400 Farrington Highway, Kapolei, HI 96707, Exit 1 off the H-1 Highway, about 35 minutes west of Waikiki; Tel. 674-9283, WILD-Wave, www.hawaiianwaters.com. Generally open 10:30am to 4pm Monday through Friday and 10:30am to 5pm on weekends. Cost: $35 (age 12 to 59), $24 (age 3 to 11), $16 (age 60 and older). Accessible by TheBus (Tel. 296-1818 for schedules and routes).

Strategically located in one of the driest and warmest parts of Oahu, this 25-acre water park is popular for its inner tube rides, slides, wavepool, and river rides. Kids love the multi-level activity pool, with its seven slides, plus lily pad walks. Hawaiian Waters Adventure Park also offers a beach volleyball court and an interactive playground featuring waterfalls, water cannons, and mini slides. Lockers, life vests, and bodyboards are available for rent, and patrons are welcome to use the changing rooms and showers. At the food court, you'll find hot dogs, pizza, ice cream, and lots of other edibles. You are not permitted to bring coolers, food, alcohol or other beverages into the park (except for infants), but there is a public picnic area (with tables and shade pavilions) just outside the front gate. As you exit the water park, be sure to have your hands stamped for same-day reentry.

SEA LIFE PARK, 41-202 Kalanianaole Highway, Makapuu Point, Waimanalo (windward coast, southeastern Oahu); Tel. 259-7933 or 800/548-6262; open 9:30am-5pm daily; admission: $26 (adults), $13 (age 4-12).

Backed by horizontally streaked cliffs and with views of the ocean and offshore islands, Sea Life Park claims a gorgeous setting. The whole windward coast unfurls itself from **Makapuu Lookout**, across the highway. At the park, mock killer whales, dolphins, penguins, sea lions, and even a wholphin (a cross between a whale and a dolphin) perform amazing feats to the delight of the audience, even when folks get splashed. Marine exhibits also include colorful local sea life as well as hammerhead sharks and other menacing creatures seen through glass in their natural habitats. Ask about the special behind-the-scenes tour.

Dolphin-lovers won't want to miss the program called Splash U. Both adults and children get the chance to sit pool side and work with one of the trainers instructing the dolphins to perform various tricks. Participants are permitted to reward the animals with fishy treats. Splash U is included in the Junior Animal Trainer Program, in which kids age 9 to 12 spend the day helping the staff with their work. Call in advance to register (note that there are addional charges for these programs).

For an added bonus for younger children, stop by the playground overlooking the stingray habitat. By the way, if you visit Sea Life Park on a hot day, be sure to bring hats or visors, sunglasses, and plenty of sun block since there is little shade in the park.

Along the coast near Sea Life Park, the water sprouts up through the rocks at **Blow Hole**, which is most dramatic when the waves are nice and rough.

SENATOR FONG'S PLANTATION AND GARDENS, 47-351 Pulama Road, Kahaluu (southern part of the windward coast); Tel. 239-6775; open 10am-4pm daily; admission $11.

These botanical gardens are also a working plantation, with many different types of fruit and nut trees. Trams amble through the 725-acre estate, taking visitors on tours. Named for Hiram Fong, the first Asian-

American to be elected to the US Senate, the gardens have a visitor center with a gift shop and snack bar. Fong's father emigrated from China to Maui to work in the sugarcane fields. His family struggling to stay afloat, Hiram Fong began working (picking kiawe beans) when he was only four years old. His industriousness landed him at the University of Hawaii. From there he moved on to Harvard Law School, and finally to the US Senate, serving under five presidents, from Eisenhower to Ford.

On Their Own

Traveling with kids between the ages of 10 and 17? Then consider sending them on a week-long adventure to **Camp Timberline**, Tel. 672-5441, www.kamaainakids.com/camp/program.html. The seven-night sleepover programs range from surf camp (in which kids sleep in tents on the beach and go kayaking and snorkeling in addition to learning how to handle their boards) to camps focusing on dance, crafts, and archery. Whether they stay in tents or cabins with electricity, kids will have showers and toilets with running water.

THE NORTH SHORE

Across the island from Waikiki and famous for its lush foliage, rural atmosphere, and beautiful beaches, the North Shore seems to be in another world. During the winter, its excellent surfing conditions draw scores of sports enthusiasts, whether they come just for fun, to compete in one of the tournaments, or simply to watch the action (and all the bodies in skimpy bathing suits).

Surfers' paradise begins with **Sunset Beach**. During the winter, this two-mile sandy expanse draws crowds of master surfers with its 20- and 30-foot waves. In the summer, when the water is "flat" (with waves a mere 10 feet tall), only experienced windsurfers and bodysurfers should attempt these sports. Even strong swimmers should not venture far from shore and no one should ever enter the water alone. Right off the road, the beach is backed by a thick row of pines.

Along with the other surfing meccas along the north shore, **Ehukai Beach Park** and the famed **Banzai Pipeline** get their share of board masters during the winter. During the championships, a festive atmosphere prevails. Blaring music sails past busy photographers, judges, and tables stacked with T-shirts. Lines form at food trucks parked along the road.

At **Pupukea Beach Park**, a marine reserve next to Sunset, snorkeling could hardly be more exciting. When you need a lift after all your aquatic action, take a drive along one of the nearby steep, narrow roads that go up into the hills. In this area, dotted with small ranches and orchards, roadside fruit stand vendors sell all kinds of fresh pickings during the summer. **Waimea Bay** has a wide, especially attractive beach.

A plantation town about an hour drive northwest of Waikiki, **Hale'iwa** is the main settlement on the North Shore. Handsome old buildings are set off by African tulip trees and palms. Turn up winding Paalaa Road, at the western end of the main road, for a scenic drive past banana plantations, private homes, and an old Buddhist temple with colorful gardens.

Looking at this small, remote town today, it is hard to believe that it ushered in tourism before Waikiki did. In 1899, Benjamin J. Dillingham, a wealthy businessman, put a stately hotel here, christening it Hale'iwa, meaning House of the Frigate Bird. This elegant Victorian lodging stood between the ocean and graceful **Anahulu River**. Fleeing Honolulu for seashore vacations, city residents climbed aboard the train that Dillingham had built for the surrounding sugar plantations and rode it here to the end of the line. The railroad, the hotel, and the sugarcane fields are now long gone. Today most newcomers arrive with surfboards tucked under their arms and head for the appealing beach park.

In 1984, Hale'iwa became a Historic, Cultural and Scenic District. However, this was just a few months too late for the rose-colored, art-deco Hale'iwa Theater, which protesters could not save from being torn down. Despite the demise of this theater, the old feeling of the frontier town has been preserved and, in some cases, manufactured. Weathered wooden buildings— both old and new—now house some exceptional boutiques, health food stores, restaurants, artists' studios, and art galleries.

In Hale'iwa, no new structures can look as though they were built after the 1920s. Dating back to 1926, **H**. **Miura** specializes in all kinds of fabrics from Japanese designs to Hawaiian *kapa* cloth patterns. The owners also run a shave ice stand next door. **Ishimoto Grocery** is in another old wooden building. **Liliuokalani Church**, erected in 1932, is one of the town's earliest buildings. Named for the queen who worshipped there, it contains a whimsical wall clock, a gift from the monarch herself in 1892. Instead of numbers on this timepiece, you'll see the 12 letters of the queen's royal name.

Spanning the river and dating back to 1921, the nearby concrete **Hale'iwa Bridge** serves as a stationary diving board for local children in the summer. During the popular August Hale'iwa Lantern Festival, delicate paper lanterns are sent floating down the river by Japanese residents to honor their ancestors. To escape into the jungle interior, some people go kayaking along this serene waterway. Houses perch on stilts along its banks while chickens scurry around yards.

Few people pass through town without stopping at **Matsumoto's**, a mom-and-pop general store, for a shave ice. Lilikoi, coconut, banana, and rainbow are the most-licked flavors. Red *azuki* beans or scoops of ice cream are often added to these snow cones. Don't be surprised if you have to wait on a wrap-around line.

ORIGINAL GLIDER RIDES, North Shore, Dillingham Airfield, Mokuleia, near the polo grounds; Tel. 677-3404 or 255-7826, www.honolulusoaring.com. Cost: $150 (two people) or $85 (one person). Reservations recommended. (Ask about the periodic promotional discounts.)

Children of any age can join their parents on these exhilarating 20-minute glider plane flights with Original Glider Rides, the operation with the most experience. A tow plane pulls the glider into the sky, then releases it. Wrapped in silence (since there's no motor), you'll float on air currents over gentle hills, the rugged Waianae Mountains, deep valleys, agricultural fields, and long broad Mokuleia Beach.

During the winter, you might even spot whales. You can generally see for more than 40 miles and sometimes as far as 80 miles, to the island of Kauai. Gliders fly seven days a week; there are only about 30 unflyable days a year. Be forewarned that occasionally people experience slight altitude sickness (drowsiness, headache, nausea). If you know you or your kids are prone to air- or seasickness, tell the pilot before you board, and he'll optimize conditions for you.

Note that there are two different glider plane companies based at the same location, so be sure to ask for "Mr. Bill" when you arrive.

POLYNESIAN CULTURAL CENTER, 55-370 Kamehameha Highway, Laie (northern windward coast); Tel. 293-3333; Open 12:30pm - 9pm daily, except Sunday; packages including the luau begin at $80 (adults) or $55 (age 3-11).

Kids (and adults) of all ages enjoy the al fresco Polynesian Cultural Center, featuring a variety of authentic recreations of traditional villages from islands all over the Pacific, a luau, and an evening performance of music and dance. Visitors get an intimate look at contrasting architectural styles and ways of life. At the "villages," the cultures of the indigenous peoples of Hawaii, Tahiti, the Marquesas, Tonga, New Zealand, Fiji, and Samoa come alive through music, crafts demonstrations, exhibits of artifacts, and historical mini-lectures.

You might watch a group of Hawaiian women pounding out bark to make *kapa* cloth, a young Tongan walking almost effortlessly up a giant palm to lop off a coconut, or a Maori warrior sticking out his "tattooed" tongue to let his enemies know he means business. The canoe ride down the "river" is pleasant. At the end of the day, visitors are serenaded by each village they pass along the way.

Wearing traditional dress, the people who work in the villages are actually from the islands they represent. Most of them are students at Brigham Young University whose Hawaii branch is run by the Mormon church, which runs the Polynesian Cultural Center. (Note that no alcohol or caffeinated beverages are served here since it would be against the Mormon religion.)

For the most rewarding part of visiting the Center, spend some time chatting with the staff between demonstrations. Many of them plan to return to their countries, while others end up marrying Americans and staying in the United States, some moving to the mainland. Once I talked to a Fijian grandmother whose daughter had married an American and moved to Philadelphia. She told me about old Fijian songs and legends that explained how these Pacific islanders had originally come from Africa.

At the **Hawaii Imax Theatre**—with a screen that is 65 feet tall and 96 feet wide — you will be able to see 40-minute, multimillion-dollar films. The huge

Hawaiian-Style Partying

Many hotels and independent companies regularly host **luau**, some in dramatic oceanfront settings. Although these feasts, with entertainment, will certainly give you a taste of Hawaiian food, music, dance, and traditions, these crowded, touristy affairs don't appeal to everyone. I prefer to steer clear of the larger feasts. Instead, I check the newspapers for fundraising luau sponsored by local churches, civic groups, or hula schools.

However, if you can't find a more local luau, the lavish production at the **Polynesian Cultural Center,** Tel. 293-3333, is an exciting way to close a day of visiting the Center's recreated villages (see above).

Another good choice is **Paradise Cove Luau Park,** Ko Olina, Ewa (27 miles from Waikiki). Tel. 842-5911 or 800/775-2683; www.paradisecovehawaii.com; held nightly; packages start at $60 (adults) and $40 (children), including round trip transportation from Waikiki. As far as commercial luau go, this is one of the most enjoyable. The food is nothing special, but the setting, the visitor participation in ancient Hawaiian activities, and the sometimes campy entertainment make the trip worthwhile.

Located on 12 acres in a beach park on Oahu's uncrowded Leeward Coast, Paradise Cove is a great spot for spectacular sunsets. Before the extensive buffet and performance, you'll be treated to live Hawaiian music and watch demonstrations such as palm frond weaving and coconut tree climbing. When it's time for the *hukilau* (net fishing), everyone watches the huge net being thrown out to sea, then helps pull it in. Guests may try their hands at husking coconuts, pounding poi, and stringing leis. They are also invited to participate in games such as *ulu maika* (Hawaiian bowling), spear throwing, and Tongan shuffleboard. If you'd rather not make the 50-minute drive yourself, you can arrange to be picked up by bus in Waikiki (you'll leave around 4pm and be dropped off at about 10:30pm).

☙

screen and the cinematography make you feel as if you're in the middle of the action. Seats are steeply terraced so that no views are obstructed by heads. One side effect: some people experience slight motion sickness. But if you close your eyes, it should pass.

After an afternoon of visiting villages, the buffet dinner or luau is followed by a musical extravaganza incorporating dances from all the islands. Like the rest of the cultural center, this colorful show is open air. Be sure to stop by the indoor-outdoor shopping complex, which sells crafts from all the islands.

Beaches

Oahu is rimmed with more than 50 beach parks, some of which have lifeguards, bathrooms, changing facilities, showers and picnic tables. Only highly skilled surfers should enter **North Shore** waters during winter months, when the waves are massive. This shore is the site of winter surfing tournaments. At all beaches, pay attention to warnings about surf conditions. Like any ocean, the extremely powerful Pacific must be handled with care.

Be sure to apply sunscreen before and immediately after leaving the water. Let the rays darken your skin slowly. Don't spend your whole first day in the sun. (But note that it may not be a good idea to find shade beneath a palm tree, since falling coconuts could klonk you on the head.) Leave your valuables in your hotel or condominium safe.

Waikiki, southeastern shore (leeward coast

The busiest and best-known beach in the entire state is actually a two-and-a-half-mile series of beaches. Although it's often difficult to catch a glimpse of the sand between all the glistening bodies lying, walking, and playing on top of it, no one seems to mind the crush. At a string of concessions along the shore, "beachboys" make arrangements for people to sail on catamarans, ride outrigger canoes and aqua-bikes, go parasailing, and learn to surf, among other pursuits. Particularly in the waters in front of the Sheraton Waikiki, you're likely to spot endangered *honu* (Hawaiian green sea turtles) swimming and feeding on the *limu* (seaweed). Most of these harmless creatures weigh anywhere from 17 to 180 pounds.

Human swimmers looking for the calmest waves and the sandiest ocean floor gravitate toward **Kahaloa** and **Ulukou** beaches, facing the Royal Hawaiian ("the Pink Palace") and the Sheraton Moana Surfrider hotels. Many people consider this section the cream of Waikiki's crop.

Kahanamoku Beach and Lagoon, in front of Hilton Hawaiian Village, is named after Duke Kahanamoku, Hawaii's beloved surfing champion and Olympic swimmer, and is a good spot for young children, since the waves are gentle. You might mix with military personnel at **Fort DeRussy Beach**, the broadest section of Waikiki Beach. Teen visitors might want to join a volleyball game here.

The Halekulani hotel overlooks calm, narrow **Gray's Beach**, once a Hawaiian retreat for spiritual healing. Surfers find great waves out past the reef. **Kuhio Beach Park**, by the Waikiki Beach Center, is an especially good spot for watching sunsets (which can be spectacular along this shore). As the sun slips into the ocean, you might catch a torch-lighting ceremony here, complete with Hawaiian music and hula. Although a sea wall that protrudes into the ocean keeps waters relatively calm at shore, swimmers must be very careful since the ocean floor is potholed with unexpected drops. Surfing and bodysurfing are good on the ocean side of the wall.

At **Queen's Beach**, near the Honolulu Zoo, the sand becomes particularly powdery. This is a popular picnic site with families. During the summer, free blockbuster movies are sometimes projected onto a 30-foot screen here at night, and vendors sell snacks and crafts. Locals flock to **Sans Souci Beach**, near the New Otani Kaimana Beach hotel, for sunning, picnicking, and more volleyball.

Unless you're a bird, the best view of Waikiki Beach is from the Hanohano Room high at the top of the Sheraton Waikiki. By day, you'll look down on the many other hotels lining the curve of beach and boat-studded water, with Diamond Head volcano at the far end. By night, the scene is lit with glittering lights from all the hotels.

Ala Moana Beach Park, just *ewa* (west) of Waikiki; across from the Ala Moana shopping center

Although this beach teems with families, couples, and singles swimming, playing volleyball and tennis, jogging, flying kites, rollerblading, fishing, and just plain socializing, it is less crowded than Waikiki, which begins on the other side of the Ala Wai Yacht Harbor. Locals and visitors congregate here for picnics. The shallow, sandy entry makes this a particularly swimmable beach for children.

Hanauma Bay, near Oahu's southeastern tip

You'll arrive here at the top of a hill, looking down on the palm-lined, mountain-backed C-shaped beach. The crater of an extinct volcano, this is one of Oahu's most beautiful settings. Even from above, you can see all kinds of coral through the transparent blue water. Both children and uninitiated adults love being introduced to **snorkeling** here at this protected cresent where smoking has been prohibited since 1993.

Even in the waist-deep water, you'll be surrounded by a blizzard of colorful tropical fish in small pools between the clusters of coral. Look for everything from longnose butterfly fish and moorish idols to potter's angelfish and iridescent parrotfish. When I first started visiting Hawaii during the 1980s, these fish stayed plump on a diet of frozen peas, popcorn, and bread nibbled from human hands. However, to help restore nature's balance, fish feeding is no longer permitted at Hanauma Bay.

Because the walk-in snorkeling is so good here, the beach remains packed most of the day. If you don't own snorkeling gear, you can easily rent some before you come. (And be sure to outfit your family with water shoes or aqua socks, since the coral can be sharp, especially on tender young soles.)

For a treat (with older children), walk around a slippery ledge to the left of the path down to the water, and you'll come to the **Toilet Bowl**, a pocket where water "flushes" in and out with the tides. But be careful, since the rush of water can be powerful.

Lanikai Beach, southeastern windward coast

You won't find many fellow vacationers on this wonderful swimming beach. Canoers and kayakers like to paddle around the two islets just offshore. To find this beach, hidden behind the waterfront houses along Mokulua Drive, you'll have to take one of the sandy paths between the homes.

Kailua Beach Park, windward coast, at Kailua

Few visitors seem to know about this four-mile palm-shaded beach, which is excellent for windsurfing, boogie boarding, and swimming. The curving shore and the mountains make it an especially scenic setting, and the calm, shallow water is great for young children. Everyone gets a kick out of the annual **sandcastle competition** each February. The safety and convenience of lifeguards, barbecue grills, public showers, rest rooms, tables, and benches draws quite a few local families on weekends. Teenagers may want to join one of the volleyball games that are always going on. Kayakers like to paddle out to Mokulua, two itty-bitty offshore seabird sanctuaries. Windsurfers and kayaks are available for rent in Kailua.

Kahana Bay Beach Park, windward coast

The shallow waters here make for better wading than swimming, so this is a good place to introduce toddlers and other children to the Pacific. This shady, picturesque site is also fine for a picnic or simple relaxation. Pandanus and ironwood trees provide ample shade. Boating and fishing are popular here as well. Not far from here is an ancient Hawaiian fish pond, which was still being used as late as the 1920s. See if you can find some ripe mangoes or bananas in lush Kahana Valley, across the road.

Hale'iwa Beach Park, North Shore

At funky little Hale'iwa, the North Shore's only town, this beach is good for swimming and snorkeling during the spring and summer, but, like all North Shore beaches, should not be entered by anyone but accomplished surfers in the winter. Feel free to join a volleyball game or to toss a Frisbee around.

Yokohama Bay, just north of Makaha, on the Waianae Coast
Never crowded, this surfing beach lies at the northern end of the leeward coast road. A prime fishing spot among locals, this broad beach also attracts young boys with boogie boards and, on weekends, picnicking families. During the summer when the water is calmest, small children splash in the waves and collect shells along the shore.

Ewa Beach Park, leeward coast, near Pearl Harbor
This long, broad strand of white sand is bathed by calm waters. Diamond Head and the skyscrapers of Honolulu and Waikiki loom in the distance. On weekends, residents flock here to swim, socialize, and play basketball on the court in the expansive grassy park. Swings, a jungle gym and picnic tables attract families. After a storm, it is not unusual to see Hawaiians gathering uprooted *limu* (seaweed) to use in salads and other dishes. Hawaiians have been cooking with seaweed for generations. Asian immigrants have added their own seaweed recipes to Hawaii's culinary melange. Park facilities also include restrooms, showers, and changing areas. To get here, you'll drive past open farmland interspersed with sprawling housing developments backed by mountains.

Sports & Other Activities

Riding the waves in an ancient Hawaiian-style outrigger canoe or learning to surf on Waikiki Beach are only the beginning of the many water and land sports available on Oahu. Snorkeling, scuba diving, boat trips, as well as tennis, golf, and other activities, can be arranged through most hotels and condominiums. Sports concessions and "beach boys" (life guards, surfing instructors, outrigger canoe paddlers, etc.) sprinkle Waikiki's sandy shore. Some beaches or adjoining parks have volleyball courts. Here is some of Oahu's best action on water and land for families with children:

Biking

Cycling on Oahu can be enjoyable, as long as you steer clear of Waikiki and the rest of Honolulu, where traffic is thick. Many airlines allow bikes on board for a small additional charge. If you haven't brought your own you can rent one; your accommodation can recommend a good bike shop.

Canoeing

Along Waikiki Beach, "beach boys" compete for the chance to take tourists out in 30- to 40-foot outrigger canoes to ride the waves as the ancient Hawaiians once did. For about $6, paddlers will allow several good waves to push you toward shore. In this sport, sometimes called "canoe surfing," boats can travel faster than 25 miles an hour.

Paddling Past

When Hawaiian kings, queens, and high chiefs used to ride their canoes or surfboards, commoners knew to stay away from the beach, lest they sully these royal sports. When a kapu (taboo) was placed on a site reserved for alii at play, a commoner foolish enough to trespass might even be put to death.

After the 1820 arrival of American missionaries, canoe surfing, along with many other Hawaiian pastimes, was almost wiped out. The god-fearing New Englanders were appalled at all the glistening skin exposed — on both men and women — during water sports. By the end of the 19th century, aquatic games had begun making their comeback, thanks in large part to King David Kalakaua, who also revived the hula and other Hawaiian traditional arts. However, canoe surfing was never quite the same as it had been. In an attempt to preserve this disappearing segment of Hawaiian culture, Alexander Hume Ford started the **Outrigger Canoe Club** in Waikiki in 1908. A rival association, called the **Hui Nalu Canoe Club**, was put together in 1911 by a group consisting mainly of Hawaiians.

Fishing

Kewalo Basin, near Waikiki, is the place most visitors go to arrange full- and half-day excursions on charter fishing boats. **Wahiawa Reservoir**, not far from Schofield Barracks in central Oahu, is home to many big peacock and black bass. **Nuuanu Reservoir**, near the Pali Highway (Route 61), just outside Honolulu, is also good for small-boat freshwater fishing.

Safety Note: You may see locals fishing from cliffs, such as at a spot near Hanauma Bay, but I don't recommend your trying this yourself since it can be very dangerous. The edges of precipices can be extremely slippery; and unexpectedly high waves can suddenly burst up from the ocean.

Golf

Oahu has more than 30 golf courses, the majority of which are open to the public. There are more courses here than on any of the other Hawaiian islands. However, since Oahu receives more visitors, many tend to be crowded. **The Ko Olina Golf Club**, Tel. 676-5300, is an 18-hole championship course that sprawls on the leeward coast, near Ihilani Resort, about a half-hour drive from downtown Honolulu. The lakes and rock gardens make this green especially picturesque. Golfers have to drive their carts under a waterfall to get to the 12th hole! Greens fees run about $150 before noon, $105 between noon and 3pm, and $80 after 3pm.

Also consider the **Hawaii Kai** courses, Tel. 395-2358, just east of Waikiki. Greens fees on weekdays are around $90 before 11am, $80 between 11am and 12:30pm; and $60 after 12:30pm; on weekends, $100 before 11am, $90 between 11am and 1pm, and $80 after 1pm. On the North Shore, about an hour and 15 minutes from Waikiki, the Turtle Bay Resort, Tel. 800/203-3650, gives you a choice between two courses, one more challenging than the other. Fees begin at about $160 before 2pm and $90 afterwards.

Helicopter Tours & Seaplane Rides

I recommend taking a helicopter ride on Oahu only if you're not going to Kauai, the Big Island, or Maui. Starting at about $100, most flights are from 30 minutes to an hour. You can make arrangements through your accommodation.

If taking off and landing on water is more your style, contact **Island Seaplane Service,** Tel. 836-6273, www.islandseaplane.com, run by a family that has been in the aviation business since the 1920s. Flights begin at $100 per person for a half hour or $170 for an hour. The office for this company floats in a lagoon just off the international airport.

Hiking

Oahu is interlaced with many good hiking trails, several close to Waikiki. From the summit of **Diamond Head** crater, for instance, your eyes will take in Koko Head, Honolulu, the Waianae and Koolau mountains, and the ocean, among other sights. The trail to the top is clearly defined. A flashlight will come in handy when it's time to enter the tunnel used by the military during WWII. For a leisurely pace, allow about an hour going up and 45 minutes coming down. The interior of the crater is surprisingly lush.

Note that facilities, open from 6am to 6pm, include drinking water and bathrooms. Start out as early as possible, before the day gets too hot. The trailhead is about a 30-minute walk (or a quick public bus ride) from the heart of Waikiki.

Other good trails near Waikiki are in the Makiki Valley, Tantalus Mountain, and Manoa Valley area. A hike through jungled vegetation will take you to **Manoa Falls**, a perfect spot for swimming and relaxing. Easily reached by bus, the **Kaneaole Trail** starts in Makiki Valley, turns west onto the **Makiki Valley Trail**, which cuts across the valley, then goes north on the Nahuina Trail, eventually coming to the Manoa Cliffs. From here you can take the **Puu Ohia Trail** northeast and go down into Manoa Valley via the **Aihualama Trail**.

Manoa Falls is less than a mile from here. The wind makes an eerie, musical sound as it blows through stands of bamboo. Bordering the trail, the leaves and branches of koa trees form a ceiling overhead. The roots of banyan trees drip to the ground like hair. Right before you reach Manoa Falls, you'll be yanked back into modern times with a view of Honolulu peeking through the woods. The trail out of the valley is just under a mile. You can catch a public bus back to Waikiki, or walk about three miles down Manoa Road to Waikiki.

For good guided hikes (including hotel pickup) to waterfalls, gardens, wildlife sanctuaries, and the rainforest, contact **Oahu Nature Tours**, Tel. 924-2473, www.oahunaturetours.com.

Horseback Riding

With **Koko Crater Equestrian Center**, Tel. 395-2628, the trail cuts across Koko Head crater, not far from Waikiki. Ask about lessons and pony rides. At **Kualoa Ranch and Activity Club**, Tel. 237-7321, www.kualoa.com, in lush Kaaawa Valley on the windward coast (across from Kualoa Beach Park), you can take trail rides with ocean views. Children must be at least 10 years old and the weight limit is 230 pounds.

Kayaking

At **Twogood Kayaks**, Tel. 262-5656, in Kailua, you can rent a one-person kayak for $40 for a half day or $50 for a full day and two-person tandem kayaks for $50 for a half day or $60 for a full day, including delivery to Kailua Beach and a lesson.

Sailing

On Waikiki Beach, you can arrange to sail on catamarans through concessions and "beach boys." Many sunset, moonlight, and dinner cruises leave from Kewalo Basin, not far from Waikiki. Sailing charters (from whale watching trips and snorkeling excursions to sunset cruises) are available through **Tradewind Charters**, Tel. 973-0311 or 800/829-4899, www.tradewindcharters.com. Charters begin at about $500 for six people on a 3-hour dinner cruise or 4-hour **snorkeling** trip on a 40-foot yacht.

Scuba Diving

Aaron's Dive Shop, Tel. 262-2333 or 888/84-SCUBA, claims to be the oldest dive shop on Oahu. Divers must be at least 10 years old. A two-tank dive or an introductory lesson and dive runs about $125. The 3-day certification course costs about $450 per person.

Snorkeling

Many hotels have snorkeling equipment for rent or loan, or will happily book you on a snorkeling cruise. While this water sport may seem intimidating to the uninitiated, it is actually very simple, even for children. Most people can catch on in just a few minutes. If you take a snorkeling excursion, you'll get a lesson that prepares you to take the plunge. Rather try on your own? Then ask someone who has snorkeled before to demonstrate. **Hanauma Bay,** Oahu's premier snorkeling site, is worth every (often crowded) minute. Be sure to wear rubber-soled shoes or dive booties in the water, because the coral can give nasty cuts.

There are various ways to get to Hanauma Bay, in addition to driving yourself. Public buses witll drop you off at the top of the hill. Be sure to rent snorkel gear from your hotel or at Waikiki Beach before you get here. *Also see* Beaches, *above.*

Surfing

The family that surfs together . . . Don't know how? Here's your chance! Try the **Hans Hedemann Surf Camp**, Tel. 808/924-7778, www.hhsurf.com/activity.html, which offers Lifeguard- and CPR-trained instructors at six locations on Oahu, from Waikiki to the North Shore; or **Sunset Suzy's Surf Camp,** Tel. 808/781-2692, www.sunsetsuzy.com/rates.htm, run by a professional surfer who is a film and television stuntwoman.

On Waikiki Beach, "beach boys" working independently (with Parks Department approval), hang out to give surfing lessons.

Most board-lovers agree that the best surfing in Hawaii is along Oahu's North Shore, from Hale'iwa to Kahuku. However, only experts should attempt to handle these monster curls. Each winter this area is pounded by some of the tallest, most shapely waves anywhere. The international surfing masters flock here each December and January for the **Triple Crown**. Each of these three contests takes five days.

The competitions kick off at the Banzai Pipeline, Sunset Beach, Waimea Bay and/or other prime surfing spots.

Yokohama and Makaha, on the northern Waianae coast, are other good locales for the sport.

Tennis

Hotels with tennis courts give guests first priority, but most are available for the use of non-guests as well. In the Waikiki area, **Ala Moana Park** has ten free public tennis courts; the **Diamond Head Tennis Center** also has ten; and **Kapiolani Park** is home to four.

Waterskiing

Try **Hawaii Sports Wakeboard & Water Ski Center**, Tel. 395-3773 or 800/690-8055. This company teaches children from age 5 up. Rates begin at $50 for 20 minutes and $60 for 30 minutes.

Whale Watching

Check with your hotel or at Kewalo Basin for winter cruises, or, for private charters, try **Tradewind Charters**, Tel. 973-0311 or 800/829-4899.

Windsurfing

One of the best places to rent equipment, take lessons, and go on group sails in **Naish Hawaii**, Tel. 262-6068, Web site: www.naish.com, based in Kailua, on the southeastern windward coast. This outfit is run by Robby Naish, a world champion windsurfer, and his family. Children as young as five can take lessons, as long as they are strong enough to hold the sail.

Working Out & Spas

For the best pampering, head to one of the spas at Hilton Hawaiian Village, the Hyatt Regency Waikiki, or the Outrigger Reef Hotel, all in Waikiki, or Ihilani Resort on the Leeward coast. These hotels, along with many others, also have fitness centers. Programs and facilities include weight rooms, exercise bikes and aerobics classes, as well as spa treatments from massages to body wraps.

Another option for working out is a non-hotel gym in Waikiki or Honolulu, such as the **Clark Hatch Physical Fitness Center**, Tel. 536-7205, in Honolulu. The health-conscious are drawn to its classes in aerobics, step, yoga, and weight training, and its stationary bikes, stairsteppers, treadmills, rowing machines, indoor pool, racquetball court, and other facilities.

I'm Hungry!

Unlike in many other vacation spots, hotel restaurants in Hawaii are some of the best places to eat. Not only do they keep visitors pouring in, but locals make a habit of returning often to their favorites as well. Now, don't get me wrong: there is also an excellent selection of independent eateries. Competition in recent decades has brought Oahu in particular and Hawaii in general a long way from the once-prevalent "Polynesian" menus that featured heavy dishes that were mainly sweet and sour.

Honolulu boasts Hawaii's widest choice of restaurants, both within and outside of hotels. They range from roadside "BBQs" and "Drive-Ins" (which are very economical, and thus popular with families) to dining rooms bathed in top-drawer elegance. Many offer "keiki menus" with smaller portions just for children. For the most part, Waikiki restaurants tend to be more expensive than elsewhere in the state, particularly for dinner. While some visitors dress up at dinner time just for the fun of it, men are asked to wear jackets at only a handful of restaurants. Casual chic is more commonly the way to go.

Head to **Chinatown** in downtown Honolulu for Vietnamese, Filipino, and (what else?) Chinese cuisine in small, family-run eateries. A stroll through Chinatown can be a gustatory adventure. Bakeries and other small shops sell everything from peanut-rice squares, custard pies, and candied papaya, coconut, lotus root, and ginger to black sugar donuts and moon cakes. Selling goodies such as *manapua* (steamed Chinese rice-flour dough stuffed with pork or black beans), lunch wagons parked near beaches cause lines to form.

Hawaii's pervasive Japanese influence shows itself in the deli-like stores that do a brisk business in sushi, tempura, and plate lunches. A hybrid culinary institution of the islands, a fast-food **plate lunch** generally includes a teriyaki or curried meat or fish entree, two scoops of rice, and macaroni salad. **Zippy's**, a fast-food chain restaurant popular among locals, serves saimin (noodle soup with meat or fish) and other Japanese and Chinese dishes, as well as burgers. Thai and Korean food are also big on Oahu.

Few children can pass through **Hale'iwa**, the little surfing town on the North Shore, without stopping at **Matsumoto's** for a **shave ice**. Known as snow cones in other parts of the world, the Hawaiian version comes doused with mango, passion fruit, coconut, and other tropical syrups.

Consider the restaurants below dubbed "Romantic Escapes" for those nights when you enlist babysitters or let your teenagers order in while you hang out.

Brunch on the Beach

If you time your vacation right, you might hit the montly "Brunch on the Beach," festivities, which turn Kalakaua Avenue, bordering Waikiki Beach, into an outdoor café, complete with live music and hula. Some of the island's best chefs whip up their specialties on the spot, from omelets to desserts, for much less than you'd pay in their restaurants. This event usually takes place on the third Sunday of the month, from 9am to 1:30pm. For more details, Tel. 808/523-CITY or 808/923-1094; www.waikikiimprovementassociation.com.

Greater Honolulu

CHEF MAVRO, 1969 South King Street (near McCully), Honolulu. Tel. 944-4714. Reservations recommended. Dinner only (6pm to 9:30pm); closed Monday. Dinner entrees: $30 to $39. *Romantic Escape.*

Named for celebrated chef George Mavrothalassitis, this restaurant offers a perfectly paired glass of wine with each menu item. In this hushed, romantic atmosphere, candlelight sets off the white table cloths, modern art, and potted plants. Yes, the prices are steep, but the Provence-inspired food is delicious. The imaginative menu is always changing. You might begin with an amazing cup of chilled carrot soup with orange essence and curry croutons, or green tea-dusted zucchini blossom tempura in a salad of Hamakua mushrooms and essence of watercress. Expect to find other creations such as charbroiled lobster and mashed sweet potatoes, squab roasted with sesame oil and wild mushrooms, or onaga baked in a Hawaiian salt crust. To clear your palate before dessert, you might be served strawberries in champagne gelatin with fresh mint. Dessert itself might include Hawaiian vanilla tapioca, lilikoi malasads (passionfruit hole-less donuts) with guava coulis and pineapple-coconut ice cream, or a chocolate dome filled with Kona coffee creme brulee.

JOHN DOMINIS, 43 Ahui Street, at Kewalo Basin, Honolulu. Tel. 523-0955. Reservations recommended. Open nightly for dinner and for brunch on Sunday. Dinner entrees: $26 to $45.

The excellent food is neck and neck with the wonderful ocean view. Surfers ride the waves in the distance while fishing boats pull up to shore. Seafood is the specialty here, and the location—right near the Honolulu Fish Market—could hardly be more convenient. A lobster-filled pond meanders through the restaurant. Treats from the sea are prepared in a variety of tasty ways, from broiled in butter to steamed with ginger. Tiger prawns—tempura, sautéed, broiled, with black bean sauce, as you wish—are a specialty. While there is no children's menu here, half portions are available and the pizza appetizer is popular with kids. Save room for a slice of Bailey's mud pie.

This upscale restaurant borrows its name from John Owen Dominis, the son of an Italian ship captain. Dominis married Hawaii's last queen, Liliuokalani, in 1862 and later became governor of Oahu.

SAM CHOY'S DIAMOND HEAD, 449 Kapahulu Avenue. Tel. 732-8645. Dinner entrees: $23 to $33.

Residents love Sam Choy's for Pacific Rim cuisine. Portions are huge, so come hungry or plan to split one dish between two adults or an adult and a couple of kids. The emphasis is on local-style seafood, such as seafood laulau, fish and veggies wrapped in ti leaves, and marinated fresh ahi salad. The menu might also include continental favorites, like bouillabaisse, with a regional twist, or roast duck with orange sauce. Expect surprises such as wontons filled with brie and served with pineapple marmalade. Children graviate toward the grilled teriyaki chicken, spaghetti and meatballs, and tempura.

THE PINEAPPLE ROOM, third floor of Macy's, Ala Moana Center, 1450 Ala Moana Boulevard. Open for breakfast Saturday and Sunday, lunch daily, dinner Monday through Saturday. Tel. 945-8881. Dinner entrees: $20 to $30. *Romantic Escape.*

Serving gourmet cuisine under the watchful eye of Hawaii's renowned chef and owner Alan Wong, the Pineapple Room is not what you'd expect to find in a mall department store. The classy menu features creative dishes such as pineapple-shaped crab cakes, miso-glazed salmed with stir-fried veggies and kimchee vinaigrette, and sweet chili-glazed short-tail red snapper. The modern dining room may be a bit more brightly lit than other restaurants at night, but this is probably because the chef wants patrons to see every bit of each artistic culinary masterpiece.

ROY'S, 6600 Kalanianaole Highway, Hawaii Kai, Honolulu. Tel. 396-7697. Reservations suggested. Dinner only. Entrees: $20 to $30.

About eight miles east of Waikiki, in the ritzy suburb of Hawaii Kai, Roy

Yamaguchi has made a culinary splash. Before coming to Hawaii, he began by thrilling diners in Los Angeles with his imaginative creations that married the East to the West. This duplex restaurant, high on my list of Oahu favorites, gazes out at the mountains and Maunalua Bay. The bar, with its outdoor tables, is downstairs. The upstairs dining room, with its tall picture windows, is always packed. In the center of the room, the gleaming white-tile and stainless-steel kitchen is open to full view of the diners at the surrounding tables. On Friday and Saturday nights, live Hawaiian music entertains patrons.

The ever-changing menu might include steamed pork dumplings served with a mustard and soy vinaigrette dressing; seafood-filled potstickers in a sauce made from sesame seeds and butter; beef stir-fried with roasted macadamias, fresh mint and Maui onions; scallops flavored with ginger and basil. One bite and you'll understand why Yamaguchi was Hawaii's first recipient of the coveted James Beard award. Pizza here is for the adventurous, who enjoy it with such toppings as marinated Chinese chicken, Japanese sprouts or shiitake mushrooms. The children's menu includes quesadillas and vegetable sticks with a main course of meatloaf, chicken, fish, or pasta, served with a chocolate sundae.

ROY'S KO OLINA, Ko Olina Resort & Marina, western Oahu, Tel. 676-7697, lunch and dinner served. Dinner entrees: $20 to $25. *Romantic Escape.*

Born in 2004, sixteen years after Roy Yamaguchi's flagship restaurant opened in Hawaii Kai, just east of Waikiki, this second Oahu offering overlooks a lagoon, waterfalls, and the 18th hole of the Ko Olina Golf course, about an hour from Waikiki. The chef's secrets are in full view in the open kitchen, but somehow ordinary mortals can't even begin to emulate the special flavors, textures, colors, and aromas of Roy's signature Hawaiian fusion cuisine. This melange of fresh local ingredients, Asian spices and culinary techniques, and European sauces might feature blackened ahi and seared ono one night, then grilled shrimp sticks and maacadamia nut chicken the next.

FISHERMAN'S WHARF RESTAURANT, 1009 Ala Moana Boulevard, on the harbor at Kewalo Basin, Honolulu. Tel. 538-3808. Reservations recommended. Dinner entrees: around $20. Open for lunch Tuesday to Friday, dinner nightly.

This seafood restaurant is so popular that many people call Kewalo Basin, the jumping-off point for many sightseeing and party cruises, Fisherman's Wharf. Fresh fish daily, lobster, and broiled oysters are their signature. The children's menu includes chicken nuggets and spaghetti.

SUNSET GRILL, Restaurant Row, 500 Ala Moana Boulevard, Honolulu. Tel. 521-4409. Reservations recommended. Dinner entrees: $18 to $33.

Kiawe-grilled chicken, fish, beef, and vegetables are the specialty of this restaurant. The fresh pastas, peppery warm spinach and calamari salad, sesame-crusted chicken breast with ginger-scented potatoes, and creme brulee are also delicious. Children choose among chicken fingers, penne, and burgers. If you're looking for a quiet place, however, this isn't it. The giggle level in this see-and-be-seen dining spot is often high. Perhaps this is because adults are invited to regress to childhood: crayons and canvases (a.k.a. place mats) are provided for each patron, whether toddler or adult. Some of the best artwork is framed and hung around the room.

L'URAKU, 1341 Kapiolani Boulevard, at Uraku Tower, Honolulu. Tel. 955-0552. Dinner entrees: $17 to $29.

Europe and Japan collide beautifully at this delightful dining spot. What a joyful place this is! The bold colors of the whimsical hand-painted umbrellas suspended from the ceiling are reflected not only in the table cloths and napkins, waiters' shirts, and bar stools, but also in the delectable dishes. So it's no surprise to learn that the artist of the umbrellas and the paintings that decorate the walls is not an artist by trade but a sushi chef.

L'Uraku wins the award for the most colorful meals around. The delicate sauce surrounding the pan-seared sea scallops is decorated with droplets of green onion chive oil, yellow tumeric oil, and orange chili oil. Moi, a fish once reserved for Hawaiian royalty, comes drizzled with hot peanut oil and topped with diced and sliced ginger, red and yellow tomatoes, and tofu. Tender veal cheeks are steamed in soy for more than three hours. Garlic mashed potatoes and taro bread complement entrees.

While there is no children's menu here, with 24 hours notice you can order a "keiki bento," which could include shrimp cocktail, rice balls, pasta with marinara sauce, or beef teriyaki, plus fruit punch and ice cream.

SAM CHOY'S BREAKFAST, LUNCH & CRAB, 580 North Nimitz Highway, Honolulu. Tel. 545-7979. Dinner only. Entrees: $15 to $40.

The home of Sam's Choy's Big Aloha Brewery, this busy, funky place is big on huge portions of delicious food. Live crabs wait for their fate in tanks. A 27-foot wooden fishing boat, complete with tables, is dry-docked in the middle of the dining room. The open kitchen gleams in stainless steel, matching the dining tables. The cuisine is plate lunch chic. Try the flash-fried poke, a scrumptious fish marinated in soy and ginger, served with rice and macaroni salad. Children like the burgers and fish and chips.

KINCAID'S FISH, CHOP, AND STEAK HOUSE, 1050 Ala Moana Boulevard, Ward Warehouse, Honolulu. Tel. 591-2005. Dinner entrees: $15 to $22.

Overlooking Kewalo Basin, this restaurant provides an upscale atmosphere and good food for down-scale prices. Ceiling fans circulate the air in attractive, spacious dining areas. The emphasis is on salads, soups, and seafood, served with wine and a wide selection of beer. Sandwiches, chicken, and fish are on the children's menu. For dessert, try the crème brulee. There's live music several nights a week.

COMPADRES MEXICAN BAR AND GRILL, 1200 Ala Moana Boulevard, Honolulu. Tel. 591-8307. Dinner entrees: $11 to $24.

This large, attractive restaurant draws a young, lively crowd. Dine outside on the balcony or indoors. Grilled fajitas (chicken, beef, vegetable, and seafood) are delicious; the ingredients are marinated in wine and tequila and sautéed with vegetables. The fresh fish tacos are popular. Along with the usual Mexican fare, you'll find hamburgers and great margaritas, as well as T-shirts and sweatshirts, emblazoned with the restaurant logo, for sale. For the younger editions, the keiki menu includes pint-size burritos, quesadillas, and tacos served with rice and beans.

SEKIYA'S RESTAURANT & DELICATESSEN, 2746 Kaimuki Avenue (across from Kaimuki High), Honolulu. Tel. 732-1656. Entrees: $9 to $13. Closed Monday.

Some residents say Sekiya's prepares the best plate lunch on Oahu. Corned beef is the specialty of this longstanding family business; corned beef hash tempura may sound unusual, but it's very popular. Whether they eat it in or take it out, patrons also enjoy Japanese dishes such as beef teriyaki, sushi, and shrimp or vegetable tempura, as well as chow fun (warm noodles with vegetables), breaded butterfish, and fried Spam.

KAKA'AKO KITCHEN AT WARD CENTER, 1200 Ala Moana Boulevard, Honolulu. Tel. 596-7488. Entrees: $8 to $20.

Jam-packed for breakfast, lunch, and dinner—particularly the breezy patio—this casual roadside restaurant updates the plate lunch, that old Hawaiian favorite. For lunch and dinner, the usual mahi-mahi and teriyaki chicken sandwiches are on the menu and can come with the expected scoops of macaroni salad and white rice. The difference is that here you can swap the pasta for a crispy green salad and the sandwiches can come on delicious purple taro buns. The menu is quite extensive as well, including everything from blackened ahi wraps and fried sweet chili chicken to grilled vegetables and tofu burgers. For children, consider the spaghetti or peanut butter and jelly sandwiches.

ONO HAWAIIAN FOODS, 726 Kapahulu Avenue, Honolulu. Tel. 737-2275. Entrees: $6 to $10. Closed Sunday.

There are only ten tables at this unassuming local favorite. Entrees include kalua pig (cooked in a pit over hot rocks), laulau, poi, butterfish, and that Hawaiian staple, Spam. Other popular choices are chicken long rice and stir-fried sliced steak with vegetables. Portions are quite generous; after lunch here, you may feel like skipping dinner.

Waikiki

LA MER, the Halekulani hotel, 2199 Kalia Road. Tel. 923-2311. Jackets required for men. Dinner entrees: $36 to $46. *Romantic Escape.*

Tables in this elegant dining room—done in warm rusts, golds, and browns—are spaced so that everyone has a view of the ocean. At night, patrons can look out to the catamarans taking the partying crowd on dinner cruises. While the walls are decorated with Hawaiian carvings, the accent of the food is French. Consider ordering the bouillabaisse, lamb chops, or the sauteed John Dory fish with avocado and orange basil butter. The macadamia vanilla coffee is also delicious.

HANOHANO ROOM, Sheraton Waikiki, 2255 Kalakaua Avenue. Tel. 922-4422. Reservations required. Jackets and ties recommended. Dinner entrees: $29 to $40. *Romantic Escape.*

A glass elevator glides from the lobby thirty floors up to this restaurant showcasing local fish and contemporary cuisine. From one of the best vantage points around, the sweeping view encompasses Diamond Head, especially dramatic at sunset, and famed Waikiki Beach. Crystal chandeliers sparkle while the mellow sounds of a combo pull diners onto the dance floor in the evening. On the menu, you might find lemongrass-crusted onaga, steamed moi in sesame soy sauce, and rack of lamb with Dijon mustard, with banana flambe or passionfruit sorbet for dessert.

KACHO, Waikiki Parc Hotel, 2233 Helumoa Road. Tel. 921-7272 or 924-3535. Reservations recommended. Dinner entrees: $24 to $40.

An excellent Japanese restaurant, Kacho serves a traditional breakfast that includes seafood and vegetable appetizers, broiled fish, pickled vegetables, steamed rice, and miso soup or okayu (rice soup), plus natto (fermented beans). For lunch and dinner, the Kyoto-style cuisine consists of sushi and sashimi, a variety of soups, tempura, and seafood. Bento boxes, featuring a variety of treats built around a beef, chicken, fish, or vegetable entrée, are also served.

ORCHID'S, the Halekulani hotel, 2199 Kalia Road. Tel. 923-2311. Dinner entrees: $20 to $53.

Right at the edge of the beach, with a view that takes in Diamond Head, this restaurant serves three meals a day. Hardwood floors, white tablecloths, and a profusion of orchids and greenery make this a particularly pleasant locale. Try the ahi seared sashimi with Cajun spices or the steamed red snapper with shitake mushrooms and ginger. The keiki menu might include grilled mahi mahi over rice and chicken yakitori. If you're in Waikiki on a Sunday, this is the place for brunch. The pastry department outdoes itself with its fresh oversized popovers and other baked goodies.

KYO-YA, 2057 Kalakaua Avenue. Tel. 947-3911. Dinner entrees: $18 to $35.

One of the most elaborate Japanese restaurants I've ever seen, Kyo-Ya, with shoji screens and enamel, looks like the headquarters of a fancy Japanese corporation. The food can be cooked right at your table (if you order at least two portions of the same dish). Try the sukiyaki or the shabu-shabu (thinly sliced beef in a noodle and vegetable broth). Deep-fried chicken, sushi, and tempura are other specialties.

CIAO MEIN, Hyatt Regency Waikiki, 2424 Kalakaua Avenue, Tel. 923-1234. Dinner only. Entrees: $18 to $29

This unusual restaurant offers the best of Europe and Asia with a menu that blends Italian and Chinese cuisines. Consider ordering the seafood funn lasagna (assorted seafood, Boursin cheese, mozzarella, spinach, eggplant, and look funn noodles with marinara sauce). Feeling less adventurous? Then go for the spicy ginger garlic shrimp.

PADOVANI'S BISTRO & WINE BAR, 1956 Ala Moana Boulevard. Tel. 946-3456. Dinner entrees: $16 to $44.

Serving a blend of French-Mediterranean and Hawaii regional cuisine, this bistro offers a vast selection of wine. Casual dining is upstairs at the wine bar. Downstairs, a more elegant atmosphere prevails. Entrees might include black prawns and mango with hearts of palm salad, and dessert might be exotic fruits with chocolate sabayon. Tasting menus allow diners to sample a variety of menu items. There's a good choice of vegetarian dishes, such as mushroom-artichoke-asparagus risotto, along with the seafood, beef, and chicken.

THE GOLDEN DRAGON, the Hilton Hawaiian Village. Tel. 946-5336. Dinner only. Entrees: $15 to $35.

A gourmet restaurant serving Cantonese and Szechuan cuisine, the Golden Dragon is on the lagoon side of the hotel's landmark Rainbow Tower (with its colorful mosaic design). As you enter between golden Chinese horses, you'll see a large tropical fish tank. Decorative carts resemble Chinese chariots. Good selections might be smoked spare ribs (smoked in a glass-enclosed chamber in the middle of the room), sharkfin soup, seafood egg rolls, and lobster with curry and haupia (Hawaiian coconut pudding). For the delicious Peking duck with plum sauce, you'll need to place your orders 24 hours in advance. Sinking your teeth into Imperial Beggar's Chicken also requires a day's notice. The bird is seasoned and stuffed, wrapped in leaves and then clay, and baked for several hours. The dish is brought to your table still encased in its shell and you're given a wooden mallet for making the first crack. This flavorful chicken is so tender.

PARC CAFE, Waikiki Parc Hotel, 2233 Helumoa Road, at Lewers. Tel. 921-7272. Dinner buffets: $15 to $26.

This brightly lit hotel dining room serves delicious gourmet creations three meals a day. The breakfast buffet includes pancakes and French toast with coconut or maple syrup, fresh fruit, muffins, croissants, eggs, assorted breakfast meats, and other goodies. Sunday brunch is more elaborate, with rotisserie chicken, eggs Benedict, and fresh catch. You'll also be treated to both a sushi station and an omelet station. Lunch or dinner buffets might begin with freshly made soup, followed by meats cooked on a rotisserie and carved to order, pasta, fish, chicken, freshly baked pastries and chocolate mousse. Salads are especially good, such as the deep-fried tofu salad. Children's rates are available for the buffets.

SINGHA THAI, 1910 Ala Moana Boulevard (across the street from Hilton Hawaiian Village), Honolulu, HI 96815. Tel. 941-2898. Reservations recommended. Dinner only. Entrees: $12 to $34.

A Thai temple guards the entrance to this excellent Thai and Hawaiian regional restaurant, which is decorated with Thai masks and golden Buddhas. During your meal, you'll be treated to a performance by elaborately costumed dancers, whose sensual belly and hand movements are truly impressive.

Vegetarians are pleased to find a variety of well-seasoned selections along with the seafood and meat on the menu. Many people choose the multi-course family-style meals, so they can sample the greatest number of dishes. For appetizers, you can't go wrong with the blackened ahi summer rolls or the chicken sate. Most dishes, such as the Tom Kah soup (lemongrass with coconut milk, chicken breast, mushrooms, and lime juice) come mild, medium, or hot. Children like the noodle dishes, sticky rice, and chicken Pad.

Among the best entrees are the spicy long eggplant with tofu and shiitake mushrooms, the red curry shrimp, the pan-fried mahi mahi with chili sauce, and the seafood Pad Thai noodles. Good sides include the vegetarian fried rice and steamed sticky rice. There's an extensive wine list, with wines chosen specifically to complement the highly seasoned food.

KEO'S WAIKIKI, 2028 Kuhio Avenue, Tel. 951-9355. Reservations recommended. Dinner entrees: $10 to $26.

Keo Sananikone has spent years building an excellent reputation with spicy Thai dishes such as crispy fried shrimp rolled in lettuce and cucumber with a delicious dipping sauce, and vegetarian spring rolls with mint leaves. Peanuts, basil, lemongrass, and other flavors perk up the palate. Among the preparations for the seafood, steaks, and chops, curries are quite popular. Children enjoy the chicken wings and the many noodle dishes. For a fruity coconut cocktail, try the Evil Princess.

RAINBOW DRIVE-IN, Kapahulu Avenue, Tel. 737-0177. Entrees: around $6.

Locals drive here for some of the best plate lunches around. The popular mixed plate includes teriyaki beef, chicken, and mahi mahi. Boneless chicken with brown gravy also moves briskly.

Elsewhere on Oahu

JAMESON'S BY THE SEA, 62-540 Kamehameha Highway, Hale'iwa, North Shore. Tel. 637-4336. Dinner entrees: $25 to $40.

Along with well-prepared seafood, evening diners are treated to fabulous sunsets at this ocean view restaurant. Torches flame at the edge of the open-air dining area. Jameson's is packed for lunch, cocktails, and dinner. Good choices include Portuguese bean soup, Boston clam chowder, the grilled crab and shrimp sandwich, veggie burgers, Thai summer rolls, Caesar salad, and Cajun chicken wings. The children's menu includes chicken teriyaki, fried shrimp, and fish of the day.

Stop at the restaurant's **crafts shop**, where you'll find all kinds of ceramic sculpture and wall hangings, cards, and paintings, along with fudge that you can have mailed back to the mainland.

KUA AINA SANDWICH, 66-214 Kamehameha Highway, North Shore. Tel. 637-6067. Inexpensive.

Residents say this place has the best hamburgers on Oahu (some claim it's the vermouth), and the fries get raves as well. Sandwiches and fish burgers are also on the menu. Packed at lunch time, this small eatery is very popular among surfers.

HALE'IWA CAFE, 66-460 Kamehameha Highway, Hale'iwa, North Shore. Tel. 637-5516. Inexpensive.

Breakfast, lunch, and dinner are served at this popular dining spot. In the morning, our kids can't get enough of the huge whole wheat and buttermilk pancakes and we love the omelets and mahi-mahi with rice. Mid-day, try the burritos, tostadas or a sandwich (such as veggies with avocado and melted cheese). If you order a tuna- stuffed tomato, no worries: the fish is "dolphin safe." Walls are decorated with original paintings and photographs for sale.

BARBECUE KAI, 85-973 Farrington Highway, Waianae, western coast. Tel. 696-7122. Inexpensive.

Since this roadside stand serving three meals a day is located right next to the Waianae Army Recreation Center Beach, one of the area's best spots for swimming, it's a good place to stop for a take-out lunch. Choose among mahi mahi sandwiches, saimin, teriyaki pork chops, sweet and sour ribs, and chicken katsu (deep fried, breaded chicken cutlet). Although the very low prices sometimes attract some down and out looking diners, the food is delicious.

Which One is My Bed?

Especially in Waikiki, Oahu's accommodations are so competitive that many are continually being renovated or redesigned in an attempt to convince travelers to choose them over others. Both on and off the beach, there is a broad range of types of hotels and condominiums. The Outrigger/Ohana chain has a slew of Waikiki hotels. Those in the Ohana line appeal to people with beer budgets while some Outriggers draw those with champagne taste. The Aston, Marc, and Sheraton chains also have some good hotels and package deals for families looking to stretch their dollars.

At Aston properties, for instance, children age 12 and younger receive free meals, admission to attractions such as Sea Life Park and HawaiianWaters Adventure Park, and merchandise (when accompanied by a paying adult).

Most of Marc's condos feature full kitchens and washer/dryers in each unit, along with barbecue areas and on-site activities.

Ask about the Outrigger/Ohana packages that include a surfboard rental and lesson, an outrigger canoe ride, or a catamaran sail. Outrigger hotels offer children age 5 to 13 programs with supervised activities that teach them about Hawaii, from lei-making to boogie boarding. In addition, this chain sponsors family programs so that parents can join their kids in the fun.

Parents are also encouraged to bond with their children at some Sheraton/Starwood programs, which include excursions plus recreational and cultural activities (from crab hunting to afternoon tea) for those aged 5 to 12. If you stay at one of Oahu's Sheratons (Sheraton Waikiki, Sheraton Moana Surfrider, Royal Hawaiian, or Sheraton Princess Kaiulani), you'll be able to charge meals and entertainment to your room while you're visiting the others. At Sheraton/Starwood properties, children under age 12 are not charged for meals when accompanied by adults who pay.

Waikiki Kids' Camps

While many Waikiki hotels offer day-camp-style children's programs, note that not all are held at the accommodations that offer the programs. These camps are often centralized, so that children staying at various hotels travel to one location.

You'd rather sleep outside Waikiki, away from the crowds? Choose among isolated beach resorts, one just east of Waikiki (Kahala Mandarin Oriental) and two over an hour away in the west (JW Marriott Ihilani Resort and Spa) and north (Turtle Bay Resort).

Breakfast is included in the rates of some hotels and children under age 18 are generally not charged for sharing a room with their parents.

Home Sweet Home on Oahu

Many families appreciate the convenience of staying in apartments or vacation homes, often in attractive residential neighborhoods. Note that most rates for condos and private homes are based on a minimum three-night to one-week stay, so nightly rates may be higher for shorter stays or lower for longer visits. Here are two reliable companies:

·**Team Real Estate**, Tel. 800/982-8602, www.teamrealestate.com.

·**Naish Hawaii**, Tel. 808/262-6068,www.naish.com—and for an added bonus, ask about windsurfing lessons for you and your kids.

Outside Waikiki

KAHALA MANDARIN ORIENTAL, HAWAII, 5000 Kahala Avenue, Honolulu, HI 96816. Tel. 808/739-8888, 808/738-8911, or 800/367-2525, www.mandarinoriental.com. 371 rooms. Rates begin at $345.

Located on the ocean in a quiet, residential area with views of both Diamond Head and Koko Head craters, the sprawling Kahala Mandarin Oriental is wonderfully tranquil and verdant. The beach is remarkably calm and protected. But the hotel is also just ten minutes from Waikiki, the heart of Oahu's action. Families appreciate the small children's wading pool and the popular children's program (for kids aged 5 to 12).

Mixing tropical and classic Asian and European decor, guest rooms (some with balconies) are decorated with handsome mahogany furniture, local artwork, and hand-loomed Tibetan rugs on teak parquet floors. Views take in the ocean, the Koolau Mountains, and Waialae Golf Course, or the Dolphin Lagoon, where friendly aquatic mammals entertain spectators during the daily feedings—and where vacationers can arrange to spend some time in the water with the dolphins. (Ask about children's dolphin encounter sessions.) When guests aren't on the beach or in the pool, they can hit the fitness center and enjoy the Jacuzzi or a relaxing aromatherapy massage.

TURTLE BAY RESORT, 57-091 Kamehameha Highway, Kahuku, HI 96731. Tel. 808/293-6000 or 800/203-3650, www.turtlebayresort.com. Rates begin at $300.

Far off the beaten path, near the famous surfing beaches of the North Shore (about a 60-minute drive from the airport), the Turtle Bay is a pleasant, self-contained resort. The beaches are beautiful here. Unlike many other North Shore beaches, which can be dangerous for swimming when the winter surf is high, calm Kuilima Cove is protected by a reef where snorkeling is good. Guests age 5 to 12 enjoy the children's program, with daytime and evening sessions. Participants are welcomed with a backpack filled with goodies such as a T-shirt, visor, and sunscreen. Activities range from Hawaiian crafts, games, and pole fishing to reef walks, night crab hunts, and horse carriage rides. A kiddie pool appeals to the youngest kids while older children gravitate toward the waterslide, as well as beach volleyball games. Adults like the exercise room and spa. Surfing, hiking, and horseback riding are other diversions that snag Turtle Bay Resort guests.

JW MARRIOTT IHILANI RESORT & SPA, 92-1001 Olani Street, Kapolei, HI 96707. Tel. 808/679-0079 or 800/626-4446, www.ihilani.com. 387 rooms. Rates begin at $275.

About a half-hour drive from the airport, Ihilani ("Heavenly Splendor") overlooks a series of calm, C-shaped, sandy lagoons. The children's program invites guests aged 5 to 12 to join treasure hunts, learn hula dancing, make leis, play sports. Ask about the periodic program especially for teenagers.

A sea water fish pond wanders through the grounds, and restaurants feature Japanese, continental, and Mediterranean cuisines. In the triangular lobby, a 15-story wall of glass brings the dramatic mountains inside. Overhead, greenery drips from railings along the open corridors outside guest rooms, most of which have views of the ocean.

The quietest guest rooms, all oceanfront, are in the shorter four-story wing. Here you can book a unit with a private whirlpool on the lanai. Other rooms gaze down on the busy circular swimming pool, the main lagoon, and the Pacific—but note, for instance, that while room 539, a minimum category room, is spacious, it has no view at all, unless you consider the roof of an adjoining building scenic. Guest room perks include a minibar, personal safe, and Japanese-style *yukatas* for use during your stay. You can even bring your favorite music for the room's CD player. The marble baths are large, with twin sinks.

Teens & Tweens

Who says teenagers and preteens can't learn to prepare and love healthy food, reduce the stress in their lives, and take better care of their skin—all while having big fun? At JW Marriott Ihilani Resort & Spa, the **Teens Club**, Tel. 808/679-0079 or 800/626-4446, specially designed for kids from age 11 to 18, periodically offers a variety of innovative sessions that teach kids about health and wellness in such enjoyable ways that they don't even realize they're learning!

With a cry of "Ladies and gentlemen, start your blenders!" kids take off on a culinary adventure during "Dueling Blenders," in which they create fruity smoothies that can serve as snacks, desserts, energy boosters, and even meals. In "The Big Chill" workshop, they learn practical ways of combating everyday stress. The "Zen Run and Morning Meditation" session teaches kids to optimize their athletic performance by bringing their bodies, minds, and spirits into balance, while "Introduction to Athletic Massage" gives them a chance to experience how hands-on therapy can improve blood circulation. In the "Skin Fitness" workshop, kids learn everything from sun protection to preventing and treating acne and the most effective over-the-counter products for healthy skin. And, of course, no Hawaiian Teen Club would be complete without "Hip, Hop Hula" lessons.

Along with six tennis courts, Ihilani has an excellent spa for indulging in treatments such as thalassotherapy, herbal wraps, facials, and massages. Facilities are extensive for both men and women. The hotel's more peaceful second swimming pool is on a sunny deck at the spa, near the exercise room and studio where fitness classes are given. (Don't forget your sneakers if you want to work out; you aren't allowed in the exercise room without them.) Transportation to the golf course is provided, and preferred tee times and special rates are available for hotel guests.

LAIE INN, 55-109 Laniloa Street, Laie, HI 96762. Tel. 808/293-9282 or 800/526-4562, www.laieinn.com. 48 rooms. Rates begin at $95.

Near the Polynesian Cultural Center, this modest accommodation is the only game in town. Some people choose to stay here before or after the long drive from Honolulu to the Center or the North Shore, but don't expect anything special. Rooms are equipped with air conditioning, refrigerators, TV, and coffeemakers. Some also have microwaves. Lanais overlook the swimming pool.

Waikiki

HALEKULANI, 2199 Kalia Road (at end of Lewers Street), Honolulu, HI 96815. Tel. 808/923-2311 or 800/367-2343, www.halekulani.com. 456 rooms. Rates begin at $445.

Perfect for honeymoons (including my own), this fabulous hotel may be a bit too hushed and elegant for very young children. But families with kids age 5 to 12 will appreciate the summertime children's program that includes learning to create pastry in a chef's workshop, studying Hawaii's marine ecosystem at the Waikiki Aquarium, fishing with traditional bamboo poles, and excursions to the Hawaiiana-packed Bishop Museum, the Honolulu Zoo, and Sea Life Park.

As tranquil as Halekulani is, it's difficult to believe that it's right in the heart of Waikiki, at the edge of the state's most crowded beach. Potted silver cup bromeliads and pink cactus blossoms decorate the white-columned porte cochere. A sweeping staircase fringed with waterfalls leads to the lobby and garden. Adjoining towers topped with high-pitched roofs enclose a grassy, palm-studded courtyard, a popular locale for weddings.

Halekulani is full of personal touches. Guests are escorted to their rooms, where they are registered in plush privacy and shown around. You're greeted with complimentary fruit baskets and chocolates freshly made in the hotel's pastry shop. In the bathroom, floor-to-ceiling mirrors slide open to the closet, which contains a safe and is separated from the bedroom by sliding louvered wooden doors. Open these doors while in the tub, and you'll drink in a fabulous view through the room's windows. Although there's a stall shower, the deep tub also has a hand-held, snake-neck nozzle. Thick terry cloth robes are provided for guests during their stay.

Lanais are very large and most look out to Diamond Head (the most impressive view) and/or the ocean. In addition to the expected color TV and mini bar/refrigerator, there are marble vanities, and both fresh flowers and complimentary newspapers appear daily. When you order breakfast room service, don't be surprised if a toaster is brought to your room so you can have your toast warm and just the way you like it.

OUTRIGGER WAIKIKI SHORE, 2161 Kalia Road, Honolulu, HI 96815. Tel. 808/923-3111 or 800/688-7444, www.outrigger.com. 188 units. Rates begin at $250, for a one-bedroom condo.

The one-bedroom apartments comfortably sleep four at this family-friendly condominium on Waikiki Beach. Accordion doors separate the bedroom, with a queen-size bed or two twins, from the living room, which has a convertible sofa. Apartments come with kitchens and washer/dryers. Guests are invited to use all the resort facilities of the full-featured Outrigger Reef hotel right next door.

THE ROYAL HAWAIIAN, 2259 Kalakaua Avenue, Honolulu, HI 96815. Tel. 808/923-7311 or 800/782-9488,www.royal-hawaiian.com. 527 rooms. Rates begin at $230.

While we've enjoyed staying here with our young kids, this elegant beachfront hotel, dating back to 1927, is best for families with older children. Affectionately known as the Pink Palace, the Royal Hawaiian was one of the first hotels in the islands. An oval swimming pool also faces the water. Tall, flourishing trees and other vegetation obscure the flashy neighboring Royal Hawaiian Shopping Center, which adjoins the grounds of this subdued hotel. It was built on the site of King Kamehameha V's summer cottage, which stood here in the mid-19th century. In the early days, the Royal Hawaiian catered to wealthy tourists who, with their servants in tow, sailed to Honolulu by steamship, often remaining for months at a time. The first registered guest was Princess Kawananakoa, who would have become queen of Hawaii had the monarchy survived. The roomy lobby is decorated with marble, crystal chandeliers, and sparkling mirrors. Picture windows draw shoppers into stores. Rooms contain colonial style furniture, including cherry wood beds, plus refrigerators, minibars, a sitting area, cut-glass light fixtures, and plush baths with marble.

OUTRIGGER WAIKIKI ON THE BEACH, 2335 Kalakaua Avenue, Honolulu, HI 96815. Tel. 808/923-0711 or 800/688-7444, www.outrigger.com. 530 rooms. Rates begin at $230.

Busy day and night, this large, modern hotel is the best known of the Outriggers. One side faces the beach while the other overlooks Kalakaua Avenue, Waikiki's main drag. Murals decorate the lobby walls. There is a whirlpool by the hotel pool, and guests are welcome to use the exercise room. Guest rooms have private lanais with varying views, refrigerators, and safes. Suites also come with minibars, wet bars, kitchenettes with microwave ovens, and two baths. Duke's Canoe Club, the hotel's popular beach side restaurant, features Hawaiian and contemporary music at night.

OUTRIGGER REEF ON THE BEACH, 2169 Kalia Road, Honolulu, HI 96815. Tel. 808/923-3111 or 800/688-7444, www.outrigger.com. 885 rooms. Rates begin at $220.

I'd probably call this Waikiki's best choice for a moderately priced yet highly attractive beach front hotel, especially for families. For one reason, a children's program that serves various Waikiki hotels is centralized here. This accommodation is often referred to simply as The Reef so as not to be confused with the many other Outriggers. The dignified lobby is graced with a rock and water sculpture, columns, and stone tile floors. Kids, and their parents, enjoy visiting the humback whale kiosk here to learn all about the giant mammals that frequent Hawaiian waters during winter months. When you aren't shopping, swimming, or out sightseeing, you can hit the hotel's fitness center. Extensive water sports are the draw by day, and lounges and restaurants provide entertainment at night. Guest rooms are contemporary, with private lanais and refrigerators. Suites feature honor bars, wet bars, kitchenettes, microwave ovens and two bathrooms each.

HILTON HAWAIIAN VILLAGE BEACH RESORT & SPA, 2005 Kalia Road, Honolulu, HI 96815. Tel. 808/949-4321 or 800/HILTONS, www.hilton.com. 2,545 rooms. Rates begin at $210.

Hilton Hawaiian Village is actually more like a small city than a village. In the grandiose, open-air lobby, handsomely uniformed porters push gleaming gold luggage carts through the whirl of activity. More than 2,500 rooms and a slew of hard-to-resist shops and restaurants are located in and around its towers, the most distinctive of which (from the outside) is the mosaic-covered Rainbow Tower, a Waikiki landmark. In varying degrees of luxury, guest rooms come with and without ocean views. Some look out to gardens and mountains. Features of all rooms include lanais, mini-bars, and refrigerators.

In the Rainbow Bazaar, many people photograph the Thai temple and the 400-year-old farmhouse that was brought from Japan in pieces and put back together here. The split-level swimming pool rambles over 10,000 square feet and is bordered by colorful blossoms and lava rock waterfalls. The grounds are also graced with fish ponds with koi, swans, and turtles, a penguin pool, Japanese sculpture on marble and granite pedestals, palm trees, and a profusion of other tropical greenery. As part of the children's program (for guests aged 5 to 12), kids get to feed the resort's fish, as well as go on trips to the zoo and aquarium in Waikiki.

At the activities desk, guests set up their itineraries, from cruises and horseback rides to tours and car rentals. Pedi boats, snorkeling equipment, canoes, Hobie cats, surfboards and other water sports equipment are rented on the beach. Be sure to spend some time at the **Bishop Museum** annex, in Kalia Tower. It may be smaller than the main museum, in Honolulu, but this satellite, packed with Hawaiian art, antiques, and artifacts, is just the right size for kids. Daily activities include music, crafts, and Hawaiian language lessons.

HYATT REGENCY WAIKIKI RESORT & SPA, 2424 Kalakaua Avenue (off Ka'iulani), Honolulu, HI 96815. Tel. 808/923-1234 or 800/233-1234, www.hyattwaikiki.com. 1,230 rooms. Rates begin at $210.

Across Kalakaua Avenue—which borders Queen's Beach, famous for its soft sand—this hotel takes up an entire block. Just look for the two connected towers. The three-story atrium has waterfalls, tropical foliage, and exotic birds. With its labyrinth of dozens of designer shops and boutiques on the property, the busy lobby gleams with rich koa wood. Rooms offer a variety of views, with Diamond Head/partial oceanfront being the most popular. The swimming pool provides an alternative to a stroll to the beach. Camp Hyatt offers children (age 5 to 12) a menu of activities from Hawaiian crafts and traditional board games to story time in the camp library with its extensive collection of classic and Hawaiian children's books.

ASTON WAIKIKI BEACH HOTEL, 2570 Kalakaua Avenue, Honolulu, HI 96815. Tel. 808/922-2511 or 800/922-7866, www.astonhotels.com. 715 rooms. Rates begin at $205.

Right next to the Honolulu Zoo, Kapiolani Park, Waikiki Aquarium, and a slew of fast-food restaurants, this is a good choice for families with children. It is also a good Kalakaua Avenue location for viewing both the June King Kamehameha Day Parade and the Aloha Week Parade in September. People fight to get seats on the terrace of the hotel's main dining room.

The beach across the street is the quieter end of Waikiki's sandy strip. A swimming pool is just off the lobby, which is one flight up from the ground floor. Since hotel towers keep most of the sun off the pool during the day anyway, many prefer to swim in the evening when other guests are out on the town. Some of the guest rooms (many of which are small) have no lanais at all, while others have either large balconies or standing lanais (just big enough for a couple of pairs of feet). The largest rooms are those that face Diamond Head. All rooms come with refrigerators.

ASTON WAIKIKI BEACH TOWER, 2470 Kalakaua Avenue, Honolulu, HI 96815. Tel. 808/926-6400 or 800/922-7866, www.astonhotels.com. 140 units. Rates begin at $200 per one-bedroom unit.

The beach is just down the street from this all-suite resort, which is probably Waikiki's most upscale condo. Grounds include a swimming pool, whirlpool, sauna, and paddle tennis court. A spacious lanai runs on two sides of each one- and two-bedroom unit. The most expansive vistas are from floors twenty and above. Apartments sport full kitchens, wet bars, and washer/dryers. Housekeepers tidy your digs twice a day and concierge service is available. You can sign for meals at a choice of nearby restaurants. Valet parking is included in the rates.

ASTON WAIKIKI SUNSET, 229 Paoakalani Avenue, Honolulu, HI 96815. Tel. 808/922-0511 or 800/922-7866, www.astonhotels.com. 362 units. Rates begin at $195 per condo.

Three short blocks from the beach and near the zoo, aquarium, Kapiolani Park, and the trailhead for the hike up Diamond Head, this all-suite condo caters mainly to families and students. The studios, one- and two-bedroom units, and penthouse suites are all comfortable, but some (such as the one-bedroom units) are on the small side. A swimming pool, tennis court and shuffleboard keep guests entertained. The restaurant serves inexpensive Japanese and American food, and the fifth-floor Mini Mart—which stocks everything from eggs and liquor to film and Nintendo for rent—is another welcome convenience. Many guests prefer rooms with more dramatic mountain views (spectacular at night with all the lights on the hillsides and in the valleys) to those with (usually partial) ocean views.

WAIKIKI BEACH MARRIOTT, 2552 Kalakaua Avenue, Honolulu, HI 96815. Tel. 808/922-6611 or 800/367-5370, www.marriottwaikiki.com. 1,310 rooms. Rates begin at $190.

Just across Kalakaua Avenue from the beach, this five-acre resort is a huge complex encompassesing a mall of shops and designer boutiques, two swimming pools, a full-service spa overlooking the ocean, a 24-hour fitness facility, and several restaurants. Comfortable guest rooms look out to Diamond Head and Waikiki Beach or the mountains. The periodic evening screenings of movies on the beach take place right across the street from this hotel, which is within walking distance of Waikiki Aquarium, Honolulu Zoo, Kapiolani Park, and Diamond Head.

SHERATON MOANA SURFRIDER, 2365 Kalakaua Avenue, Honolulu, HI 96815. Tel. 808/922-3111 or 800/782-9488, www.moanasurfrider.com. 793 rooms. Rates begin at $180.

The first hotel on Waikiki Beach, the 75-room Moana debuted in 1901. Its first guests paid a whopping $1.50 a night. By 1918, two added wings had enlarged it to more than 200 rooms and created the lovely courtyard you'll see cupping a sprawling banyan tree that was planted in 1885. "Hawaii Calls," the famous radio program, was broadcast from the 1930s to the '70s from this courtyard, near where the swimming pool now is. Don't miss the elaborate buffet breakfast or afternoon tea here on the oceanside Banyan Verandah.

Now combined with the SurfRider, the beautifully restored Moana is known as the Banyan Wing. This four-story Italian Renaissance building, once one of Hawaii's tallest, has been on the National Register of Historic Places since 1972 and has also been named one of the Historic Hotels of America. Twenty 15-foot columns stand in the dazzling white and oak lobby. Front-desk attendants wear Victorian ivory and lace dresses. Copies of turn-of-the-century antiques were made from prized native koa wood. To see nearly a century of Moana memorabilia, stop by the hotel's Historical Room.

If you want to be surrounded by the most atmospheric architecture and furnishings, be sure to request one of the Banyan Wing rooms. Done in muted tones, they are decorated with wood and wicker. Each has an armoire with a television, refrigerator, mini bar and safe hidden inside. All rooms come with terry cloth robes and slippers for guests' use during their stay. Baths are modern, some with art deco touches. Room service is available all day and night. Note that guest rooms throughout the hotel vary greatly in size, decor, and view, so make sure you know what you're getting when you make your reservation. Ask about the year-round children's program (for those aged 5 to 12).

SHERATON WAIKIKI, 2255 Kalakaua Avenue, Honolulu, HI 96815. Tel. 808/922-4422 or 800/782-9488, www.sheraton-waikiki.com. 1,852 rooms. Rates begin at $175.

While this busy beachfront hotel, with two connected towers forming a V, is popular among tour groups and conventions, it also boasts many repeat guests. The comfortable guest rooms differ in price according to view. Most look out to the Pacific. Beach activities include sailing, canoe and catamaran rides, snorkeling, and surfing. One of the two swimming pools is shaped like the head of a mushroom, while the other is round. Hawaiian music entertains poolside each evening while the sun sets. A glass elevator whisks guests up to the Hanohano Room, 30 stories in the sky, with a fabulous view of Waikiki Beach. Periodically, kupuna (elder) craftspeople demonstrate lauhala weaving, Hawaiian quilting, coconut frond weaving, lei-making, and other traditional arts on the lobby level. The hotel offers a year-round children's program (for those aged 5 to 13).

OHANA WAIKIKI TOWER, 200 Lewers Street (at Kalia Road), Honolulu, HI 96815. Tel. 808/922-6424 or 800/688-7444, www.ohanahotels.com. 439 rooms. Rates begin at $150.

In one of Waikiki's busiest areas, this hotel is just across from the plush Halekulani Hotel and a brief stroll from the beach. Ask about the status of the renovation that is scheduled to turn the modest individual rooms into suites that are well-suited to families with children. All kinds of street action is on view from the street-level restaurant.

MARC DIAMOND HEAD BEACH HOTEL, 2947 Kalakaua Avenue, Honolulu, HI 96813. Tel. 808/922-1928 or 800/923-1928, www.marcresorts.com. 52 rooms. Rates begin at $140.

If you'd like to be on Waikiki Beach, but can do without the crowds, this small hotel is a good choice. The artificial beach here is petite, but good stretches of sand are on either side of the hotel. Guests don't pay anything to use the boogie boards and snorkeling gear. Rooms are comfortably furnished. Families often book the units with kitchenettes. A light breakfast is included in the rates. Really want to feel at home? Take advantage of the washer/dryer. Be sure to ask about special discounts, which can cut the room rate in half!

OHANA REEF TOWER, 227 Lewers Street, Honolulu, HI 96815. Tel. 808/924-8844 or 800/688-7444, www.ohanahotels.com. 480 rooms. Rates begin at $135 (for studios with kitchenettes).

The convenient location—on a palm-lined block near the beach and in the thick of Waikiki hurly-burly— makes this a good choice. Although this property is slated to become a timeshare, units will remain available for rent. There isn't much to see from the windows of the comfortable guest rooms, but who cares? Just step outside, and you can see (and do) as much as you'd like. At this hotel at night, you might even find a musical revue or performance by a comedian at the showroom.

SHERATON PRINCESS KA'IULANI, 120 Ka'iulani Avenue (off Kalakaua), Honolulu, HI 96815. Tel. 808/922-5811 or 800/782-9488, www.princess-kaiulani.com. 1,150 rooms. Rates begin at $120.

Discount rates (and convenient connecting rooms) make this hotel a good choice for families with children. Sheraton's children's program runs year-round. The Honolulu Zoo, Waikiki Aquarium, and Kapiolani Park (where night-lit tennis courts are open to the public at no charge) are all within walking distance. The cheery guest rooms vary greatly according to size and view. Some rooms have twin beds and no lanais. Other rooms contain king-sized beds and writing desks. So when you make your reservations, be sure you are clear about exactly what you are getting.

Adjoining a lounge alive with greenery, the large pool patio of this Sheraton opens to Kalakaua Avenue, which borders the beach. Arrangements for golf, guided tours, rental cars, and other activities can be made in the lobby, which is decorated with plants and elaborate floral arrangements. Prominently displayed in the lobby is the handsome portrait of Princess Ka'iulani, the namesake of the hotel. Heartbroken by the overthrow of Hawaii's kingdom, she died at the tender age of 23.

HAWAIIANA HOTEL, 260 Beachwalk, Honolulu, HI 96815. Tel. 808/923-3811 or 800/367-5122, 95 rooms. Rates begin at $110.

While this small hotel is rather simple in decor, it is a half block from Waikiki Beach. Its low-rise wings surround colorful gardens, which sit just outside guest room doors. Some of the air-conditioned studio and one-bedroom units have lanais, and all contain kitchenettes and safes. You'll be treated to fresh pineapple when you arrive. In the mornings, juice and kona coffee are served on the pool side patio. Guests are welcome to use the washers and dryers.

THE BREAKERS HOTEL, 250 Beach Walk, Honolulu, HI 96815. Tel. 808/923-3181 or 800/426-0494, www.breakers-hawaii.com. 63 rooms. Rates begin at $110.

Stretching from Beach Walk to Saratoga Avenue, and halfway between Kalia Road and Kalakaua Avenue, this hotel is close to both the ocean and the main shopping thoroughfare. The Breakers is a pleasant surprise along a strip of low budget hotels. Shingled roofs cover a handful of buildings. Banana trees, palms, and other tropical greenery add color to the pool patio. Attractively furnished in rattan, bright guest rooms surround the pool. You'll find books for borrowing at the nearby open-air front desk. Each air-conditioned unit has a kitchenette, TV, and safe. While most units here sleep three people, some are two-room suites that sleep four.

Chapter 10

MAUI WITH KIDS

The second-largest member of the Hawaiian archipelago, at roughly 729 square miles, Maui is also the second-most visited—and with good reason, particularly for families. When, and if, you can tear yourselves away from the beach, exciting road trips are not only short and sweet, but they can take you quickly to and through a boredom-busting array of contrasting attractions and settings. For instance, the drive from sea level to the 10,023-foot summit of Haleakala volcano can transport you from the heat of summer to the chill of winter, from lush fields to a stark moonscape, in just 90 minutes. And while Maui is the second-most developed of the islands after Oahu, it is packed with glorious regions where Mother Nature still reigns. For serious low-key action, you can even take a ferry ride or a brief flight to the nearby island of Lanai or Molokai.

Long ago, Hawaiians say, the sun sped across the sky too swiftly for anyone to put in a good day's work. For instance, night always fell before the *kapa* cloth that women pounded from water-soaked bark had had a chance to dry. Maui is named for the demi-god who put an end to all that by standing on the rim of Haleakala and throwing a long rope with a hook that snared the yellow ball of fire and slowed it down.

Once actually two separate islands, Maui consists of two volcanic peaks divided by lush valleys thick with agricultural fields. From the air, it looks as if a pair of mountainous cookies, one much smaller than the other, had been placed too close together when they went into the oven. Maui's shape is sometimes described as the head and torso of a short-haired woman in profile. Her head forms West Maui, dominated by Kahalawai (commonly called the West Maui Mountains). Her neck is the six-mile isthmus that slopes gently toward Mount Haleakala, which commands larger East Maui—her bust, shoulder and side.

Along with prime scuba and snorkeling sites, buff-colored (and black sand) beaches ring the island. Many families are lured by the mountain bike excursion down Haleakala volcano, horseback riding in the crater, scenic hiking trails, good camp sites, and excellent waves and windsurfing breezes. In addition to all kinds of land and water sports, this island welcomes visiting families with surprises for kids such as spa treatments designed especially for teenagers. Maui also boasts worthwhile art galleries, theaters, and small museums that appeal to the whole family.

The historic, picturesque port town of Lahaina offers a glimpse into Hawaii's 19th century whaling days. During the winter, this island is the whale-

Maui's Whopping Whale Watching

From around December through June, migrating humpback whales bound through Hawaiian waters. Maui provides the state's best vantage point, with hundreds coming to its waters. Growing as long as 45 feet and weighing as much as 40 tons, these are the fifth-largest of the great whales. Scientists believe that they travel the 3,000 miles from Alaska to breed in Hawaii's warmer climate, giving birth 12 months later. Baby whales weigh only about 2,000 pounds (!) and spend the winter fattening up off Maui's shores.

While whale-watching cruises depart several times a day from Lahaina and Maalaea harbors, conservationists encourage people to view these aquatic giants from land (and with a good pair of binoculars, you'll do just fine). The sound of so many people-packed boats can interfere with the whales' mating. There are lots of good vantage points on terra firma, such as the top of the cinder cone at Big Beach in the Makena area. You'll still have a great view as these giant creatures fluke (lift their tails into the air), breach (jump partially out of the water), and spurt water from their blowholes.

However, if you're determined to see the whales from out in the ocean, try one of the boat trips run by the **Pacific Whale Foundation**, Tel. 879-8811, www.pacificwhale.org, a nonprofit research, conserva-tion, and education organization based in Maalaea Harbor. A marine biologist, on board for every trip, shares lots of fun facts. For instance, each male whale has its own distinctive song, which changes each year. (You can buy CD recordings of whale music in the gift shop.) Unlike other outfits, Pacific Whale Foundation boats all use bio-diesel (made from vegetable oil) so, instead of the usual vessel fumes, the emissions from these boats smell like French fries!

ð

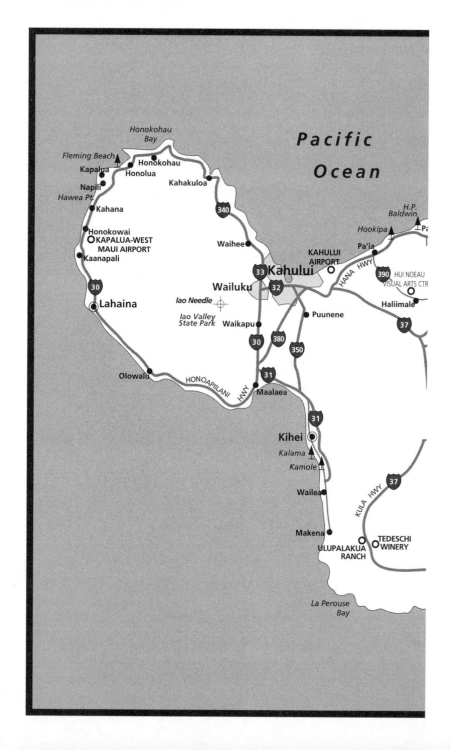

Maui

N

↑ = ...Beach Park

Pauwela
36
360 ✗ Twin Falls
Ulumalu
400 Kaupakulua
Kailua
Honomanu Bay
Keanae
Kaumahina ✗ State Park
Wailua
Kokomo
Makawao
Keanae Valley State Park
Nahiku
HANA AIRPORT
Waianapanapa State Pk. ✗
Puaa Kaa Falls Park ✗
360
HANA HWY
Hana Bay Pk. ✗
377 Olinda
Pulehu
Waiakoa
378
HALEAKALA PARK HQ
Hana
31
Kula
Haleakala National Park
Hamoa Beach
Puuiki
Haleakala Crater
Wailua Falls ✗
Oheo Gulch ✗
Haou
Kipahulu
Kaupo
31

watching capital of the state. In fact, if you arrive in Maui between December and June and drive to the Kaanapali resort area from Kahului Airport, you might even spot whales from the sea cliffs along northwest West Maui. Cars are often pulled over while people stand on the nearby bluffs to get good looks at the mammoth mammals.

Getting Around

Most travelers fly into Kahului Airport, just east of the neighboring towns of Kahului—Maui's commercial and industrial center about 35 minutes from Lahaina—and flourishing Wailuku. Rental car agencies that aren't located at the airport provide shuttle service between their parking lots and the baggage claim area. Taxis and shuttle buses to hotels are also available at the airport. The smaller Kapalua-West Maui Airport is convenient for many visitors flying to or from other Hawaiian islands since it is close to Kaanapali, Honokowai, Kahana, Napili, and Kapalua. Hana is reached by air from either airport or by car.

From Kahului, the drive to Lahaina is about 45 minutes (depending on traffic); to Kaanapali, about an hour; to Kihei, 25 minutes; to Wailea, 40 minutes; to Makena, 50 minutes; and to Hana, at least two hours. Lahaina (about 15 minutes south of Kaanapali) is some 45 to 50 minutes north of Kihei and Wailea and an hour from Makena. Small planes fly into Hana Airport, from both airports as well as from other Hawaiian islands.

In East Maui, the region between about 3,000 and 7,000 feet up along the north, west, and southwest slopes of Haleakala volcano is known as upcountry Maui. However, exploring this area and driving to the volcano's summit should be done on separate days. The land here is given over to cool breezes, agriculture, small towns, rodeos, and ranches for cattle, sheep, and horses. Although upcountry sits just above the beach resorts of Kihei, Wailea, and Makena, people coming from those areas must take the one paved route through Kahului.

Although Maui has no island-wide public transportation system, shuttle service is available to guests of various hotels. In Kaanapali, these buses run between accommodations, Whalers Village Shopping Center, and the town of Lahaina. Kapalua, Makena, and Wailea also offer local bus service within each resort. When you want to venture beyond the resorts, try **Speedy Shuttle**, *Tel. 875-8070*, a van service that is less expensive than using taxis.

To go upcountry and other less developed parts of the island, it's best to rent a car. Make your reservation as far ahead of your arrival as possible, especially if you're vacationing during the summer or between late December and the end of February. Traffic along the roads connecting Lahaina, Kaanapali, and Kahului is particularly sluggish during rush hours. There is no road, at least not a drivable one, that will take you around the whole island of Maui. Therefore, you will find yourself doing a fair amount of back tracking

Island Hopping

When you're vacationing on Maui, exploring beyond this island is a cinch. Inter-island ferries connect Maui with both Lanai and Molokai for convenient day trips. Call **Expeditions**, Tel. 661-3756, about $50 (adults) and $40 (children age 11 and younger) round trip, for schedules of the 45-minute rides between Lahaina and Lanai, where it's not unusual to spot dolphins at the Hulopoe Bay beach. For the hour-and-45-minute ride to Kaunakakai, Molokai's sleepy town, board the **Maui Molokai ferry**, Tel. 866-307-6524. Roundtrip fare is about $85 for adults, $43 for children ages 4 to 12, and free for kids age three and younger. However, the water is sometimes rough, so those who get seasick may prefer to take a brief flight to Lanai or Molokai.

if you plan to do extensive touring. Allow at least two hours from the Wailea area to the summit of Haleakala and about 2.5 hours from Lahaina.

A four-wheel-drive vehicle is best for getting to some of Maui's most scenic hideaways, such as Polipoli State Park, on the slopes of Haleakala volcano, the fishing village of Kahakuloa on West Maui, and La Perouse Bay, south of Makena resort. Although it is against rental agreements to take even four-wheel-drives onto unpaved roads, many visitors ignore these rules so as not to miss some of Maui's best sights.

Where Are We Going Now?

With plenty to explore on a pair of once-separate land masses, Maui is like getting two islands for the price of one. The rugged West Maui Mountains have had lots of time to become expertly sculpted by the elements. Their last volcanic eruption probably occurred some 5,000 to 10,000 years ago. Greener than the resort areas of East Maui, West Maui is the busiest section of the island. It is home to Kapalua, which draws affluent vacationers, many of whom are avid golfers; peaceful, residential Napili, with its beachfront condos; Kaanapali, the island's main resort area; the town of Lahaina, the old whaling port; and jungled Iao Valley (great for hiking). From Kaanapali Beach, along the west coast, there are striking views of the islands of Molokai and Lanai.

Dominating East Maui, Haleakala volcano is thought to have spewed lava as recently as 500 to 1,000 years ago. Hugging the gentle slopes of the volcano, upcountry Maui is a picturesque region of cowboys and ranches, flower farms and scenic neighborhoods, and peaceful, winding roads. East Maui offers a diverse group of resort areas along its largely arid western coast: lively Kihei, with its moderately-priced, architecturally uninspired high-rise condos; more subdued Wailea, clearly a planned resort, where you'll find several luxury accommodations; and upscale Makena, a newer, less developed region at the southern end of Maui's western coast; plus flourishing, tranquil Hana, isolated way over on Maui's more verdant eastern coast.

Sights & Adventures

LAHAINA-KAANAPALI AND PACIFIC RAILROAD, Kaanapali area and Lahaina, West Maui. Tel.661-0080. Cost: about $16 (adults) and $10 (ages 3 to 12) roundtrip.

Also known as the Sugar Cane Train, this steam-engine takes vacationers on a 12-mile ride back and forth between Kaanapali and Lahaina. This railroad was inspired by the turn-of-the-century trains that carried cane to the mills. You'll chug along the highway past areas thick with sugarcane fields until 1999. Although the narrated tour is piped through all the cars, you'll hear it best if you sit in the same car as the guide. While you listen to the historical and geographical tidbits about passing sights, you might have a chance to see and touch an actual stalk of sugar cane. Several round-trip excursions run daily between Puukolii (Kaanapali area) and Lahaina. The ride is just over 30 minutes each way. If you time it right, you'll be able to have a leisurely amble through Lahaina before catching the return train to Kaanapali, or you can go back right away—that is, after passing through the Lahaina station gift shop.

WHALERS VILLAGE MUSEUM, Whalers Village, Kaanapali Parkway, Kaanapali, West Maui. Tel. 661-5992. Admission: free. Open 9am to 10pm daily.

In an open-air, oceanfront mall, this petite museum gives families a worthwhile break from all the shops and restaurants. Among the intriguing displays are 19th century whaling implements, vintage photos, scrimshaw, the skeleton of a 30-foot sperm whale, and replicas of old whaling ships. Videos provide additional information about Maui's lucrative whaling years.

Rent a Friend

When you're away from home, what could be more fun than having friends take you to all their favorite places? No getting lost trying to find what you're looking for, no arguing over whether to stop to ask for directions. If you don't know anyone on Maui, don't worry. Through **Guides of Maui**, Tel. 877-4060, www.guidesofmaui.com, based in Kahului, a guide will drive you (in your rental car) wherever you want to go ($235 for a day). For an extra charge, you can even arrange to be met at your hotel or condo. Families rave about these personalized tours because sights and stops are tailored to their specific interests. Guides are happy to share their favorite hideaways—secluded beaches, waterfalls, back roads, and other little-known scenic spots.

Buying it on Maui

While the larger hotels have clusters of boutiques on the premises, I find it more fun (and more economical) to wander in and out of the small stores along Front Street in Lahaina. If you're in the market for locally produced ceramics, jewelry, clothing, candies, and other items, keep an eye out for the **Made on Maui** logo.

Shopping centers tend to stay open as late as 9pm or 10pm. To go where residents go, head for the **Kaahumanu Center** in central Kahului. The indoor **Lahaina Cannery,** at the north end of Lahaina, is reminiscent of the 1919 Baldwin Packers pineapple cannery that once stood on this site. Toward the southern end of Lahaina are **The Wharf** and **505 Front Street. Whalers Village** is an open-air collection of shops and boutiques, some of them designer, and waterfront restaurants right on Kaanapali Beach. At **The Shops at Wailea,** an attractive, sprawling mall south of Kaanapali, you'll find well-known retail stores along with worthwhile restaurants and art galleries.

If you love lavender, be sure to visit **Maui Kula Lavender**, Tel. 808/878-3004, upcountry in Kula, with spectacular views in a cool, serene setting. Sip some lavender tea while relaxing on the lanai as the kids sample lavender lemonade. This is the place to try or buy everything from lavender scones, lavender seasoning, and lavender lilikoi (passionfruit) jelly to lavender soap, lavender aromatherapy candles, and lavender-scented note cards.

LAHAINA, just south of Kaanapali, West Maui.

Much of it now a National Historic Landmark, Lahaina was the first royal capital of the Hawaiian islands. The town is composed of only about four mile-long streets, which run parallel to the waterfront. Most of the sights are found on or adjacent to a half-mile section of Front Street. Plan to spend a couple of hours poking around here.

If you're vacationing in June, the kids will love Kamehameha Day and Lahaina's yearly King Kamehameha Parade, a *ho'olaule'a* (street party) in honor of the monarch who unified the Hawaiian islands. During the 1800s, Lahaina was a flourishing whaling port. *Moby Dick* author Herman Melville was among the hundreds of sailors who passed through. Today, along handsome Front Street, sunlight glints off the windows of the refurbished or recreated wooden buildings that now house a jumble of restaurants, cafes, T-shirt shops, jewelry stores, and clothing boutiques. Take the time to wade through the touristy souvenirs and you'll find a welcome array of quality goods. Most of Maui's major art galleries are in Lahaina, many along the main street.

The town was named for the relentless sun (*la haina*) that can be especially merciless in the afternoon. However, afternoon is also the time when you're likely to see rainbows, if you look *mauka* (toward the mountains). The town is most crowded during the cooler, earlier part of the day. Don't even think about trying to find a parking space then. Opt for the Sugar Cane Train (described above) or one of the shuttles that run between town and accommodations in neighboring Kaanapali.

BALDWIN HOUSE MUSEUM, 120 Dickenson (on Front Street), Lahaina, West Maui. Tel. 661-3262. Open 10am-4pm daily. Admission: $3 (adults); free for children age 17 and younger.

This museum is a good place to stop as soon as you get to Lahaina, since members of the Lahaina Restoration Foundation supply free walking tour maps of the historic town. The name of a prominent local family with missionary roots, "Baldwin" crops up frequently in Hawaii. Respected for giving generously to the islands that gave them their wealth, this clan has owned *The Maui News* and built schools, parks, and other public institutions.

The 19th-century home of the Reverend Dwight Baldwin, M.D., this whitewashed stone building contains furnishings that once belonged to this missionary physician, his children, and grandchildren. From the mid-1830s through the late 1860s, Dr. Baldwin and his family welcomed countless patients, fellow missionaries, whaling captains, and members of the congregation who came to chat or to seek medicine or advice.

Today, visitors are invited to take a look at the 1859 Steinway piano; the imported china on display in the dining room; the gleaming four-poster *koa* wood bed and the monkeypod crib; and Maui's first toilet. Outside the master bedroom is the grape arbor under which Mrs. Baldwin taught sewing and Bible classes for Hawaiian women and children.

OLD BANYAN TREE, across from the Pioneer Inn, Lahaina, West Maui.

It may look like a forest, but it's really just one tree! Covering nearly an acre of land right in town, this sprawling banyan was planted in 1873 to celebrate the 50th anniversary of the arrival of Protestant missionaries in Hawaii. Thrown wide like many open arms, the branches drip vertical shoots that grow into additional trunks resembling elephant legs. The wealth of branches provides plenty of shade for the scattered benches in this peaceful setting. Many kids (including ours!) find it difficult to obey the signs that forbid climbing the long, thick horizontal branches, some of which are propped up with poles.

Greatest Groceries

If you're staying in a condo or vacation home, consider taking care of your grocery shopping in residential Kahului or Wailuku, where prices are the lowest on the island. ❧

MAUI OCEAN CENTER, off Route 30, Ma'alaea, West Maui. Tel.270-7000. Open daily 9am to 5pm. Admission: $20 (adults), $13 (age 3 to 12).

Our kids love spending time here at one of the world's largest tropical aquariums. Rent a magic wand and a narrator will take you from exhibit to exhibit at your own pace. Filled with thousands of fish, turtles, rays, and sharks, the three-acre Maui Ocean Center features a tunnel though an open-ocean tank, and the interactive Whale Discovery Center. Allow at least two hours to fully explore this indoor/outdoor facility—you'll need more than 30 minutes just for the Whale Discovery Center. Traveling with young children? Don't miss the touch tank.

BAILEY HOUSE MUSEUM, 2375-A Main Street (Route 32), Wailuku, West Maui. Tel. 244-3326. Open 10am-4pm, Monday to Saturday. Admission $5 (adults), $1 (age 7 to 12).

Best for children age seven and older, Bailey House Museum is an old missionary house built of lava rock and local wood in 1833. Now headquarters of the Maui Historical Society, it contains the island's most extensive public collection of Hawaiian artifacts (some from before the arrival of Europeans), including feather work, stone and shell tools, kapa cloth, and bone fishhooks. On display as well are furniture and clothing used by missionaries, along with old paintings of 19th century Maui. Ask about special programs at the museum, such as Hawaiian music, hula, and crafts lessons. Stop by the gift shop and you might find something you like among the local handicrafts, clothing, and Hawaiian books and music.

HAWAII NATURE CENTER IAO VALLEY INTERACTIVE SCIENCE ARCADE, 875 Iao Valley Road, Wailuku, West Maui. Tel. 244-6500. Open daily 10am-4pm. Admission $6 (adults), $4 (age 4 to 12).

On your way to flourishing Iao Valley State Park, be sure to stop at this enjoyable hands-on museum. More than two dozen exhibits and activities bring Hawaii's natural history to life, from touch pools and aquariums to live insect exhibits and a dragonfly ride. Families love the twice-daily guided nature walks. During the mile loop, you'll learn all about the medicinal uses of various plants and fruit, and hear about days gone by in the valley.

IAO VALLEY STATE PARK, Iao Valley Road, Wailuku, West Maui.

You'll know you've reached Iao Valley State Park when the highway dries up. The valley began as the crater of the West Maui volcano and was enlarged by wind and rain. Rising 1,200 feet from the ground, **Iao Needle** points to the sky like a giant green finger. There are about ten major botanical zones on Maui, ranging from desert to soggy, from the tropics at sea level to an alpine region at the summit of Mount Haleakala. Each area contains a different group of plants. In tropical Iao Valley, bathed by about 150 inches of rainfall a year, the variety of plant, animal, and insect life is greater than anywhere else on the island.

This is a wonderful area for hiking, especially if you enjoy picking fruit. Apple, banana, mango, guava, and coffee trees grow wild. This last plant produces red coffee berries in the fall. Remove the skin from the berry and suck on the two beans in each. The coating has a candy-like flavor. But don't try to eat the beans! If you happen to be hiking in July or August with dirty hair, look for the three-inch red bulbs of the shampoo ginger plant, which contain a clear liquid that can serve as a natural shampoo; there won't be any suds, but it will leave your hair soft and silky. (The Paul Mitchell hair care company has even marketed it commercially.)

An Intimate Look at Maui

There's nothing like getting to know Maui through the eyes of a photographer. With **Open Eye Tours,** Makawao, Tel. 808-572-3483, www.openeyetours.com, you and your family can have a private, customized adventure that you'll never forget. Barry "Pono" Fried, an outdoorsman, certified SCUBA diver, language teacher, and musician as well as a published photographer, loves getting children of all ages involved in the fun whether he is leading visitors to the island's most popular spots or to nooks and crannies they might never find on their own.

He might show the kids how to play his ukulele, string a lei, or fashion a fish from a palm frond. While sampling poha berries and bananas during a wooded hike, you might learn all about edible plants used for healing. As you examine the ancient remains of heiau (Hawaiian temples) and petroglyphs (rock carvings), Barry might tell intriguing Hawaiian legends. If you're lucky, he might even let your kids feed the hens, chickens, or rabbits on his farm, where he grows his own herbs and vegetables. A long-time resident, Barry shares his infectious passion for Maui as he guides you to refreshing swimming holes, craggy desserts, dramatic shorelines, hidden waterfalls, misty rain forests, and rugged mountain trails. When he takes vacationers to his favorite artists' studios, crafts shops, and handsome mansions, he seems as excited as if he too were seeing them for the first time.

Not only will Barry teach you Hawaiian words, chants, and songs, but you can even brush up on your French or Spanish as you wander through some of Maui's most spectacular settings. No worries about your family's designated photographer being left out of your photo album. You'll have plenty of pictures of your entire family since Barry is always happy to shoot the whole gang against the most dramatic backdrops.

≈

MAUI TROPICAL PLANTATION, Route 30, Waikapu, just south of Wailuku, West Maui. Tel. 244-7643. Open 9am-5pm daily. Tram tour $10 (adults), $4 (ages 3 to 12).

These 112 flourishing acres are a working plantation. Children love feeding the ducks in the fishpond (you can buy food at the water's edge) and watching monkeys romp around in a cage. Take a narrated tram tour and you'll learn about both agriculture and aquaculture on Maui. You'll also have a chance to taste freshly cut sugar cane and various tropical fruits. Protea, orchids, and anthuriums blossom in the flower nursery. Fresh fruit and gifts are on sale in the plantation's market.

HALEAKALA NATIONAL PARK, Haleakala Highway, Route 37, East Maui.

The largest dormant volcano in the world, massive Haleakala ("House of the Sun") rises two miles into the sky in Haleakala National Park. It hasn't erupted since 1790. This mountain ensures that Maui's climate is schizophrenic: lush in the north and east, parched in the southwest. Pushed across Maui by northeasterly trade winds, rain clouds bump up against Haleakala. Moving up along the slopes into the cooler air, they let loose their water on northern and eastern Maui. By the time the clouds make it to the southwestern portion of the island, they have spent most of their rain.

Thirty miles from Kahului, Maui's main town (about a 90-minute drive through upcountry Maui), the crater is spectacular at sunrise. Biking down its winding road after watching the sun come up has long been a favorite adventure among visitors. However, while visibility at the summit is best early in the day, that's also the chilliest time to visit. So don't forget to bring some very warm clothing: a jacket and/or thick sweater, gloves, a hat, long pants, heavy socks—no, I'm not kidding. While it might be 65 or 70 degrees at sea level, it could be 35 or 40 degrees at this high altitude! Also, note that it's not uncommon for the weather to be dry and sunny in coastal areas while rain pours down at the summit.

Note: children aged 5 to 12 are invited to take part in the **Junior Ranger program**. Stop at the park's headquarters (open 7:30am to 4pm) to pick up the free booklet of activities that teach Hawaiian words and phrases while educating about the delicate ecosystem of this unusual region. When the children finish the tasks in the booklet, they are awarded badges and sworn in as Junior Rangers.

Outside the headquarters, toward the back of the building, you might see some *nene geese*, Hawaii's state bird. **Kalahaku Overlook**, at 9,325 feet, is one of few places where you can see rare, endangered silversword. Resembling a cone-shaped, gray or purple sea anemone, this delicate yet hearty plant thrives where few others can, at high altitudes with extreme temperature fluctuations. Even when the thermometer hits the 90s here during the day, snow can fall that night. These plants take anywhere from 10 to 20 years to reach maturity and their full 8- or 10-foot height. They die after blooming only once and scattering their seeds. The best time to see them is from May, when the flowers begin to look like silver puffs, through August, when the stalk has grown and the blossoms have sprouted yellow and magenta. From this overlook, there are thrilling views of the stark, lumpy crater.

Ten miles from Park Headquarters, the glassed-in Haleakala Visitor Center is perched at 9,745 feet. It is generally open from 6:15am to 3:30pm. This is the place to be for the most spine-tingling views of the crater's lunar landscape. It's a prime spot for sunset watching. The ebony lava looks like petrified molasses and the cinder cones resemble licorice gumdrops. Rocky formations come in chocolate brown, reds, oranges, sooty black, golden, charcoal gray, and even some greens. Throughout the day, the sun alters the crater's hues. (The view is especially intense during the morning or late afternoon.)

Unless you're in a plane or a helicopter, you can't get any higher than the Puu Ulaula observation point, at Haleakala's 10,023-foot summit. When the weather is clearest, the wrap-around view takes in the crater, the rest of the island, Lanai, Molokai, the Big Island of Hawaii, and Oahu. The nearby domes of Science City, which is not open to the public, house a research and communications center for scrutinizing the sun and moon, tracking satellites and missiles, and testing lasers.

THE ROAD TO HANA, Route 36, East Maui.

When your kids ask, "Are we there yet?" you'll be able to answer, "Yes" even while you're still driving. The road to Hana is as much of an adventure as Hana itself, perhaps even more so. Affectionately called a "highway," this road came into being when the feet of ancient Hawaiians pounded out a path. Convicts broadened it during the 1920s, but it wasn't paved until 1962 and couldn't accommodate regular traffic until it was further improved in 1982.

Hana is some 52 twisting, turning, climbing, cliff-edge miles from Kahului, the main town. The road hugs the edge of a precipice, high above dark sand beaches, pitch black boulders, and deep blue waters with vigorous white surf. Hundreds of sharp curves lead to dozens of one-lane bridges over rocky streams and past quiet settlements, thick rain forests, waterfalls, swimming holes, a riot of blossoms, and flourishing state parks where people pause for picnics. Just off the road, many trails are popular with hikers. Hit with about 100 inches of rainfall a year, this coast is extremely lush.

The air is perfumed by wild ginger, plumeria, orchids, and mangoes ripening on trees. Buttercup-like *hau* blossoms open yellow in the morning and turn red as the day goes by. Thick ferns form roadside walls and the wind whistles through stands of bamboo. One of the most striking (and fragrant) trees you'll see is the rainbow eucalyptus, whose smooth bark is vertically striped with red, yellow, green, and brown, as if someone had sat in its branches and poured paint down the trunk. You'll pass a lone house or church here and there. Along the craggy lava coast, you might see local fishermen casting nets into the ocean just as ancient Hawaiians did. Grazing beef cattle add clumps of brown and beige to the many shades of green.

Near Kahului, **Pa'ia** is the last town you'll come to before reaching Hana, so it's your last chance to fill up on gas or any other necessary supplies. The

Maui Arts

In Kahului, the **Maui Arts & Cultural Center,** One Cameron Way, Tel. 242-2747, hosts performances in dance, music, and theater by national touring companies as well as local artists. You might see a slack key guitar festival one day, a show with popular Hawaiian songs another evening, and a circus extravaganza the next. Tickets are half price for children age 12 and younger.

While commercial, touristy artwork can certainly be found on Maui, the island is better known for its many accomplished artists producing quality paintings, sculpture, and other appealing pieces. Maui sports dozens of galleries, mostly in Lahaina. Art exhibits and other cultural events take place throughout the year. A few hotels are virtual museums, such as the Westin Maui (with all kinds of antiques and its oversized marble Asian and European replicas) and the Hyatt Regency Maui (where an 18th century Burmese Buddha is only one item in the hotel's multi-million dollar collection). Both of these resorts are in Kaanapali Beach Resort.

At **Hui Noeau Visual Arts Center**, 2841 Baldwin Avenue, Makawao, Tel. 572-6560, www.mauiarts.org, free admission, open 10am to 4pm daily, shows and classes are open to visitors. If you miss one of the periodic exhibitions, don't worry. Artwork and crafts are always on sale in the gift shop, which carries baskets, local posters, ceramics, hand-painted clothing, and other imaginatively rendered items. Workshops might be held on lei-making, Chinese calligraphy, photography, jewelry-making, and sculpture.

A nonprofit art institute, Hui Noeau was begun in 1934 by a group of 21 women, headed by Ethel Baldwin, a prominent member of one of Maui's leading families. Located upcountry, just outside the center of the paniolo (cowboy) town of Makawao, it is housed in Mediterranean-style Kaluanui, the old Baldwin estate built in 1917.

This gracious, sunny two-story building, now a historic landmark, rests on the upper slopes of Haleakala volcano, providing a perfect vantage point for a panoramic vista of the island. Near the entrance to the driveway, you'll see the ruins of one of Maui's first sugar mills. The nine acres of grassy grounds are studded with tall Cook Island pines and camphor trees. A reflecting pool sets off a scrupulously trim garden filled with colorful flowers.

☙

historic main street in this former sugar plantation town is lined with a collection of old and new Western frontier-style buildings. Some of the original turn-of-the-century structures have been converted into boutiques, restaurants, bakeries, antiques stores, bookstores, natural foods shops, and art galleries.

Just beyond Pa'ia, you'll come to **Hookipa Beach County Park,** one of Maui's premier surfing and windsurfing spots, with waves often reaching 15 feet. Then the road begins to meander roller-coaster style over hills and through valleys. At almost every turn, a new waterfall and swimming hole appears.

GARDEN OF EDEN ARBORETUM, mile marker 10 1/2, Hana Highway, Route 36. Tel. 572-6453; admission $8; open daily 9am-2pm.

If you're ready to stop for a picnic, see strutting peacocks, or bone up on your vegetation, visit this 26-acre drive-through or hike-through botanical garden. As you wander along the two miles of quiet trails, see how many of the hundreds of colorful marked trees and plants you already know. At the end of the trail, stand on a ridge overlooking **Puohokamoa Falls**. Back on the main road, you'll see quite a few cars parked by this waterfall, which thunders into a rocky stream, bordered by picnic tables.

KAUMAHINA STATE WAYSIDE PARK, about 24 miles northwest of Hana, Hana Highway, Route 36.

We've never been here after dark, but we're told that if we were to stick around after sunset, we could see the moon coming up over the ocean from here—hence the name that means "the rising moon." In addition to picnic tables and shelters, you'll find drinking water and toilets here. The crunch of tourists usually thins out by 3pm or so. Like the bony, interlacing fingers of dozens of hands, roots cover the ground, so be careful when walking. Across the road from the park, a lookout point affords a sweeping view of the royal blue Pacific and Keanae Peninsula. A quilt of taro patches spreads across this flat jut of land, the site of a Hawaiian village.

After another mile, massive **Honomanu Valley** sprawls to the right, with its 3,000-foot cliffs and plummeting waterfall. Bright African tulips dapple the highway's greenery with reddish-orange blossoms. Dipping down to sea level, the road passes un-peopled black sand **Honomanu Beach**, where the waves are excellent for surfing. Mountain apple trees are abundant along this stretch. The small, red pear-shaped fruit has a delicious white pulp inside.

KEANAE OVERLOOK, near mile marker 17, Hana Highway, Route 36.

Before you reach this spot after leaving Kaumahina State Wayside Park, Hana Highway takes a steep climb, then comes to **Keanae Arboretum**, where you can splash in **Piinaau Stream**. A hike into the arboretum, filled with many native as well as introduced plants, will give a glimpse of pre-modern, natural Hawaii. Various kinds of *taro* grow in patches and tropical trees provide shade. When you reach the Keanae Overlook, a favorite among shutterbugs, you'll gaze down on smooth, rectangular taro patches and the ocean. Haleakala volcano is visible in the distance. Almost a mile after mile marker 20, **Wailua Lookout** provides a vista of Wailua Canyon and small Wailua Village, with its tiny church.

Fruit to Go

There are many fruit stands near Wailua Lookout. When the vendors are absent, it's not unusual for them to leave the fruit beside an honor box where customers are trusted to drop in their money.

MAUI CAVE ADVENTURES AT KA'ELEKU CAVERNS, Ulaino Road, off the 31 mile marker, Hana Highway, Route 36. Tel. 248-7308, Web site: www.mauicave.com. Cost: $30 and up.

Maui's largest lava tube system dates back some 30,000 years when a volcano belched East Maui into existence. Guides will lead you into the eerie subterranean passages of Ka'eleku Caverns, filled with stalagmites, stalactites, gas bubbles, ledges, and overhead "windows." Some chambers are taller than 40 feet. You'll be most comfortable wearing sturdy closed-toe shoes, long pants, and a T-shirt. Rates include use of hardhats, lights, gloves, and hippacks with water bottles. The hour and 15 minute tours are good for those aged 6 and up, while the two and a half hour tours are reserved for those aged 15 and older since these explorations include crawling and climbing.

WAIANAPANAPA STATE PARK, three miles north of Hana, East Maui.

Sit on the grassy rise overlooking the black sand beach or climb down to the ebony sand. Pronounced *Why*-ah-*nah*-pah-*nah*-pah, the name means "glistening water." The swimming can be good and there is an abundance of hiking trails and wild fruit waiting to be plucked. If you decide to poke around the caves, be careful!

HANA, three miles south of Waianapanapa State Park, East Maui.

Tucked away on the isolated east coast, the agricultural town of Hana is removed from the rest of the island by far more than geography. Actually, it's a bit of an exaggeration to call it a town since it consists of one luxury hotel and a handful of small accommodations, a couple of restaurants, a post office, a ranch, and a few stores and gas stations. Some of the first Polynesians to arrive in Hawaii settled here. In fact, it was from this area that King Kamehameha the Great first set out, in 1795, to conquer the rest of the Hawaiian Islands (a mission he didn't accomplish until 1810).

Too many vacationers pop in and out of Hana in a single day. We think this flourishing region of Maui is best appreciated when you stay for at least a couple of days. This way, you get a taste of the intoxicatingly low-key ambiance that blankets Hana before and after the day-trippers swarm the town. You have time to go hiking, horseback riding, and swimming at the black sand beach. You and the kids are able to unwind, and talk story with some of friendly the people who live here.

The jagged mountains, green expanses, and explosion of flowers seem to have changed little since the ancient Polynesians called this area home. With its many Hawaiian residents, this is the part of Maui where you are most likely to hear people speaking Hawaiian, an unfortunate rarity these days in most of the state. When the population is not swelled by itinerant tourists, it hovers around a mere 1,200. The majority of residents earn their living through fishing or ranching. Verdant Hana has attracted celebrities from actors and comedians to musicians, many of whom have bought houses in the vicinity. This is also where famed aviator Charles Lindbergh chose to be buried.

For a sweeping view of Hana, hike up to the huge white cross on the hill overlooking Hotel Hana-Maui and the rest of the town. Just be sure to steer clear of the cows and cow dung.

HANA CULTURAL CENTER MUSEUM, up the hill from Hana Bay, East Maui. Tel. 248-8622; open 10am to 4pm daily; suggested donation: $3.

Small enough for child-size attention spans, this museum features out-door replicas of the hale (houses) in a Hawaiian chief's compound. In the old days, when it was the job of Hawaiian men to cook for the women, only males age 14 and older were allowed to enter the thatched roof men's eating house. However, men, women, and children were all permitted into the sleeping house, where the door was made tiny to protect them from intruders.

The second name of this museum, Hale Waiwai 'O Hana, means "House of Treasures of Hana." Among the relics of days gone by are everyday Hawaiian implements such as poi pounders (resembling large wooden ironing boards), kapa cloth (made from bark), Hawaiian quilts, and old canoe paddles. Local children enjoy visiting the museum to see the huge portraits—shot during the 1970s—of their grandparents, aunts, and uncles, all labeled with their names. Next door, the Hana District Police Station and Courthouse, now on the National Register of Historic Places, was used from 1871 to 1978.

VENUS POOL, between Hana and Oheo Gulch.

If you're traveling with older, sure-footed children, consider a visit to one of the most gorgeous sights on Maui. Look for the cars parked by a pasture on the makai (sea) side of the road. Take the path through the field, then head down the rocky path. Your view will suddenly open up to a stunning pool, far below, with dramatic rock formations, white surf bursting into the air, and the open ocean beyond. There was a lone man swimming the last time we visited and a mother was telling her three children about how she used to come here to swim as a child but that climbing down the rocks to the water is very dangerous. Don't even think about getting into the water here. The beauty of this peaceful setting is exciting enough.

OHEO GULCH, Route 31, several miles south of Hana.

Frequently referred to as "Seven Pools" or "Seven Sacred Pools," these volcanic swimming holes are actually closer to 30 in number and no one ever considered them sacred. As it heads for the ocean, the Oheo Stream flows down the valley, spilling into a series of volcanic holes in the rocks. The best time to visit Oheo Gulch is early in the morning, before the van- and car-loads of tourists arrive. From a bridge, you'll look down on a handful of people cooling off, and depending on when you arrive, diving into the holes in the charcoal colored rock. I don't recommend your following the lead of locals and diving in, since hidden rocks can be deadly if you're not familiar with the holes. For a real treat, hike to upper pools and waterfalls. Makahiku Falls is about a half-mile from the parking lot, while Waimoku Falls is about a mile and a half farther.

CHARLES LINDBERGH'S GRAVE, near Oheo Gulch.

A couple of miles beyond Oheo Gulch along the narrow, bumpy road, Kipahulu is the site of Charles Lindbergh's grave. Extremely fond of Hana, this master aviator chose to be buried here, at difficult-to-find **Palapala Hoomau Congregational Church**. On your way here, you'll pass houses ranging from plush to small and weather-beaten, **St. Paul's Church**, and the tall chimney (partially obscured by vegetation) of a crumbling sugar mill. Just beyond the

That's Entertainment, Hawaiian-Style

Most **luau,** all with plentiful authentic Hawaiian (plus modified Hawaiian) foods, feature lively Polynesian revues.

For a comfortable balance between commercial and intimate, try **The Feast at Lele**, 505 Front Street, Lahaina, Tel. 667-5353 or 866/244-5353; cost: $100 (adults), $70 (ages 2 to 12). With the ocean as the backdrop, this dinner and show features the music and dance of Hawaii, Tahiti, Tonga, and Samoa. As each of the four island groups is celebrated, diners sample delicacies from that culture, such as poi, kalua pork, and steamed moi (a fish once reserved for Hawaiian royalty), Tahitian poisson cru (raw marinated fish and vegetables), Samoan shrimp and avocado with passion fruit, and Tongan sea salad and barbecued beef.

In another beachfront setting, **Old Lahaina Luau**, 1251 Front Street, Lahaina, Tel. 667-1998 or 800/248-5828; cost: $86 (adults), $55 (ages 2 to 12), also makes a pleasant evening. Guests may choose between sitting at tables or on *tatami* mats, all arranged in semi-circles and terraced toward the ocean. Everyone has an excellent view of the graceful hula dancers on stage, which is backed by the Pacific. From the purple sweet potatoes to the *haupia* (coconut custard), the food is as delicious as the sunsets.

~

mill and a pasture, you'll come to a steel gate and a road that leads to the church. Inside, you might find a program from a recent service containing hymns written in Hawaiian. This plain, one-room house of worship was built in 1864 on a cliff high above the Pacific. You'll find Lindbergh's tombstone in the small graveyard. Of the many places he had been around the world, he is said to have found Hana the most beautiful. Against his doctor's advice, he left his sickbed in New York and returned to Hana to die in 1974.

Beaches

Two of Maui's most beautiful beaches are at the island's extremes: Kaanapali in western West Maui and Oneloa (Big Beach) in southwestern East Maui. Spend some time driving around the island to see the variety of sandy (or sometimes rocky) shores.

Kaanapali, West Maui

This is where most of Maui's visitors congregate—and with good reason. A broad, 3-mile, palm-edged crescent, Kaanapali (Maui's premier resort area) is lined with attractive hotels and condominiums. All kinds of water sports facilities are available here. There's also a healthy selection of restaurants and shops, both in accommodations and in oceanfront Whalers Village Shopping Center.

Oneloa, Makena, East Maui

Often called **Big Beach**, this 100-foot-wide, 3,000-foot-long beige sandy strip faces the islands of Kahoolawe and Molokini. Even though a family we know was staying in gorgeous Kaanapali, they took the 70-minute drive to this beach every day! They explained that they loved the low density of fellow bathers, especially during the week. Most of the people who use this beach are locals, and my friends enjoyed getting into conversations with residents here.

This area is full of cacti, jade plants, and *kiawe* (mesquite) trees, with huge gnarled trunks bent over by the wind. Like a giant thimble, **Puu O' Lai** (cinder cone) stands guard over the beach. On the other side of this volcanic hill is **Little Beach**. This isolated pocket lures nude bathers even though police periodically remind them that public nudity is illegal in Hawaii.

Napili Bay, northern West Maui, at Napili Kai Beach Club

Trimmed with palms, this gorgeous, tranquil, sandy crescent is what Hawaii is all about. An offshore reef ensures that the water remains calm and that snorkeling is excellent. The facilities of the accommodation, however, are for guests only.

Olowalu Beach, off Route 30, south of Lahaina, West Maui
There are no facilities here and you'll have to park at the edge of the road, but this sandy beach is one of the island's best snorkeling spots. Petroglyphs are found in the Olowalu area.

Papalua State Wayside Park, south of Olowalu, West Maui
The offshore reef makes for calm waters and good snorkeling at this sandy stretch bordered by kiawe trees.

Awalua Beach, near Olowalu, West Maui
Locals flock here for the swimming and new surfers try to hone their craft.

Kamaole Beaches, Kihei, East Maui
If you want your kids to meet some local children, these three beach parks are a good place to start. You might stumble upon a soccer game or see families flying kites.

Hookipa, near the town of Pa'ia, not far from Kahului, East Maui
Many people stop here on their way to Hana, but most come for the windsurfing and surfing, which boardsailors swear by. You can rent sports equipment in shops in the town of Pa'ia. Championship international competitions in both sports are held here each year.

Baldwin Beach Park, near Pa'ia, East Maui
Backed by the West Maui mountains, this eye-pleasing beach (named for one of Maui's oldest and wealthiest families) is hard to resist—so don't even try.

Hamoa Beach, just past Hana, toward Kaupo, East Maui
An unspoiled stretch of salt-and-pepper sand backed by thick greenery and rolling hills, this beach is lapped by exceptionally clear water. Lots of young surfers and boogie boarders put on a good show. Young children will love riding the waves in your arms. Water can be shallow for quite a distance out, depending on the tides, but the surf is always rough. The calmest time of day is the morning.
The Hotel Hana-Maui uses this beach, and its facilities are reserved for guests. However, as with all of Hawaii's beaches, the sand and water are public property.

Black Sand Beach, Waianapanapa State Park, near Hana, East Maui
This ebony sand was created when hot lava hit cold ocean water. This cove sits at the bottom of a cliff edged by jagged black lava sculpture-like formations. The electric blue water, bursts of white surf; and bright green

vegetation against the tar-black lava and sand is a fabulous sight. A path winds down to the crescent, which is often scattered with smooth black rocks and driftwood.

To the right (if you're facing the water) is a small cave. Adults have to squat to enter. Once inside, you may be able to straighten up and walk all the way through to the surf crashing on the other side. Lava pebbles crunch underfoot. Bordered by greenery, a hole in the ceiling shows a piece of the sky.

Sports & Other Activities

Maui offers a host of ways to keep in shape, most of them aquatic. Arrangements for sailing and fishing charters can be made at the Lahaina harbor, as well as for scuba and snorkeling excursions, parasailing, and cruises to watch whales or to visit neighboring Lanai and Molokini crater (for snorkeling). If you and your family want to rent jet skis, go surfing, or try water-skiing, head to Kaanapali Beach, which also has excellent golf courses and tennis courts.

Biking—Down a Volcano!

Traveling with older children? One of the most enjoyable things to do on Maui is cycle 38 miles down Haleakala volcano, especially after watching the sun rise over the crater. The temperature, landscape, and aromas all change dramatically from top to bottom. Cold, rocky, and brown at the summit, the volcano gives way to expanses of wheat-colored grass and the air grows warmer. Views of the West Maui Mountains and patchwork farmland open up in the distance.

With each hairpin turn, more tufts of green appear. Mail boxes stand in front of houses set back from the road. A wonderful fragrance envelopes bikers as they pass through a eucalyptus forest. The sweet perfume of plumeria blossoms wafts by. Suddenly everything is green and the steep mountain slopes have flattened out considerably. With heads bent to the ground, lethargic cows and horses stand in pastures behind fences made of branches and wire. By the time you reach the bottom, you'll be wearing shorts and T-shirts after stripping off the gloves, hats, sweaters, and windbreakers you needed at the summit.

There are two versions of this mountain bike excursion: the sunrise expedition and the later morning trip. You'll be picked up in the middle of the night (around 3am) if you plan to get to the summit before the sun does. Vans carry passengers and the mountain bikes you'll be given at the top. It's freezing up there, so even though the bike companies provide windbreakers and gloves, be sure to bring your own warm layers as well. A breakfast of pastries is served while the sun starts to bathe the crater in light. After riding down, you'll have a picnic or brunch at a restaurant. Those who don't want to drag themselves out of bed can take the later morning trip, which also ends with a picnic or meal in a restaurant.

Most of the riding is coasting so it's more fun than hard work. The leader keeps in touch by walkie-talkie with the driver of the van, who follows the train of bikers, watching to make sure everyone is okay. Through hand signals, the leader tells riders to slow down, stop, or pull over when necessary. If anyone gets tired, they are welcome to ride in the van.

Contact **Maui Downhill**, Tel. 871-2155, Mount Haleakala; about $150 per person (age 12 and older). For the sunrise trip, ask the person who books you to be sure to notify you in a timely fashion if the ride is canceled due to bad weather at the summit.

Fishing

Deep-sea fishing enthusiasts on Maui are rewarded with catches of mahi-mahi, Pacific blue marlin, tuna, and other game fish. No licenses are required. The harbors in Lahaina and Ma'alaea (southern West Maui) are the places to make arrangements for charters. Trips are usually four or eight hours and boats provide all gear, including bait and ice. Try **Hinatea Sportfishing**, Tel. 667-7548, or **Finest Kind Sportfishing**, Tel. 661-0338. For shore fishing, the most sheltered spots are along the southern coast.

Golf

Maui has quite a few top-rated championship courses, in both East and West Maui. Hugging the lower mountain slopes of West Maui, the **Kaanapali North Golf Course** was designed by Robert Trent Jones, Sr. Both this course and its sister, the **Kaanapali South Golf Course**, Tel. 661-3691 for either, are graced with wonderful ocean and mountain scenery. If you're staying at a hotel in Kaanapali, green fees on the North Coarse will run you $130 before 2pm and $77 afterwards; or, on the South Course, $105 in the morning and $65 in the afternoon. While the afternoon rates are the same for non-resort guests, morning rates for outsiders are $160 in the morning at the North Course and $130 at the South Course.

My husband and I may not be golfers, but we could spend hours on the gorgeous championship courses at the **Kapalua Golf Club**, Tel. 669-8044. The fourth hole on the Bay Course here is in a stunning location atop a lofty peninsula enclosed by the ocean. Complete with duck-filled ponds and rolling hills, these courses are considered among the world's best by the pros. They play host to popular annual tournaments. Bay Course green fees are $190 before 1:30pm and $85 afterwards. At the newer Plantation course, fees run $225 before 1:30pm and $90 afterwards.

Make reservations at any one of the dramatically located **Wailea Golf Club** courses, Tel. 875-5111. The Blue Course ($95 in the morning, $70 in the afternoon) is a popular, relaxing course. The Emerald Course has a panoramic ocean view. The challenging Gold Course is set in a natural terrain of Hawaiian grasses, lava fields and wili wili trees. Fees at both Emerald and Gold run $185 before 1pm and $125 afterwards for outsiders or $145 in the morning and $115 in the afternoon for Wailea resort guests, who may reserve tee times at any Wailea Golf Club course up to 30 days in advance.

Maui's public courses are less expensive, but their views are no less expansive. **The Pukalani Country Club**, Tel. 572-1336, sprawls in Kula, upcountry Maui. Note that the high altitude may make you somewhat light-headed. In an arid part of the island, **Elleaire Maui Golf Club**, Tel. 874-0777, sits in Kihei near Wailea; fees are $100 in the morning and $80 after 1pm. At **Waiehu Municipal**, Tel. 243-7400, by the beach at Wailuku, fees are $26 on weekdays and $30 on weekends.

Helicopter Rides

Since these whirls can be so expensive, you should choose your tour carefully, and only plan a flight if your children are old enough to appreciate it. If you're planning to visit the Big Island of Hawaii or Kauai, I recommend that you wait to take a helicopter tour over one of those islands. On Maui, the most exciting tours are the flights over Hana and Haleakala volcano. The whirlybirds pass over inaccessible flourishing valleys and thundering water-falls, as well as Haleakala volcano, with a crater the size of Manhattan.

Ask about buying a videotape of your trip to take home. Try **Blue Hawaiian Helicopters**, Tel. 871-8844 or 800/745-BLUE, or **Sunshine Helicopters**, Tel. 871-0722 or 800/544-2520. Helicopter flights begin at about $125 for 30 minutes.

Hiking

Maui offers countless scenic hiking trails, some near resort areas. Many families enjoy walking in the tropical rain forest of **Iao Valley** in West Maui, with its prominent green Iao Needle rock formation.

About six miles beyond **Twin Falls** on the Hana Highway, the **Waikamoi Ridge Trail Nature Walk** is some two miles round trip. You'll know you've come to the beginning of the trail when you see a parking area and a picnic table on a cliff overlooking the highway to the right. Passing through a bamboo forest, this trail also goes by mahogany, tree ferns, guavas and many other kinds of vegetation.

Kaumahina State Park provides flush toilets, drinking water, shelters and picnic tables. The crowd of tourists here usually disappears by 3pm or so. This park sits on a blutf with a dramatic view of the Keanae Peninsula.

If you hike into the **Keanae Arboretum**, beyond Kaumahina State Park and Honomanu Beach, you'll find all kinds of labeled native and imported plants, as well as many varieties of taro growing in patches.

Hiking about a quarter-mile to the caves at **Waianapanapa State Park**, near Hana, is a popular pursuit. At **Oheo Gulch** (a.k.a. Seven Pools or Seven Sacred Pools), beyond Hana, don't stop at the lower pools that are usually crowded with visitors. The first of the upper falls is only about a half-mile from the parking lot.

One of the best outfits for guided treks is **Hike Maui**, based in Kahului, Tel. 808/879-5270. These half-day, full-day, and overnight rambles along coasts, through rain forests, or into the mountains are designed for adults and children over age 6. Swimming is often part of the trip. Along the way, your guide will identify plants, flowers, birds, and animals, plucking fruit for hikers to sample. A picnic lunch may be included, as well as roundtrip transportation from central Maui. Groups are kept small, from four to ten people. Prices for day hikes run from about $60 to $155.

Horseback Riding

Pony Express, Tel. 667-2200, www.ponyexpresstours.com, (age 10 and older), specializes in horseback rides into Haleakala Crater. The most popular of these trips runs for about five hours ($165 per person) and covers 7.5 miles to and from the crater floor, where riders unsaddle themselves for a picnic lunch. For families with younger children, Pony Express also offers leisurely one-hour rides ($65) through the rolling hillside and through a eucalyptus forest along the slopes of Haleakala volcano. The two-hour paniolo ride ($95) will take you through Maui's largest working cattle ranch. A scenic lunch is part of the 2 +-hour picnic ride ($115). This company keeps its groups small, so be sure to make reservations at least several days in advance.

In Hana, you can trot along the rugged coast or into the mountains with horses from Hana Ranch, through **Hotel Hana-Maui**, Tel. 248-8211, (age 7 and older). Bring your camera—the guide will be happy to take shots of you and your family against dramatic backgrounds. The one-hour ride costs $50 per person, while the two-hour excursion will run you $90 each.

Scuba Diving

In addition to Maui's coasts, there are some wonderful dive sites off neighboring Lanai and Molokai. Full certification (starting about $350 for a 3-day course) is available on Maui in PADI, NAUI, and SSCI training programs. For adults and children age 10 and older, one-day introductory scuba programs begin at about $100 including a one-tank dive and $150 for two tanks.

Among the most experienced dive operators are **Ed Robinson's Hawaiian Reef Divers**, Tel. 879-3584; **Captain Nemo's Scuba Shack**, Tel. 661-5555; **Lahaina Divers**, Tel. 667-7496; and **Maui Sun Divers**, Tel. 879-3337.

Snorkeling

Some of Maui's best (though often crowded) snorkeling and diving is at **Molokini**, a partially submerged volcano whose crater just breaks the surface of the ocean. Depths here range from 10 feet to more than 60 at the drop-off. The sail to Molokini takes about 45 minutes. Schools of butterfly fish, triggerfish, yellow tang, bluespine, pinktail durgeon, unicorn fish, and even zebra moray eels swarm snorkelers and divers. Porpoises often frolic in these waters. From November to April, there's a good chance you'll also spot humpback whales. Even if you don't see one of these gigantic mammals, you may hear them calling out to each other when you're under water.

A variety of companies offers snorkeling or scuba trips to Molokini as well as to Turtle Arches, a coral garden where green turtles hang out. Try the **Ocean Activities Center**, Tel. 879-4485, which offers a five-hour trip including breakfast, lunch, drinks, and two snorkel or dive sites, and costs $70 (adults) and $40 (children); the 3-hour excursion, including continental breakfast, costs $40 (adults) and $30 (children).

The nonprofit **Pacific Whale Foundation**, Tel. 879-8811, hosts another good five-hour snorkeling trip to Molokini crater and Turtle Arches, including breakfast and a barbecue lunch, for $70 (adults), $22 (age 7 to 12), and free for children age 6 and younger. If you're traveling with older children, consider the longer sail to the island of Lanai, where a photo safari will give you a chance to capture spinner dolphins on film.

Family-owned and -operated, **Trilogy Excursions**, Tel. 661-4743 or 800/874-2666, also offers excellent trips to Molokini Crater, Turtle Arches, and other locales. The homemade cinnamon rolls served at breakfast are legendary and lunch might consist of teriyaki chicken, salad, corn on the cob, and freshly baked bread. Another company to consider is **Island Marine**, Tel. 866/307-6524.

Submarine Rides

To explore the lower depths (but only if you're not going scuba diving), board the 48-passenger **Atlantis Submarine**, Tel. 800/548-6262, which takes the 100-foot plunge off Lahaina Harbor. Rates begin at $80 for adults and $40 for children, who must be at least 3 feet tall. (Note that although you'll be underwater for 45 minutes, this excursion includes a boat ride to the sub; so you should allow about 90 minutes for the whole deal.)

Surfing

Hookipa Beach, in northern East Maui, is probably the most popular surfing (and windsurfing) spot on Maui. Championship surfing competitions are held here every year. **Honolua Bay**, in northern West Maui, also has excellent waves, which can rise up to 15 feet during the winter. For an overview of the hot-dogging surfers, drive down the red dirt road at Lipoa

Point. You'll cut through agricultural fields before reaching the 200-foot cliffs that serve as a perfect vantage point for the surfers' aquatic ballet. During the summer, Ma'alaea Harbor, in southern West Maui, and Big Beach (a.k.a. Oneloa), in southwestern East Maui, draw many surfers.

To learn to surf, contact **www.MauiSurf.com,** where you'll find two-hour lessons for around $80 (adults) and $45 (children).

Tennis

There are tennis courts all over Maui, in hotels, condos, and elsewhere. The **Wailea Tennis Club** has the greatest number: three grass courts, nearly a dozen hard surface courts, and a 1,000-seat tennis stadium; call the Club for details about clinics for both adults and children. The **Royal Lahaina Tennis Ranch** at Kaanapali boasts 11 courts, six of which are lighted. You'll find six lighted public courts at **Lahaina's Civic Center** and two in **Hana**. **Kapalua Tennis Garden** has 10 lighted courts on which tennis attire is required. In southern Maui is the six-court **Makena Tennis Club**.

Whale Watching

See the "Maui's Whopping Whale Watching" sidebar at the beginning of this chapter.

Windsurfing

Maui's best beach for boardsailing is **Hookipa Beach**, in northern East Maui, about 35 miles from Lahaina. International competitions take place here throughout the year. Windsurfing gear is sold at stores in nearby Pa'ia. Wind and wave conditions are also excellent at **Honolua Bay**, in northern West Maui. Most of the larger hotels give windsurfing lessons, and many won't charge you for the land demonstration on a simulator.

Maui Sports Unlimited, Tel. 877-7778, offers lessons for children as well as adults. During June, July, and August, vacationers age 6 to 17 may attend the Windsurfing kids' camp, held for three hours each Wednesday, Thursday, and Friday (cost: $150 for 9 hours). Throughout the year, one-on-one lessons for children are $50 an hour or $55 for adults. Consider this great deal for two parents and a child, or two children and one adult: Group lessons run $80 total for up to three people.

Working Out & Spas

Many of the larger hotels have exercise rooms, fitness centers, or aerobics classes. Some charge a fee for use of the exercise equipment, but often only for non-guests. Some hotels also have wonderful full-scale spas with treatments ranging from healthful to pure pampering, including the **Westin,** the **Hyatt Regency,** the **Grand Wailea,** the **Four Seasons,** the **Fairmont Kea Lani,** and **Hotel Hana-Maui.**

I'm Hungry!

Maui's restaurants are concentrated in West Maui and northwestern East Maui. Kahului and Wailuku are home to a selection of good, casual eateries patronized mainly by locals. Some of them serve Hawaiian cuisine. You'll notice that, unless you're at a luau, contemporary "Hawaiian food" usually includes items such as Spam and eggs, Portuguese sausage, and *saimin* (noodle soup with vegetables and meat)—a reflection of the islands' varied ethnic influences. More than a few Maui restaurants serve one version or another of hula pie. What is it? Ice cream on a crunchy cookie crust with macadamia nuts and whipped cream—real low calorie! While many of the island's dining rooms offer keiki (children's) menus (along with diversions such as crayons and paper), others simply serve smaller portions or appetizers for kids.

When you need some adult time without the younger editions, make a reservation at one of the restaurants below marked "Romantic Escape."

Kapalua

SANSEI SEAFOOD RESTAURANT & SUSHI BAR, The Shops at Kapalua, 115 Bay Drive. Tel. 669-6286. Reservations recommended. Dinner entrees: $16 to $30.

Located in an upscale mall, Sansei dazzles with Euro-Japanese surprises, such as caterpillar-shaped eel and avocado maki that is almost too pretty to eat. Another winner is the pan-seared opakapaka (pink snapper) with warm truffle potato salad and caviar butter sauce. Also consider the Asian rock shrimp cake topped with thin crispy noodles and black sesame seeds. Chicken skewers and noodles are particularly popular with children. This restaurant gets quite crowded at dinnertime.

Sansei has a second location in Kihei, at the Kihei Town Center, 1881 South Kihei Road, Tel. 879-0004.

Kahana

ROY'S KAHANA BAR & GRILL, Kahana Gateway Center, 4405 Honoapiilani Highway. Tel. 669-6999. Reservations recommended. Dinner entrees: $25 to $30.

After making a name for himself with his Honolulu restaurant, Roy Yamaguchi opened another one on Maui. Look for imaginative creations such as blackened *ahi* (tuna) with spicy soy mustard, teriyaki grilled pork tenderloin, and rack of lamb. On the keiki menu, hibachi salmon, chicken teriyaki, and quesadillas make good choices for children.

Desserts might include fresh peach creme brulee, dark chocolate soufflé, or apple cobblers with blueberries or peaches. Easy listening music plays in the background while talkative diners watch the chefs at work in the open kitchen.

Kaanapali

SWAN COURT, Hyatt Regency Maui, Kaanapali Beach. Tel. 661-1234. Reservations recommended. Breakfast and dinner only. Dinner entrees: $16 to $35. *Romantic Escape.*

Swans float past tables near the lagoon in this elegant open-air dining room. This truly is an exceptional place to for a meal, whether for dinner or the breakfast buffet. Focusing on continental dishes with Asian touches, the menu is always changing.

HULA GRILL, 2435 Kaanapali Parkway, Building P, Whalers Village, Kaanapali Beach. Tel. 667-6636. Reservations recommended. Dinner entrees: $13 to $20.

Chef Peter Merriman first made a big splash with Hawaii's new regional cuisine on the Big Island, starting at the Mauna Lani Bay Hotel, then moving to his own restaurant, Merriman's. Now he brings to Maui this exciting melange of Pacific, Asian, and European cooking styles, emphasizing fresh local produce. Try to reserve an oceanside table and arrive before dark so you can watch the sun set. Outrigger canoes hang from the rafters of this open-air restaurant. Before meals, guests relax in a hammock or in the cozy library stocked with old books about seafaring Hawaii. At night, fire flickers on torches while hula dancers move fluidly to Hawaiian music. The children's menu comes with washable markers for coloring it. (Meals are free for kids age four and younger.) Tears from the little ones? Your waiter might rush over offering some colorful tropical drink umbrellas to restore the peace.

I love the chili pepper dipping sauce served with the foccacia bread (you can even buy a bottle to take home). Seafood is the focus of the menu. You might begin with scallop and lobster potstickers, sashimi, or macadamia nut and crab wontons. The brown rice salad with Thai peanut sauce is another delicious choice. Seared on the outside and raw in the middle, the wok-charred ahi resembles rare roast beef. The firecracker mahimahi is baked with chili and cumin aioli and served with a relish made from black beans, Maui onions, and avocado. A good choice for pasta is the Kula vegetable primavera in a garlic cream sauce. The free range jerk chicken breast with tropical fruit chutney is also delicious. For dessert (but only if you promise to jog an extra mile or two the next day), consider the coconut creme brulee or the ice cream sandwich (vanilla ice cream, macadamia nut brownies, raspberry puree, and whipped cream!).

LEILANI'S ON THE BEACH, Whalers Village, Kaanapali Parkway. Tel. 661-4495. Dinner entrees: $16 to $26.

You may have a long wait for a table on weekends, but most of the food is worth it. Decorated with local art, some walls are paneled in golden brown wood. Others are made of exposed rugged lava rock. Many enjoy dining on the curved terrace overlooking the water. My family and I have had the best luck with the charbroiled teriyaki ahi (tuna); ginger chicken; coconut-crusted prawns; and baby back pork ribs. Grilled cheese, burgers, and chicken teriyaki are on the keiki menu. Downstairs at the beachside grill (which offers a lighter, less expensive menu featuring burgers and salads), tables are lit by the dancing flames of torches.

Lahaina

GERARD'S, The Plantation Inn, 174 Lahainaluna Road. Tel. 661-8939. Reservations required. Dinner entrees: $27 to $37.

This casual restaurant began as a small bistro near Front Street. It is now ensconced in plusher digs in a wonderful turn-of-the-century-style inn. The inner dining room is graced with stained glass over French doors, brass, and oak. The lanai is enclosed by Victorian pillars, an elegant balustrade, and delicate latticework. Try the roasted opakapaka (snapper) with star anise, orange, and ginger, the duck confit, the filete of beef, or the rack of lamb in a mint crust. Steak, pasta, fish, and chicken are prepared in portions small enough for children.The creme brulee and the macadamia nut chocolate cake are popular for dessert.

DAVID PAUL'S LAHAINA GRILL, Lahaina Inn, 127 Lahainaluna Road. Tel. 667-5117. Reservations recommended. Dinner entrees: $26 to $39. *Romantic Escape.*

The atmosphere is always cheery and elegant, with white table linen, delicate china, and small crystal vases with fresh flowers. Expect to find "new American cuisine" with Pacific Rim flair, such as tequila shrimp with firecracker rice, sauteed mahi-mahi with Kula spinach and garlic mashed potatoes, or pan-seared ahi. Linguini with lemon pepper is delicately seasoned. The crab meat appetizer arrives looking like a sundae topped with avocado and caviar. While there is a keiki menu, which offers corn dogs, shrimp, fish, chicken nuggets, pasta, and beef kebabs, many adults enjoy David Paul's romantic atmosphere sans kids. Be sure to save room for dessert. Don't pass up the Kona coffee ice cream topped with chocolate fudge, coconut flakes, and macadamia nuts.

I'O, 505 Front Street. Tel. 661-8422. Dinner only. Entrees: $29 to $34. Reservations recommended. *Romantic Escape.*

Chef James McDonald (who also brings Maui the Feast at Lele luau and Pacific'O restaurant) outdoes himself at this beachside restaurant that puts an Asian twist on Euro-American cuisine. It's all in the details. First the nautical décor: The lights behind the curved, hand-formed bar are portholes filled with cracked glass. Lifted from an old walk-in refrigerator, the door leading behind the bar looks like a ship's galley door. Etched glass windows are illuminated to resemble aquariums. A ship's railing is found along the interior folding glass doors. Stainless steel ceiling fans stir the fresh air.

As in the ambiance, no detail is overlooked in the food. Take a peek through a large window into the high-tech kitchen and you'll catch Chef James or one of his partners at work. You might begin your evening with crab tempura or Silken Purse (steamed wontons stuffed with roasted peppers, mushrooms, spinach, macadamia nuts, and tofu). Another hard-to-resist starter is shrimp satay (grilled prawns with a Korean barbecue sauce). For your main course, consider the foie gras crusted fish or the Tiger by the Tail (roasted tiger prawns with mushroom, asparagus, and pea shoots in lilikoi sauce). And you don't even have to be a vegetarian to love the spicy organic tofu with Maui onions, mushrooms, and polenta with a lavender yogurt accent. If you decide to bring your kids, the keiki menu offers fish and chips, cowboy ribs, and skewered fish.

PACIFIC'O, 505 Front Street. Tel. 667-4341. Reservations recommended. Dinner entrees: $24 to $38. *Romantic Escape.*

Unlike its sister restaurant, I'O (which is just across the walkway), Pacific'O also serves lunch, and every Thursday, Friday, and Saturday evening, live jazz accompanies dinner. At night, tall flickering torches and illuminated palm trees draw your eyes upward, toward the star-scattered sky. Lava flows may be found on many a menu, but here this pina colada with fresh strawberry juice is particularly delicious. Another winner from Chef James McDonald, this beachside locale is celebrated for its shrimp-and-basil wontons and its imaginative fish; among the bestselling preparations for the fresh catch are coconut-macadamia nut crusted, tempura, or sesame-seared. Chef James gives his dishes refreshing twists: Surf and turf comes with a tiger prawn, mahi mahi, and sesame-crusted lamb instead of beef. Both white jasmine rice and black Thai rice accompany some entrees. Despite all the ingredients in each dish, the food is surprisingly light. On the keiki menu, you might find a seared chicken or fresh fish sandwich or grilled fish with salsa. Good choices for dessert include mango cheesecake and crème brulee.

LONGHI'S, 888 Front Street. Tel. 667-2288. Dinner entrees: $18 to $33.

The accent is on the Italian at this noisy waterfront dining spot that serves breakfast, lunch, and dinner, and sells T-shirts emblazoned with its logo. Despite its long-standing popularity (rumor has it that Prince ate here every night during a recent week-long trip to Maui), some meals I've had here have been disappointing. My bland pesto penne, for example, was totally devoid of zip. Most of the ingredients are Maui-grown. Some of the pasta is made on the premises. Although greasy, the pizza bread with jalapenos is delicious. The midday menu might feature lobster, shrimp, or Greek salad, lobster cannelloni, or pasta marinara. Breakfast begins with freshly squeezed orange juice and freshly ground Kona coffee.

KIMO'S, 845 Front Street. Tel. 661-4811. Dinner entrees: $16 to $30.

A great place for drinks and sunset watching, Kimo's is a popular steak and seafood restaurant. Sit upstairs or downstairs on the lanai at the water's edge. Potted plants and flaming torches add to the pleasant atmosphere. The selection of local fish is broad, from *hapu* (Hawaiian sea bass) and *ulua* (deep-sea pompano) to *a'u* (broadbill swordfish) and *ahi* (Hawaiian big game yellowfin tuna). Preparation of the fish is your choice, from broiled in lemon butter to parmesan-crusted. Also on the menu are lobster tails, teriyaki sirloin steak, hamburgers, and Koloa pork ribs glazed with plum sauce. The keiki menu offers shrimp, steak, chicken, and ribs. If you leave room for dessert, try the macadamia nut ice cream, hula pie, or the lilikoi (passion fruit) sherbet.

MOOSE McGILLYCUDDY'S, 844 Front Street. Tel. 667-7758. Dinner entrees: $12 to $18.

Sit on the second-floor lanai, and you'll overlook Front Street action. For breakfast, you'll get a poster-sized menu offering pancakes, all kinds of omelets, and other delicious choices. The New York steak and chicken fajitas are popular. Children zero in on the chicken strips, cheese burgers, fish and chips, and pasta. Drawing a lively crowd, this place gets pretty wild after dark, with entertainment until 2am.

BUBBA GUMP SHRIMP COMPANY, 889 Front Street. Tel. 661-3111. Dinner entrees: $12 to $18.

This loud, busy, crowded restaurant sits right on the water, just the way Forest Gump himself would like it. His namesake movie plays continuously at the entrance, near storyboards and costume sketches from the film. At the tables, children entertain themselves with crayons and coloring paper while parents are periodically quizzed by waiters testing patrons' knowledge of trivia from the movie. The drink menu comes on a ping pong paddle. Food, from Lt. Dan's drunken shrimp to Dixie-style baby back ribs, is served in tin pails in "newspaper."

LAHAINA COOLERS, 180 Dickenson Street, Tel. 661-7082. Open for breakfast, lunch, and dinner. Dinner entrees: $10 to $22.

Start your day with a papaya or fresh pineapple with low fat granola topped with sliced banana or order a Portuguese sausage omelet with onion, tomato, and sour cream. The kids might enjoy some macadamia nut pancakes or French toast made with soft, sweet Molokai bread. For lunch or dinner, you might find crab wontons, tempura calamari with blue cheese ranch dip, or spinach and feta cheese quesadillas. The fish tacos are legendary. From Portobello mushroom sandwiches, ahi burgers, kalua pig, and hibachi chicken with soy glaze to chocolate tacos for dessert, it's all here. Sit in a courtyard under umbrellas or in the al fresco inner dining room under ceiling fans. Inside, the kids will get a kick out of the huge marlin on the wall and the colorfully-painted surfboard that hangs over the bar.

COOL CAT CAFÉ, 658 Front Street, #160, upstairs at the Wharf Cinema Center. Tel. 667-0908. Dinner entrees: $10 to $20.

Overlooking Front Street, this retro restaurant takes you back to the 1950s and
'60s with tables shaped like record albums and food with names such as Jailhouse Rock and La Bamba burgers, Ricky Ricardo salads, Jerry Lewis tuna sandwiches, Great Balls of Fire chicken sandwishes, Rockin' Robin turkey

melts, and Porky Pigs (shredded pork sandwiches with barbecue sauce). Hot dogs, grilled cheese, chicken strips, and burgers are on tap for kids. Walls are decorated with magazine and record album covers, front page articles from old newspapers, and movie posters.

THAI CHEF, Lahaina Shopping Center. Tel. 667-2814. Closed for lunch Saturday and Sunday. No alcohol. Dinner entrees: $10 to $16.

This casual, low-profile restaurant is a good place to take a break from shopping in Lahaina. Tucked away in a very local shopping center, it serves ginger coconut soup; spring rolls; red, green, or yellow curry chicken; garlic vegetable shrimp; beef broccoli; pad Thai (a noodle dish); vegetarian selections; and other well-seasoned favorites. Try the Thai tapioca pudding for dessert. If you want alcohol with your meal, you'll have to bring your own.

SUNRISE CAFE, 693 Front Street, near the library and Baldwin Home Museum. Tel. 661-8558. Reservations recommended. Open 6am to 6pm. Entrees: $10 to $15.

This tiny cafe emphasizes light, healthy eats, such as gourmet sandwiches, plate lunches (kalua pork or roasted chicken, perhaps), pastas, and filling salads. It's a good choice for an early breakfast (try the French toast or chocolate waffles), a late lunch, or an early supper. The children's menu includes burgers, pizza, macaroni and cheese, chicken strips, and shrimp.

Olowalu

CHEZ PAUL, West Maui (Highway 30, about 4 miles south of Lahaina). Tel. 661-3843. Reservations required. Dinner entrees: $30 to $36. *Romantic Escape.*

With just over a dozen tables—each sparkling with china and crisp linen—this is one of Maui's finest restaurants. Mirrors enlarge the cozy dining room, lit by flickering candles. Featuring local catch and produce, the imaginative, artistically presented French-inspired dishes are always changing. One day you might find rack of lamb with fruit chutney or carmelized salmon while another you might run across crispy boneless duck or mahi mahi poached in champagne.

Wailuku

TASTY CRUST, 1770 Mill Street. Tel. 244-0845. Lunch and dinner entrees: $4 to $7.

Sit in a booth at this local roadside diner, and you'll feel like a resident. Start your day with an omelet made with shrimp, Vienna Sausage, SPAM, or cheese. Try some fresh papaya on the side. The plate-size hotcakes are absolutely delicious as well, and locals swear by the saimin for lunch or dinner, along with the chow fun, won ton, and miso soup. Other good choices include the honey-dipped chicken, chicken katsu, curry stew, teriyaki pork, salads, and sandwiches.

Pa'ia Area

MAMA'S FISH HOUSE, 799 Poho Place. Tel. 579-8488. Reservations recommended for dinner. Dinner entrees: $32 to $49.

Just outside Pa'ia, popular Mama's Fish House is located along the Hana Highway. While it is something of an institution, some diners have thought it overpriced and touristy, and a few say it serves up more hype than good food. But you would probably do well to try the sweet potato fries (served at lunch) and the stuffed mahi mahi.

CAFÉ DES AMIS, 42 Baldwin Avenue. Tel. 579-6323. Open for breakfast, lunch, and dinner (until 8:30pm). Dinner entrees: $8 to $15.

France meets India at this excellent eating spot where people line up for the sweet crepes: Try the Maui cane sugar with lime juice, the pineapple with mango sauce, the honey and toasted almonds, or the banana and chocolate. Crepes also come filled with ham and scrambled eggs or gruyere cheese; lentils, tomatoes, pesto, and mozzarella; spinach with feta cheese; and Mediterranean vegetables. A variety of curries, served in wraps or just with rice and chutneys, is also on the menu: shrimp and coconut; beef and mushroom; chicken; mixed vegetable; and mahi mahi. Wash it all down with a smoothie made from strawberries, blueberries, and bananas; or peaches, bananas, and raspberries. While no alcohol is served, you are welcome to bring your own wine or beer. Since everything is made to order, this is a far cry from fast food, so be prepared to wait.

PAIA FISH MARKET, 110 Hana Highway (corner of Baldwin Avenue). Tel. 579- 8030. Dinner entrees: $7 to $20.

This casual local hot spot is often packed with diners chowing down on the ono and mahi fish burgers and "dinner plates" featuring fish either charbroiled, sautéed, served Cajun style, or blackened. Along with fish and chips, the menu offers shrimp and chips and even calamari and chips. Stuffed with beans, rice, salsa, lettuce, sprouts, tomatoes, and cheese, the veggie quesadillas move quickly. Fish or chicken soft tacos are other good choices. Whet your appetite with blackened sashimi or New England seafood chowder, then try a salad and a fajita or the seafood pasta. Portions are large, so be sure to come hungry. Many people are pleased with the extensive beer and wine list here.

FRESH MINT, 115 Baldwin Avenue. Tel. 579-9144. Dinner entrees: $8 to $10.

Casual and friendly, this Vietnamese restaurant is top of the line. So what are beef, chicken, ham, and fish doing on this vegetarian menu? They are all made from vegetables, and served in delicious dishes such as "chicken" curry; spicy "beef" with lemon grass, onions, carrots, and mushrooms tossed with sweet pineapple and vermicelli; seared "fish" with sesame or mint ginger sauce; and fried rice with "ham." If you don't need faux meat to make a meal, go for the grilled eggplant with basil; the tofu stuffed with onions, mushrooms, and bean thread; or the green papaya salad. For dessert, sample the mung bean coconut tapioca or the banana fritter.

HANA HOU CAFÉ, 810 Haiku Road #404, Haiku, near Pa'ia. Tel. 808/ 575-2661. Open 10am to 10pm. Entrees: $5 to $8.

Located in the parking lot of Haiku Cannery, this local favorite is a great place for families with children. While the adults go for the beer, wine, and pupus (appetizers), kids enjoy the burgers, fish and chips, and haupia (coconut pudding). Among the Hawaiian specialties, you might find lau lau (meat steamed in taro leaves), chicken long rice, and lomi salmon, along with a variety of plate lunches. Six nights a week, a guitarist plays and sings Hawaiian music. If you're lucky, one of the waitresses might be moved to put on a hula performance.

Makawao Area

HALI'IMAILE GENERAL STORE, 900 Hali'imaile Road, Hali'imaile. Tel. 572-2666. Reservations required. Dinner entrees: $18 to $40.

Located upcountry, this restaurant snags many residents as well as vacationers on their way to and from Haleakala Crater. (However, note that it closes between lunch and dinner.) This gourmet dining spot seems just a bit out of place in the middle of pineapple fields. Born as a plantation store back in 1925, it was turned into a restaurant in 1988 by a successful local caterer, Beverly Gannon, and her husband, Joe. Fresh flowers and artwork splash the bright, spacious dining room with color. The window above the bar is etched with a depiction of the building.

For dinner, you might start with sushi or with fish cakes with a ginger cilantro remoulade, then move on to Szechuan barbecued salmon with caramelized onion and orange peel or rack of lamb Hunan style with sesame and black beans. Duck is also prepared in innovative ways. The children's menu includes macaroni and cheese, ribs, barbecued chicken, pizza, and burgers. For dessert, don't miss the Kona coffee cheesecake and other freshly baked goods.

CASANOVA'S DELI AND RESTAURANT, 1188 Makawao Avenue, Makawao. Tel. 572-0220. Deli open 7:30am to 6:30pm; restaurant open for lunch and dinner. Dinner entrees: $12 to $24.

A funky little Italian eatery, the deli is the place to find a variety of fresh breads and pastries along with pasta and pizza. Sandwiches range from smoked salmon, chicken breast with mozzarella and pesto sauce, and salami and cheese to marinated zucchini and goat cheese or veggie burgers. Soups, salads, and bagels are also on the menu. Dine on the lanai, where residents often relax behind newspapers.

For heavier fare, head into the restaurant. The ricotta and spinach dumplings and the tube pasta with chicken, broccoli, and sun-dried tomatoes in a cream sauce are both really good. Other good selections are the brick-grilled Cornish game hen and the Creole ahi served with mango salsa. Entertainment Wednesday through Saturday nights brings the party crowd. Music ranges from salsa and disco to local Hawaiian.

Kula

KULA LODGE, Haleakala Highway, Route 377. Tel. 878-1535. Dinner entrees: $20 to $30.

Perched on the edge of a cliff upcountry, this rustic dining spot yields a fabulous view of the island. If you're on your way back from watching the sun rise over Haleakala Crater, consider stopping here for breakfast. Try the Belgian waffles with fresh tropical fruit topped with coconut syrup. For lunch, the bacon and blue cheese burger is a good choice. For dinner, consider starting with the seared ahi sashimi and then ordering the seafood lasagne or the macadamia nut-crusted mahi-mahi.

GRANDMA'S MAUI COFFEE, 9232 Kula Highway, Keokea. Tel. 878-2140. Entrees: $7 to $9. Open 7am to 5pm daily.

A family-run bakery and restaurant, this eatery serves coffee that is grown on Maui and roasted by owner Alfred Franco himself. He uses a roaster that was passed down from his great-great grandmother and is more than a century old. The recipes for the delicious baked goods have also been around for generations. Consider stopping here for breakfast. Other crowd pleasers are the sandwiches, and teriyaki chicken or other daily specials.

Kihei

SANSEI SEAFOOD RESTAURANT & SUSHI BAR, Kihei Town Center, 1881 South Kihei Road. Tel. 879-0004. Reservations recommended. Dinner entrees: $16 to $30.

This is the younger sibling of the Kapalua location (above). Expect to find the same delicious, artful food, since the menu is a clone of the original.

THAI CHEF, Rainbow Mall, 2439 South Kihei Road. Tel. 874-5605. No lunch served Saturday or Sunday. Dinner entrees: $9 to $14.

Not to be confused with the restaurant with the same name in Lahaina, this is another friendly, casual Thai restaurant. It serves ginger coconut soup; spring rolls; red, green, or yellow curry chicken; garlic vegetable shrimp; beef broccoli; Pad Thai (a noodle dish); vegetarian selections; and other well-seasoned favorites. Try the Thai tapioca pudding for dessert.

JOY'S PLACE, Island Surf Building, 1993 South Kihei Road. Tel. 879-9258. Monday to Saturday, 10am to 5pm.

For those who like their food both healthful and delicious, this grocery and deli offers a wide selection of "mostly organic" sandwiches, soups, wraps, veggie burgers, salads, and fruit smoothies. Vegan and raw food choices satisfy those with strict diets while fish and poultry selections appeal to others. On your way to the beach, pick up some hummus avocado sandwiches on sprouted grain tortillas, falafel burgers, ginger lemonade, and wheat-free vegan oatmeal cookies. Or try a bowl of vegetable chili with rice or a free-range turkey sandwich with pesto.

Wailea

SPAGO, Four Seasons Resort Maui at Wailea. Tel. 879-2999. Dinner only. Reservations recommended. Dinner entrees: $32 to $48. Credit cards accepted. *Romantic Escape.*

World-renowned master chef Wolfgang Puck brings his culinary artistry to Four Seasons Resort Maui. Spago's menu is an appealing blend of Pacific Rim, Hawaiian, and California cuisines. You might find pan-roasted opakapaka with lobster crusted potatoes, lamb chops grilled with Hunan eggplant, or whole Big Island moi (the fish once reserved for *alii—Hawaiian* royalty) with chili. Complementing the food is an excellent selection of American, European, Australian, and South American wines. Highlighted by stone, wood, glass, and art pieces, this restaurant overlooks Wailea Beach. So the tables on the lanai are snapped up quickly. If you're in the mood for fine dining but don't want to spring for a babysitter, Spago could be the place. The children's menu includes chicken fingers, pizza, pasta, and grilled cheese.

JOE'S BAR AND GRILL, 131 Wailea Ike Place, Wailea Tennis Center. Tel. 875-7767. Dinner only. Entrees: $20 to $42. Reservations recommended.

The folks who have made such a big splash with Hali'imaile General Store, in upcountry Maui, get more raves at this Wailea dining spot overlooking the tennis courts. The casual, chatty atmosphere is friendly and inviting. Stained glass hanging lamps illuminate tables. Consider starting dinner with the paper-thin ahi (tuna) carpaccio or crab dip with flour tortillas. Follow it up with a crisp salad of baby field greens, toasted pecans, Maui onions, and sherry vinaigrette. For the main course, meatloaf comes seasoned with barbecue sauce with garlic mashed potatoes on the side and jumbo shrimps are skewered with rosemary. Another good choice is the herb grilled chicken breast wit artichokes and sun-dried tomatoes. The keiki menu serves the usual children's favorites.

Hana

HANA RANCH RESTAURANT, hours are limited and varied. Inexpensive.

This take-out window, with a few picnic tables on a rise overlooking the ocean, is a tasty and inexpensive alternative to meals at nearby Hotel Hana-Maui. While waiting for the fish sandwiches, burgers, chicken katsu, saimin, or hot dogs to be ready, our children love watching the horses in the neighboring corral as the ranch hands rope and shoe them.

Which One is My Bed?

Along with many luxury accommodations, you'll find a good selection of inexpensive-to-moderate sleeping quarters on Maui, including hotels, condominiums, and vacation homes. The island's oldest and busiest resort area, palm-studded Kaanapali Beach is a beautiful sandy strand. Most of Maui's action—by day and by night—takes place here and in neighboring Lahaina, on the west coast of West Maui. There's a wide array of restaurants, hotels and condominiums, along with excellent golf courses and tennis courts. The only problem with all these convenient diversions is that during the most popular seasons (the summer and Christmas through Easter), Kaanapali and Lahaina are teeming with tourists—but these vacation playgrounds are still far less crowded than Oahu's Waikiki.

Families that find Kaanapali and Lahaina too busy can choose among several other quieter, less-developed resort areas. To the north are Kapalua and Napili, while Kihei, Wailea, and Makena lie to the south. Many of these resorts come complete with their own tennis courts and golf courses. And it's not difficult at all to find un-peopled sandy shores along the miles of tranquil, beautiful beaches that stretch from Maalaea, on southern West Maui, to Makena, on southern East Maui. For the utmost in seclusion, head to remote Hana, on the far eastern coast of the island.

Lovely and understated, Napili is conveniently located right next door to the fancy boutiques, gourmet restaurants, golf, and tennis of the upscale Kapalua Resort. Residential Kihei is far more laid back than Kaanapali. It stretches for about six miles along both sides of South Kihei Road. Stay at one of the many condos here, and you'll be right near one of the sunny Kamaole waterfront parks that attract snorkelers, scuba divers, and big-game fishing enthusiasts. Visiting teenagers can meet their local peers at oceanside baseball and soccer games in Kalama Park. While most of Kihei's accommodations are rather undistinguished-looking from the outside, many are perfectly comfortable inside and the majority of them are moderately-priced.

Unlike Kihei, where each developer seems to have done as he pleased, Wailea, just south, is a meticulously planned resort. About a 50-minute drive from Kaanapali, Wailea is greener than Kihei and offers five separate beaches along a mile and a half of shore, plus excellent golf courses and all kinds of other activities. Since it is larger than Kaanapali but less built-up, the artfully designed hotels, condos, and shops have lots of elbow room.

Continue south and you'll come to the Makena resort, just over an hour's drive from Kaanapali. If you want to be in a deluxe hotel or condo off the beaten path, but within striking distance of mainstream action, book a room here in Maui's youngest and most peaceful beach resort, complete with golf, tennis, and other fun.

Home Sweet Home on Maui

Like the idea of living like a local—moving at your own pace in your own space, especially around meal times? Then consider renting an apartment or a vacation home. Most rates for condos and private houses are based on a minimum three-night to one-week stay, so nightly rates may be higher for shorter stays or lower for longer visits. We've had good experiences with these rental companies on Maui:

- Bello Realty, Tel. 800/541-3060; Web site: www.bellomaui.com, with economical beach cottages and condos in Kihei, East Maui.
- Condominium Rentals Hawaii, Tel. 800/367-5242, Web site: www.crhmaui.com, with moderately-priced beachfront condos, mainly in Kihei
- Destination Resorts Hawaii, Tel. 800/367-5246; Web site: www.drhmmaui.com, with one-, two-, and three-bedroom condominiums in Wailea, East Maui
- Maui Beachfront Rentals, Tel. 888-661-7200; Web site: www.mauibeachfront.com, with affordable oceanfront condos and vacation homes in West Maui resorts from Maalaea up to Kapalua

Kapalua

THE RITZ-CARLTON KAPALUA, 1 Ritz-Carlton Drive. Tel. 808/669-6200 or 800/262-8440, www.ritzcarlton.com. 548 rooms. Rates begin at $400.

Although the Ritz-Carton does have a children's program, the hotel's hushed elegance may be off-putting to families with even slightly rambunctious children. So this is probably a better choice for those with older kids. You'll find all kinds of extras here—nightly turn down service; bathrobes; a marble bath with a separate shower and a telephone; mini bar and refrigerator. On these fifty sprawling acres, you'll have several bars and excellent restaurants to choose from. Guests on the concierge floor head to the lounge (grab a table on the balcony) for light (and delicious) renditions of breakfast, lunch, dinner, hors d'oeuvres, and dessert.

Along with tennis courts, sports facilities and equipment include snorkel gear, scuba, windsurfers, and sail boats. At the three-level swimming pool, you may have to make a reservation for one of the popular shady cabanas, but attendants walk around offering everyone fresh pineapple and ice-cold towels scented with mint. Picturesque trails have been designed for jogging and strolling. Set on a gentle slope above the white sand beach, the hotel borders one of Kapalua's three championship golf courses with views of a picturesque chapel, the Pacific, and the cloud-capped island of Molokai. If you're vacationing in April, you may be just in time for the three-day arts festival dedicated to Hawaiian culture.

KAPALUA BAY HOTEL & OCEAN VILLAS, 1 Bay Drive. Tel. 808/669-5656 or 800/367-8000. www.kapaluabayhotel.com. 194 rooms. Rates begin at $300.

Nestled at the shore in an area where tall pines stud grassy slopes, the

Kapalua Bay Hotel has long been one of Maui's most tasteful resorts. The open-air lobby looks out to the pool and the ocean. Boutiques are found in a breezy arcade. The manicured grounds are set off by palms, bright flowers, a waterfall-fed stream, and a wooden footbridge over a pond. Parties are often held at the coconut grove by the beach. Guests enter their attractive, spacious rooms through wide double wooden doors. Baths are done in marble and the twin sinks are opposite each other; there are bath a tub and a stall shower; and the toilet is in a separate room within the bath. Connecting rooms are available for families with older chidren.

A couple of Maui's best restaurants are on the premises. The resort is also adjacent to three of the island's most challenging golf courses, and tennis courts and an exercise room are available. The seasonal children's program, for those aged 5 to 12, features Hawaiian arts and crafts, yoga, and sand castle contests, among other activities. Staying at Kapalua Bay Hotel & Ocean Villas entitles guests to complimentary use of the fitness centers, short-term parking, and other facilities and services of the two sister hotels: the Westin Maui and the Sheraton Maui, both just ten minutes away in Kaanapali.

KAPALUA VILLAS, 500 Office Road, Kapalua, HI 96761. Tel. 808/669-8088 or 800/545-0018. www.kapaluavillas.com. 520 units. Rates begin at $200 per unit.

Looking like residential suburbia, various groups of villas are scattered across the sprawling grounds of this condominium complex. Some of the one- and two-bedroom units are elevated on verdant slopes, while others are closer to the water or the golf course. Handsome furnishings, modern kitchens, lofty ceilings with exposed beams, and spacious bathrooms make these apartments a pleasure to come home to. Guests have signing privileges throughout the Kapalua Resort, and are welcome to use all its facilities, including its beaches, pools, golf courses, tennis courts, children's program, and shuttle bus.

Napili

ONE NAPILI WAY, 5355 Lower Honoapiilani Road, #101. Tel. 808/669-2007 or 800/841-6284, www.onenapiliway.com. 14 units. Rates begin at $320 per three-bedroom condo. One-week minimum stay required.

If you'd like to stay in one of Napili's most attractive condos, book a vacation rental here. Arriving guests are greeted with small baskets of goodies. Many of these units have been sold as time shares, so only three-bedroom apartments are available for rent. These bright, spacious units come with large screen TV and VCR, Jacuzzi in the master bath, roomy closets, and washer/dryer. Sparkling kitchens are equipped with everything from microwaves to blenders and ice cream scoops. The swimming pool, whirlpool, and barbecues are fenced in for the safety of young children. Cribs, high chairs, and strollers are available for rent. A sandy beach, at Napili Bay, is a short stroll away.

NAPILI KAI BEACH RESORT, 5900 Honoapiilani Highway. Tel. 808/669-6271 or 800/367-5030, www.napilikai.com, 163 rooms. Rates begin at $235 per unit.

If you're in the market for a small, friendly, low-rise resort sprawled over a hilly stretch of land with a quiet, palm-trimmed crescent beach, this is it. For me and my family, Napili Kai Beach Resort is what a vacation in Hawaii is all about. Book well in advance to secure one of the sunny, modern units, the vast majority of which come complete with kitchens (including microwaves). All but six rooms have private lanais and only six do not have ocean views. For large families or groups of friends, you can connect up to three rooms. This resort is popular for family reunions, perhaps in part because wheelchair accessibility makes it comfortable for members of all generations. Most vacationers here are repeat guests. We met a man with his ten-year-old daughter who told us that the first time he stayed at Napili Kai he was ten himself.

Children under age 14 are not allowed on the adult putting green, unless accompanied by an adult—and adults are not permitted on the children's putting green, unless accompanied by a child. Across from the entrance to the boutique, which sells estate jewelry along with resort wear, you'll find posted on the wall the names of everyone who has broken par on the putting green since 1968. Adults who break par are rewarded with mai tais, while children get soft drinks.

In addition to the two 18-hole putting greens, Napili Kai offers four swimming pools (one that attracts teenage guests), a jumbo whirlpool overlooking the ocean, an exercise room, and, at the nearby Kapalua resort, golf and tennis. Ask about renting tennis racquets.

This is the kind of place where staff members often address vacationers by name since they take the time to get to know their guests. What's that honking sound every day at 10am? The blowing of the conch shell announces the gathering of staff and guests to "talk story" (chat) and answer questions over coffee, ice tea, lemonade, and fresh pineapple. One morning a staff member might show guests how to crack coconuts, another he might teach them to weave baskets and hats from palm fronds. Speaking of palms, each day the temperature and times of sunrise, sunset, high tide, and low tide are posted on a palm tree. Excellent for snorkeling, sand castle building, and relaxing, the gorgeous, peaceful beach is off-limits to motorized vehicles and boats. Use of snorkels and masks is complimentary to guests, but you'll need to rent or bring your own fins. Amid the scores of reef fish, you might spot turtles, eels, and even an octopus.

The oceanfront restaurant serves three delicious meals a day—and some of the best tropical cocktails I've had anywhere in Hawaii. Don't miss the weekly Polynesian dinner show, during which local children, age 6 to 18, perform hula. Children of guests may join them on stage if they have taken the morning hula class (which our daughter loved). The local children are part of a group set up by a non-profit foundation (supported solely through donations) to teach Hawaiian arts, crafts, language, music, dance, and history.

During spring vacation, the summer, Thanksgiving, and Christmas time, Napili Kai offers complimentary children's activities. Hawaiian games, hula lessons, storytelling, lei-making, nature walks, sand castle building, and parent/child golf putting contests are all part of the fun. While your kids are busy elsewhere, get a massage or a facial at the Massage & Body Work Center.

HALE NAPILI, 65 Hui "H" Drive, Lahaina. Tel. 808/669-6184 or 800/245-2266, www.halenapili.com. 18 units. Rates begin at $140 per condo.

On Napili Bay, this economical condo is convenient to the beach and within walking distance of resort shopping at Kapalua Bay and restaurants. Perched above the shoreline, rooms have spectacular views. Expect to find king or queen-size beds, pull-out sofas, ample closets, full kitchens, and stall showers. This place books up quickly, so you'll need to make your reservation anywhere from six months to a year in advance.

Kahana

SANDS OF KAHANA, 4299 Lower Honoapiilani Road. Tel. 808/669-0400 or 888-669-0326, www.kapalua.com. 189 units. Rates begin at $130 per condo.

One-, two-, and three-bedroom apartments are available at this beachside condo looking out to the islands of Molokai and Lanai. Views from most private lanais are oceanfront or ocean view; the least expensive rooms have no view. Families like the large apartments, which come with cable TVs and VCRs, washer/dryers, and full kitchens. In addition to a swimming pool and a wading pool for children, there's also a hot tub, putting green, three lighted tennis courts, and a fitness room. Breakfast, lunch and dinner are served at the poolside restaurant.

Honokowai

EMBASSY VACATION RESORT, 104 Kaanapali Shores Place. Tel. 808/661-2000 or 800/669-3155, www.mauiembassy.com. 413 suites. Rates begin at $384 per suite.

Each unit in this resort is a luxurious suite, with one or two bedrooms, a living room (with a full-size sofa bed), two telephones, a lanai and a kitchenette. Culinary gadgets include a microwave oven and coffee maker (with complimentary coffee), and there's also a wet bar. The bedroom-sized baths are decked out with two marble vanities, a stall shower, and a tub. For indoor entertainment, suites are equipped with two remote control TVs (19" in bedrooms and 35" in living rooms), VCRs (the resort has a video library), stereos, and cassette decks. Room service is available until 11pm. Most suites have views of the ocean.

Guests are invited to indulge themselves in a complimentary full breakfast every morning and the manager's al fresco cocktail party every afternoon. Small bridges span streams filled with fish. Lilies, bird of paradise, and hibiscus flourish in gardens. A 54-foot waterslide ensures that giggles accompany the act of getting into the one-acre swimming pool. After a workout in the fitness center, sore muscles can be soothed by the whirlpool or a massage. The year-round children's program, for kids aged 5 to 10, focuses on Hawaiian arts and crafts, from beach sand art and leaf painting to decorating coconuts.

ASTON KAANAPALI SHORES, 3445 Honoapiilani Highway. Tel. 808/667-2211 or 800/922-7866, www.astonhotels.com. 463 units. Rates begin at $190 per condo.

This condominium is located just north of Kaanapali. The lobby opens to a lush, jungled courtyard with waterfalls, red ginger, crotons, and palm trees. A garden foot path winds along a fish-stocked pond. Lanais of first-floor rooms lead to the beachwalk. Ceilings are high and living rooms (in the one- and two-bedroom apartments) are spacious. Studios with kitchens and hotel rooms with refrigerators, wet bars, and microwave ovens are also for rent. Laundry facilities, storage closets, cable TV, and kitchens with dishwashers are features of one- and two-bedroom units. However, in the one-bedroom apartments, the only telephone is in the living room, along with the one television.

The two swimming pools make this resort especially appealing. Two whirlpools, a sauna, a putting green, and a restaurant and lounge are also on the grounds. Guests receive a discount at the fitness center. The three lighted tennis courts are open until 10pm and the closest golf course is only about three miles away. Sessions of the children's program are available Monday through Friday mornings and afternoons, as well as Friday nights. Children aged 5 to 10 enjoy the scavenger hunts, kite making, sand art, hula lessons, swimming, and ukulele demonstrations, among other activities.

Kaanapali

SHERATON MAUI, 2605 Kaanapali Parkway. Tel. 808/661-0031 or 800/782-9488, www.starwoodhawaii.com. 510 rooms. Rates begin at $360.

It's hard to believe that when Sheraton Maui opened in 1963, it was the only full-scale hotel on Kaanapali Beach, a stretch now lined with snazzy resort hotels and condos. The first guests paid just $15 a night for their rooms! Today various buildings, none taller than six stories, are spread over 23 beautifully landscaped acres. The sunny lobby welcomes vacationers with a panoramic view of the 80-foot-high black lava Pu'u Keka'a rock formation, the islands of Molokai and Lanai floating in the dark blue water, and gorgeous white sand. Koa wood, local artwork, bright floral arrangements, and Hawaiian kapa cloth decorate the lobby. All of the upscale guest rooms and suites come with lanais and most face the ocean. Not only are fifteen rooms accessible to visitors in wheelchairs, but 10 are designed for people with impaired hearing.

Instead of a mere swimming pool, here a wonderful swimming "lagoon" (ranging in depth from 4' to 7') meanders under bridges and past waterfalls. The fabulous keiki (children's) section is shallow enough for toddlers to stand. Speaking of kids, little people find stuffed animals in their rooms when they first arrive. Facilities also include three tennis courts (lit for night play), a fitness center, and a seaside salon and spa. Here you can arrange to have a fresh fruit facial or an oceanside massage. Scuba diving, sailing aboard a catamaran, and other diversions are easily arranged at the Beach Activities Desk. One of Maui's best snorkeling areas is right in front of the hotel, around Pu`u Keka`a (a.k.a. Black Rock). Kaanapali golf courses are within walking distance.

Travelers have three restaurants to choose from, and, at night, live Hawaiian music entertains people at the Lagoon Bar. Sheraton Maui is particularly attractive to families since folks age 12 and younger staying at the resort with adults aren't charged for meals. Consider booking one of the special family suites: Two adjoining rooms with a kitchenette in the living/dining area. The seasonal Keiki Aloha program, located at the nearby Westin Maui, a sister hotel, offers a slew of special activities for children. Marriott guests are welcome to enjoy the Westin Maui pools and other facilities, along with those of Kapalua Bay Hotel, the other sister property, up north in Kapalua.

Each evening begins with the Marriott's dramatic torch lighting and cliff-diving ceremony, which recreates the legend of Pu'u Keka'a. This symbolic ritual honors the spirits who have come to the farthest point west on the island to dive off the rock from this world into the next. No matter what guests are doing, they pause to observe this impressive moment.

MAUI MARRIOTT RESORT & OCEAN CLUB, 100 Nohea Kai Drive. Tel. 808/667-1200 or 800/763-1333. www.marriott.com. 608 rooms. Rates begin at $350.

Toward the southern end of Kaanapali, this large beach hotel delights parents and children alike with its fabulous aquatic playground that is terraced down toward the ocean. Young children love the ship built for climbing at the edge of the children's pool, which has a sandy bottom. Parents and older children enjoy floating under bridges and past waterfalls, and zipping down the waterslide. The hotel's grounds are bright with lush plantings and lily pads float on a pond. Work out in the health club, be pampered in the spa, or hit the beauty salon. Play some tennis or golf.

While the Marriott boasts attractive guest rooms, note that the walks to some are down surprisingly long corridors. The Monday through Friday children's camp, for kids aged 5 to 12, turns "learning" and "fun" into synonyms. Activities include excursions to the whale museum, rides on the Sugar Cane Train to the historic town of Lahaina, bamboo pole fishing and sand castle building on Kaanapali Beach, storytelling through dance, and Hawaiian arts and crafts.

KAANAPALI ALII, 50 Nohea Kai Drive. Tel. 808/667-1400 or 800/642-6284, www.kaanapali-alii.com or www.classicresorts.com. 264 units. Rates begin at $350 per condo.

Much quieter than many of its neighbors, Kaanapali Alii offers complimentary children's activities to guests during the summer. Artfully landscaped grounds surround the small free-form swimming pool. There are also a Jacuzzi, exercise room, and saunas. Surfing and body surfing is all the rage at the beach in front of this condo.

Unlike in many condos, the front desk is open 24 hours a day, and a special security key is necessary to enter buildings. A concierge is on hand to arrange sports, tours, and other activities. The four buildings have six one- and two-bedroom apartments on each floor. Spacious rooms look out to the mountains, the garden, and/or the ocean. In some units, the master bathroom has a whirlpool. Other facilities include microwaves, dishwashers, trash compactors, blenders, and coffee makers. All rooms have the use of washers and dryers. In Building #3, oceanfront two-bedroom apartment #3106 is fabulous. The full ocean view provides excellent whale watching from the lanai, especially at sunset.

Although there is no food and beverage facility on the property, Kaanapali Alii guests may charge meals at the Kaanapali Golf Course Clubhouse as well as at Maui Marriott and Westin Maui restaurants.

HYATT REGENCY MAUI RESORT & SPA, 200 Nohea Kai Drive. Tel. 808/661-1234 or 800/233-1234, www.hyatt.com. 815 rooms and suites. Rates begin at $325.

Our kids thought they were in a zoo when we first entered the Hyatt's lobby, where parrots and macaws perch uncaged on brass rings. When we went outside and saw the rotund penguins and huge koi waddling and darting around various pools, there wasn't anything we could say to convince our son and daughter that this is indeed a hotel. Then they decided we must be in a museum. Buddha heads and other sculptures stand on pedestals. Near the Napili wing shops, a glass-covered coffee table serves as a showcase for New Guinea headdresses, headbands, and shell necklaces. Art and artifacts from Burma, Thailand and China, among other places, are displayed here and there.

A swinging rope-and-wood-plank bridge spanning a section of the sprawling-half-acre swimming pool got our children thinking we were in an amusement park. They were certain of this when they spotted the Keiki Lagoon, where they could enter the 1 + foot deep pool via a choice of slides, turtle statues spout water, fountain streams do a rhythmic dance, and mist looks like a volcanic eruption. Then when our daughter had her first manicure and pedicure at age five, our children just knew the Hyatt had to be a beauty salon. At the sprawling Spa Moana, which also offers keiki (children's) yoga classes, some treatments are designed especially for teenagers, such as the "Rock Star Package," which includes spray-on hair color, a pedicure, a toe ring, and a temporary tattoo. Mind you, adults are also welcome to try everything from massages to body wraps based on ancient Hawaiian healing techniques.

Neighboring the Kaanapali Golf Courses, the Hyatt is many things to many people. It thrills vacationers with its lava tube waterslide into the pool, boogie boards, kayaks, bikes, six tennis courts, and sails on a 55-foot catamaran. Camp Hyatt organizes a variety of activities for children aged 5 to 12, including Olympic-like games, obstacle course racing, tug-o-war on the beach. Stargazers should ask about the hotel's astronomy program.

In rooms, the TV and refrigerator are hidden in handsome armoires, and dressing areas are spacious. Yukatas (Japanese robes) are provided for guests to use during their stay.

THE WESTIN MAUI RESORT & SPA, 2365 Kaanapali Parkway. Tel. 808/ 667-2525 or 888-625-4949, www.westinmaui.com. 758 rooms. Rates begin at $295.

Next door to Whalers Village shopping center, this lavish resort is graced with waterfalls, swan-filled ponds, huge statues and urns, plus five swimming pools. Guests delight in swimming under the cascades and whizzing down the water slides. Send your kids off to the hotel's camp (ages 5 to 12) and you'll have time for an oceanside massage in an open-air cabana. While guest rooms are surprisingly small, they are elegantly decorated. Each room has a coffee maker, iron and board and a refrigerator. Accents include marble- and glass-topped tables and heavy, wide chaise lounges.

A variety of restaurants and lounges, along with dramatically decorated suites, add to the overall elegance. Guests are invited to take advantage of the fitness center and a full range of beach activities. Stay at the Westin Maui and you can get a change of scenery every three days: Westin guests may use the facilities at the nearby Sheraton Maui and Kapalua Bay Hotel, in Kapalua.

KAANAPALI BEACH HOTEL, 2525 Kaanapali Parkway. Tel. 808/661-0011 or 800/262-8450, www.kbhmaui.com. 430 rooms. Rates begin at $180.

Upon check-in, children receive passports that lead them to various parts of this appealing and distinctively Hawaiian resort. At each destination, the passport is stamped with a Hawaiian word and the child receives a special gift. Centrally located, Kaanapali Beach Hotel offers other complimentary children's activities, including lei making classes, hula lessons, and lauhala weaving. Young children can stay in the shallow end of the large swimming pool. Refrigerators in rooms and the availability of connecting rooms are other reasons families find this a good choice. Varying mainly in terms of views, rooms are quite spacious, with dressing rooms, coffee makers, and lanais.

The two restaurants are known for their generous portions and good prices for home-style food. Serving breakfast and dinner, the Tiki Terrace is the place to go for taro pancakes with coconut syrup and macadamia nuts or an omelet with salmon and white rice. Breakfast, lunch, and dinner are served buffet-style at the Mixed Plate. Be sure to ask about the dinner theater show, which is generally geared to people of all ages. You might be treated to the magic show that delighted my husband and me as much as it fascinated our three- and five- year-old children.

Each evening at sunset, guests can witness the lighting of the hotel's torches. Kaanapali Beach Hotel encourages its staff to become knowledgeable about Hawaiian culture by providing time to attend classes. This commitment allows staff to better respond to curious guests. When guests check out, staff members often gather in the lobby to perform a brief, yet very moving farewell ceremony of appreciation.

Maui's Most Hawaiian Hotels

At some hotels in Hawaii, it's easy to forget that you're *in* Hawaii—in fact, as attractive as many of these accommodations are, you could almost be anywhere in the world. So it's refreshing to know that several of Maui's resorts do a particularly good job of incorporating Hawaiian cultural programs, arts, and traditions into the daily lives of guests, especially the Kaanapali Beach Hotel, along with the Ritz-Carlton Kapalua and the Wailea Marriott Resort.

Lahaina
LAHAINA SHORES BEACH RESORT, 475 Front Street. Tel. 808/661-4835 or 800/642-6284, Web site: www.classicresorts.com. 199 units. Rates begin at $180 per condo.

Conveniently located at the end of Lahaina boardwalk, this six-story condominium is the only accommodation in town that is on the beach. Teenagers like the proximity to surfing lessons. While a medley of stores and restaurants are nearby, this is one of the least crowded parts of Lahaina. The large plantation-style building has tall columns and a beautiful arched porte cochere. Trimmed in oak, the attractive lobby is spacious and simply furnished. As in major hotels, someone is on duty at the front desk 24 hours a day. The swimming pool is just off the lobby. Public tennis courts and a basketball court are across the street, while a 10-minute drive will take you to the closest golf courses.

Although the studio and one-bedroom ocean view or mountain view apartments are uninspired, they are perfectly comfortable. Note that while some units have two full-size beds, most have either two twins or one queen, but rollaway beds can be requested. Guests have a choice of excellent restaurants next door at the 505 Front Street complex.

OHANA MAUI ISLANDER, 660 Wainee Street. Tel. 808/667-9766 or 800/462-6262. Web site: www.ohanahotels.com. Rates begin at $125.

You can't beat the location of this modest hotel. Perfect for families that are watching their pennies, Ohana Maui Islander sits in a quiet residential neighborhood just a block from the action of Lahaina's Front Street and harbor, once the Pacific's busiest whaling port. A vacation here puts you right in the middle of a wide choice of excellent restaurants and shops. With a swimming pool and lighted tennis courts, this hotel offers units (some with kitchens) on the first and second floor. Families make good use of the barbecue and picnic areas.

Kula
KILI'S COTTAGE, Off Highway 37. Tel. 808/985-7488 or 800/262-9912, www.bestbnb@aloha.net. 1 cottage. Rates begin at $110. Minimum 2-night stay.

Perfect for a family, this three-bedroom, two-bath cottage is a good starting point for the drive to the summit of Haleakala. The sweeping views from the wraparound deck are wonderful, since the cottage sits at the 3,000 foot elevation. You'll feel at home with the well-equipped kitchen, gas barbecue, and washer/dryer. Remind your children that they can admire the colorful lei-making garden, but that they must ask the owners before plucking any of the blossoms.

Kihei
KIHEI BEACH RESORT, 36 South Kihei Road. Tel. 808/879-2744 or 800/367-6034, www.kiheibeachresort.com. 54 units. Rates begin at $160 per condo.

This six-story concrete building contains one- and two-bedroom apartments that are pleasant enough. Lanais look out to Maalaea Bay, frequented by whales during the winter, the West Maui Mountains, Haleakala volcano, the beach and uninhabited Kahoolawe island. In addition to the sandy shore, there's a swimming pool. Kitchens are outfitted with dishwashers, microwaves, and garbage disposals.

NONA LANI COTTAGES, 455 South Kihei Road. Tel. 808/879-2497 or 800/733-2688. 8 units. Rates begin at $100.

These one-bedroom shingle-roofed cottages are set on an appealing grassy lawn across the road from the beach. Flowers and fruit trees flourish here. Guests relax on their lanais, which gaze out to the ocean. Each unit can sleep four. Kitchens are fully equipped. Barbecue grills and laundry facilities are available. Kihei's restaurants and stores are conveniently located nearby.

KIHEI AKAHI, 362 Huku Lii Place #204, Kihei, HI 96753. Tel. 808/879-2778 or 800/367-5242, Fax 808/879-7825. 140 units. Rates begin at $80 per condo. Four-night minimum stay required. Major credit cards.

This centrally located condominium is affordably priced, an attraction for families. Units come as studios as well as one- and two-bedroom apartments. Some are only partially air-conditioned (either the bedroom or the living room) and others are not air conditioned at all. Along with two swimming pools, facilities include a tennis court and barbecue area. Guests can learn about local vegetation along the marked flower and plant trail.

Wailea

GRAND WAILEA RESORT HOTEL & SPA, 3850 Wailea Alanui Drive. Tel. 808/875-1234 or 800/888-6100, www.grandwailea.com. 780 rooms. Rates begin at $480.

With nearly 800 rooms (all of them ocean view), this hotel stands on a beach, but the ocean almost seems mundane next to the other bodies of water here. The main swimming pool, set off by a fountain that is lit after dark, takes up 15,000 square feet. A 2,000-foot-long river pool boasts the world's first water elevator; gushing water pushes a basket-like cubicle through a tube with rock on three sides and a glassed-in aquarium on the fourth.

Complete with a computer center, a whale-shaped wading pool, a crafts room, and a movie theater, the children's camp is a hit among young guests. Activities include sand sculpting contests, guided tidal pool and reef exploration, nature walks along the beach, and swinging from ropes to splash into the water. When you and your mate would like to go out alone together at night, just sign your child up for night camp.

Vacationers at Grand Wailea have a choice of restaurants, including an authentic Japanese inn and a thatched roof ohia wood seafood restaurant on a lagoon. The spacious, full-scale health spa tempts visitors to keep in shape and be pampered. Scuba lessons are available in a specially designed pool. Guest rooms—which each have a private lanai, three telephones, and a bathroom with a tub and separate shower—are quite large.

Note that this hotel books quite a few large conventions. If you'd rather not be bombarded by these often invasive groups, when you make your reservation, ask if any are scheduled for the time you'd like to vacation.

THE FAIRMONT KEA LANI MAUI, 4100 Wailea Alanui. Tel. 808/875-4100 or 800/866/5577, www.kealani.com. 450 suites; 37 villas. Rates begin at $445 per suite.

This luxury resort sits on Polo Beach. The white Mediterranean-style buildings are set against 22 acres of colorfully landscaped grounds. Each oceanfront villa has its own plunge pool. One-, two-, and three-bedroom villas are available along with one-bedroom suites. Huge, elegant marble baths come with tubs and separate showers. Guests may watch the large screen color TV in the living room, with a VCR, or the TV in the bedroom. There is an extensive video library. Units also come with CD and audio-cassette players as well as AM/FM radio stereos. Kitchenettes are equipped with refrigerators, microwave ovens, and coffee and tea.

Two of the three swimming pools are joined by a water slide and one pool is reserved for adults only. If you need to work off that midnight snack, you'll be happy to know that the fitness center, complimentary for hotel guests, is open around the clock. Worked that body a little too intensely? Then visit the spa, where a la carte services include massages and hydrotherapy.

For guests aged 5 to 12, the children's program emphasizes the indigenous culture and the ecosystem of Hawaii.

FOUR SEASONS RESORT MAUI AT WAILEA, 3900 Wailea Alanui Drive. Tel. 808/874-8000 or 800/334-MAUI, www.fourseasons.com. 380 rooms. Rates begin at $365.

The elegant lobby, done in polished and unpolished marble and granite, sets the tone for this gracious beachfront hotel. The Four Seasons Resort Maui is known for its exceptional cuisine. Even the smallest guest rooms are large and comfortable teak furniture decorates lanais. The brightly lit bathrooms are fabulous, all with glass-enclosed, marble-tiled stall showers, bath tubs, double sinks, and endless counter space. Room service is available around the clock.

Talk about serious pampering! Sit by one of the swimming pools and attendants periodically bring you ice towels and glasses of ice water, and they might even spritz you with Evian. (It's easy to understand why celebrities such as Elton John and Arnold Schwartzenegger have chosen to stay here.) The upper pool, complete with a waterfall, has a section for children designed so that parents can be in the deeper area while keeping an eye on the kids. With two Jacuzzis, the main pool has a fountain in the middle. At sunset, Hawaiian music wafts out from the poolside cafe.

Have morning coffee and tea in the library or browse through the wide selection of books and periodicals when you need a quiet moment. Live dance music draws people to the Lobby Lounge at night. A pool table, large screen TV, and full bar are found in the game room. Along with an exercise room, massage rooms (your body will love you after a lomi lomi massage), and a steam room, the health club has a centrifugal dryer so you can work out or take a swim on your last day without having to pack a wet bathing suit.

Designed for kids age five to twelve, the children's program is complimentary to guests. Activities might include hula lessons, story-telling, games, crafts, and music. Kids aged twelve and up can get to know each other over complimentary scuba clinics, snorkeling trips, whale watching excursions.

MARRIOTT WAILEA RESORT, 3700 Wailea Alanui. Tel. 808/879-1922 or 800/367-2960, www.marriott.com. 516 rooms. Rates begin at $280.

The original hotel in the Wailea area, this is a group of seven low-rise buildings and an eight-story main building scattered across 22 acres. (Be sure to check out the maps around the property to avoid getting lost on the sprawling grounds that slope to the ocean's edge.) Sporting koa wood rocking chairs and Pacific art, the attractive ocean view lobby resembles a living room without walls. Most guest rooms face the ocean and contain commodious dressing rooms. All have lanais. Floor-to-ceiling mirrors serve as sliding closet doors. The L-shaped junior suites are especially nice.

Swimming pools are on various levels of the terraced grounds, along with a couple of whirlpools. Adults have a choice of two water slides: The steeper one sends you hurtling into a deep tank at a *really* high speed, while the longer one brings you to a gentler horizontal stop at the end of the slide. This is an excellent hotel for families with children. During our last trip, our two young children couldn't get enough of the slides, sprinklers, ladders, and platforms of the impressive oceanview aqua-playground, complete with a kiddie pool with a sandy bottom. The hotel's children's program (available several days a week) also attracts families to the resort. At check in, kids are welcomed with a frisbee, beach ball, and water bottle. Through the children's program, visiting young people learn all about Hawaii through crafts, music, dance, and other activities.

Many guests spend time on the three Wailea golf courses and eleven tennis courts, the lounge, the Mandara Spa, and the restaurants. Once a week in the lobby, you can buy handicrafts made by local artists. In addition to lei-making classes and other crafts demonstrations, what is among the area's best luau is held at the water's edge four times a week. Attend this Hawaiian feast, and chances are, you'll see a breathtaking sunset during the festivities. Many agree that the centerpiece of the action is the award-winning fire dancer.

THE PALMS AT WAILEA, 3200 Wailea Alanui Drive, Wailea, HI 96753. Tel. 808/879-5800 or 800/688-7444, www.outrigger.com, E-mail: pwr@outrigger.com. 150 units. Rates begin at $215 per condo. Major credit cards.

One of Wailea's nicest condos, the Palms offers contemporary apartments attractively decorated and with open, airy layouts. Life-like silk plants are among the furnishings. Lanais are large, with lots of seating as well as tables for dining al fresco. Kitchens are modern, complete with icemakers, blenders, toasters, and coffee makers. A washer/dryer comes with each unit and there is lots of closet space. You'll find a swimming pool and whirlpool on the grounds, and the extensive facilities of the Marriott Wailea are right across the street. Golf, tennis, shopping, and the beach are all nearby.

My only problem with the Palms is that bedrooms are air-conditioned, but living rooms have ceiling fans instead and can get a bit warm.

WAILEA GRAND CHAMPIONS VILLAS, 3750 Wailea Alanui. Tel. 808/879-1595 or 800/367-5246, www.destinationresortshi.com. 188 units. Rates begin at $185 per condo.

A moderate price tag, roomy units, and the fact that you can literally tee off in your backyard draw families with children to this condo. Guest units, in two-story buildings, are right on the green of Wailea's Blue Golf course. There are also Laykold night-lit tennis courts. Kitchens of these one- and two-bedroom units open onto lanais overlooking the golf course—but there are plenty of restaurants nearby if you don't intend to put fire to any pans. Master bedrooms have their own lanais, and living/dining areas are spacious. On the attractive 11-acre grounds are two pools, two Jacuzzis, and barbecue areas. The closest beaches are a two-minute drive away and beach towels are provided for guests' use. Families with little ones are encouraged to make arrangements through the concierge for participation in children's programs based elsewhere.

Makena

MAUI PRINCE, 5400 Makena Alanui. Tel. 808/874-1111 or 800/321-6284, www.mauiprincehotel.com. 310 rooms. Rates begin at $220.

The high standard of service, the unobtrusive staff, and the spare, stylish decor bring many repeat guests to this attractive beach front hotel. In the open-air lobby, tall wooden louvered doors are pushed back by day to expose the central octagonal courtyard below. Gaze down, and you'll see a garden with a waterfall, streams, and lush plantings. The Prince Court is the hotel's signature Hawaii regional restaurant. Complete with a sushi bar, Hakone is an excellent Japanese dining spot.

Al fresco corridors outside guest rooms overlook the garden courtyard and the volcano propping up clouds in the distance. Most rooms have views of the Pacific from their lanais. Special touches include, video cassette or CD players, refrigerators stocked with complimentary fruit juices and bottled water; slippers and robes for guests' use during their stay; and handheld shower nozzles. Room service is available from 6am to midnight.

The two round pools near the two golf courses are small and shallow—great for young children. A landscaped pathway leads to the hotel's beach and other beaches are also nearby. Note that golfers can reserve their tee times when making their hotel reservations. Tennis (on six courts) and horseback riding can also be arranged. Ask about the sports and activities package. Children aged 5 to 12 are invited to participate in the Prince Kids Club, which includes activities such as painting coconuts, feeding fish, sand castle-building, bamboo pole fishing, arts and crafts, and scavenger hunts.

Hana

HOTEL HANA-MAUI, Tel. 808/248-8211 or 800/321-4262, www.hotelhanamaui.com. 67 rooms. Rates begin at $395.

Once on our last day here, our five-year-old daughter burst into tears upon hearing that the lauhala weaving class had to be postponed until the afternoon, after we were scheduled to leave. Something had come up, so the teacher couldn't make it in until later, we were told. The next thing we knew, there was Auntie Kuulei setting up her weaving as originally scheduled. She explained to our delighted daughter that she had heard that someone cried, so she had rearranged her conflicting family business to come in.

It is this level of caring and consideration that makes Hotel Hana-Maui such a wonderful place for families. There are no TVs in guest rooms, so you'll have a chance to bond over nature walks, swimming, and fine dining (as well as a take-out window at the ranch). In a lush, remote part of Maui, this is the kind of place many people picture when they think of Hawaii. Travelers sleep in individual rooms, suites, cottages, and a restored nineteenth-century plantation house that rests on a hilltop. Bathtubs have views of gloriously colorful patios or gardens. Rooms also have refrigerators, ice-machines, and wet bars.

Hot tubs are found on lanais at Sea Ranch Cottages, among the most luxurious of the hotel's accommodations. They were built to resemble old plantation houses. One swimming pool and the hot tub sit on a rise overlooking the cottages and the rocky shore. This is where you'll find the Wellness Center, where you can work out on exercise machines, take an aerobics class, or have a spa treatment. Massages are even available for children, as long as they are accompanied by a parent. The garden swimming pool is near the original guest rooms. The more scenic beach is about 2.5 miles away, but there's also another one a brief stroll down the road.

Note that some months are adults-only months at this hotel.

HANA KAI-MAUI, 1533 Uakea Road. Tel. 808/248-8426 or 800/346-2772, www.hanakaimaui.com. 16 units. Rates begin at $170 per condo.

If you want to be right on a beach in Hana, this condominium is the place to stay. Unfortunately, however, the picturesque shore here is rocky and thus better for sunbathing than swimming. Overlooking the beach, a spring dribbles into a lava rock decorative pool. All with large oceanfront lanais and kitchens, the apartments vary in size. The largest sleeps up to six people. Guests enjoy the waterside barbecue grill and picnic area. Truly a place to get away, Hana Kai-Maui has no TVs or telephones in rooms, but some units have clock radios.

Chapter 11

THE BIG ISLAND
WITH KIDS

Alternatively lush and stark, the island of Hawaii is one of the most unusual-looking and diverse places I've ever seen. Its striking appearance is due in part to the fact that it is still growing. Kilauea, the world's most active volcano, continues its periodic spurts of lava, which solidifies and adds to the island's land mass. From safe lookout points and helicopters, both adults and children love watching the magnificent pyrotechnics. Recent and ancient lava flows, ebony or chocolate in color, and moonscapes of volcanic craters stretch for miles in some regions.

In other areas, waterfalls plunge into jungled valleys and mist clings to rolling hills. Flower nurseries, macadamia nut orchards, and coffee plantations thrive in the rich volcanic soil. Beaches come in white, black, salt and pepper, and even green! And with its paniolos (cowboys), rodeos, and herds of Herefords, this island is home to one of the largest privately-owned cattle ranches in the United States.

On the western side of the island, heading north from Kona International Airport on Queen Kaahumanu Highway (named for Kamehameha I's feisty, favorite bride), you may think you're driving through a vast wasteland. No buildings or even gas stations border the road. As far as you can see, stark lava flows sprawl on both sides of the highway. Here and there the barren charcoal landscape is interrupted by hay-like pill grass, kiawe trees and cascades of colorful bougainvillea, which create a brilliant contrast. The Big Island version of graffiti also decorates some roadsides. Kids use white coral rocks to spell

Which Island is This?

So as not to be confused with the whole state, Hawaii is commonly referred to as the Big Island. And, at about 4,000 square miles in size, big it is. Even if all the main islands in the chain were placed within its borders, they each would have plenty of elbow room. Some outsiders are under the mistaken impression that, because of its size and name, Hawaii is the main island in the chain and thus the home of the capital, Honolulu (which is actually on Oahu).

out phrases such as "Fred loves Noelani" on the black lava expanses, most of which resulted from the last eruption of Mt. Hualalai in 1801.

What could philanthropist Laurance Rockefeller possibly have been thinking when he decided to build the Mauna Kea Beach Hotel in this desolate area in 1965? Well, his idea caught on, and other developers have followed suit. From most of the road, there's no sign of these plush resorts. They are tucked neatly out of sight at the water's edge, beyond the lava flows that stretch between the highway and the Pacific. Despite the ruggedness of the region, the grounds of these well-spaced hotels are startlingly green, with flowers in every hue and smooth lawns and golf courses.

But don't worry—you need not be a Rockefeller to enjoy the Big Island's bounty. The oceanfront town of Kailua-Kona, south of the airport, and Hilo, the verdant capital (on the east coast, near Volcanoes National Park), offer a wide array of accommodations, many of which have moderate rates, some even inexpensive.

Getting Around

The Big Island's two main airports are Hilo International Airport (a.k.a. General Lyman Field) in the east (closer to Volcanoes National Park) and Kona International Airport in Kona on the west coast (closer to most hotels and beaches). Hilo International is barely five minutes from most of Hilo's hotels

Sky High Snow

Mauna Kea, a dormant volcano 13,796 feet above sea level, and active Mauna Loa, 13,677 feet above the ocean, are the world's tallest mountains (if measured from their aquatic bases). Rising 30,000 feet from the ocean floor, they beat Mt. Everest by a few hundred feet. During winters when there is enough snow, experienced skiers can actually whiz down the slopes of Mauna Kea!

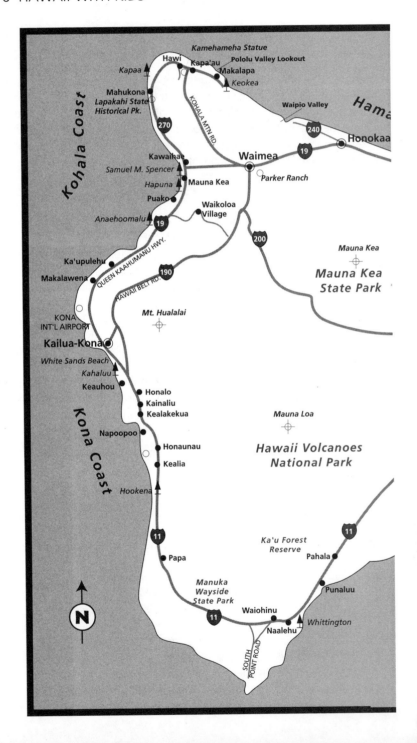

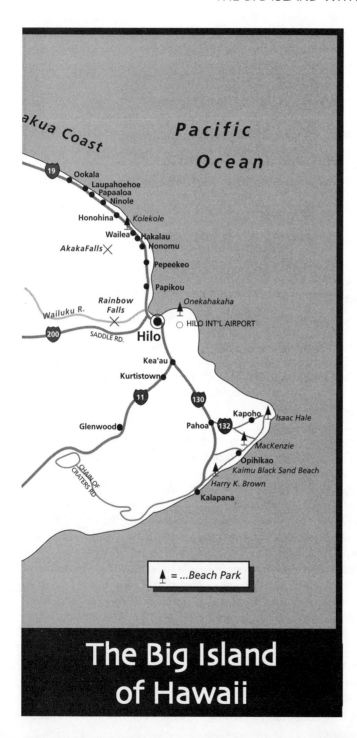

The Big Island
of Hawaii

and about 30 minutes from Volcano. From the Kona airport, the drive is about 35 to 50 minutes to Kona-Kohala hotels, 10 minutes to Kailua-Kona, and 20 to Keauhou. Taxis and rental car stands are found at the airport. Some accommodations on the Kona-Kohala Coast and in Kailua-Kona and Keauhou provide transportation to and from Kona International Airport.

Many first-time visitors are struck by the landscape they see as they swoop down on this airport, which is built on top of a desert-like lava flow. The black runways cut through ebony and dark brown expanses punctuated by tufts of dry yellow grass. Along the roads to and from the airport, the green palms and purple, red, and orange bougainvillea provide a stunning contrast to the dark, barren terrain.

Planning Your Stay

To really appreciate the Big Island of Hawaii, you'll need to stay at least a week. You may want to divide your time among a hotel on the Kona-Kohala Coast (if you can afford it), one in Kona, and one in Hilo.

While there is no island-wide bus system on the Big Island, public buses periodically travel between Kailua-Kona and Hilo daily (except Sunday when there is no service). Along the Kohala Coast as well as in Keauhou and Kailua-Kona, shuttle buses take guests between hotels, condos, golf courses, restaurants, and other locales.

Rental cars provide the most flexibility. It's best to reserve autos well in advance of your arrival, especially if you plan to travel between November and March, during August, the week before Easter (when the Merrie Monarch Festival takes place in Hilo), or in October (during the annual Ironman Triathlon World Championship). Remember, sights, attractions, and gas stations can be far apart on the Big Island. Many residents have no problem with driving 50 miles just to visit a friend for an evening or to eat at a particular restaurant.

One main road goes around the southern portion of the island. Two roads cut across the northern segment: Saddle Road (Highway 200) runs between Mauna Kea and Mauna Loa volcanoes from Hilo to South Kohala. Here it joins Highway 190 to head north to Waimea or south to Kailua Kona; and after following the Hamakua Coast in the east, Highway 19 heads inland, then meets Highways 250 and 270 for the journey to North Kohala, or follows the western coast (on Queen Kaahumanu Highway) down to Kailua-Kona.

Where Are We Going Now?

For such a huge place, the Big Island is sparsely populated and has a great deal of undeveloped land. It is nearly twice as large as the other main islands combined, yet only about ten percent of the state's residents call it home.

The Kohala Coast, along the northwest, is treated to the least amount of rainfall in all of the inhabited Hawaiian chain. The Big Island's most expensive resorts are found here, hugging beaches once frequented by Hawaiian monarchs at play. From royal fishponds and burial caves to heiau (temples) and petroglyphs (rock carvings), intriguing remnants of Hawaii's past are well-preserved along this coast, and some have been incorporated into the grounds of these luxury hotels.

Northern Kohala is the birthplace of Kamehameha the Great, the ambitious Big Island king who brought the whole archipelago under his rule. The kingdom's seat of government was moved from the Big Island to Lahaina, Maui, in 1820, and finally to Honolulu in 1845. Today in this area, pastures speckled with Holstein cows have replaced the sugarcane fields that once blanketed the area; the quiet streets of Hawi, the northernmost town on the Big Island, are lined with low Western front buildings.

To the south, the town of Kailua-Kona is a jumping off point for excellent marlin fishing and the headquarters for international fishing tournaments. There are few sandy beaches here along the Kona Coast, where the dramatic shore is trimmed in craggy black lava set off by green lawns and palms. However, some of the island's best snorkeling sites can be found here.

On the other side of the island, not far from partly flourishing, mostly desolate Volcanoes National Park, Hilo is the island's capital and largest town. While this low-key residential community does have some hotels, agriculture and shipping contribute far more heavily to its economy than tourism does. This is because the few nearby beaches are rocky and Hilo receives a great deal of rain. Even when the weather is dry, the sky is often gray. However, Hilo is home to a couple of worthwhile museums and this eastern side of the island

Big Island Driving Tips

It's certainly true that at 93 miles at its longest and 76 miles at its widest, the Big Island lives up to its name. It takes some seven hours to drive the nearly 250 miles of road that ring the island. Mainly 2-lane, the roads are slim and curvaceous with no shoulders in some sections.

Since the island is so expansive, Big Islanders are used to spending a great deal of time behind their wheels. However, you and your family may not be. When you're planning excursions, make sure you have a good idea of how long it will take you to get from point A to point B, especially if you don't want to be driving after dark. Even though you can certainly drive around the island in a single day, I don't recommend this exhausting endeavor. You'll have much more fun if you explore the Big Island in chunks over the course of several days.

is wonderfully lush, sprouting lots of tropical fruit and hundreds of varieties of orchids.

The drive from Kailua-Kona to Hilo should take about 2-1/4 hours via the northernmost route and 3-1/4 hours via the southern route. Driving from Kona to Hilo on Saddle Road (the middle route) will take roughly 2-1/4 hours. Some visiting families choose to spend a night or two in Hilo when they're ready to visit Volcanoes National Park and the Hamakua Coast. Volcanoes National Park is only a 30- to 45-minute drive from Hilo, while it is about two hours from Kailua-Kona. Waimea is approximately 1-1/4 hours from Hilo and 50 minutes from Kailua-Kona.

Sights & Adventures

KING KAMEHAMEHA STATUE, Kapaau, east of Hawi, North Kohala.

The imposing King Kamehameha Statue, erected in 1878, stands in front of the North Kohala Civic Center in Kapaau. On King Kamehameha Day in June, residents drape the monarch with scores of brightly colored leis. The statue bears a striking resemblance to the one in front of the Judiciary Building in Honolulu. This is because that statue was copied from this one. Intended for Honolulu, the original was modeled by an American sculptor in Italy, cast in Paris, and lost during a shipwreck off the Falkland Islands. So the replica, which now stands in Honolulu, was made. Then the original turned up. It

A Scenic Northern Island Drive

The 21-mile drive from **Kamuela** (a.k.a. **Waimea**) north along the Kohala Mountain Road (Highway 250) to **Hawi**, the sleepy town at the island's northern tip, is one of the island's most scenic routes. Just outside Kamuela/Waimea, stop at the lookout point that offers an expansive view of the Kohala Coast. Along the inland road, an eerie mist often hangs over the towering ironwoods, open fields and country lanes. You'll pass Kahua Ranch, which sports windmills. The *paniolo* (Hawaiian cowboys) here are as likely to round up cattle on motorcycles as on horseback and as adept at growing produce as they are at raising sheep. At the outskirts of Hawi, the feathery branches of casuarina pines create a shady tunnel over the road. Cattle graze in lime green meadows and on the lower slopes of forest green hills.

Continue past Hawi to the **Pololu Valley Lookout**, where the main road grinds to a halt. Awe-inspiring cliffs drop into the deep valley, where wild boars, goats, pheasants, and horses roam freely. A rugged three-mile hiking trail dips into Pololu and eventually makes its way to distant Waipio Valley, where Kamehameha I (Kamehameha the Great) was raised.

seemed appropriate to erect it near the birthplace of the first ruler of the Hawaiian Kingdom.

PARKER RANCH, Kamuela/Waimea, Tel. 885-7655 or 885-2303, Web site: www.parkerranch.com. Visitor Center and Museum: open Monday to Saturday, 9am to 4:45pm (last admission at 4pm); admission (including 25-minute movie): $7 (adults), $5 (children). Wagon Tours: Tuesday to Saturday, 10am to 2pm, $14 (adults), $12 (children).

At 175,000 rolling acres surrounding the town of Kamuela/Waimea, this working ranch is one of the largest privately owned cattle ranches in the US. The word *paniolo,* a corruption of Españoles (Spanish people) meaning Hawaiian cowboy, entered the local vocabulary after cowboys from Mexico and South America were brought in as ranch hands. Wild rodeos are periodically hosted by the ranch.

If you're traveling with kids age 16 or older, ask about the 4x4 all-terrain-vehicle rides with fabulous views of sprawling land backed by mountains and glimpses of wild pigs, pheasants, and wild goats. For horseback riding through Parker Ranch, the minimum age is 7. Families also enjoy riding carriages pulled by Belgian draft horses (10am to 2pm, Tuesday through Saturday).

The ranch got its name from John Palmer Parker, a sailor who jumped ship in Hawaii in 1809. He found a job cleaning fish ponds for King Kamehameha I. In 1816, Parker married Princess Keliikipikaneokaloahaka, Kamehameha I's granddaughter, called Kipikane for short. Thus, the New England Euro-American became a member of the Hawaiian royal family.

Back in 1788, Captain George Vancouver had come to the islands with Captain James Cook, the man who let Europe know that Hawaii existed. When Vancouver returned in 1793, he brought Mexican longhorn cattle as a gift for Kamehameha. The king put a kapu on killing cows, decreeing that anyone who disobeyed the law would be put to death. But the cows reproduced so rapidly, trampling and eating such great quantities of vegetation on Mauna Kea's slopes, that they soon threatened nearby communities. Kamehameha enlisted Parker, his American grandson-in-law, to control and shrink the herd. In exchange, he gave Parker two acres of land. In 1847, the ex-sailor and his wife established Parker Ranch.

After Parker's death, ownership of these lands fell into the hands of a 14-year-old descendant, Thelma Parker. She grew up to be the mother of the late Richard Smart, the great-great-great-grandson of the founder and the most recent owner of the ranch before it was taken over by a trust.

The Museum at the Parker Ranch Visitor Center was started by Thelma Parker Smart. On display are her jewelry, a well-used family Bible, and the blue gown she wore to the opera at Covent Garden in England when George V was crowned king in 1911. Exhibits also include old saddles, bridles and bits, branding irons, iron pots, brass plates, and an old wind-up telephone mounted on the wall. Portraits, photographs, and a short video tell the history of the ranch and the Kamehamehas, as well as of other relatives and family friends.

What's in a Name?

Waimea was the ancient Hawaiian name for the area surrounded by Parker Ranch, but it was dubbed **Kamuela** (the Hawaiian version of Samuel) after Colonel Sam Parker, the son of Parker Ranch founder John Palmer Parker. However, many people continued to call it Waimea and since there are Waimeas on both Oahu and Kauai, the US Post Office requested that the name be officially changed. So much for officialdom: This upscale ranching town is still commonly known by both names.

One way to get here is to turn mauka (inland) onto Kawaihae Road (Highway 19). This route will also take you across to the east side of the island, down the lush Hamakua Coast and to Hilo, the Big Island's largest town, where pleasant rainfall is abundant, especially in the evening.

KAMUELA/WAIMEA, northern Hawaii, tucked within Parker Ranch.

At the crossroads of the island's main highways (routes 250, 19 and 190), Kamuela, a.k.a. Waimea, rests in the Kohala Mountains. Nearly 3,000 feet above the dry, sunny Kohala Coast (a 45-minute drive away), it is about an hour's drive from Hilo (along Saddle Road). Rainbows often span its verdant fields where horses graze, enclosed by fences made of stones or rough logs. Horseback riding past cattle in open fields or into forests thick with ferns and aromatic ginger is a popular pastime. Houses with gingerbread trim are complemented by neat, colorful gardens. Small churches coexist peacefully with modern mini-malls.

Kamuela/Waimea was born as a shopping and services area for ranch employees. As drowsy as this village is, development is happening too quickly for many long-time residents. They complain about the new homes and shopping centers that keep cropping up. Others are pleased with the changes. More than a few people from Honolulu and other busy parts of Hawaii have relocated to Kamuela/Waimea. They've been lured by the prospect of living in the country, yet being able to take advantage of Kamuela/Waimea's chic boutiques, smattering of gourmet restaurants (several of which are owned by former chefs at some of Hawaii's most upscale resorts) and art galleries.

Over the years, another draw for affluent families has been private Hawaii Preparatory Academy, which is one of the best schools in the state. It was founded in 1949 by an Episcopal bishop. Two of its four campuses—an elementary school and a middle school—are in central Kamuela/Waimea, and one (the high school) sprawls across more than 80 acres of Parker Ranch land.

THE ONIZUKA CENTER FOR INTERNATIONAL ASTRONOMY VISITORS' INFORMATION STATION, Saddle Road, Mauna Kea volcano, Tel. 961-2180; no admission charge.

At Mauna Kea's 9,300 foot elevation, about an hour's drive from Hilo or Waimea/Kamuela and two hours from Kailua-Kona or Kohala, the Onizuka Center is dedicated to Ellison Onizuka, the astronaut from Hawaii who was killed in the 1986 Challenger explosion. Exhibits illustrate the work of the scientists who use the massive telescopes at Mauna Kea's 13,796-foot summit. Every evening from 6pm to 10pm, you can gaze at the heavens through the powerful telescopes at the Center. Temperatures at this elevation can be in the 40s and even 30s, so bundle up! And watch out for cattle along the road as you drive here and back.

More than 1,600 years ago, Polynesians used their knowledge of astronomy to guide them over thousands of miles of open ocean to Hawaii, first landing on the Big Island. Today, some 12 observatories on the 13,796 foot summit of Mauna Kea help contemporary scientists learn more about the heavens. The dry, generally cloud-free weather here on Hawaii's loftiest peak creates such prime conditions that scientists from Great Britain, the Netherlands, France, Canada, and Japan, as well as NASA, have built their countries' major telescopes here. More than 90 percent of all the stars visible from anywhere on the planet can be seen from this perch.

Children under age 16 are not permitted to visit the summit of Mauna Kea (which you'll need a four-wheel-drive to reach)—and some adults (like me) experience altitude sickness there. However, people of all ages can look through the telescopes at the Onizuka Center at the 9,300-foot level and some hotels offer evening stargazing, with special telescopes provided.

WAIPIO VALLEY, northeast coast.

One of my favorite places in all of Hawaii is Waipio Valley, cupped by 2,000-foot cliffs. Kamehameha the Great (Kamehameha I) spent his formative years here. Located just northwest of Honokaa, it can be reached from both the Hamakua and Kona-Kohala Coasts (a 90-minute drive from either Hilo or Kona). At six miles long and a mile wide at the shore, this is the island's largest valley. In its heyday, 40,000 people called it home. Now, barely a few dozen live here, most of them taro farmers.

Roads are rocky riverbeds, bordered by aromatic jasmine and ginger, mango and guava trees, taro fields, and edible fern shoots. You might catch a glimpse of wild horses. A visit here makes an invigorating day trip, especially if you hike in. The walk down into the valley is less than a mile, but the road is nearly vertical, so the hike back out is hard, particularly on the hottest days. But the payoff is that hoofing it is the only way you'll be able to treat yourselves to a visit to the gorgeous black sand beach, since it is *kapu* (off-limits) to the commercial transportation that takes visitors on tours of the valley. Rental cars aren't allowed into the valley at all—they must stop above at the overlook.

While the ocean is too rough for swimming at the black sand beach, it's fine to take a dip in the fresh-water stream that bisects the beach, which is scattered with driftwood and backed by pines. (However, don't drink the water!) Some visitors simply like feeling the ebony sand between their toes and taking in the drama of their surroundings. A waterfall pours down one of the cliffs. Arrive early enough and you might see master local surfers in action. Here at the beach and elsewhere in Hawaii, look for the white naupaka flowers that also grow in the mountains. Half the petals of each blossom seem to be missing. The story goes that these flowers were once lovers whose families forbade them to marry, banishing one to the seashore and the other to the mountains.

Jeep tours are the most popular mode of transport into the valley. Contact the **Waipio Valley Shuttle**, Tel. 775-7121, $45 (adults), $20 (children 11 and younger), for a 90-minute four-wheel-drive tour. Other enjoyable ways to see the valley are on a mule-drawn wagon with **Waipio Valley Wagon Tours**, Tel. 775-9518, $45 (adults), $23 (children older than 3); and on horseback through **Waipi'o Na'alapa Trail Rides**, Tel. 775-0419, $75 (children must be at least 8 years old) for the two-hour trail ride, plus 30 minutes for transportation in and out of the valley. Your guide will tell you all about the passing sights, explaining ancient uses for plants and flowers, describing the formation of the black sand beach, and relating old Hawaiian legends.

THE HAMAKUA COAST, northeast, between Waipio Valley and Hilo.

The lush, rural Hamakua Coast is one of the island's most stunning regions. You can approach Hamakua from the Kohala Coast or from Hilo. Several good curio and antiques shops have cropped up in the sleepy town of **Honokaa**. About six miles north of Hilo, you'll come to **Old Mamalahoa Highway Scenic Drive** (off Highway 19), after passing through endless agricultural fields that melt into the verdant mountains. This four-mile stretch is bordered by royal palms, poincianas, breadfruit and African tulip trees. Flourishing ravines come into view and bridges span rocky streams. The road passes weathered former sugar plantation towns, with old fashioned movie theaters, tin-roofed houses, and wooden-frame churches. Stop at the bluff that gazes down on **Onomea Bay**, with its distinctive rocky formations.

DOLPHIN QUEST HAWAII, Hilton Waikoloa Village, 69-425 Waikoloa Beach Drive, Waikoloa, Tel. 808/886-1234 (x2875) or 800/248-3316, www.dolphinquest.org. Sessions begin at $125 for 30 minutes.

Local students, visiting children (age 5 and older), and vacationing adults all flock to Dolphin Quest programs to get up close and personal with these gentle marine mammals. In addition to getting right in the shallow water with the dolphins to stroke their smooth, warm skin, participants learn about many aspects of ocean life, including conservation and what they can do to help protect dolphins' natural environments. Some animal lovers object to keeping dolphins in captivity for programs like these, but others applaud the educational component and say the dolphins here live healthy lives free from the dangers of the wild.

KAILUA-KONA, just south of Kona International Airport.

Although it caters primarily to tourists, the lively town of Kailua-Kona is a pleasant place to spend some time. Most of its low buildings are found along the mile or so segment of oceanfront Alii Drive between Hotel King Kamehameha in the north and the Royal Kona Resort in the south. Many of its boutiques and restaurants are housed in a variety of shopping arcades (some rather atmospheric).

Visitors wander in and out of stores selling island specialties such as macadamia nuts, jewelry made from coral and shells, billowy color-splashed muumuus, guava jelly and lilikoi (passion fruit) jam, ceramic chimes and, of course, gourmet Kona coffee grown in surrounding plantations.

Kailua-Kona also offers several attractions that played important roles in Hawaii's history, including Hulihee Palace and Mokuaikaua Church (details below). Once the summer haunt of Hawaiian royalty, Alii Drive is shaded by immense gnarled banyan trees with dripping shoots, and branches that reach all the way across the street.

Kailua Pier is the departure point for yacht charters, glass-bottom-boat cruises, sunset sails, submarine sightseeing rides, parasailing and fishing charters. The catch is sometimes weighed here at the end of the day, most often during fishing tournaments. Local fishermen still cast their lines or nets from the seawall along Alii Drive, where vendors often sell hats, bags, mats and other lauhala weavings.

Time & Money

As in other tourist areas in the state, beware of the Kailua-Kona booths disguised as information and activities centers that are actually time-share sales counters. They'll offer free excursions or discounted luau in exchange for sitting through a two-hour-plus hard-sell presentation at the time-share resort.

HULIHEE PALACE, 75-5718 Alii Drive, Kailua-Kona, Tel. 329-1877; open 9am to 4pm Monday to Friday, 10am to 4pm Saturday and Sunday; admission: $6 (adults), $1 (age 18 and younger).

For a trip into the regal past, visit two-story Hulihee Palace, made of coral and lava, in a beautiful setting at the edge of Kailua Bay. It was built in 1838 for John Adams Kuakini, governor of the island. Over the decades, many members of Hawaiian royalty spent several months a year relaxing at this vacation home. King David Kalakaua later bought it and had it remodeled and enlarged. He filled its rooms with Victorian furniture, imported rugs, and delicate china. After its new owner died in 1914, the palace fell into ruin. The Daughters of Hawaii, a group of women whose foreparents had been Hawaii's first American missionaries, convinced the territorial government to buy the building. In 1927, the Daughters themselves took over its restoration and turned it into the museum it is today.

Along with feather work and kapa cloth, much of Hulihee's original furniture is on display. Its prize pieces include a table inlaid with nearly two dozen different kinds of native wood and an artfully carved four-poster bed whose posts once resided in Kamehameha's grass palace. It is clear from the size of some of the chairs how large Hawaiians were. Kamehameha I is thought to have been nearly seven feet tall. Both Queen Kamamalu and rotund Princess Ruth Keelikolani were said to have been a towering six feet. The missionary influence is apparent in the architecture and furnishings.

MOKUAIKAUA CHURCH, across from Hulihee Palace, Kailua-Kona, Tel. 329-0655.

Built by American missionaries, this is the oldest Christian church in Hawaii. This house of worship symbolizes the merging of two cultures: The lava stones in its walls came from an old heiau (Hawaiian temple) that was no longer in use. Founded during the 1820s, the church was completed in 1837 by Hawaii's original group of New England missionaries. Inside, be sure to take a look at the model of the *Thaddeus*, the ship on which these Americans arrived, and the copy of the writings of one of the missionary wives explaining how she felt about her new life.

Home Cooking?

If you're staying at a hotel or condo with cooking facilities, residents say you'll find the best grocery prices at the supermarkets on Palani Road in Kailua-Kona.

ATLANTIS SUBMARINE, Kailua Pier, Kailua-Kona, Tel. 329-3175 or 800/ 548-6262. Cost: $80 (adults), $40 (children age 12 and under who are at least three feet tall).

I'd recommend this dip only if you're not planning any snorkeling or scuba diving during your vacation, or if you take the sub during the winter when you might spot humpback whales as the *Atlantis* descends about 140 feet. First of all, these trips ain't cheap, especially for a family. True, a slew of colorful fish—zebra-striped Hawaiian sergeants, monogamous butterfly fish, yellow tangs, balloon-like puffer fish, blue-striped snapper—do swim right up to the portholes. But seeing them is more fun when you're actually in the water with them. You'll meet at Kailua Pier in Kailua-Kona for the ten-minute catamaran ride out to the sub for the 45-minute underwater exploration.

ROYAL KONA COFFEE MILL MUSEUM, off Highway 11, Hononau, Kona Coast, about 20 miles south of Kailu-Kona, Tel. 328-2511, open 8am-5pm.

Inland, the road winds through coffee country, along the lower slope of Mauna Loa volcano. Hawaii is the only part of the US where coffee is grown commercially. Stop here at this museum and visitor center to have a steaming cup. Kids love walking through the lava tube on the grounds, seeing the coffee drying, and walking around the gift shop. Highway 11 cuts through fertile land, with many different kinds of trees along the road; see how many different types your kids can identify: macadamia nut, wide-leafed breadfruit, mango, and tall skinny papaya.

A note on coffee in Hawaii: It was 1825 when coffee—soon to be Hawaii's black gold—first found its way to the islands. The coffee plants, picked up during a stop in Brazil, arrived at Kona on a British warship. First the coffee was planted in Manoa Valley on Oahu. Then, in 1828, farmers tried it on the Big Island. Kona's dry climate provided perfect conditions and it flourished as never before. Large-scale coffee growing eventually fell victim to rising labor costs, droughts, and dropping world coffee prices. In the late 1970s, people around the globe began developing a voracious taste for gourmet coffee, and the market began to soar once again.

PUUHONUA O HONAUNAU NATIONAL HISTORICAL PARK, Honaunau, Kona Coast, about 20 miles south of Kailua-Kona, Tel. 328-9877; admission $5 per vehicle; or $3 walk-in (adults), free for children under age 16; Visitor Center open 8am-4:30pm daily; park open 6am to 7:30pm Monday to Thursday, and 6am to 11pm Friday to Sunday.

When you head to this historic spot, be sure to bring your bathing suits and picnic goodies: two tidepools at the picnic area in the southern part of the park are great for a dip, especially for kids. In a game of tag, children know that they are safe if they get to home base before their pursuers catch them. For 12th century Hawaiians, this waterfront site provided similar asylum for religious and political refugees.

Kapu (the taboo system) governed everything ancient Hawaiians did, from dietary habits and to land ownership. These taboos were believed to be divine will, and going against the gods could have far-reaching consequences for all Hawaiians. Therefore, the punishment for transgressors could be severe—often death. However, people who broke these sacred laws could be spared if they reached Puuhonua O Honaunau before being caught. Refugees were protected here by the *mana* (spiritual power) that remained in the bones of the dead chiefs who were buried in nearby *heiau* (temples). Through a ceremony performed by a *kahuna* (priest), the lawbreaker would be absolved of all guilt.

This refuge is adjacent to the ancestral home of the Kamehameha line. After a fight with Kamehameha I, Kaahumanu, his number one wife, is said to have hidden from him at Puuhonua O Honaunau, only to be given away by the barking of her pet dog. As usual in their tempestuous relationship, the loving couple finally made up. The land remained in the hands of Hawaii's royal family until the late 19th century, when it was bought by Charles R Bishop. Also called Place (or City) of Refuge, this 180-acre site—the most revered of Hawaii's religious sanctuaries—was restored and turned into a national historic park in 1961.

Big Island Big Time Shopping

Particularly if you're traveling with young children, consider stopping at **Ukulele House**, at King's Shops in Waikoloa on the Kohala Coast, which sells as many as forty child-size ukuleles a day. Ask for a pocket-sized instruction book and a pick, and the salesperson might give a mini-lesson on the spot. Another great shop for children in this mall is **Giggles**, which has a tempting selection of Hawaiian shirts, dresses, handbags, water gear, toys, and books.

When you're visiting nearby Waimea/Kamuela, be sure to stop by **Cook's Discoveries**, a wonderful little gift shop selling everything from distinctive jewelry and clothing to toys.

Another pleasant place to spend some time—and money—is **Alii Gardens**, on Alii Drive, just south of downtown Kailua-Kona (open only Wednesday through Saturday, 9am to 4pm). This outdoor market is packed with high-quality goods and handmade crafts, including koa wood products and black pearl jewelry at some of the best prices in Hawaii. You might find nuts, cookies, and soap at **Goodies From Hawaii**, kites, wind socks, and banners at **Gems of the Sea**, or sculpture, paintings, and other artwork from Indonesia, Tonga, or Australia at **Island Pleasures**. If you'd like to share some of the Big Island's tropical blossoms with friends back home (or ship some to yourself to welcome you when you get back), visit **Hawaiian Island Flowers**. For sarongs in unusual patterns and unique sandals decorated with beads and island shells, try **Chrysalis**.

Both you and your children will appreciate the baked goods at Alii Gardens' family-owned **Tropical Dream Macadamia**. You'll find it hard to believe that the delicious macadamia-nut-flour cookies (in flavors such as guava, coconut, Kona coffee, chocolate chip, and shortbread) are actually sugar-free, sweetened only with honey or syrup. Kids also love hanging out at **Doodlebugs**, where they can color "doodlebugs" and enter their creations in a contest. For refreshments, the deli serves sandwiches (including veggie choices), saimin, milkshakes, fruit bowls, smoothies, and ice cream.

☙

Sights include the Kaahumanu stone (where the regent hid during her tiff with Kamehameha), a reconstructed heiau (temple), old-style thatched roof *hale* (houses), burial caves, a stone for playing *konane* (a royal game something like checkers), a royal fishpond, and a royal canoe landing. Be sure to wear sturdy shoes if you plan to walk through the lava fields to see the petroglyphs. Exhibits cover various aspects of ancient life, and traditional skills and crafts are demonstrated by staff members.

At the end of June or early July, a three-day cultural festival is held in the park. Transformed into royalty, the staff is decked out in elaborate feather capes and helmets. Vacationers are invited to try their hands at lei making, lauhala weaving, poi pounding, and tying fishing nets. They can even help pull in a load of fish.

MANUKA STATE PARK, southern Kona Coast.

Much of the land is desert in the **Ka'u** region, the southern portion of the Big Island. However, Manuka State Park, near the lower end of the Kona Coast, flourishes with an arboretum and its trails wind through greenery. Picnic pavilions make this a relaxing stop.

This is a good place to stop on your way to **Ka Lae** (South Point), with its unusual green sand beach, which is the southernmost tip of the United States. (It's about a two-hour drive from Kailua-Kona.) As Hawaiians have always believed, historians have concluded that this is the part of the archipelago where the ancient Polynesian settlers first stepped ashore. Some experts say that these original inhabitants arrived between A.D. 700 and 750, while others point to evidence that indicates they were here as early as A.D. 300 or even A.D. 150. Just 30 miles offshore, by the way, a new volcanic island, Loihi, should break the ocean's surface in a few thousand years.

NAALEHU, southeast coast, about 40 minutes from Volcanoes National Park Visitor Center.

Flat, pretty Naalehu, a former sugar plantation town, is backed by scenic hills. Several handsome churches are clustered in this tiny town. Stop at a food stand here for *malasadas*, Portuguese hole-less doughnuts. Or watch bakers at work at Punalu'u Sweetbread Bakeshop and Visitor Center, then sit in the garden to eat a sandwich made with the bread. Although Naalehu is known as the most southern town in the US, you won't hear any drawls, but you'll sense the hospitality.

A thrill for many visitors is stretching out under a palm on the coal black sands of **Punalu'u Beach,** just northeast. From Punalu'u to Hawaii Volcanoes National Park Visitor Center, the drive is about 30 minutes.

HAWAII VOLCANOES NATIONAL PARK, southeast. Tel. 985-6000 (general information, updates on eruption activity, camping, and weather from recorded messages); admission $10 per car, $5 for bikers and hikers—keep your receipt, since it's good for re-admission for one week; Visitor Center open 7:45am-5pm daily; park open 24 hours a day, year round.

Whether you're coming from Hilo or the Kona-Kohala Coast, plan at least a full day for a trip to Hawaii Volcanoes National Park. Start at the Visitor Center, where a brief video helps children (and adults) understand what they are about to see. Ranger-guided tours can be fun for families with children. They are a good way to ensure that you see the some of the most dramatic sights in the park. Routes change daily, depending on volcanic activity, so call before 9am for details. This 359-square mile park is interlaced with 150 miles of hiking trails and scenic drives. Maps are available at the gate. Be sure to carry a good supply of bottled water, even for short hikes and strolls, especially in the summer.

A national park since 1916, the island's most visited attraction encompasses **Kilauea** and **Mauna Loa** volcanoes. More than two million people pour into the park each year, the majority arriving when eruptions are in progress. The terrain ranges from moonlike craters, steaming fire pits, and hissing fumaroles to thick rain forest. Picnic grounds and camping cabins help lure vacationers to this otherworldly landscape, about 4,000 feet above sea level. In the heat of the day, it's hard to imagine that temperatures can dip into the 40s at night.

Volcanoes National Park even boasts a golf course and a hotel. During a visit here, Mark Twain quipped, "The surprise of finding a good hotel in such an outlandish spot startled me considerably more than the volcano did."

It surprises many to learn that fatalities from Hawaii's volcanic eruptions have been few. Some of the last in recent history occurred in 1790, when a group of warriors battling Kamehameha I was wiped out by flying boulders, poisonous gases and fire. A hiking trail from the highway by the western edge of the park leads to an area where footprints of members of the retreating army can still be seen in the petrified lava.

Kilauea volcano's longest recorded series of eruptions began on New Year's Day of 1983. In early April, lava swept away the first house to be destroyed by the volcano in a quarter century. By the end of that year, more than a dozen homes and hundreds of housing lots had been smothered by the flow. After witnessing an eruption of the 4,090-foot Kilauea, Mark Twain remarked, "I have seen Vesuvius since, but it was a mere toy, a child's volcano, a soup-kettle, compared to this." Mauna Loa got in on the act in 1984, the first time it had erupted in nine years, and the first time both volcanoes had performed together in 65 years. Lava oozed onto the highway in 1986. Early the following year, just two months after the highway had been rebuilt, the road was swallowed by lava once again—to the delight of tourists with cameras. Highway 11 cuts through the park, and has been aptly named **Chain of Craters Road**, where you'll see old sections of the highway that were partially covered with lava.

During a fiery 1989 eruption, the former visitor center went up in smoke and a new one had to be built. By July of 1990, the lava flow had destroyed

If You Have Only One Day...

Kilauea's caldera alone is two and a half miles long, two miles wide, and 400 feet deep. If you only have a day or several hours to spend in the park, take the 1l-mile **Crater Rim Drive**, the park's main attraction. You'll see Halemaumau (the 300-foot-deep fire pit inside Kilauea), where Pele, the hot-tempered volcano goddess, is believed to live. Kamehameha II abolished the islands' restrictive religion in 1819. However, many Hawaiians continued to worship the old gods, even after American missionaries arrived the following year and began converting people to Christianity.

In 1824, Queen Kapiolani, who had readily converted, decided to prove to those who had not yet embraced Christianity that Pele did not exist. She stood at the rim of Halemaumau and ate some red *ohelo* berries, known to be sacred to the goddess, without offering any to Pele first. When the queen was not struck down on the spot, she told her people that this showed that there was no such thing as Pele, or any other Hawaiian god.

Yet some contemporary Hawaiians maintain that Pele continues her wandering, sometimes in the form of a wizened old woman, other times as a beautiful girl with flowing hair. From politicians and business people to educators and reporters, residents have told of sightings of a mysterious woman just before eruptions. Thus, many people take very seriously the warning not to remove any rocks or volcanic sand from Hawaii, lest they anger the powerful goddess.

most of the town of Kalapana and eventually swallowed up famed Kaimu Black Sand Beach. A trucking company volunteered to move the historic Star of the Sea Painted Church, whose walls and ceilings are covered with colorful religious murals done in 1931. Luckily, town residents were safely evacuated.

Along **Devastation Trail**, you'll see the serious damage hot volcanic ash did to a dense rain forest. The trail along the boardwalk (15 minutes each way) takes you through a vast expanse of what looks like charcoal dust strewn with sun-bleached branches that were stripped of their bark by bursts of volcanic debris. Ohia trees and other new vegetation have begun to sprout up from the ashes. The trail ends at the edge of **Kilauea Iki Crater**. If you wish to walk only one way, have your mate drive here to meet you. Then he or she can walk back and be met by you at the other end.

On the rim of Kilauea Crater, the **Thomas A. Jagger Museum**, Hawaii Volcanoes National Park (three miles past entrance), Tel. 967-7643; no admission charge; open daily from 8:30am-5pm, displays the highly accurate seismographs used to pick up volcanic activity, even far below the earth's surface. Be sure to bring a pocket of quarters for the telescopes (located just outside the museum), which offer close-up views of the vents and, at night, the stars.

Across the street from Volcano House (the current hotel) is **Volcano Art Center**, in a building that began life in 1877 as the park's lodge. The work of local artists sold here includes wood carvings, photographs, and paintings done on T-shirts, silk, and canvases. Within walking distance of Volcano House, you'll find **steam vents** and the yellow, sour smelling **sulphur banks**.

About four miles from the hotel, take a brief stroll through a bird-filled rain forest thick with cushiony mosses and huge *hapuu* ferns, their long stems tightly curled into spirals at the top. Then you'll come to gigantic **Thurston Lava Tube**—a real hit with kids—and into a dense, ginger-scented fern forest. This cool, damp walk-through tunnel was created when hot lava continued to pour through an outer shell of cooled lava. Watch out for puddles. A couple of miles west of the hotel, **Kipuka Puaulu** is a lush oasis that was spared by the surrounding lava.

Lava Tree State Park is an eerie reminder of the power of Pele. In a 1790 volcanic eruption, lava surged through an ohia forest, leaving mounds, swirls, and rolls of lava that sparkle like iridescent crystal. Once lush with green leaves, trees trapped and ensnarled by molten lava are now bone dry and ghostly white. Branches stick out as if they tried to free themselves. Be careful of cracks and indentations while walking.

Yes, It's Safe to Visit

With a highly sensitive warning system, volcanic eruptions and the path of lava flows can now be predicted. This means that sightseers are kept far away from any dangerous areas and homeowners are advised if they need to evacuate. Although a haze called vog (volcanic fog) hangs over the island during and after an eruption, this volcanic dust helps create some of the state's most dramatic sunsets (along the Kona-Kohala Coast).

HILO, east coast, thirty miles from Volcanoes National Park.

Thirty miles from Volcanoes National Park, Hilo is a quiet waterfront town with a handful of modest hotels. The verdant rolling hills, flamboyant blossoms, carpet-like lawns, and grassy plains tell you that rain is no stranger to this side of the island. However, most of it falls either at night or in brief showers during the day. If you're driving along the highway from Volcanoes National Park between June and December, you'll be treated to a fragrant explosion of white and yellow ginger growing wild. Although most of Hilo's shores are rocky and its skies are more often gray than blue, its proximity to east coast attractions makes spending some time here worthwhile.

Many of Hilo's easygoing residents are descendants of the Filipino, Japanese, and Chinese laborers who immigrated to work on the surrounding sugar plantations, once the foundation of Hilo's economy. In some of the cluttered, tin roof stores, merchants use abacuses instead of—or to double check—vintage cash registers. Sugar cane fields have been replaced by macadamia nut farms and the omnipresent flower nurseries that bloom with orchids, anthuriums, and ginger. Visitors are welcome to tour the grounds of some of the nurseries and to buy inspected plants, cuttings, or seeds to mail to the mainland.

The cultural heart of the Big Island, Hilo is the site of the annual Merrie Monarch Festival, held each March or April at the Edith Kanakaole Tennis Stadium. Plays, concerts, and other local performances take place at the University of Hawaii-Hilo campus. The college, which has an art gallery, also sponsors periodic lectures and demonstrations on kapa making, lauhala weaving, and other Hawaiian traditions.

Most of Hilo's hotels are clustered along Banyan Drive, where the old Chinese trees, dripping hairy shoots, were planted by notables such as Amelia Earhart and Cecil B. de Mille during the 1930s. With huge leaves, all kinds of plants grow up the water tank-sized trunks of the banyans. A small footbridge from Banyan Drive will take you across to tiny **Coconut Island** in Hilo Bay. Studded with palm trees, it's a popular setting for picnics and plain relaxation.

LILIUOKALANI GARDENS, Hilo Bay, off Banyan Drive, Hilo.

Japanese-style pagodas, bridges, and ponds grace this tranquil park. Spend some time in the shade of a flat-topped monkeypod tree. With its intense light and long shadows, the early morning is a particularly pleasant time to visit. In addition to a friendly lunch bunch, the park attracts local children who fish in the ponds with bamboo poles and neighborhood fishermen who catch opae (Hawaiian shrimp) with nets to use as live bait, as well as local wedding parties who come to have their pictures taken here. Although the park is named after Hawaii's last monarch, it was actually designed as a tribute to Hilo's first Japanese immigrants, who arrived as laborers in the sugar cane fields. A visit to Kyoto, Japan, inspired the white plantation managers to build this artfully landscaped Japanese garden.

The many-tiered stone lanterns, one of them 10 feet high, were given to the park by Japanese officials in the early 1900s. In Asia, they were first used to illuminate evening religious services, then later found their way into private homes. A symbol of wealth, they were carved from granite or marble. These sturdy treasures were about the only part of the pond and bridge-filled park that was not washed away in the 1946 tsunami. The park was rebuilt, only to be swept away again in the 1960 tidal wave. Still, some of the stone lanterns remained intact, if mud-covered. In 1968, to commemorate the 100th anniversary of the Japanese presence in Hawaii, the government of Japan donated a wooden torii gate, two stone lion gates, and 13 more lanterns to the park.

MOKUPAPAPA: DISCOVERY CENTER FOR HAWAII'S REMOTE CORAL REEFS, 308 Kamehameha Avenue, downtown Hilo, Tel. 808/933-8195; Open Tuesday to Saturday, 9am to 4pm. No admission charge.

At nearly 100,000 square miles, the Northwestern Hawaiian Islands Coral Reef Ecosystem Reserve is the largest conservation project in the United States. This discovery center allows visitors to appreciate the magic and majesty of the delicate habitats within this region. Targeted at children age 8 and older, the interactive exhibits are designed to get kids excited about conserving Hawaii's marine world, among the last and most impressive wild places on earth. Displays, including videos of virtual dives, offer lots of buttons to push. A 2500-gallon saltwater aquarium swarms with tropical fish and coral reefs in cartoon colors.

A highlight for most little people is the exhibit with robotic arms that demonstrates how to pick up rock samples from the ocean floor. In a state where the original tongue is rarely seen in anything but names, the descriptions of displays here are in both Hawaiian and English.

PACIFIC TSUNAMI MUSEUM, 130 Kamehameha Avenue (at Kalakaua Avenue), downtown Hilo; Tel. 935-0926; www.tsunami.org. Open Monday to Saturday, 9am to 4pm. Cost: $7 (adults), $2 (children age 6 to 17).

While the displays in this museum may be too disturbing for young children, older kids will love the drama of learning just how powerful nature can be. A digestible mix of scientific detail and personal testimonials bring the history of Hawaii's tsunamis (tidal waves) to life. It is comforting to note that today a highly sensitive warning system keeps residents safe from the devastation of the past.

Tsunami!

In Hilo, a thick wall of coconut palms stands across from the stores along **Hilo Bay**, which is bordered by parks and gardens. In 1946, an Alaskan earthquake set off a *tsunami* (tidal wave) that quickly moved toward Hawaii. Traveling across the open ocean at perhaps more than 600 miles an hour, the series of waves slowed down—but grew in height—as the ocean floor rose toward shore. Gathering steam, the first wave suddenly sucked the water out of Hilo Bay. Some people ran into the dry seabed, delightedly scooping up the fish that had been stranded. Then, in a flash, the monster wall of water hit the shore. One hundred and fifty-nine people lost their lives and 163 were hurt. The *tsunami* also caused more than 25 million dollars in property damage. Another tidal wave struck Hilo in 1960. Today however, a very sensitive scientific warning system has been devised and is used throughout the state.

LYMAN MUSEUM & MISSION HOUSE, 276 Haili Street, Hilo, Tel. 935-5021, www.lymanmuseum.org. Admission (including guided tours): $10 (adults), $3 (children age 6 to 17); open 9:30am to 4:30pm Monday to Saturday.

Built in 1839, restored Lyman House was once the home of Hilo's first Christian missionaries, the Reverend David and Sarah Lyman. The museum, which opened in 1973, displays antiques from the days of Hawaii's monarchy and items from the early 1900s. Some pieces date back to the time before Westerners arrived. In addition to Hawaiiana, exhibits also spotlight missionary life and the various ethnic groups that populated the islands. The gift shop makes for good browsing.

PANAEWA RAIN FOREST ZOO, just south of downtown Hilo, Tel. 959-7224; open daily from 9am-4pm; no admission charge.

Not many visitors know about this small zoo, where a Bengal tiger and two giant anteaters are the stars of the show. Kids love the tiger feedings, held each afternoon. Every Saturday from 1:30pm to 2:30pm, the petting zoo thrills the young crowd. Peacocks have the run of the grounds. You might also see the nene goose, Hawaii's rare state bird, as well as parrots and spider monkeys.

MAUNA LOA MACADAMIA NUT ORCHARD, Highway 11, between mile marker 5 and 6, five miles south of Hilo. Tel. 966-8618; Web site: www.maunaloa.com. Open daily 8:30am to 5pm.

Macadamia trees line one side of the long entry road and stately pines border the other. Take the free self-guided tour, watch the video of macadamia nut harvesting and processing from beginning to delicious end, then pick up a can or two of macadamia nuts to take home. Particularly in late September and October, you can also see factory workers in action. The nature trail is a good place for children to run and stretch their legs.

RAINBOW FALLS, Wainuenue Avenue and Rainbow Drive, Wailuku River State Park, just outside Hilo.

When the sun cooperates, a colorful shimmering arc is caught in the mist at this crashing waterfall. The best time to come is early in the morning.

Just up the road, near Hilo Hospital, you'll come to **Boiling Pots**. These churning pools and series of cascades are created by the water rushing into large pits in the lava of the riverbed. The park here is a scenic spot for a picnic.

HAWAII TROPICAL BOTANICAL GARDEN, Onomea Bay, off the Four-mile Scenic Drive, Hamakua Coast just north of Hilo, Tel. 964-5233; open 9am-4pm daily; admission $15 (adults), $5 (children age 6 to 16); or $35 for a family (mother, father, and any number of children), with 10% discount at gift shop.

The visitor center and museum are only part of the fun at this non-profit nature preserve. In a tropical rain forest, it is filled with birds, marine life, jungle vegetation, streams, and waterfalls. The bright heliconias, bromeliads, and ginger are particularly striking. The garden sprawls along a craggy ocean

Big Island Hula and Luau

If you're planning to vacation around Easter, consider attending the **Merrie Monarch Hula Festival**, Tel. 935-9168, the state's most important hula competition, which takes place over several evenings in Hilo. Both modern and traditional hula and chanting are performed. The program is named for Hawaii's last king, David Kalakaua, dubbed the Merrie Monarch for his love of the arts and of having an all-out good time. During his 1874 to 1891 reign, he was largely responsible for bringing back the hula and other Hawaiian traditions that had been banned by American missionaries. You'll need to order tickets months in advance.

The festival also includes free activities such as midday hula shows; a parade with floats and marching bands; a Hawaiian cultural fair with crafts, music, and food booths; and displays of Hawaiian quilts, artifacts, historic photographs, and antique furniture.

When this festival began during the 1960s, only women's halau (hula groups) competed. The event soared in popularity after a men's hula division was added in 1976. (Men, by the way, were the original dancers of hula in ancient Hawaii.) Today, it features both kahiko hula (ancient) and auana hula (modern) styles, accompanied by mele (ritual chants). Some halau (hula schools) spend years on the waiting list to participate.

While most groups are from the various Hawaiian islands, some come all the way from the mainland. Throughout the year, visitors on all islands should keep an eye out for any fundraising **luau** hosted by hula halau to cover the cost of the costumes, leis, food, and transportation they'll need to take part in the festival. These luau tend to be more down to earth than the more commercial affairs hosted by hotels and other tourist-oriented groups.

If you don't come across one of these truly local luau, the next best thing is an evening at **Uncle Billy's Hilo Bay Hotel**, Tel. 961-5818, where dinner at the restaurant most nights includes a hula show. For a much larger-scale affair at Hawaii's most Hawaiian-looking resort, make reservations (as many days in advance as possible) at **Kona Village Resort**, Tel. 325-5555, on the Kona Coast, just north of Kona International Airport. The plentiful food, elaborate performance of music and dance, and rustic surroundings sweep visitors into the past. Some topped with thatched roofs, Polynesian *hale* (cottages housing guest rooms) stand on stilts above black lava flows or at the edges of beaches or lagoons. This special event takes place on Friday nights. A highlight of the show is the hula performance by the children of hotel guests.

coast. The flat trails are easy walking; insect repellent and umbrellas are provided.

AKAKA FALLS STATE PARK, ten miles north of Hilo, near Honomu Village.

Here water plummets more than 400 feet over a volcanic cliff. If it's a choice between Rainbow Falls and these cascades, make this 66-acre park your destination. A long (sometimes steep) trail winds up and down through a thick rain forest, with towering bright yellow bamboo stalks, banyan trees, and flowers. Before you reach the main falls, you'll pass mini-cascades that flow under bridges. Benches are placed at strategic locations for rest stops.

LAUPAHOEHOE TRAIN MUSEUM, Highway 19, Laupahoehoe, northeast coast, mauka side, Tel. 808/962-6300. Open Monday to Friday 9am to 4:30pm, Saturday and Sunday, 10am to 2pm. Admission: $4.

Take a look around the displays celebrating the bygone days of the Hilo Railroad when the sugar industry dominated Hawaii, then board an old train engine for a quick ride. This choo-choo was rescued and revived after the railroad was destroyed in the 1946 tsunami (tidal wave).

Especially in the late-afternoon sun, nearby **Laupahoehoe Point** is a beautiful spot. Its name means "leaf of lava," and indeed this is a narrow lava peninsula that is lapped by the Pacific. Local families enjoy barbecues in the stone pits here. Picnic tables and shelters are also provided. At the edge of the water is a monument to the 20 schoolchildren and their teachers who were killed here by that 1946 tidal wave.

Beaches

Although the Big Island was the first part of the archipelago to be inhabited, it is the geological baby of the bunch. It's been around for only about a million years, as opposed to the first main island, Kauai, which was created more than five million years ago. Thus, the Big Island hasn't had time to develop as many beaches as its older siblings. However, it boasts enough sandy shores for any family vacation and beaches here come in a variety of colors: eggshell, pitch black, salt and pepper, and (believe it or not) even green (from olivine crystals).

Although most of the hotels and condominiums with moderate to inexpensive rates are clustered in Kailua-Kona and Keauhou (in the southwest), the majority of sandy beaches are along the 40-mile Kohala Coast (in the northwest), where resorts are plusher and far more spread out. Kohala is also the best area for whale watching, since the ocean is deeper closer to shore than elsewhere. However, while beaches in Kailua-Kona and Keauhou tend to be rocky, these shores are still wonderful for swimming and snorkeling.

In geographical order (starting in the north and moving counter-clockwise), here are my picks for the island's nicest beaches for families with children:

Keokea Beach Park, North Kohala.

The pleasant drive along a winding road takes you past private homes, a graveyard, and a bright green pasture. When you reach the park, you'll see red cliffs set off by verdant vegetation and electric blue water with frothy white surf. One covered picnic area is elevated, affording a panoramic view of the rocky cove. During the summer, the water is calm enough for snorkeling and fishing. Locals often gravitate here on weekends. In addition to a campsite at the water's edge, the park has restrooms and showers.

Mahukona, Northern Kohala.

Don't look for sand here. Instead, you'll have a good view of the island of Maui from the rocky shore and a grassy expanse that is great for picnics as well as for running around. We once met a man here who had been camping his way around the Big Island and said that this was one of his favorite spots. Scramble over the rocks and you'll find some good swimming, snorkeling, and scuba diving in these waters (during the summer only, though). Restrooms and fresh water are provided.

Lapakahi Park, Northern Kohala.

When the water is calm enough, the snorkeling is good here off **Lapakahi State Historical Park**, Tel. 882-6207, open 8am-4pm; trail closes at 3:30pm. This spot will satisfy families who want more than sun and sand. Dating back to the late 1300s, this fishing village was established on a rugged, isolated segment of the coast. As you enter, pick up a map at the guide station. Wear sturdy shoes to wander along the rocky, red dirt trails through the remains. The longer of the two marked routes is a mile. Identification signs and directions are carved into logs and rough tree trunks, so they blend into the natural landscape. You'll pass a palm-fringed beach scattered with black lava rocks and white chunks of coral. Most of the ruins are lava stone walls, dramatically set against pandanus trees, palms, and the choppy white surf.

You'll also come to a konane board (the Hawaiian answer to Chinese checkers), nets, ancient tools and utensils, canoe sheds and other thatched roof shelters. Although there are benches here and there, you'll find little shade, and the sun can be quite strong. Be sure to bring plenty of water.

Spencer Beach Park, Kohala.

Overlooked by nearby Puukohola and Mailekini, the remains of two of the island's most important *heiau* (temples), this white sand beach is just north of the Mauna Kea Resort. Since it is protected by reefs, its waters are good for swimming. Camping is permitted and there are restrooms, fresh water, a paved volleyball court (great for teens), tennis courts and a red-roofed pavilion for parties and picnics.

Kaunaoa Beach, Mauna Kea Beach Hotel, Kohala.

The presence of the Mauna Kea Beach Hotel does not detract from the beauty of this ivory curve. Like all of Hawaii's beaches, this one is open to the public. However, the hotel has its own beach facilities. During the winter when the surf is high, stick to the sand for sunbathing and other dry pursuits.

Hapuna Beach State Park, between Mauna Kea and Mauna Lani resorts, Kohala.

Some people consider this Hawaii's most gorgeous beach. Although its white sands certainly draw a fair number of swimmers, snorkelers, and sun worshipers, it is rarely crowded. During the winter, bodysurfing is big here. The water is calmest in the summer, when it is most popular with families with young children. Rocky outcroppings enclose the half-mile stretch. At the northern end, where it looks as if the beach stops, find the shallow hidden cove. Kids enjoy splashing in the tidal pools here.

Puako, Kohala.

Take a dirt road down to this white sand beach where kiawe trees provide shade. In the northern section, you'll find rewarding **snorkeling** around the tidal pools. A 20-minute walk leads to the petroglyphs (rock carvings) off Puako Road.

Anaehoomalu Bay, Kohala.

The nearby Hilton Waikoloa Village may have all the glitz, but the older, more sedate Waikoloa Beach hotel here has the best beach. Picturesque salt-and-pepper Anaehoomalu is bordered by coconut palms and a restored ancient fishpond that was once reserved for the alii (Hawaiian royalty). Commoners had to fish in the ocean. Bathers are welcome to rent equipment here for windsurfing, sailing, scuba diving, snorkeling, and surfing. Kids love spotting sea turtles among the other marine life. Restrooms, showers, and picnic tables make this a family favorite.

Magic Sands (a.k.a. Disappearing Sands or White Sands), Alii Drive, between Kailua-Kona and Keauhou.

Called by whatever name, the white sands of this beach come and go with the tides, often vanishing completely in the winter. Near petite St. Peter's Catholic Church, this is one of the island's best offshore snorkeling sites. Don't wear jewelry while swimming or leave it on your towel. Even when it appears calm, the water can be rough enough to separate you from your rings and chains. And waves can suddenly wash across your sunbathing spot. Local young men consider this a prime place for diving for tourists' jewelry. One resident told us he found a gold ring that brought him $5,000! When not in the water, stretch out on the smooth black lava rocks or play volleyball.

200 HAWAII WITH KIDS

Kahaluu Beach Park, Alii Drive, between Kailua-Kona and Keauhou.

The pavilion and rocky salt and pepper sands here draw many locals on weekends. The swimming and snorkeling (in only three to six foot depths) are fine during the summer (once you get past all the slippery rocks), but the surf is high in the winter. Our kids love looking for the green sea turtles, an endangered species, that are often spotted here, very close to shore, almost as much as they love getting shave ices from the oceanside vendors. Restrooms and fresh water are provided. This beach is next door to Keauhou Beach Resort.

Ke'ei, just south of Kealakekua Bay, Kona.

Beside the village of Ke'ei, this salt and pepper strand gives way to shallow waters. The swimming is fine here and the snorkeling is even better. After taking the road that leads to Kealakekua Bay, turn left at the bottom of the hill. Drive another half-mile, then make a right onto a road through a lava flow and continue another half-mile to the shore.

Teen Trek to Green Sand

Papakolea, or Green Sand Beach, in Kae Lae (South Point), is one of the most difficult beaches to get to on the island—and one of the most rewarding. If you're traveling with older teenagers, consider this exciting trek. The unusual color of the sand comes from the olivine crystals created in volcanic eruptions. After driving about an hour and 45 minutes from Kailua-Kona, you'll turn off the highway for 12 more miles to the boat yard where people leave their non-four-wheel-drive vehicles. Cupped at the bottom of steep cliffs, the petite cove is about three miles (an hour's hike) from here. A four-wheel-drive will get you closer, but you'll still have a good walk.

As you gaze down from above, the kelly green sand, the multi-hued blue of the Pacific, and the orange earth create a vibrant collage. However, your first thought will probably be, "How will we ever get down there?" Some people find the step-like section of rough, black lava boulders on the side or the smooth terraced rock at the back of the beach and climb down. Others slide down the nearly vertical sandy wall at the back. Whichever route you take, be careful! Even when there are others around, people often strip down to their skin in this beautiful, secluded spot.

Note that there is no shade, water, or restrooms here and the inviting-looking waters can be dangerous for swimming.

જ

Puuohonua O Honaunau National Historic Park, south of Kailua-Kona.

Climb into the bay at the Place of Refuge from the boat ramp near the park complex. Both the scuba diving and snorkeling are good here. Many people combine a swim with a visit to the exhibits at this fascinating historic park that once provided sanctuary for ancient Hawaiians who broke kapu (taboos).

Hookena, South Kona.

The sand is steel-colored at this beach that is good for swimming during most of the year. The two-mile road to the shore is steep and slim, so drive with caution. Near the end of this street, the gas lampposts have been standing since the early 1900s. When Mark Twain visited the island during the 1860s, more than 2,000 people lived in the settlement here. Today the village could hardly be more quiet. Picnic tables, fresh water, and restrooms are provided at the beach.

Punaluu Black Sand Beach, Ka'u, southeast coast.

These picturesque pitch-black shores are overlooked by condominiums with tennis courts and a golf course. In the adjacent beach park, you'll find picnic and camping facilities. Endangered (and thus protected) green sea turtles, which you'll see swimming off-shore, lay their eggs in the dark sand. Snorkeling is exciting here, that is, when the currents are not too strong for swimming (which is generally in the summer). Walk *mauka* (inland) and you'll come to fish ponds and remnants of a *heiau* (temple). At one end of the park, you'll find pavilions and campsites equipped with restrooms. Visitors enjoy browsing among the lei stands, where vendors also provide information about the turtles and sell knickknacks and snacks.

Kamoamoa Black Sand Beach, southeast coast.

One of the world's newest beaches, this half-mile black beauty was born during volcanic eruptions that took place between January and April of 1988.

Don't Offend the Gods!

Big Island residents often ask visitors not to offend Pele, the volcano goddess, by taking any rocks or sand—no matter how tempting the ebony and green sand are on this island. Many vacationers who scoff at this warning have nothing but bad luck after returning home with their stash. Post offices regularly receive rocks that have been mailed back by travelers desperate to undo their insult to the fiery-tempered goddess. Shells, on the other hand, make fine souvenirs, since they are part of the sea, not the land.

☙

Here you'll see a recent example of how flaming lava explodes into tiny fragments when it meets the cold water.

Onekahakaha Beach Park, Hilo.
About three miles from Hilo, this calm white sand beach draws many picnicking families. It's probably Hilo's most popular scenic swimming beach. The shallow depth (only one to four feet), sandy ocean bottom, and calm water protected by a breakwater make it a great spot for children. Lifeguards are on duty and facilities include pavilions, showers, and restrooms.

Richardson Beach Park, Hilo.
Packed with coral, sponges, reef fish, eels, and octopi and visited by dolphins, this marine reserve is an excellent snorkeling site. The shallow bay area at the center of the shoreline is where you'll see the most colorful underwater scenery. Lifeguards are on duty every day, and restrooms are on hand.

Reeds Bay Beach Park, Hilo.
Lapped by tranquil waters, this beach is known for its Ice Pond, fed by chilly freshwater springs. Restrooms and showers are on the premises.

Coconut Island, Hilo.
Overlooking Hilo Bay, with 13,796-foot Mauna Kea in the background, these palm-shaded shores are frequented by picnickers. A small bridge from Banyan Drive will take you to this isle.

Sports & Other Activities
Like everything else on the Big Island, sports come in a wide variety. Hawaii is renowned for its excellent deep-sea fishing, particularly for marlin and tuna, along the Kona Coast. Anglers come from all over to attend the annual **Hawaiian International Billfish Tournament** in the summer. Kailua-Kona is the mecca for water sports enthusiasts.

On land, hiking, camping, and biking are popular pastimes among both visitors and residents. In the fall, the island plays host to the **Ironman Triathlon World Championship**.

Biking
For rentals, try **Kona Bike Works**, Tel. 326-2453, which offers some bikes small enough for 12- or 13-year-olds, **Dave's Bikes**, Tel. 329-4522, or **Hawaiian Pedals**, Tel. 329-2294, all in Kailua-Kona.

Fishing
The Kona Coast is famous for its deep-sea fishing. While tournaments are held on the Big Island throughout the year, the July or August Hawaiian

International Billfish Tournament, centered in Kailua-Kona, is the star attraction. Some of the Big Island's best fishing spots are off the beach at Samuel M. Spencer Beach County Park; off Kailua Pier in Kailua-Kona; in Kealakekua Bay; offshore at Napoopoo Beach County Park; and at Punaluu Beach County Park.

Boats are available year-round for marlin fishing. Most depart from Honokohau Harbor, not far north of Kailua-Kona. For fishing charters, try **Blue Hawaii Sportfishing**, Tel. 895-2970, **Kona Charter Skippers Association**, Tel. 329-3600, or **Medusa Sport Fishing**, Tel. 329-1328, all based in Kailua-Kona.

Golf

Particularly along the Kona-Kohala Coast, where black lava flows provide a wonderful contrast with the green swards, this island has some of the state's most appealing courses, all with dramatic ocean or mountain views—sometimes both. Many consider the **Mauna Kea Beach Golf Course**, Tel. 882-7222, on the Kohala Coast, among the world's best. For hotel guests, greens fees are about $130 before 1pm and $110 afterwards; for non-guests, $195 before 1pm and $175 afterwards. The **Hapuna Golf Course**, also on the Mauna Kea Resort, was noted by the US Golf Association for being particularly environmentally sensitive. Here greens fees run about $110 before 1pm and $90 afterwards for guests, and $145 before 1pm and $125 afterwards for non-guests. With greens fees of about $185, the 18-hole Jack Nicklaus course at the **Hualalai Golf Club**, Tel. 325-8000, is open only to guests of the Four Seasons hotel, on the Kohala Coast. At the Francis I'i Brown Golf Course at the **Mauna Lani Resort**, Tel. 885-6655, also in Kohala, greens fees run about $120 before 3pm and $75 afterwards for Mauna Lani guests, and $185 before 3pm and $75 afterwards for non-guests.

Waikoloa sports three beautiful courses. The first two were designed by Robert Trent Jones, Jr.: the **Waikoloa Village Golf Course**, Tel. 883-9621, on the mauka (mountain) side of the road ($100 before 1pm and $55 afterwards), and the **Waikoloa Beach Golf Course**, Tel. 886-6060 ($125 before 2pm and $75 afterwards for resort guests, or $175 before 2pm and $75 afterwards for non-guests), adjoining the Hilton Waikoloa Village and the Waikoloa Beach hotels. The third course, the **King's Course**, Tel. 886-7888 ($125 before 2pm and $75 afterwards for resort guests, or $175 before 2pm and $75 afterwards for non-guests)), is also at the Hilton Waikoloa Village.

In the Keauhou-Kona area, the **Kona Country Club**, Tel. 322-2595, offers an ocean course ($135 before noon or $100 afterwards) and a mountain course ($115 before noon or $85 afterwards). It comes as a surprise to many visitors that there is even a course in Hawaii Volcanoes National Park: **Volcano Golf and Country Club**, Tel. 967-7332 ($63). In Punaluu, known for its black sand beach, you'll find the **Sea Mountain Golf Club**, Tel. 928-6222 ($50), on the grounds of a condominium development.

Helicopter Tours

A wonderful way to experience the Big Island, helicopter tours are best for kids age 10 and up. Seats are expensive, and except for the 15 minutes spent hovering above volcanoes, younger children tend to be bored by all the pretty scenery, no matter how spectacular it is to adults. Flying above Kilauea (the most active of Hawaii's two active volcanoes), in Hawaii Volcanoes National Park, you can often hear the bubbling, crackling, and hissing, and see red hot fountains of lava and ribbons of the fiery molten rock flowing from the crater. Actually, with its steaming pits, lunar terrain, and pockets of verdant rainforest, this park is amazing even when the volcanoes are quiet.

All helicopter companies offer variations on the following routes: Kilauea or Mauna Loa (the island's second active volcano); the Kona-Kohala coastline, the town of Kamuela/Waimea, Parker Ranch, the Hamakua Coast, Waipio and Waimanu Valleys, black sand beaches, and remote white-sand coves. In the north, you might hover near sheer cliffs pocked with an ancient burial cave that still contains skulls and bones. Some flights combine the Kona Coast with a whirl above Puuhonua O Honaunau (Place of Refuge), Captain Cook Monument and Kealakekua Bay, and Hawaii Volcanoes National Park.

The Mom and Pop owners of **Sunshine Helicopters**, Tel. 808/882-1223 or 800/469-3000, www.sunshinehelicopters.com, have more than 30 years of aviation experience and their company has been around for more than two decades. Sunshine has the island's best safety record. Perhaps this is because it is a member of TOPS (Tour Operators Program of Safety), which goes above and beyond FAA standards for tour helicopters, including requirements for the experience of both pilots and ground crew as well as for the maintenance of the helicopters. Rates range from about $200 per person for a 50-minute flight to $400 for an hour and 45 minutes. Cameras are on board and passengers are invited to purchase copies of the video of the flight afterwards ($20).

Hiking

Trails lead through virgin valleys, lava fields, and dense wilderness. Routes range from the rugged to the relaxing. Many footpaths cut through **Hawaii Volcanoes National Park**. Since lava can be thin, brittle, and wickedly sharp in places, be sure to stick to marked trails and always wear sturdy closed shoes. Trail maps and other information are available at the Hawaii Volcanoes Visitor Center.

We love hiking in green **Waipio Valley**, on the northeast coast, especially because the only way to get to the gorgeous black sand beach there is on foot (since no commercial traffic is allowed on the beach). While the hike down into the valley is less than a mile, the road back up is very steep and particularly taxing on hot days. With its colorful botanical garden, **Manuka State Park**, in south Kona, is good for more easygoing hiking.

Horseback Riding

Kids love pretending to be cowboys as they ride through Parker Ranch, in Waimea/Kamuela. You'll see where the first paniolos (Hawaiian cowboys) settled in the 1800s and watch 5,000 head of cattle being herded. Cinder cones seem to have fallen out of the sky onto the vast, flat land backed by distant hills in endless shades of green. Rainbows are common in this misty region. Contact **Cowboys of Hawaii,** Tel. 885-5006, $80 per person (age 7 and older), next to the Parker Ranch Visitor Center.

Kohala Na'alapa Trail Rides, Tel. 889-0022 (rates begin at $55 for the 90-minute ride and $75 for the 2+ hour ride) leads scenic trail rides in the Kohala Mountains. You'll ride through a working cattle and sheep ranch, with views of rolling hills, the coast, and, on a good day, the island of Maui. Children must be at least eight years old.

Paniolo Riding Adventures, Tel. 889-5354, offers private guided rides for families ($115 per person for 2+ hours) that are particularly good for younger children (who must be at least four feet tall). As they ride through the open range on a working cattle ranch in Kamuela/Waimea, kids (and their adults) receive lots of personal attention and riding instruction.

An unforgettable Big Island experience is seeing remote Waipio Valley with **Waipi'o Na'alapa Trail Rides**, Tel. 775-0419; ($75; children must be at least 8 years old). Don't forget your camera. During the scenic ride, your guide will tell you all about the history, legends, facts, and folklore of the Big Island in general and the valley in particular. In a van, you'll descend the steep, winding dirt road and pass through the river to reach the valley floor where your horse will be waiting for you.

You'll clippity-clop through waist-deep irrigation canals and past rushing streams. Waterfalls tumble hundreds of feet from mountainsides. Since the majority of the (few) people who live in the valley are taro farmers, you'll see plenty of plots where this root (used to make poi) is grown. Your guide will point out all kinds of vegetation, including jabon trees, which bear a fruit that's a cross between an orange and a grapefruit. Be sure to have a taste. You might also spot wild horses and rare birds such as the koloa. You'll spend two hours on horseback, plus a half hour going in and out of the valley.

Scuba Diving & Snuba

Underwater exploration is concentrated along the Kona Coast. Try **Big Island Divers**, in Kailua-Kona, Tel. 329-6068, or **Kona Coast Divers**, about three miles north, Tel. 329-8802 or 800/KOA-DIVE. Certification courses start at about $350 per person. For a one-day introductory course, plan to spend about $150, including two dives. Children must be at least ten years old.

If you and your children are not quite bold enough (or old enough) to try scuba diving, consider snuba, a safe and easy shallow-water alternative. Contact **Snuba Big Island, Inc.,** Tel. 326-7446, to explore the underworld while your source of air floats above you, connected to you by a long tube. You'll have a choice between a shore dive (about 45 minutes underwater during the 90-minute adventure; $70 from age 8 up or $60 for ages 5 to 7) and a dive from a boat (about 45 minutes underwater during the 3-hour cruise; $110 from age 8 up or $100 for ages 5 to 7). This outfit is based at the Kona Beach Hotel in Kailua-Kona.

Snorkeling

For a fun-filled, family-friendly snorkeling trip on a 60-foot two-level catamaran that carries 106 passengers, contact **Fair Wind**, Tel.322-2788. You'll visit the crystal waters near the Captain Cook Monument at Kealakekua Bay, where Cook (who "discovered" Hawaii for Europe) was killed in 1779. If you're as lucky as we were, a playful school of porpoises will swim along as you sail. Winter vacationers are sometimes treated to the sight of whales. The most popular excursion is the 4+-hour morning trip, including breakfast, lunch, and use of snorkel gear, available in children's sizes, as well as water toys ($90 for adults, $55 for children under 12).

For those who'd rather steer clear of the crowds, Fair Wind also offers Kealakekua snorkeling trips on a 28-foot hard-bottom inflatable raft that holds just 14 people ($77 for adults or $70 for kids aged 6 to 12 on this four-hour trip that includes snacks and beverages). Also with rafts that zip in and out of sea caves, **Captain Zodiac Raft Expeditions**, Tel. 329-3199, offers a similar Kealakekua Bay excursion ($85 for adults, $70 for children aged 5 to 12). These bouncy inflatables carry sixteen folks max, and children must be at least five years old.

You don't need to board a boat for some of the best views of the underworld. The Kona-Kohala Coast is also great for snorkeling right off shore. **Kapaa Beach Park** in northern Kohala is one of the best places for swimming among multi-colored coral and other marine life. Between Kailua-Kona and Keauhou, the waters of **Magic Sands Beach** (a.k.a. White Sands or Disappearing Sands), which vanishes in the winter, are always teeming with many different kinds of tropical fish. At nearby **Kahaluu Beach Park**, along with snorkeling gear, families can rent all kinds of flotation devices, including boogie boards with built-in child-size viewing windows, as well as beach chairs and umbrellas.

Surfing

At Kahaluu Beach Park, between Kailua-Kona and Keauhou, surfing lessons are available from 8am to 5pm. To make a reservation for a group lesson (maximum of four people) or a one-on-one, stop by at least a day a head

Old-Style Canoes

For an exhilarating trip to the past, consider a 2 + hour snorkeling and/or fishing sail on a traditional **double-hulled canoe** carved from trunks of koa, Hawaii's largest native trees. This spacious canoe carries four to six passengers. As you ride the waves, the crew tells you all about the navigational skills that Polynesians once used to travel throughout the Pacific. You'll get a glimpse of the Kohala Coast the way ancient Hawaiians saw it—well, except for those hotels and other buildings along the shore. Contact the Fairmont Orchid hotel in the Mauna Lani resort, Tel. 885-2000, to make a reservation for one of these sails, which will run you about $100 per person.

of time, then, on the day of the lesson, call to confirm, since lessons may be cancelled depending on surf conditions (even on days that appear calm to the uninitiated).

Tennis

On the Big Island, you may choose among scores of courts, especially along the Kona-Kohala Coast. However, while many of the larger hotels have tennis courts, some allow only their guests to use them. Open to the public, courts at **Kailua Playground** are convenient to the Kailua-Kona area. On the Kohala Coast, the **Waikoloa Beach Marriott,** Tel. 808/896-4576, Web site: www.cindyhill.usptapro.com, offers both group and individual keiki lessons. Courts are also open to non-resort guests at the **Royal Kona Resort, Waikoloa Village**, **King Kamehameha's Kona Beach,** and **Sea Mountain Resort**.

In Hilo, you can play at **Hilo Tennis Stadium, Waiakea Racket Club**, or **Lincoln Park**.

Volleyball

Especially among teenagers, beach volleyball is all the rage in the oceanfront pit by the Royal Kona Resort on Alii Drive in Kailua-Kona.

Whale Watching

Especially between December and April, you can catch glimpses of the massive humpback whales that migrate to Hawaii from cooler climes. Throughout the year, other whales—pilot, false killer, and melon-headed among them—sometimes visit these waters as well. Some tour companies take sightseers on jeep excursions to elevated vantage points while others take people out on the sea. A good pair of binoculars comes in handy. You can book ocean or land whale watching tours through your hotel activity desk, or try **Fair Wind**, Tel. 322-2788.

Working Out & Spas

Most of the larger resorts, particularly along the Kohala Coast, have extensive exercise facilities and health spas, such as **Fairmont Orchid Hawaii, Mauna Lani Resort, Hilton Waikoloa Village, Mauna Kea Beach Hotel, Hapuna Beach Prince Hotel, Kona Village,** and **Four Seasons Resort Hualalai**. If you're looking for programs and facilities especially for children age 3 to 15, try the **Keiki Gym and Family Fitness Center**, Tel. 329-9600, in the heart of Kailua-Kona and within a 10-minute drive of most Kailua-Kona accommodations.

I'm Hungry!

Whether upscale or not, in hotels or on the street, many Big Island restaurants cater to families with kids. From keiki menus and table toys to free meals for those under age five, they roll out the welcome mat. However, for those evenings when you crave adults-only nights out, you'll also have plenty of choices. See the restaurants I've marked "Romantic Escapes," below. Here are some of our favorite dining spots, with and without children in tow.

Kohala

THE BATIK, Mauna Kea Beach Hotel, Mauna Kea Beach Drive, Tel. 882-5810. Reservations required. Dinner only. Nights open vary. Entrees: $38 to $50. *Romantic Escape.*

Whether you have a taste for curry, French-Mediterranean cuisine, or Indonesian food, this waterfront restaurant serves delicious creations amid elegant surroundings. Enclosed in glass, this split-level dining room is the culinary showpiece of the hotel and many of its staff members have worked here for more than a decade. Seafood and meat come both delicately and pungently flavored with lively ingredients such as lemongrass, coconut, mango, and macadamia nuts.

DONATONI'S, Hilton Waikoloa Village, Waikoloa Resort. Tel. 886-1234. Reservations recommended. Dinner only. Entrees: $29 to $42.

In addition to pasta and gourmet pizza, children enjoy the chicken breast and grilled mahi mahi. Vacationers, residents, and food critics alike rave about the Northern Italian cuisine here. The imaginative desserts bring any meal to a sweet end. Reserve early if you'd like a table by the window or on the large lanai. The sunsets are fabulous from here and you can watch the boats along the canal.

ROY'S WAIKOLOA BAR & GRILL, The King's Shops, 250 Waikoloa Beach Drive, Waikoloa Beach Resort. Tel. 886-4321. Reservations recommended. Dinner entrees: $20 to $36.

With a lanai providing a tranquil panoramic view of Waikoloa's Beach Golf Course, Mauna Kea, and the Kohala mountain range, Roy's offers an appealing setting for enjoying the famed Hawaiian regional cuisine of renowned chef and restaurateur Roy Yamaguchi. Friendly, knowledgeable waiters assist diners in selecting the perfect pairing of food and wine. The use of fresh, local ingredients, including seafood, fruit, and vegetables, means that the menu changes daily, depending on what is available.

At lunch, you might consider the Thai fish satay salad with sweet chili lemongrass vinaigrette, the Waimea tomato and smoked bacon sandwich, the teriyaki chicken, or the spicy fish burrito. For dinner, you might find cayenne crusted ono (the local fish) with cumin black beans and sweet shallot honey sauce, mahimahi with Tahitian vanilla shrimp and gingered sweet potato, or rack of lamb glazed with caramel rum. Roasted garlic mashed potatoes might be served with organic tomato relish. For children, choices include cheese quesadillas and pasta. While kids might go for the ice cream sundaes for dessert, adults prefer the chocolate soufflé and the homemade sorbet.

Big Island Treats

Visitors who can't live without that first cup of coffee will want to take home a bag or two of those famous Kona beans. Some of the fancier hotels stock guest rooms with fresh Kona coffee beans, grinders, and coffee makers. Another Big Island specialty is macadamia nuts, sold all over the island. Among the many sweet treats at the **Kailua Candy Company** are macadamia nuts in a variety of incarnations. At the **Tex Drive Inn** restaurant in Honokaa, few can limit their consumption of hot, sweet *malasadas* (Portuguese balls of fried dough) to only one. Also best when warm, **Aunty Peaches' Onolicious Poi Balls** are delicious sweet and chewy snacks sold at roadside stands. You might be able to pick up a stick of three or a box of these treats in front of Wal-Mart in Kona or by the Ace Hardware store in Kamuela/Waimea. And by the way, just in case you've tased the soupy poi served at luaus and decided you don't like it, these fried snacks taste nothing like it.

For a cool sweet, try the **Shave Ice Company** on Alii Drive and Palani Street in Kailua-Kona. You'll find some of the island's best ice cream at **Hilo Homemade Ice Cream**, next to Tropical Gardens and Gallery in Hilo. You might sample flavors such as ginger, lilikoi (passion fruit), mud pie, rocky road, and green tea. Particularly popular among Asians, **mochi ice cream**, sold in some supermarkets, is a dough made of rice flour and sugar that is filled with ice cream, sort of like a dumpling. Uncooked and served frozen, it is as much a part of many island New Year's celebrations as apple pie is to a mainland Thanksgiving.

☙

MERRIMAN'S MARKET CAFÉ, King's Shops, Waikoloa, Tel. 886-1700, open 11am to 9:30pm. Dinner entrees: $14 to $30. Reservations recommended.

While this indoor-outdoor restaurant featuring local, organic produce is a more casual version of its sister restaurant in Waimea, the food is just a wonderful. Outside, wrought iron tables with umbrellas give the place a very European feel. The sautéed opakapaka with garlic and mushrooms has quickly made a name for itself. Old favorites come with unexpected twists: For instance, French fries, with the skin on, are dipped in homemade ketchup with olive oil and herbs, broccoli is served spicy and slightly crunchy, and coffee, Merriman's own house blend, is made in a French press. The word "spectacular" has been used by more than a few diners to describe the lilikoi (passionfruit) cheesecake.

CAFE PESTO, Kawaihae Center. Tel. 882-1071. Open daily, Sunday-Thursday 11am - 9pm, Friday and Saturday until 10pm. Dinner entrees: $14 to $30.

With dishes on the kids' menu with names such as "Shrek's Caesar," "Potter's Pizza," and "Tigger's Turkey," Café Pesto is a favorite among young children as well as their parents. The portions of pasta and designer pizza (in an array of varieties, from Kalua pork and pineapple to shrimp and garlic) are generous here. For pasta, try the crab primavera with artichokes, roasted garlic, peppers, wild mushrooms and pesto; or the Cajun shrimp with sausage. Maybe you'll decide to begin with soup or salad and end with cornbread shortcake with blueberry topping or pecan pie. The artwork on the walls of this attractively decorated cafe is for sale.

KAWAIHAE HARBOR GRILL & SEAFOOD BAR, Kawaihae Harbor, Tel. 882-1368. Lunch, dinner, and pupus (extensive appetizers). Dinner entrees: $9 to $28.

Housed in what was built in the 1850s as a store and hotel, this casual family-friendly restaurant feels like authentic Hawaiiana. Kids enjoy coloring the keiki menu, which offers fish or chicken and chips, grilled cheese and fries, hot dogs, and spaghetti. Adults gravitate toward the wide selection of pupus (crab cakes, steamed artichoke, Cajun seared ahi sashimi, papaya stuffed with chicken, for instance), steak, ribs, red Thai seafood curry, and sautéed fresh fish, along with the salads, soups, and sandwiches. A winner for dessert is the homemade Kona coffee crème brulee.

At the Seafood Bar upstairs, the more elegant décor is highlighted by bamboo chairs and tropical fabrics. Live music entertains patrons on Sundays. You can easily make a meal of the wide variety of pupus. Try the seafood pizza, shrimp spring roll, mushrooms stuffed with smoked marlin, the Thai beef salad, or the tofu spinach salad.

BAMBOO RESTAURANT AND GALLERY, Akoni Pule Highway, downtown Hawi. Tel. 889-5555. Closed Mondays. Dinner entrees: $9 to $25.

Some folks come here just for the lilikoi (passion fruit) margaritas, but I also love the Asian-influenced fresh fish and other seafood. The potstickers, slightly sweet with peanuts, are delicious, and the grilled shrimp is nicely seasoned. Shrimp Alfredo is another popular choice. Children enjoy the butter noodles, teriyaki chicken, and Bamboo burgers. Both lunch and dinner are served, as well as Sunday brunch. Live music entertains guests on Friday and Saturday nights.

MATTHEW'S PLACE, Kohala Town Center, Kapaau. Tel. 889-5500. Open 10am to 7pm, closed Sundays. Entrees: $6 to $14.

This tiny, mainly take-out restaurant is a good place to stop for local favorites such as plate lunches and Italian treats from pasta to pizza. Each pizza is freshly made, so expect to wait about 30 minutes after ordering one.

Kamuela/Waimea

DANIEL THIEBAUT, 65-1259 Kawaihae Road. Tel. 887-2200. Dinner entrees: $18 to $35. Reservations required. *Romantic Escape.*

In a lovingly restored wooden building that was born as a general store for paniolo (cowboys) in 1900, this exceptional restaurant serves French-Asian food. During the years before it closed in 1995, this building served as a snackbar, a gas station, a bakery, and a dress shop, in addition to housing the family that ran the original general store. Today each of the various dining rooms offers a different mood and décor.

Consider starting with a vegetable roll, a bowl of lobster bisque flavored with brandy, or a spicy chicken wonton with ginger soy dip. The lamb chop Hunan style is prepared with goat cheese and thyme. Mini-pizzas, stir-fried chicken, and local fish are on the children's menu. Among the tempting vegetarian choices, you might find a crispy avocado spring roll with smoked tomato coulis and bean relish, or tofu crusted with macadamia nuts. The wine list is excellent here. For dessert, you might find macadamia nut and chocolate bread pudding with vanilla sauce or coconut ice cream over mango flambe. Even going to the women's room, with its original clawfoot bathtub, is an experience here.

MERRIMAN'S, 65-1227 Opelo Road, Opelo Plaza II (Route 19 and Opelo Road). Tel. 885-6822. Reservations suggested; at busy times of year, you might have to call a day in advance. Dinner entrees: $15 to $28. *Romantic Escape.*

Peter Merriman opened this dining spot with his wife in 1988, after drawing raves at the Mauna Lani Resort's Gallery restaurant (where he became executive chef when he was only 28). Showcasing Hawaii regional cuisine, he has joined forces with farmers so that his produce can be as exotic and fresh as possible. Entrees even come garnished with edible flower blossoms.

You might begin your meal with chicken satay or poisson cru (a Tahitian dish made with raw fish marinated in coconut milk, lime, and onions). Entrees might be grilled chicken with mango glaze or sesame-crusted fresh local fish with lilikoi sauce. The wok-charred ahi, Merriman's signature dish, is delicious (singed around the edges, and raw in the center, it resembles a slice of roast beef). You can't miss with the coconut creme brulee for dessert.

Helpful waiters take the time to explain the often-extensive ingredients and elaborate preparation of each dish. Tall potted plants, floral designs on the walls, and local artwork (for sale) make this a colorful, tropical setting.

Honokaa

PANIOLO PLANTATION INN, Mamane Street. Tel. 775-9298. Dinner entrees: $7 to $20.

Since 1908, this building has housed a restaurant and hotel. If you have a taste for some local flavor, this is the place. You might stumble upon a lively discussion about the ballgame on the large screen TV in the bar. Huge picture windows overlook corrugated tin roofs, trees, and the ocean. Nineteen-fifties prints of tropical flowers decorate the walls. Dinner might be a chicken cutlet or shredded lobster tail mixed with onions and celery and served in the shell. A children's menu is available for the young crowd. On weekends, there's musical entertainment.

TEX DRIVE INN, Highway 19. Tel. 775-0598. Dinner entrees: $6 to $8.

Stop at this casual hillside restaurant for breakfast, lunch, or dinner while you're exploring the scenic surroundings. Famous for its malasadas (Portuguese hole-less donuts) and plate lunches, Tex Drive Inn serves up delicious home-style food. Locals flock here for the chicken katsu (boneless, deep-fried), ahi (tuna) burgers, curry stew, Portuguese bean soup, and vegetable-chicken wraps. Salads, hamburgers, and saimin are also on the menu. Kids often order the chicken nuggets and French fries. While you're waiting for your food, peer through the picture window into the bakery to watch malasadas being made. Eat inside or outside with a view of a sliver of ocean beyond the trees. Browse around the adjacent boutique, which sells everything from dried tropical fruit, dry roasted macadamia nuts, and chocolate covered roasted coffee beans to handmade soap, koa bracelets, and Zen pocket stones.

Kailua-Kona Area, Keauhou, & South Kona

PAHU I'A, Four Seasons Resort Hualalai, 100 Ka'upulehu Drive, near Kona airport. Tel. 325-8000. Breakfast and dinner only. Reservations required. Dinner entrees: $32 to $48. *Romantic Escape.*

The fine-dining restaurant of what is arguably Hawaii's best resort for families (if you can afford it), Pahu i'a showcases the island's finest produce from local fishermen and farmers. For instance, ingredients in these scrump-tious contemporary Pacific dishes might include taro from Waipio Valley, corn from Waimea, or goat cheese from Puna. The hearts of palm salad might come with candied macadamia nuts and Asian pear slices. Shiitake mushrooms might accompany the steamed snapper. A strolling musician adds a romantic touch while yellow tangs and pink wrasses dart around the giant aquarium and diners absorb the dramatic sunsets against the sand and surf.

BEACH TREE BAR & GRILL, Four Seasons Resort Hualalai, 100 Ka'upulehu Drive, near Kona airport. Tel. 325-8000. Reservations recommended. Dinner entrees: $30 to $37.

Bring young children to this casual oceanside restaurant and they might be given a basket of toys to capture their attention while awaiting their pizza or chicken strips. At lunch, adults enjoy the fish and sandwiches, while the evening meal might bring shrimp marinated in citrus vodka and green-olive vinaigrette among other treats in an extensive buffet. As you watch the sun set from this al fresco spot, you might be entertained by a slack-key guitar player or a hula dancer.

KONA INN RESTAURANT, 75-5744 Alii Drive, Kailua-Kona. Tel. 329-4455. Dinner entrees: $20 to $40.

Open to the ocean breezes, this waterfront restaurant is decked out in gorgeous, carved koa wood (walls, partitions, tables, and ceilings). Peacock chairs, oriental rugs, and slow-moving ceiling fans further enhance the atmosphere. Small birds alight on the tops of chairs and the edges of tables. The perky young waitresses are happy to make suggestions about their many local fish dishes. For lunch, try the sauteed calamari sandwich or the seafood cobb salad. The Lemongrass Curry Soup is also popular. Kona Inn serves a delicious version of mud pie. Sunset watching is a popular activity here.

BUBBA GUMP SHRIMP CO., 75-5776 Alii Drive, Kailua-Kona. Tel. 331-8442. Open for breakfast, lunch, and dinner. Dinner entrees: $14 to $17.

Among the favorite family dining spots in Kailua-Kona, this amusing oceanfront restaurant is packed with "Forest Gump" paraphernalia and waiters periodically quiz diners on trivia from the movie. Drink menus come on ping pong paddles. For the best views, try to be seated on the verandah. While shrimp dishes are certainly the most popular, the kitchen also does a decent job with steak, ribs, chicken, and burgers. Save room for the key lime or mud pie for dessert.

MICHAELANGELO'S ITALIAN SEAFOOD RESTAURANT AND DANCE CLUB, Waterfront Row, 75-5770 Alii Drive #2, Kailua-Kona. Tel. 329-4436. Reservations recommended. Dinner entrees: $11 to $14.

If you like your Italian food with an ocean view, book a table here. From pizza and pasta to seafood and steak, the menu is extensive. Homestyle favorites include chicken cacciatore, spaghetti & meatballs, and lasagne. Among the vegetarian pastas, you might find linguini with sun-dried tomato pesto or manicotti with parmesan and mozzarella. Children like the pasta, cheese sticks, and pizza. Seafood lovers should consider the smoked salmon with a creamy mushroom and tomato sauce over fetuccine or the macadamia nut sea scallops.

BIANELLI'S GOURMET PIZZA & PASTA, 75-5653 Olioli St., Kailua-Kona. Tel. 329-7062. Open for lunch and dinner Monday to Friday; Saturday and Sunday, dinner only. Dinner entrees: $10 to $22. Reservations recommended.

Bianelli's tasty Italian cuisine features freshly made pasta, salads crafted from locally-grown organic lettuce and homemade dressings, and freshly baked breadsticks. With more than a dozen selections of toppings, pizzas come Chicago style (deep dish) and New York style (hand-tossed) in different sizes to match different size appetites. Children may also choose among smaller portions of pizza, grilled cheese, pasta, and chicken nuggets. A wide array of sandwiches is on the menu as well. If you manage to save room, try the rich chocolate cake, the macadamia nut pie, or the cheesecake—the lilikoi (passionfruit) and raspberry are delicious.

SAM CHOY'S RESTAURANT, 73-5576 Kauhola Street, Kaloko Light Industrial Park, just north of Kailua-Kona. Tel. 326-1545. Open daily for breakfast and lunch only. Lunch entrees: $8 to $13.

Located in a complex of warehouses between the airport and the harbor, this restaurant is off the beaten path. But Sam Choy's is very popular among both visitors and residents, in part because of the generous portions of delicious regional food. For breakfast, you might have Sam's Ultimate Stew Omelet (filled with beef stew), fried rice and eggs, banana hotcakes, or a Belgian waffle sandwich. Fried poke (fish flash-cooked on the outside), available only here, is a lunch favorite. You might also like the Chinese duck with honey sauce or the macadamia nut chicken with mahi-mahi. For dessert, the poha berry white pineapple ice cream is great.

BIG ISLAND GRILL, 75-5702 Kuakini Hwy, 75-5702 Kuakini Highway, Kailua-Kona. Tel. 326-1153. Open for breakfast, lunch, and dinner, Monday through Saturday. Dinner entrees: $7 to $19.

Here everything comes in B.I.G. portions. Very popular among residents, this restaurant is often so busy that you might wait as long as 45 minutes for your food, but most people agree that it's worth the wait (and the weight!). For instance, the outstanding B.I.G. Saimin comes with two very large tempura fish, and you could make a meal out of a single dessert, such as the delicious guava chiffon cake, which you scoop from a halved guava. The Caesar salad with grilled shrimp is another good choice, along with the orange-glazed roast duck with fresh veggies, the broiled fish sandwich, and the fried chicken.

L & L DRIVE-INN, Lanihau Center, 75-5595, Palani Road, Kailua-Kona. Tel. 331-2401. Entrees: $5 to $8.

Ask a resident to direct you to the best plate lunch in Hawaii, and chances are you'll end up here. While your children are focused on the burgers and hot dogs, you can consider the shrimp curry, fried mahi-mahi, BBQ chicken, or teriyaki pork chops. The sweet and sour spareribs are also popular, along with the stir-fried garlic shrimp, chili, and saimin. This is a good place to stretch your dollars.

KEEI CAFÉ, Highway 11, just south of Kainaliu, South Kona. Tel. 322-9992. Dinner only. Entrees: $12 to $25. No credit cards. No dinner on Mondays. No lunch on Saturdays. Closed Sundays. Reservations recommended. *Romantic Escape.*

Locals share this secret with a few lucky visitors. A homey restaurant run by a husband and wife team, Keei Café weaves Asian, European, and South American themes throughout the artfully prepared dishes. Sample the ahi (tuna) with red Thai curry or the Brazilian seafood chowder. Sip a local beer from Kona Brewing Company.

QUINN'S, 75-5655A Palani Road, Kailua-Kona. Tel. 329-3822. Dinner entrees average $23.

This restaurant is just across the street from the Hotel King Kamehameha parking lot. After walking through the bar (where a few people will probably be watching TV), guests come to the garden lanai where they dine al fresco with greenery spilling over rough lava rock walls. The teriyaki chicken and the seafood brochette are popular, as well as the pepper steak with brandy. Quinn's does a landslide business in fish and chips. Burgers and sandwiches are also served (such as the vegetarian number with avocado, sprouts, tomato and onions). The children's menu includes grilled cheese, fish, and pasta.

HUGGO'S, 75-5828 Kahakai, Kailua-Kona. Tel. 329-1493. Entrees: $25 to $30.

A popular local hangout for sunset watching and after-dinner drinks, Huggo's looks out onto the rocky shore. At night, the crashing waves are illuminated and flaming torches hang off the oceanside balcony. The water is clear enough to see fish, sea turtles, and manta rays—and (after 9:30 every night when waiters throw them scraps) an impressive tangle of slithering eels! Kids love the show! Live music is played in the bar. Steak and seafood are the main attractions at this busy dining spot. Teriyaki steak marinated in beer has been on the menu since Huggo's opened in 1969. Also consider the Cajun seared ahi or the sizzling rock shrimp. Dessert here can be a meal in itself. The Hualalai Pie—Kona coffee ice cream, chocolate sauce, and whipped cream—is you've-got-to-be-kidding huge! A single slice could easily feed a hungry family of four.

OCEAN VIEW INN, Alii Drive, Kailua-Kona. Tel. 329-9998. Open for breakfast, lunch, and dinner, except Mondays. Entrees: $7 to $11.

With the atmosphere of an old-fashioned diner, this no-frills restaurant is often packed, especially with residents. People stream in from morning to night. Owned and run by a family, it serves Hawaiian, Chinese, and American food. Kids—whether visitors or local—love the chocolate malts.

Time to Make the Donuts!
Children love watching how donuts are born at **Daylight Donuts,** at the Keauhou Shopping Center, just south of Kailua-Kona. Made fresh daily, these delicious treats are served nice and warm.

TESHIMA'S RESTAURANT, Highway 11, Honalo, southern Kona. Tel. 322-9140. Open for breakfast, lunch, and dinner. Entrees: up to $16.

Serving three meals a day, this Japanese restaurant is an island favorite. About a twenty-minute drive south of Kailua-Kona, this family-run restaurant serves local comfort food, such as shrimp tempura, homemade tofu, and a fried rice omelet. For dessert, try the apple or pumpkin pie.

MANAGO RESTAURANT, Manago Hotel, Captain Cook. Tel. 323-2642. Open for breakfast, lunch, and dinner, except Mondays. Entrees: $7 to $12.

There's nothing fancy about the dining room of this old hotel that seems plucked from a bygone era. But the food is well worth the trip—witness the number of locals always eating breakfast, lunch, and dinner here. Specializing in fish, Manago also serves pork chops and hamburgers.

Naalehu

PUNALU'U SWEETBREAD BAKESHOP, Mamalahoa Highway, Naalehu, Tel. 929-7343. Open 9am to 5pm.

The aroma of baking bread will snag you on your way to or from Hawaii Volcanoes National Park, about 40 minutes away. This is the birthplace of the sweetbread you'll find at many local restaurants throughout the island. You can even watch the bakers at work and learn about the various stages from flour to loaf. Stop to relax in the colorful gardens while snacking on plate lunches or sandwiches made with the fresh bread. Varieties include taro, guava, and cinnamon raisin with macadamia nuts. You can buy a whole loaf, or pick up macadamia nut pies, cookies, coffee, and ice cream; jams and jellies made from guava, pineapple, and papaya; macadamia nuts in all their incarnations; and T-shirts and sweatshirts.

Hawaii Volcanoes National Park

KILAUEA LODGE AND RESTAURANT, Volcano Village, Old Volcano Road (near the entrance to the park). Tel. 967-7366. Dinner only. Reservations recommended. Entrees: $25 to $35. *Romantic Escape.*

For a change of pace from sand and surf, try dinner at this cozy, wooded mountain lodge. If it's nippy enough outside, flames flicker in the fireplace during meals. Brass chandeliers hang from a wood-paneled ceiling and attractive rugs decorate the floor. Complimented by an extensive wine list, the food is as delicious as the setting. With duck l'orange the star of the show, the rotating menu might also include French fried island zucchini, mushrooms stuffed with crabmeat and cheese, or fried brie coated with herb butter and coconut flakes as appetizers; and, among the entrees, paprika lobster, veal shank in wine and tomato sauce, pepper steak made with beef from Parker Ranch, broiled fish with papaya-ginger sauce, and eggplant seasoned with peppers, onions, tomatoes, and cheese. Rabbit, venison, and even ostrich also make appearances on dinner plates at this restaurant. Pasta and chicken teriyaki are on the children's menu.

Hilo

SEASIDE RESTAURANT, Kalanianeole Avenue, across from James Kealoha Park, 1/4 mile from Onekahakaha. Tel. 935-8825. Dinner only. Entrees: $20 to $30. Reservations recommended.

Started in the early 1900s, this family-run restaurant was washed away by the 1946 tidal wave that devastated Hilo. The grand re-opening was in 1947, and it's been going strong ever since. Dishes retrieved from the ocean floor by a scuba diver are preserved behind glass at the entrance. Both a dining spot and an old-style Hawaiian fish farm, the restaurant is surrounded by pine trees and a natural pond stocked with rainbow trout, catfish, koi (carp), mullet, and others. Guests may tour the pond while waiting for their individually prepared meals.

Seaside claims to be the only restaurant in Hawaii that serves aholehole, a rare local fish that is raised in the pond here. Demand is so great for this sweet white fish that if you'd like to try it, you'd better call a day or two ahead to reserve yours. Other choices include steak, shrimp, and mullet steamed in ti leaves. Chicken and rice and teriyaki chicken are on the children's menu. Dessert might be warm apple pie or sherbet.

KEN'S HOUSE OF PANCAKES, 1730 Kamehameha Avenue. Tel. 935-8711. Open 24 hours a day. Entrees: $5 to $20.

One of Hawaii's few restaurants open around the clock, this popular eatery serves breakfast, lunch, and dinner. The huge menu for the morning meal includes the macadamia nut, banana, and coconut pancakes that made Ken famous; fluffy waffles; hearty omelet; and Ken's corned beef hash. Lunch could be a sandwich, a burger, a bowl of saimin or a local Hawaiian favorite: a beef patty, mahi-mahi filet, or slab of Spam topped with a fried egg and thick brown gravy on a bed of rice. At dinner time, the teriyaki chicken moves quickly. Macaroni and cheese, eggs, and burgers come in child-size portions. For dessert, try the macadamia nut or lemon coconut custard pie.

Which One is My Bed?

On the sunny western shore of the Big Island, the Kona-Kohala Coast has some of the world's most sumptuous resorts. Scattered along the Big Island's prime beaches, these hotels reflect the diversity of the rest of the island. Guests are accommodated in high style, whether they're in multi-story complexes or thatched-roof Polynesian-style hales. While there are many tennis courts, championship golf courses, and endless water sports facilities, the resorts' special touches are what really make them stand out.

Following the lead of the Mauna Kea Beach Hotel, some of these hotels are virtual museums of art and artifacts from the Far East, the South Pacific, and Hawaii. Many remnants of Hawaii's past remain in this area, which is peppered with heiau (temples), petroglyphs (ancient rock carvings), and royal fishponds. Hotels including the Mauna Lani Bay Hotel & Bungalows and Kona Village Resort have incorporated some of these fishponds and petroglyphs into their grounds.

More moderately priced hotels are found along the rocky shore of Kailua-Kona and Keauhou, where beaches are few. However, many travelers don't mind cooling off in swimming pools overlooking the waves thrashing the craggy lava coast. Cruises for snorkeling, diving and sightseeing are easily arranged, and golf and tennis are also excellent in this area. Most of the island's stores and restaurants are in the waterfront town of Kailua-Kona.

A hotel in Hilo or Volcano will make a closer base for exploring Volcanoes National Park than an accommodation in Kohala, Kailua-Kona, or Keauhou. However, visiting the Park is certainly manageable no matter where you stay on the Big Island. Some families enjoy dividing their time between a beach resort and a vacation home, such as a mountain cottage.

Home Sweet Home on the Big Island

Staying in apartments or vacation homes, often in friendly residential neighborhoods, is particularly convenient for families with children. Most rates for condos and private homes are based on a minimum three-night to one-week stay, so nightly rates may be higher for shorter stays or lower for longer visits. Here are three good rental companies on the Big Island:

• Hawaii Resort Management, Tel. 800/622-5348, www.konahawaii.com, with properties in Kailua-Kona and Keauhou.
• South Kohala Management, Tel. 800/822-4252, www.southkohala.com, on the Kohala Coast.
• Chalet Kilauea Collection, Tel. 800/937-7786, www.volcano-hawaii.com, offering accommodations just outside Volcanoes National Park.

Honokaa Area

KALOPA HOMESTEAD GUEST HOUSE, Kalopa, Tel 808/775-7167 or 877-825-6185, www.hawaiivacationcottage.com. One cottage. Rates begin at $110 for three people. No smoking.

Neighboring Kalopa State Park, this homey pine mountainside cottage (1,700 feet in the sky) is surrounded by eucalyptus and coffee trees. Nights are cool and lit by more stars than we thought existed. Children love all the animals—dairy goats raised by the owner, dogs, and cats. With two bedrooms, a double-sized futon in the living room, a large kitchen, and a bath and half, the cottage can accommodate six people. There's a Jacuzzi spacious enough for two in the larger bathroom. (If you're lucky, you'll find goat's milk and macadamia nut soap handmade by the owner, who says it's wonderful for the skin.) The living room bay window overlooks a small tropical fish pond. Chilly nights are warmed by the wood-burning stove. Amenities include a TV, VCR, private telephone, washer, and dryer. Note that mosquitoes can be a problem here during the summer, so bring insect repellent (or Avon's Skin So Soft bath oil) and keep the doors closed. If you'll need a crib or high chair, you can make arrangements when you make your reservation.

Kamuela/Waimea

TINA'S COUNTRY COTTAGE, Kamuela/Waimea, Tel. 808/985-7488 or 800/262-9912, www.bestbnb.com. One cottage. Rates begin at $150 for three people.

While listening to music from stereo speakers, sit in the couch on the porch of this two-bedroom, two-bathroom cottage overlooking a sprawling lawn, bordered with flowers, and the private rodeo, backed by scenic hills. If you're lucky, you and your family will be treated to a show in the horse arena. A full kitchen, TV, private telephone, and wood stove make vacationers feel right at home. The hospitable owner and her family live on the grounds. Restaurants and shops are less than a mile away.

Kohala Coast & Northern Kona

KONA VILLAGE RESORT, Ka'upulehu, just north of airport. Tel. 808/ 325-5555 or 800/367-5290, www.konavillage.com. 125 cottages. Rates begin at $658 for two adults and a child, including three meals a day (with award-winning luau on Friday nights) and daily children's program.

Stay at what has to be the most distinctively Hawaiian resort in the state and chances are, you'll run into more than a few young children whose parents vacationed here when they themselves were kids. As you drive along the chocolate-colored lava road that twists and turns through a wasteland strewn with dark crumbly boulders, your first thought is likely to be, "What have I gotten myself into!" Then you'll see the *hales* (HAH-lays), bungalows built in the architectural styles of a variety of Polynesian peoples, from Hawaiians and Tahitians to Samoans and Fijians. Some with thatched roofs, these cottages stand on stilts above rugged lava flows, at the edges of beaches, or overlooking a lagoon. Built on the site of an old fishing village, this is the kind of place where sandy paths invite bare feet, and guests need not worry about misplacing their room keys—because there aren't any. As you wander around the peaceful grounds at night, you might hear the plaintive cries of wild donkeys.

Just as when Kona Village opened in 1965, guest rooms contain no telephones, radios, TVs, or air conditioners. Tradewinds and ceiling fans keep vacationers comfortable in rooms decorated with colorful batiks and other Pacific textiles and artwork. Some hales have glass-enclosed showers and whirlpool bathtubs. In yours you'll find 100% Kona coffee, a coffee maker, and a refrigerator (replenished daily with tropical juices, soda, and bottled water). When you don't want to be disturbed, simply place the hale's coconut outside your door. While you won't receive a room key, an in-room safe is provided. By the way, if you lock your door at night, be sure to press the button that unlocks it before leaving the next day, or you'll find yourselves locked out as we once did!

Breakfast, lunch, and dinner are included in the room rates, but guests who dine at the Hale Samoa, the more upscale restaurant, pay a surcharge. Sunsets are especially picturesque through the floor-to-ceiling windows of the main dining room. If you're here on a Friday night, you'll be treated to the legendary outdoor luau. Vacationing children are invited to learn the hula beforehand so that they can perform on stage during the show.

By day, you can tour petroglyph fields and fish ponds near where the luau is held. Sandy shores come in black, salt and pepper, and beige. There are two swimming pools, each with an adjacent children's pool (our kids love the mini-cave and waterfall), two whirlpools, and three night-lit tennis courts. Use of the fitness center, glass bottom boat rides, and all resort sports and sports equipment (from tennis to kayaks and snorkeling) are complimentary, as is transportation to golf. Room rates also include the children's programs (one for those aged 6 to 12 and a periodic teen program for those aged 13 to 17). Note that during May and September, however, there are no children's programs, activities, or special rates.

FOUR SEASONS RESORT HUALALAI, 100 Ka'upulehu Drive, just north of airport. Tel. 808/325-8000 or 888/340-5662, www.fourseasons.com/hualalai. 243 rooms. Rooms begin at $560.

It's difficult to find a better place for families with children, from infants to teenagers. When kids age 6 months to eight years old check into their rooms at beachfront Four Seasons Resort Hualalai, they are greeted with cookies and milk in the bedroom and their names spelled out in colorful sponges in the bathtub. They can relax in miniature lounge chairs around the children's pool, with its sandy bottom and water toys. Parents are welcome to borrow the hotel's jogging strollers and regular strollers, and swim diapers are easy to come by. Guests may request bottle warmers, microwave ovens, and cribs in advance. The resort provides bumper pads, a quilt, and a supply kit including powder, shampoo, baby wipes, and a few diapers (in your child's size!).

Rooms for children under age three are equipped with child-proof netting across the lanai railings, outlet protectors, night lights, and pads for glass coffee tables and end tables. Car seats are available as well. Complimentary washers and dryers (with free detergent) are strategically located throughout the resort. As if this weren't enough, staff members stroll the grounds offering kids ice pops, and the youngest children are given colorful blocks and crayons to keep them occupied during meals.

The complimentary Kids for All Seasons program offers children aged 5 to 12 supervised activities from gecko hunts and kite flying to a chance to feed eagle rays in the fish-packed King's Pond. Fed by the ocean, this swimming, snorkeling, and scuba diving instruction pool was carved from lava rock. Kids love the beach-like sloping sandy entry. Along with pint-sized snorkeling gear, attendants also provide floats with kid-sized viewing holes for watching all the colorful sea creatures.

Filled with computer games, Hawaiian musical instruments, and a variety of board games and puzzles, the Tsusami room, adjacent to an outdoor pool table and ping pong table, keeps teenagers happy when they are on dry land. Here a large-screen television continually plays popular DVDs.

Along with a half-mile stretch of beach and the unique King's Pond, the lush grounds are graced with other distinct bodies of water. For instance, the Beach Tree Pool, surrounded by a teak deck, is reserved for quiet pursuits—you can even borrow a book here from the roving library. The nearby Beach Tree Bar & Grill is no ordinary casual dining spot. Expect to find surprises such as creamy New England clam chowder served in a hollowed out round loaf of bread or spicy gazpacho decorated with yellow swirls of vegetable puree. We were thrilled to discover that at restaurants throughout the resort, certain menu items are marked vegetarian or "Alternative Cuisine," which means these selections are lighter and more nutritious than others—but just as delicious as the higher calorie choices.

In the teak and mahogany open-air lobby, where a three-tiered chandelier hangs over a glistening koa wood table, huge picture windows behind the front desk offer a dramatic view of Mauna Kea. At night, hundreds of torches light the grounds. The Hawaiian art and artifacts that decorate this resort span the years from 1775 to the present. At the heart of the Four Seasons is Ka'upulehu Cultural Center, where staff members are always happy to tell you about the fascinating Hawaiian heritage displays.

Housing spacious guest rooms, the resort's two-story buildings blend beautifully into the natural surroundings. With lanais or patios, rooms overlook the beach, the King's Pond, or the 18th hole of one of the two golf courses. You may have a hard time leaving your marble bathroom; the tubs are some of the deepest I've ever seen and stall showers are large enough for the whole family. In rooms on the bottom level, showers open to private gardens where there is a second, outdoor shower.

The Hualalai Sports Club & Spa—complete with indoor/outdoor aerobics, a 25-meter lap pool, outdoor massage huts (the perfect treat while the kids are at the day camp), and lighted tennis courts—is great for working out or being pampered. Consider sampling the spa's signature indulgence, lomi ho'ola—a combination of traditional Hawaiian lomilomi massage and hot rock treatment.

Note: Be sure to book your room at Four Seasons Resort Hualalai many months in advance, since the hotel is always full.

HAPUNA BEACH PRINCE HOTEL, 62-100 Kauna'oa Drive, Mauna Kea Resort, Kohala Coast. Tel. 808/880-1111, 800/735-1111, or 800/882-6060, www.hapunabeachprincehotel.com. 350 rooms. Rates begin at $360.

The somewhat stark contemporary design of the Hapuna Beach Prince Hotel is a counterpoint to the natural setting of the ocean and the manicured gardens. All the guest rooms and suites, some quite spacious, have private lanais and views of gorgeous Hapuna Beach and the ocean. Those in the ocean view category provide prime locations for whale watching during the winter months, when the water is too rough for swimming. At that time of year, head to Spencer Beach Park, about five minutes north. The hotel's elegant Hawaiian decor is understated, with light wood and subtle colors in the rooms and imported marble and tiles in the baths.

Here on the grounds of the Mauna Kea Resort, you'll find a swimming pool, a good selection of restaurants, various boutiques, and all kinds of water sports, along with the excellent Hapuna Golf course, the acclaimed Mauna Kea Golf course, a fitness center, and 13 tennis courts. Hapuna Beach Prince guests can sign for meals at restaurants at the neighboring Mauna Kea Beach Hotel, where the children's program takes place. In fact, from May through September, children under age 10 eat free at certain restaurants at both hotels when dining with adults. A shuttle and a 30-minute hiking trail link the two hotels. Since nearby homeowners take advantage of the facilities of both hotels, there's a friendly, family-like atmosphere among staff, guests, and residents.

Hapuna's Ocean Terrace restaurant is the setting for the bountiful weekly seafood buffet, with live Hawaiian music and jazz. Hapuna Beach Prince Hotel is a half-hour from the airport, about 40 minutes from the village of Kailua-Kona, and a 15-minute drive from the pleasant town of Kamuela/Waimea.

MAUNA KEA BEACH HOTEL, 62-100 Mauna Kea Beach Drive, Mauna Kea Resort, Kohala Coast. Tel. 808/882-7222 or 800/882-6060, www.maunakeabeachhotel.com. 310 rooms. Rates begin at $360.

Built in 1965 by philanthropist and environmentalist Laurance Rockefeller, the Mauna Kea Beach Hotel set the tone for the phenomenal Kohala Coast hotels that followed. Classical details are blended with beautifully crafted woods and varied textures of natural fibers that reflect elements of Hawaii. A melange of cultures is displayed in the decor of the very large rooms, each with a huge private lanai, and in the public spaces, with their soaring open-air design. More than a thousand pieces of Pacific and Asian art adorn both public areas and guest rooms, including traditional Hawaiian quilts, which Rockefeller first envisioned as wall hangings instead of mere bed covers. The hotel's weekly art tour is a fascinating way to spend some time. While families with young children may find Mauna Kea Beach Hotel a bit too formal, older children and adults may appreciate the hushed atmosphere and extensive gifts for the eyes.

Whether or not they participate in the children's program (for those aged 5 to 12), all children who check in to this hotel receive a "welcome kit." For younger kids, it consists of a toy-filled sand pail while older children receive an activity book, crayons, a water bottle, and a Frisbee. All guests are treated to dramatic views, from mountain to ocean to the gorgeous white sand beach. The bar here is a hit with kids, since it serves thick Ovaltine milkshakes. Two outstanding golf courses, 13 tennis courts, a fitness center, a pool, and a variety of water sports keep vacationers active. You can also take a yoga class on the oceanfront lawn. Horseback riding can be arranged in Kamuela/Waimea, 12 miles away. When you've sampled all the Mauna Kea hotel's restaurants, you can sign for meals at the neighboring Hapuna Beach Prince, a shuttle ride or a 30-minute scenic hike away. Children under age 10 eat free at some of the restaurants at both hotels when dining with adults from May through September. The Mauna Kea is a half-hour's drive from the airport, 40 minutes from Kailua-Kona, and a 15 minute drive from the charming town of Kamuela/Waimea.

MAUNA LANI BAY HOTEL AND BUNGALOWS, 68-1400 Mauna Lani Drive, Mauna Lani Resort, Kohala Coast. Tel. 808/885-6622 or 800/356-6652, Web site: www.maunalani.com. 350 rooms. Rates begin at $335.

The personal touches are part of what makes this hotel so special. For instance, arriving guests are seated individually at a small check-in desk before being escorted to their rooms. The airy lobby is set off with white columns and a blue-tiled staircase (bordered by waterfalls) that leads down to a palm-rimmed pool. Vegetation spills over balustrades and fragrant flowers are everywhere. Hawaiian musicians and hula dancers perform by the gardens in the afternoon and early evening while at night a combo plays jazz by the lobby bar. Walking tours are conducted of the historic fish ponds that meander throughout the property. Kids love watching the baby sharks dart back and forth.

With sprawling grounds including two miles of coastline, Mauna Lani Bay offers children (and adults) a huge outdoor classroom. A visiting historian, as well as day camp counselors, teach kids about Hawaiian cultural traditions, myths, and legends, take them to visit petroglyphs (ancient rock carvings), and instruct them in lei making. Children can even learn how to feed the fish (poi—like huge goldfish) in the lobby. One evening a month, kids can enjoy storytelling in the Eva Parker Woods Cottage, a mini-museum. The day camp playroom is packed with all kinds of supplies for arts and crafts, as well as books, videos, and games.

Named for one of Hawaii's best known golfers, the Francis I'i Brown Golf Courses are two of the most attractive and challenging in the state. In addition to a large swimming pool, there are ten tennis courts, a complete lineup of water sports at the beach, and an extensive fitness center. Book a babysitter and spend an evening in the Jacuzzi. Or have a private massage or a salt glow scrub in one of the health spa's serene huts along a winding path.

The stark architecture and sparse decor of guest rooms and public areas are in dramatic contrast with the hotel's lush outdoors. All with lanais, guest rooms sport teak furniture and louvered doors, and ceiling fans as well as air conditioning. For the ultimate splurge, book one of the two-bedroom oceanside bungalows, each with its own swimming pool and Jacuzzi. The hefty price tag includes a chauffeured limousine, a butler around the clock, and a maid who unpacks, irons and repacks you clothes. Double koa wood entry doors open to a huge living room with a pink polished granite bar, potted plants, and koa wood or marble tile floors. Meals are catered to guests' tastes. Scenic lagoons encircle the bungalows in this five-acre complex.

Free the Turtles!

In saltwater ponds at **Mauna Lani Bay Hotel and Bungalows**, *honu* (Hawaiian green sea turtles) have been raised for release since 1989 in a successful preservation effort. If you're planning a summer vacation, you might be just in time for Turtle Independence Day, on the 4th of July. At this event, everyone age 9 and older can help carry the turtles on gurneys to the ocean to set them free. Turtle tattoos, face painting, balloon animals, spiritual hula on the beach, and canoe rides are all part of the festivities.

FAIRMONT ORCHID HAWAII, One North Kaniku Drive, Mauna Lani Resort, Kohala Coast. Tel. 808/885-2000 or 800/845-9905, www.orchid-maunalani.com. 534 rooms. Rates begin at $300.

When you check in, you and your family may find yourselves lingering in the reception area to look at the Hawaiiana display—old books, lauhala woven bowls, shell leis, wood carvings. On a pleasant sandy cove, this wonderful beach resort sprawls across 32 acres. Waterfalls spill into beautifully landscaped ponds. Particularly because this resort uses only non-toxic cleaners and does not use pesticides, toddlers and babies who love to crawl around on the grass and in their rooms are perfectly safe.

Snorkeling is great just beyond the reef. Calm and shallow, the lagoon is great for young or timid kids. Teenagers amuse themselves with beach volleyball. On Hawaii Tattoo Day, you'll see more than a few kids decorated from head to toe. Children enjoy watching the turtles that often make their way to shore at sunset. Every evening, nearly two hundred torches are lit around the grounds and kids follow the torch lighter around like the Pied Piper.

Facilities include a swimming pool, tennis courts, several restaurants, two neighboring golf courses, a fitness center, and the Spa Without Walls—don't pass up a massage by the ocean's edge or in the private Teahouse by a waterfall. Another revitalizing spa treatment is almost edible: the aromatic vanilla and coffee exfoliation scrub.

The large guest rooms are elegant but comfortable, with hardwood furniture and lanais (most with ocean views). In some, twin closets and dressing areas lead to baths (tiled in marble, floor to ceiling), which have double sinks, and a separate tub and shower. Extras come in the form of robes for guests' use during their stay, a third telephone in the bathroom, remote-control TV and honor bars. Among the many amenities are valet parking during the day and golf bag storage. Ask about the two-hour excursion in a sailing canoe.

MAUNA LANI POINT, 68-1310 Mauna Lani Drive, Mauna Lani Resort, Kohala Coast. Tel. 808/885-5022 or 800/642-6284, Fax 808/ 885-5015, www.maunalani-point.com or www.classicresorts.com. 60 units. Rates begin at $260 per unit.

Located on a peaceful corner of the resort, this plush condominium is run somewhat like a hotel. All desk clerks act as concierges. Guests have signing privileges at some of the resort's non-hotel restaurants and sports facilities. Complimentary shuttle service is provided around the resort.

Many of the individually decorated one-, two- and three-bedroom apartments feature sunken living rooms; baths with sunken tubs, double sinks, and rosewood trim; kitchens with ash wood cabinets, built-in cutting boards and wine racks, and microwaves. All come with lanais or patios. Some units and the adjacent golf course have wonderful views of whales during the winter (especially February and March). The swimming pool, Jacuzzi, and dry sauna are tranquil even when the property is full. A barbecue pit and an open-air kitchen adjoin the pool.

HILTON WAIKOLOA VILLAGE, 425 Waikoloa Beach Drive, Waikoloa Resort, Kohala Coast. Tel. 808/886-1234 or 800/HILTONS, www.hiltonwaikoloavillage.com, 1240 rooms. Rates begin at $200.

This spectacular 62-acre playground, where tropical gardens are aflutter with cockatoos, macaws, and parrots, will put you in mind of Disneyland. Hotel towers are connected by the aptly named mile-long Museum Walkway. It is decked out with everything from six-foot tall urns and antique marionettes to weathered spears from Papua New Guinea. You can be transported to and from your room in space-age monorails or boats along the lagoon. Note, however, that if you happen to forget something, it can take ages to retrieve it, whether you walk or ride. If the boat comes while you're waiting for the tram or vice versa, you'll have to run across a bridge to attempt to catch the other mode of transportation.

The restaurants are top notch and most offer children's menus. Among the wide selection, Donatoni's for Italian food and Imari for Japanese cuisine have built excellent reputations. Families gravitate toward the food court in the Ocean Tower, which offers quick, healthful meals and snacks, gourmet coffees, and smoothies that won't empty your wallet.

Guests spend much of their time at the two golf courses, 18-hole seaside putting course, eight tennis courts, racquetball/squash court, spacious health spa, and three swimming pools. They can even interact with a group of Atlantic bottlenose dolphins. (To do so, contact **Dolphin Quest**, Tel. 808/886-2875. Children must be at least 5 years old.)

There's no real beach here, just a slip of sand at the edge of a lagoon—but the pools (complete with waterslides) and plenty of beach toys keep kids and their parents happy. Also, a beautiful beach is a brief walk or a shuttle ride away. While kids never want to leave the fun-filled day camp, parents also enjoy spending time there visiting with their children and meeting other parents.

An astronomy seminar, introductory scuba lessons, and power walks are all complimentary. There is valet parking and the hotel's circular driveway is small, so be sure to call ahead when you're ready for your wheels so your car will be waiting for you by the time you get to the front door.

WAIKOLOA BEACH MARRIOTT, 69-275 Waikoloa Beach Drive, Waikoloa Resort, Kohala Coast. 545 rooms. Tel. 808/886-6789 or 800/228-9290, www.waikoloabeachmarriott.com. Rates begin at $200.

With a far nicer beach than its splashier neighbor, Hilton Waikoloa Village, this appealing hotel overlooks the gorgeous bay. Here families entertain themselves with all kinds of water toys, from hydro-bikes and boogie boards to snorkeling gear. Both of the resort's restaurants offer keiki menus, and at Nalu, every child's meal comes in a plastic bucket with a shovel that they can later use at the beach. Upon check-in, children also receive backpacks complete with goodies such as sunglasses, binoculars, a pen, and a diary for immortalizing their adventures.

Families enjoy hiking along the King's Trail (a.k.a. the Ala Mamalohoa), where they can see historic fish ponds and petroglyphs (ancient pictures) carved in the lava. Guests also amuse themselves with the pool, the adjacent tennis courts, and Waikoloa Resort's two 18-hole golf courses. The children's program is quite popular here. Held twice a week, the hotel's luau is worth an evening.

Note that at press time this hotel was scheduled to be sold, so the name may have changed by the time you read these words.

Kailua-Kona & Keauhou Area

ASTON KONA BY THE SEA, 75-6106 Alii Drive, Kailua-Kona. Tel. 808/327-2300 or 800/922-7866, www.astonhotels.com or www.konabythesea.com. 86 rooms. Rates begin at $260 per unit.

On a dramatic rocky shore, this pleasant condominium boasts spacious upscale one- and two-bedroom units. Book a unit close to the water if you like being lulled to sleep by the sound of crashing surf. Well-manicured vegetation thrives around the freshwater oceanfront pool and Jacuzzi. In the second pool, also overlooking the sea, guests splash around in water from the Pacific.

OUTRIGGER ROYAL SEA CLIFF RESORT, 75-6040 Alii Drive, Kailua-Kona. Tel. 808/329-8021 or 800/688-7444. 154 units. Rates begin at $215.

The entrance to this stark white terraced condominium is on the fifth floor. Balconies outside rooms overlook the sunny lobby that is lush with greenery and scattered with sitting areas. Gardens, a waterfall, and fish ponds add to the tropical ambiance. The waterfront here is rocky, but there are two swimming pools to choose from (one salt, one fresh), a whirlpool, and a tennis court. Golf packages are available. The spacious, individually decorated units (some of which are time shares) come as studios and one- or two-bedrooms. All have ample lanais, but if you want a sun deck as well, book a corner apartment. When you're ready for some excellent shopping, Alii Gardens—an excellent market selling handcrafted goods, jewelry, and fresh produce—is within walking distance. A grocery store is also nearby, though you'll pay for the convenience of not having to go into town. At check-in, children (aged 5 to 13) of families staying at least three nights receive backpacks loaded with "great stuff."

KANALOA AT KONA, 78-262 Manukai Street, Keauhou-Kona. Tel. 808/322-9675 or 800/688-7444, www.outrigger.com. 166 rooms. Rates begin at $200.

These one-, two-, and three-bedroom condos overlook the golf course or the ocean. In the individually decorated apartments, special features include koa wood cabinets, marble, and whirlpool tubs. The modern kitchens come with microwave ovens and there's a restaurant on the premises, along with a cocktail lounge. Guests can keep in shape at the two tennis courts and three swimming pools. Children age 5 to 12 receive a backpack complete with a journal, pen, and other fun items.

OUTRIGGER KEAUHOU BEACH RESORT, 78-6740 Alii Drive, Kailua-Kona. Tel. 808/322-3441, 800/462-6262, or 800/688-7444, www.outrigger.com. 311 rooms. Rates begin at $190.

Rocky Kahaluu Beach, known for its excellent snorkeling, is a brief stroll from this resort that was built on royal land. The oceanfront side of the seven-story building overhangs a lagoon, affording an aquarium-like view of the water below. At low tide, take a walk to see the petroglyphs. The pool patio is the first place you'll want to stop even before you check into your room. The view of the ocean, the beach, the Royal Kuakini Grove all in one sweep is nothing less than breathtaking. There's also a small pool for children. The upbeat music of a live band and the convenience of a full-service bar may make it difficult for you to tear yourself away.

Guest rooms, with lanais, are pleasantly done. Amid the lush gardens, you'll find the reconstructed 19th century summer cottage and royal bathing pool of King Kalakaua; the frame building now houses a petite musem. There are six tennis courts on the premises and championship golf courses aren't far. The oceanfront town of Kailua-Kona is just a few miles north.

SHERATON KEAUHOU BAY RESORT & SPA, Keauhou, South Kona. Tel. 888/488-3535, www.sheratonkeauhou.com or 522 rooms. www.starwood.com/hawaii. 522 rooms. Rates begin at $175 (introductory rate).

This luxury hotel sits along a dramatic coast edged by craggy black lava and thrashing white surf. From viewing spots at sunset, guests can look down on the manta rays that come each evening to swim gracefully along the shoreline as they feed right in front of the hotel. Guests may even go snorkeling or scuba diving after dark to get a closer look at these impressive sea creatures, some with wing spans of more than twenty feet. A meandering, multi-level swimming pool makes up for the lack of a beach. Kids craving sand can head to the children's pool, with its beach-like bottom. To pump up the volume on the fun even more, there's a 200-foot-long lava tube water slide. Sheraton Keauhou Bay Resort & Spa offers a year-round children's program (for guests aged 5 to 12) and play center, and keiki menus make restaurant dining a breeze. Parents will appreciate the large spa, 24-hour fitness center, tennis courts, and two golf courses. Biking tours, snorkeling, storytelling, and hiking are among the other activities for vacationers. You'll find refrigerators and 100% Kona coffee in your room, along with other top amenities.

KONA SEASIDE HOTEL, 75-5646 Palani Road, Kailua-Kona. Tel. 808/329-2455 or 800/560-5558, www.konaseasidehotel.com. 217 rooms. Rates begin at $120.

This family-owned and -operated hotel in the center of Kailua-Kona is a convenient place to stay at modest rates. The attractively but simply decorated rooms all have air conditioning, ceiling fans, cable TV, and kitchenettes. Connecting rooms are available. After a swim in one of the freshwater pools, you can easily stroll to the nearby shops in "town."

ROYAL KONA RESORT, 75-5852 Alii Drive, Kailua-Kona. Tel. 808/329-9532 or 800/919-8333, www.royalkona.com. 452 rooms. Rates begin at $110.

Ideally located, this hotel sits at the edge of Kailua-Kona, away from the hustle and bustle but close enough to the many good restaurants and shops. The three six-story towers—housing rooms complete with lanais, safes, refrigerators, and coffee makers—command 11 acres of lush coastline. At the restaurant, overlooking the Kona shore, children aged 5 to 11 eat free with paying adults. The luau is also free for kids accompanied by adults. Although this hotel is four miles from a sandy beach, it sports a small human-made sandy lagoon, connected to the ocean. Kids love snorkeling here, as well as swimming in the pool. Tennis courts are also on the premises, and golf, scuba diving, and other activities are easily arranged. If you're traveling with teenagers, this is a great choice, since the volleyball court right across the street is popular for meeting and greeting over games.

KEAUHOU RESORT, 78-7039 Kam III Road, Kailua-Kona. Tel. 808/322-9122 or 800/367-5286. www.sunquest-hawaii.com. 48 units. Rates begin at $100.

Located on the golf course at Keauhou Bay, this resort allows you to live like a resident of the island in this lovely, quiet, laid back family-friendly condo community. Each of the spacious units is individually decorated. All have awning-shaded lanais and lush ocean views partially obscured by colorful array of foliage and flora. The small shallow swimming pool is great for young kids, who receive a backpack when they check in.

UNCLE BILLY'S KONA BAY HOTEL, 75-5739 Alii Drive, Kailua-Kona. Tel. 808/329-1393 or 800/367-5102,www.unclebilly.com. 143 rooms. Rates begin at $95.

Across from sandy Kailua Bay, this is a centrally located hotel. In the shape of a half moon with an island in its center, its layout ties in perfectly with its Polynesian decor of thatched roofs, bamboo, and tropical flowers. There is an atmosphere of fun and friendliness in this very informal, homey, colorful family inn. With a five-foot-deep circular pool, Uncle Billy's will be happy to arrange all kinds of other activities. The simply decorated bedrooms, with lanais, are perfectly comfortable.

Hawaii Volcanoes National Park Area

KILAUEA LODGE, P.O. Box 116, Volcano. On Old Volcano Road, one mile from park entrance. Tel. 808/967-7366, www.kilauealodge.com, 14 rooms. Rates for two-bedroom cottage begin at $180 for three people. No smoking.

Thick woods, tall cone-shaped pines, and giant ferns enclose this mountain lodge. A block from the main building, Tutu's Place is a former summer cottage with two bedrooms and a living room equipped with a TV, VCR, gas fireplace, full kitchen, and a pleasant garden. Also good for families, Pi'i Mauna House, a cedar cottage, sleeps up to six people. Since the two bedrooms are in two separate wings connected by a lanai, this is probably best for families with older children. A TV, gas fireplace, full kitchen, and hot tub are all on hand here. The popular restaurant in the main house serves continental food nightly. Kilauea General Store and Volcano Golf Course are both nearby.

CARSON'S VOLCANO COTTAGE BED & BREAKFAST, Volcano. Tel. 808/967-7683 or 800/845-LAVA, www.carsonscottage.com. Five rooms and five cottages. Rates begin at $155 for three people.

A rose garden, peach and plum trees, bromeliads, and tall ferns all flourish amid these alternately jungled and manicured grounds. The two cottages with full kitchens appeal to families more than the other units. Built in the 1940s, the original cottage is nicely done with attractive curtains and other soft furnishings. The one large room contains one queen-sized and one double bed as well as a woodburning stove. The Kau Room, with a queen sized bed, has a very high ceiling. Pictures of old Hawaii adorn the Kahaualea Room, which sports a queen-sized bed. An added bonus of staying at Carson's is being able to lounge in the hot tub in the open-air pavilion in the midst of the forest. For pet lovers, there are friendly dogs and cats. A delicious full breakfast is served in the dining room.

VOLCANO HOUSE, P.O. Box 53, Hawaii Volcanoes National Parks. Tel. 808/967-7321. 42 rooms. Rates begin at $95.

Perched at the rim of Kilauea Crater, 4,000 feet above sea level, this lodge is a convenient place to stay when you're visiting Volcanoes National Park. The original Volcano House was a thatched-roof grass structure built during the 1840s that had room for 40 guests. In 1877, it was replaced by a Western-style inn with only four bedrooms in addition to its dining room and parlor. Queen Liliuokalani, Robert Louis Stevenson, and Mark Twain were among its guests.

The rustic inn that stands here today was built in 1941. Visitors gather around the stone fireplace in the main building, which is usually crowded with sightseers. Anyone so inclined may pick out a tune on the koa piano here. Cafeteria-style meals, including some vegetarian selections, are served in the dining room. Uncle George's Cocktail lounge offers a magnificent view of the crater. You can also absorb your unusual surroundings while teeing off at the Volcano Golf Course. Guest rooms are decorated with koa rocking chairs and other furniture and traditional Hawaiian quilts. Some connecting rooms are available. Don't look for televisions or refrigerators, but some rooms have private lanais. A couple come with full baths but most have stall showers. Make reservations six months in advance if you're planning to vacation in the winter and three months ahead for other times of year.

Hilo

HAWAII NANILOA HOTEL, 93 Banyan Drive, Hilo. Tel. 808/969-3333 or 800/367-5360. www.nailoa.com. 325 rooms. Rates begin at $100.

Across the street from the nine-hole Naniloa Country Club Golf Course, Hilo's largest hotel sports two freshwater swimming pools and a fitness center. Four Mile Beach, considered to be the town's best sandy stretch, is about two miles away. The nicest rooms are those that gaze out to the harbor. The pleasantly decorated rooms are air-conditioned and comfortable. Most have private lanais and views are of the bay, gardens, or mountains. If you need a refrigerator, be sure to book a deluxe garden view room. Connecting rooms can be reserved.

Chapter 12

KAUAI WITH KIDS

Think tropical fantasy, and you've got Kauai on your mind. The oldest of the main Hawaiian Islands, this aging beauty has had plenty of time to be sculpted by the elements. Its 553 square miles are embellished by some of the state's most stunning scenery, from meandering rivers and streams to breathtaking 4,000-foot sea cliffs and the l0-mile-long, two-mile-wide, 3,600-foot-deep crevice that Mark Twain dubbed the "Grand Canyon of the Pacific." Jagged mountains slip into smooth green cow-studded meadows. Monk seals bask on deserted sandy crescents. Waterfalls crash into natural pools and rainbows span bays.

Thanks to the fact that Kauai receives more rain than the rest of Hawaii, it is covered with a multitude of flowers and other flourishing vegetation. Shrouded in mist, lopsided mountain peaks and verdant expanses take on a mystical beauty when showers hit. The sunniest regions are along the southern coast, where the Poipu resort area is located, and the western shore, where 15-mile Polihale (the island's longest beach) is found. Hanalei and Princeville, in the north, are the resorts where rain is most frequent, so the north is wonderfully green.

Getting Around

Your plane will land in Lihue, Kauai's capital. Find out if your accommodation provides complimentary transportation to and from the airport. If not, you can get where you're going by bus, van, taxi, limousine, or rental car. The major auto rental agencies have desks at Lihue Airport. Guests are transported in vans to and from the cars.

Kauai's Star Power

Once you see this gorgeous island, you'll understand why it has long played a starring role in blockbuster movies. Even *Lilo and Stitch* (2002), the Disney animation, was set on Kauai. Here are just a few of the films that have been shot on this island over the years:

- *South Pacific* (1958)
- Elvis Presley's *Blue Hawaii* (1961)
- *Raiders of the Lost Ark* (1981)
- *Hook* (1991)
- *Honeymoon in Vegas* (1992)
- *George of the Jungle* (1997)
- *Mighty Joe Young* (1998)
- the *Jurassic Park* series (1993, 1997, and 2001)

The town of Lihue, in the southeast, is a five-minute drive from the airport. To Poipu on the south shore, the ride from the airport should last about 30 minutes. To Hanalei and Princeville, in the north, it's just over an hour from Lihue. Wailua and Kapaa hotels and condos, on the east coast, are about 15 minutes from where you'll land. Plan to spend at least 90 minutes on the road to get to the lodge and cabins in wooded, mountainous Kokee, in the west.

The Kauai Bus, the island's public bus system, runs daily from 5am to 6pm. However, stops, frequency, and luggage capacity are very limited. The fare is about $1.50 for adults; $0.75 for children ages 7 to 18 and for seniors; free for children age 6 and younger. Taxis are available, but they are practical only for short rides or for travelers with money to burn. So renting a car is your best bet.

Just one main road goes around most of Kauai. Since it doesn't encircle the island completely and since no roads cut all the way across the interior, you'll have a second chance to see whatever you missed the first time you passed it. I never mind backtracking, since Kauai's scenery is spectacular coming and going. But if you'd rather not cover the same territory twice, consider moving from a hotel in one part of the island to an accommodation in another.

Where Are We Going Now?

Allow at least three days for leisurely exploring—one for Poipu up the east coast to Kapaa; another for Kapaa up along the north shore through Hanalei and Princeville to Haena, where Kuhio Highway (Route 56) ends; and the third for the southern coast west of Poipu, up to Waimea Canyon, Kokee State Park, and Kalalau Lookout.

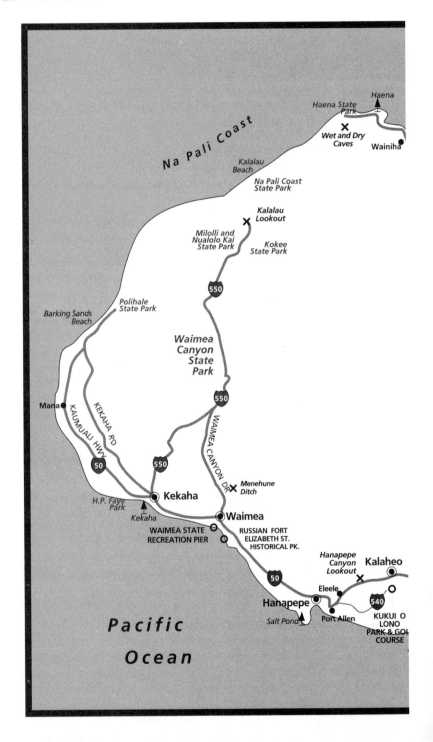

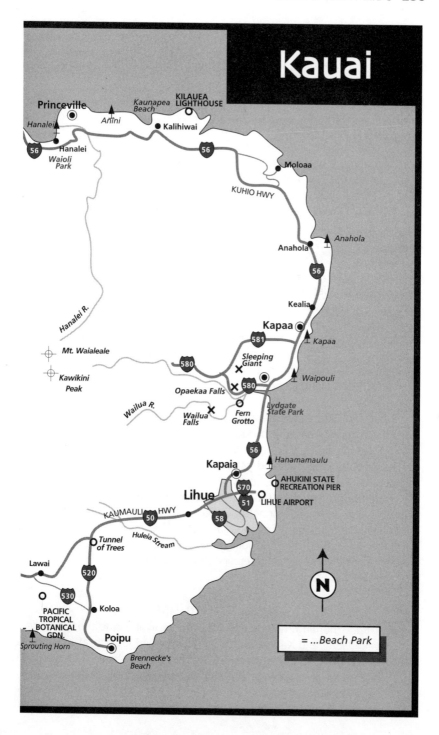

Kauai

Princeville

Kaunapea Beach

KILAUEA LIGHTHOUSE

Aníni

Hanalei

Kalihiwai

56

Hanalei

Waíoli Park

Moloaa

KUHIO HWY

Anahola

Anahola

56

Kealia

Mt. Waialeale

Kapaa

581

Kapaa

Kawikini Peak

580

Sleeping Giant

Waípouli

580

Opaekaa Falls

Hanalei R.

Wailua R.

Wailua Falls

Fern Grotto

Lydgate State Park

56

Hanamamaulu

Kapaia

570

AHUKINI STATE RECREATION PIER

Lihue

51

LIHUE AIRPORT

KAUMAULI HWY

50

58

Tunnel of Trees

Huleia Stream

Lawai

520

530

Koloa

PACIFIC TROPICAL BOTANICAL GDN.

Poipu

Sprouting Horn

Brennecke's Beach

N

= ...Beach Park

You may want to spend another day or an afternoon on Polihale beach on the west coast. For the many travelers based in Poipu, driving time to Waimea and Kekaha is about an hour; to Kapaa, about 45 minutes; to Hanalei, about 90 minutes.

Sights & Adventures

TUNNEL OF TREES, the south, north of Poipu.

This dramatic passageway is lined with stately eucalyptus whose branches reach out to each other overhead. If you're staying in the Poipu beach resort, you'll first see the Tunnel of Trees on your way from the airport after you head west on Highway 50 and turn south onto Highway 520, a.k.a. Maluhia Raod.

KOLOA TOWN, the south, just north of Poipu.

Established in the 1830s, Kauai's first sugar plantation once thrived where Koloa Town now stands. You'll see the timeworn smokestack and other remnants of the mill. Attractively refurbished or re-created 19th century wooden buildings give the town a Western frontier look. Some of the boutiques and galleries housed inside are better for browsing than for buying, since the upscale jewelry, clothing, and other goods come with (very) upscale price tags. Collectively, these stores are known as Old Koloa Town. Plaques outside the old plantation buildings tell their history and original use. One was a barber shop, another the site of a taro processing factory, and still others an ice cream and soda fountain, a music store, a fish market, a bar.

SPOUTING HORN, end of Lawai Road, south shore, just west of Poipu Beach Park.

Many families can't resist photographing each other in front of this huge oceanfront geyser. Forced into a lava tube, waves have nowhere to go but up—*way* up into the air. Don't venture off the paved walkway, since the rocks can be dangerously slippery. Vendors are usually here selling an eclectic mix of inexpensive T-shirts and rare, costly Niihau shell leis.

Note: Before you invest in a rare **Niihau necklace**, sold by vendors at Spouting Horn in Poipu, among other places, make sure it's authentic. Some fakes have been passed off as the real deal. If the vendor will not provide a certificate of authenticity (including a contact name, address, and phone number in case you ever need repairs), then move on.

Kauai Driving Tips

During morning and afternoon rush hours, avoid Lihue and the road between Lihue and Kapaa, unless you don't mind moving at a crawl. When you're going on sightseeing drives (such as to Waimea Canyon), it's best to leave as early as possible so that you don't end up stuck behind exhaust-spewing tour buses.

☙

Niihau, off the southern coast of Kauai, is the only island where these minuscule shells, decorated with delicately detailed natural designs, wash ashore in significant quantities. Each lei takes anywhere from 20 to 200 hours to complete, since the tiny shells must be picked out of the sand, sorted by size, shape, and color, then cleaned, drilled with holes, and strung into intricate patterns. The rarest colors are red and deep pink. The painstaking work, the scarcity of the shells, and the beauty of the necklaces account for the hefty price tags. These leis can cost hundreds—even thousands—of dollars each!

HANAPEPE, the south, near Salt Pond Beach Park, west of Poipu.

Weathered wooden buildings border the streets of Hanapepe, which is reminiscent of an old Western town on the mainland. Chickens do their jerky dash back and forth across the road. A few upscale shops struggle to keep afloat on the often deserted streets. This agricultural town once bustled with energy. Then came a highway that bypassed it, and a shopping center was built nearby. Along the makai (ocean) side of the main highway **Kauai Soto Zen Temple** makes an eye-catching landmark. At the end of Lele Road, you'll come to **Salt Pond Beach Park**, where salt was dried in the sun for generations. From nearby **Burn's Field**, you can arrange to take off in a glider plane or a helicopter.

Along Highway 50, **Hanapepe Overlook** brings cars and tour buses to a halt. Lush vegetation and bright green geometric plots of farmland cover deep Hanapepe Valley. Smooth hills roll gently in the distance. In stark contrast, the dramatic canyon cliffs are a vivid orange. Here in this chasm in 1824, the son of Kauai's King Ka-umu-ali'i was the leader of the island's final military maneuver. Most of the land in this area belongs to the Robinson family, the Caucasians who own **Niihau**, the offshore island where the population, language, and lifestyle are Hawaiian. The Robinsons, who speak fluent Hawaiian, also claim about a third of the land on Kauai itself.

WAIMEA CANYON, the west, north of Kekaha Beach Park.

An immense, craggy chasm, Waimea Canyon is a study in pinks, reds, oranges, greens, browns, and golds. The intensity of color changes with the moving sun. In one of Mother Nature's amusing coincidences, these hues are repeated in the bright plumage of the wild chickens that greet visitors in the parking lot. Goats move effortlessly along the rocky, nearly vertical edges of the cliffs. You can see this vast natural wonder by helicopter, by driving to the Waimea Canyon or Puu Hinahina Lookouts, or by hiking to other vantage points in and around **Kokee State Park.** (Also see *Hiking*, in "Sports & Other Activities," below.)

Along the road up to the lookout, cacti are scattered across the dry hills. Yellow tufts of grass sprout from the prairielike terrain. After some hairpin curves, you'll see the ocean and the island of Niihau in the distance. The road continues to snake uphill, past silky oak trees with their bright red-and-yellow blossoms, the pink flowers of banana poka vines, pines, and koa trees (once used to make canoes). Consider stopping at rustic Kokee Lodge, farther up, for lunch.

Especially during winter months, be sure to take a sweater when you visit what Mark Twain called "The Grand Canyon of the Pacific." To Waimea Canyon, Kokee State Park, or **Kalalau Lookout**, you can turn *mauka* (inland) up Waimea Canyon Drive. For another route, turn *mauka* (toward the mountains) at Kekaha onto wider Kokee Road (Highway 550). Waimea Canyon Drive and Kokee Road meet each other near Waimea Canyon Lookout.

KALALAU LOOKOUT, northwest, north of Waimea Canyon.

When the weather cooperates, the Kalalau Lookout, at about 4,000 feet, affords views of serrated mountains, waterfalls, treetops in the sprawling valley, and the beach-rimmed ocean. If you're traveling with rugged older kids, try to rewarding hiking trail that starts here. In ancient times, Kalalau was one of Kauai's major settlements. The crumbling *heiau* (temples) where religious sacrifices were made and the agricultural terraces where taro and other crops once grew are virtually all that remain of the villages today.

Many *Who?*

Kauai is famous for its tales of *Menehune* (meh-nay-WHO-nay), the race of miniature people who were the Hawaiian version of European leprechauns or trolls. The difference is that the Menehune truly may have existed. According to a census taken toward the end of the 1700s, 65 Menehune living in Wainiha Valley were under the domain of Kauai's King Ka-umu-ali'i. These hairy, dark-skinned people were said to be a mere two or three feet tall, with red faces, wide noses, overhanging foreheads, and scraggly straight hair.

Fond of dining on taro and shrimp, the Menehune weren't big on conversation—but when they did speak, their deep gravely voices sounded like dogs growling. They got a real kick out of playful activities such as rolling down hillsides into the ocean. With their compact, muscular bodies, they were well suited for their celebrated stone masonry. For instance, impressive **Menehune Ditch**, in southwestern Kauai, is believed to have been built by members of this nocturnal race in just one night.

The Tahitian word for "Menehune" means "commoner." Some historians theorize that the Menehune were inhabiting Tahiti when the Polynesians first arrived there and that these little people eventually made their way to Hawaii. Legend says that when their chiefs began to worry that too much interbreeding with Hawaiians would dilute their race, the Menehune sailed away on a floating island.

ॐ

KILOHANA PLANTATION, route 50, near Lihue; Tel. 245-5608.

Since 1986, this Wilcox family sugar plantation estate has welcomed the public to its 35 landscaped acres. Art galleries, jewelry stores, crafts shops, and other boutiques fill the rooms of the beautifully restored Tudor mansion. A flower-lined courtyard has been transformed into an attractive restaurant. Children enjoy the agricultural displays and **carriage rides** powered by Clydesdale horses as well as a **wagon ride**, Tel. 246-9529.

GROVE FARM HOMESTEAD, route 58, just outside Lihue, Tel. 245-3202; tours conducted at 10am and 1pm on Monday, Wednesday, and Thursday; reservations required at least one week in advance.

The home of the wealthy Wilcox family from 1864 to 1978, these 80 acres are now a living museum giving visitors a glimpse of old Hawaii. Still a working farm, Grove Farm Homestead was once a sugar plantation. It was started by George Wilcox, one of the sons of missionary teachers Abner and Lucy Wilcox, who had moved to Hawaii from Connecticut during the 1840s. This family helped revolutionize agriculture in the islands. In the days when it took a ton of water to produce a pound of sugar, they were among the first to begin using irrigation ditches, railcars instead of oxcarts, and plows that were powered by steam instead of oxen. Note that young children will probably not last for the two-hour tours.

WAILUA FALLS, the east, Wailua, near Lydgate Beach Park.

From Highway 583 or from Maalo Road (off Highway 56), gaze down on the dramatic 80-foot cascades that were used in the opening of "Fantasy Island," the 1970s television series. The cliff here served as a diving platform for daring alii (chiefs) who would plummet into the pool below the falls.

OPAEKAA FALLS, the east, Wailua, near Lydgate Beach Park

Off Highway 580 is the lookout for these falls, whose name means "rolling shrimp falls." The crustaceans once lived at the bottom of these mammoth cascades. Across the road and far below, the **Wailua River** wends its way between the mountains. At the end of Highway 580, **Keahua Arboretum** is a good place for a picnic or a hike to a private swimming hole.

SMITH'S TROPICAL PARADISE, the east, Wailua. Tel. 821-6895. Botanical gardens only: $6 (adults), $3 (age 2 to 12); open 8:30am to 4pm (doors close at 3pm). Gardens and luau: $60 (adults), $20 (age 3 to 6), $30 (age 7 to 13); held here several days per week, beginning with the 6pm imu ceremony. (Arrive by 5pm to tour the gardens.)

The 30 tropical acres of flowers, plants, and trees make visitors feel as though they have stepped into old Hawaii. While riding in the tram or walking through the grounds, you'll pass several lily ponds. The first is huge, with a large rocky fountain. Royal palms, banana trees, crotons, and bougainvillea surround the water. Hundreds of birds flutter around the rain forest garden, filled with stalks of bamboo, red ginger, scarlet lobster claws, pineapples, and papaya trees. Allow about an hour to explore the **botanical gardens**.

Before the evening **luau**, everyone observes the outdoor *imu* ceremony: The boned kalua pig, the centerpiece of the meal, is removed from its oven—a hole in the ground that has been heated by red-hot rocks. Featuring Hawaiian, Maori, Samoan, Tongan, Japanese, and Chinese music and dances, the performance takes place on a stage across a lily pond from the audience. The Samoan fire dancers are a big hit. While the bleachers are covered, the stage is open to the sky.

FERN GROTTO, the east, Wailua Marina, off Highway 56; Smith's Motor Boat Service, Tel. 821-6892; $16 (adults), $8 (under age 12).

While both the ride along the Wailua River and the visit to the flourishing cave are beautiful, such a naturally serene setting would be much more appealing with fewer people around: Up to 150 tourists are packed into each of the flat-bottom boats. The leisurely ride, between jagged mountains and cliffs with orange earth showing through the greenery, is almost as picturesque as the fern-covered cave itself. Along the way, a band plays and passengers are coaxed into ensemble hula lessons. The ridge known as the Sleeping Giant gazes down on the water. Lining the banks are "scrambled egg trees," with their fluffy, butter-colored flowers, and blossoming hau trees, with their tangle of low-growing, crisscrossed branches.

As passengers walk along the path to the cave, wild chickens parade by. Their long red and orange feathers look too bright to be real. Other birds rustle through the bushes of this extremely lush forest. At the cave, musicians from the boats perform "The Hawaiian Wedding Song" to show off the acoustics of the grotto. The song is quite appropriate, since dozens of weddings take place here each year. Hundreds of ferns grow from the cave walls and water trickles from above. Even on sunny days, the light is dim here, so be sure to use a flash or fast film if you take photos. This excursion takes about an hour and twenty minutes, round trip.

The Big Sleep

The mountain ridge known as the **Sleeping Giant** is visible from Waipouli and the town of Kapaa. Hawaiian legend has it that the overgrown Puni fell into his slumber after a hard-fought battle. Another story explains that the giant simply gorged himself at a luau and never woke up from his nap. From Kapaa, it will take about an hour to hike to Puni's chin. A picnic table invites trekkers to relax a spell. Between June and October, the guavas are ripe for plucking off their trees. If you take the left-hand path just before the trail ends, you'll come to an overlook with a sweeping view of Kauai's eastern shore.

❧

KILAUEA POINT WILDLIFE REFUGE, the north shore, Kilauea; Open 10am-4pm, except holidays.

Erected in 1913, the **Kilauea Lighthouse** had a beam that could be seen for 20 ocean miles and planes could spot it 90 miles away. Today it's the landmark for the bird sanctuary that is a nesting place for frigates, boobies, and other seabirds. Bring your binoculars or a telephoto lens for eyeball-to-eyeball views of red-footed boobies, frigates, laysan albatross, and red-tailed tropic-birds. More seabirds nest along the rugged cliffs of this promontory than anywhere else in the main Hawaiian islands. Called *a* in Hawaiian, red-footed boobies usually build their homes in shrubs or small trees. These birds are two feet long and white in color. *Iwa*, or frigates, like to swoop down on boobies and other birds in flight to steal the fish they're carrying.

Big black-and-white *moli*, or laysan albatross, pass most of their time hunting for squid and fish. They only step on dry land when they're ready to court or breed. Until these birds mature, they can spend as many as *six years* on and above the open ocean without touching terra firma. Thus, they are less than graceful on land. Their slow, goofy-looking waddle makes them an easy catch for wild dogs and other predators.

Kilauea Point, the promontory with wraparound views high above the crashing ocean, is also a great place for spotting dolphins, monk seals, green sea turtles and—from December to May—humpback **whales**. If you're very lucky, you'll see one of these 45-foot mammals jump completely out of the water.

PRINCEVILLE, the north shore.

Developed as a vacation resort, the community of Princeville is one of Kauai's most scenic regions. Sprawling across the tops of cliffs, the 11,000 acres overlooking valleys are sprinkled with upscale condominiums, private homes, and the beautiful **Princeville** hotel. Made up of three 9-hole greens designed by Robert Trent Jones, Jr., the **Princeville Makai Golf Course** is considered one of the best in the world. The 18-hole **Prince Golf Course** is another top place for teeing off. From many parts of town, the striking Makana mountain peaks can be seen. Immortalized in the movie *South Pacific*, they are still commonly known as **Bali Hai**. In Princeville Center, a post office is conveniently located just inside the grocery store.

The **Princeville** area was once a sugar plantation belonging to Robert Crichton Wyllie. Originally from Scotland, he became minister of Foreign Affairs for the Hawaiian kingdom in 1798, holding the position for nearly seven decades. He chose the name Princeville for his plantation in honor of young Prince Albert, the child of King Kamehameha IV and Queen Emma. Wyllie was known for his no-holds-barred entertaining. In 1862, he threw the four-year-old prince a royal birthday party, highlighted by a grand parade of 200 costumed Hawaiian men and women on horseback.

HANALEI VALLEY OVERLOOK, the north shore.

Gaze down on a breathtaking view: The snaking Hanalei river, which cuts through a tapestry of taro patches and other farm plots carpeting a valley set against a backdrop of irregular mountain ridges. Also down below, the Hanalei National Wildlife Refuge offers 900 acres of protection for endangered waterfowl. On its way into the valley, Highway 56 passes along a creaky, arched, one-lane bridge that was built in 1912. Despite its elderly appearance, residents are too attached to it to replace it. Kayaking is common on the river here and cows graze in a pasture along the bank.

HANALEI, the north shore.

This verdant part of the north shore couldn't possibly be as beautiful as it is without a healthy dose of rain. In fact, the slim, winding, dipping road to Hanalei is sometimes closed for hours (even days on rare occasions) when the river rises in a heavy deluge. Schools have been known to close and people have had to sleep in their cars until they could get home. Artists, poets, and other creative types are drawn to the selection of imaginative boutiques and galleries in Hanalei. Perhaps the town's artistic leanings are a holdover from the early 1970s, when Hanalei was flooded with hippies (a.k.a. "flower children"), mostly from the mainland. Continue driving to **Haena Beach** and **Ke'e Beach State Park**, where the road dries up, and you'll cross some wonderfully scenic one-lane bridges.

WET & DRY CAVES, the north shore.

Gaping at the side of the road, **Maniniholo Dry Cave** sits along Highway 56, past Limahuli Garden. You can walk deep inside this high-ceilinged grotto that is nearly as large as a football field. Lunch wagons wait to serve people at **Haena State Park**, across the road from the cave. **Haena Beach**, great for shelling, is also good for strong swimmers when the water is calm. Local children and adults swim in the rocky stream by the Haena State Park sign on the roadside. A waterfall trickles into the natural pool here. By the old houses in this area, you might see goat and pig skins hung out to dry like laundry, with birds perched on the lines. Some people believe that **Waiakapalae** and **Waiakanaloa Wet Caves** were scooped out by Pele, the fiery volcano goddess. Although the stagnant water is no longer safe for swimming, the caves are impressive sights.

Highway 56 dries up at **Ke'e Beach State Park**, where the 11-mile **Kalalau Trail** along Na Pali Coast begins. From the beach, you'll have a fabulous view of the cliffs. A trail from the beach leads to **Lohiau's Dance Pavilion**. This stone shrine honors Laka, the hula goddess. Present-day hikers sometimes come across offerings left at the altar by contemporary dancers and worshippers.

NA PALI COAST, the north shore.

Meaning "the cliffs" in Hawaiian, Na Pali Coast is accessible only by foot. However, you can enjoy spectacular views of it from both the air and the sea.

Whether this ruggedly beautiful coastline is seen from a boat or raft, through a helicopter window, or while hiking along it on the Kalalau Trail, no traveler should miss an opportunity to visit the region.

When the water is calm enough (in the spring and summer), sightseeing-boats cruise by 4,000-foot precipices and past old valleys. (Some cruises include lunch and snorkeling.) Rubber rafts skirt waterfalls and zip into the caves behind the cascades. Towering over small sandy coves, the striated mountains and cliffs are a melange of greens, oranges, and browns. Huge patches of red earth are visible where chunks of the cliffs have broken off and tumbled into the sea over the centuries. The tiny moving figures boaters see in valleys and along the cliff-top Kalalau trail are goats and hikers. Sometimes following boats, pairs of dolphins show off by spiraling out of the water in unison or rolling on their backs and slapping their tails on the ocean's surface. Huge sea turtles poke their heads out of the Pacific.

Only families with older children will want to try hiking the 11-mile Kalalau Trail, the first two (strenuous) miles of which will take you to a wonderful beach. While the popular **Captain Zodiac**, Tel. 826-9371, raft trips may be too bumpy for the youngest children (and pregnant women), others will enjoy the thrill. And by the way, don't let the word "raft" put you off. These motor-powered craft are actually just small boats.

Bird's Eye View

If you're considering a helicopter ride and you're not going to the Big Island (with its active volcano), then Kauai is where you should board a whirlybird.

MT. WAIALEALE, center of the island.

Rising more than 5,000 feet, Mt. Waialeale (why-ollie-ollie) stands at the center of the nearly round island of Kauai. This extinct volcano is considered among the wettest spots on earth. Almost 500 inches of rain (about 40 feet!) fall on this misty mountain each year, and its dark green slopes are striped with white cascades. But this precipitation is surprisingly localized. Just a few miles west, there's an arid region that receives a mere six inches of rain a year. **Aloha Kauai Tours**, Tel. 245-6400 or 800/452-1113, www.alohakauaitours.com, uses small four-wheel-drive vans to travel the back roads of Kauai. Older children may enjoy the half-day or full-day four-wheel-drive and guided hike in the flourishing Blue Hole area on Mt. Waialeale—especially when they see where scenes from the movie *Jurassic Park* were filmed. The bumpy ride takes you along trails across streams and through thick greenery. Then, on foot, you'll take in fragrant wild flowers and stop at stunning lookout points.

HAWAII MOVIE TOURS, Tel. 822-1192 or 800/628-8432, www.hawaiimovietour.com. Prices begin at $101 (adults), $82 (children under age 12), including lunch.

If you've ever thought you or your kids oughta be in pictures, here's your chance. Re-enact the scene from *Raiders of the Lost Ark* where Indiana Jones swings on a vine above a river to escape his enemies or visit the beach where Mitzi Gaynor vowed to "wash that man right outa my hair" in *South Pacific*. Hawaii Movie Tours will pick you up at your accommodation in a custom-built mini-van complete with a surround-sound system and TV monitor. As you sit back in reclining seats, you'll see scenes from films shot on Kauai, then visit the actual locations. The 4X4 vehicles will take you onto back roads and off roads to see some virtually inaccessible areas.

Beaches

The sandy shores in the north are absolutely gorgeous, but during the winter their waves are much too rough for swimming, snorkeling, or diving. At this time of year, head south to Poipu—the island's most popular resort area—where the water remains much calmer throughout the year. Most of the beaches along the eastern shore are usually not good for swimming since they have high waves and strong currents. These shores also sometimes attract jellyfish—so pay attention to the posted warning signs. Frequented by residents more than visitors, some of the quietest beaches are along the western shore, past Kekaha. Here are Kauai's best beaches for families with children:

Polihale, west coast.

Mid-summer is the safest time to swim in these waters. During the rest of the year, the long, broad, white sand beach watched over by soaring Na Pali sea cliffs is best used as a sunbathing and picnic spot. Dune buggies kick up the sand on weekends, but the beach is refreshingly empty and quiet at other times. Since there are no trees, there is no natural shade—just a few picnic shelters by the base of the cliffs. So you may want to bring an umbrella. Restrooms and showers are provided. Camping is permitted here in tents. When you turn left at the end of Highway 50, you'll be on a bumpy dirt road that winds through seemingly endless fields. Looming ahead, the horizontally striped cliffs bear a strong resemblance to Mount Rushmore.

Note that some car rental agencies prohibit drivers from taking vehicles onto dirt roads.

Kekaha Beach, southwest shore.

The sound of dune buggies often slices the air along this long, narrow, sandy stretch off Highway 50. The undertow is strong and there are usually many breakers. But when the water is calm enough, this is a popular spot for teaching local children to surf. Picnic tables are provided. Camping is permitted.

Salt Pond Beach Park, Hanapepe, south shore.

Families gravitate to this beautiful spot, since the relatively flat waters are fine for swimming. Take advantage of the picnic tables. Unlike some beaches in the area, the sand along this curve is white instead of dark.

Brenneke's Beach, Poipu, south shore.

Bodysurfing and boogie-boarding are all the rage here at one of Kauai's most popular beaches.

Poipu Beach Park, south shore.

Very busy on weekends, Poipu Beach is excellent for surfing. Snorkeling is also rewarding here, and waves are usually manageable for bodysurfing. The shallow natural pool off to one side of the bay seems to have been designed for toddlers and other young children. There are also a playground and a grassy lawn. Lifeguards scan the water. Showers and restrooms are available. See if you can find the petroglyphs (ancient Hawaiian rock carvings) in the park. Be sure to take a spin in this neighborhood; you'll see some beautiful homes.

Kalapaki Beach, Nawiliwili Park, southeast coast.

The swimming is excellent at this sandy curve fronting the lavish Kauai Marriott Resort. Windsurfing is popular among locals here.

Ahukini, east coast.

Stop here if you're in the mood for some good snorkeling.

Lydgate State Park, Wailua, east coast.

In the old days, Hawaiians who had broken kapu (taboos) fled to the Place of Refuge here, thus avoiding punishments that could include death. This beach is much calmer than most of the others along the east coast. Swimmers and snorkelers enjoy splashing around in the rock-enclosed natural pool that's about the size of a football field. Restrooms and a playground across from the shore make this a popular spot for families.

Wailua Beach, east coast.

When the waves are small enough, this is a good spot for swimming or for novice surfers to get the hang of hanging ten.

Anini Beach, north shore.

This protected beach is one of the best north shore strands for swimming during the summer. Windsurfers enjoy this spot. During the winter, however, waves should be left to master surfboarders.

Hanalei Beach Park, north shore.

Hanalei ("crescent bay") aptly describes the namesake sandy cove cupped by mountains. This narrow roadside beach is good for swimming and snorkeling near the pier, where the water is calmest. Across the road from the water, vacation rentals are scattered here and there.

Lumahai Beach, north shore.

It was on this lovely mile-long cliff-enclosed stretch that Mitzi Gaynor sang about washing that man right out of her hair in South Pacific. You can gaze down on this cove from the road or carefully pick your way down the steep trail to the sand. Although this beautiful beach is a great place to spend some quiet time sunbathing, picnicking, or searching for (green) olivine crystals in the sand, it's not safe for swimming..

Makua Beach, north shore.

If you plan to cruise along Na Pali Coast, you'll board your boat or Zodiac here. The view of the cliffs is wonderful, especially in the late afternoon. Since the waters are protected, swimming and snorkeling are fine here during the summer.

Ke'e, north shore.

You'll know you've found this beach when Highway 56 grinds to a halt. This pristine crescent near the beginning of the Kalalau Trail along the top of the Na Pali sea cliffs is calm enough for children during the summer. But be careful of the slabs of rock at the water's edge.

Hula Goddess Hike

A jungled path from **Ke'e Beach** leads to an ancient hula platform, where the blessings of Laka, the hula goddess, are still sometimes invoked. You might see offerings left by recent dancers. The walk is about 10 minutes each way, but only attempt it if the sea is calm and if you're traveling with older children who are experienced hikers. To find the rocky oceanside path, go left (facing the water) around the point. You'll pass some homes and turn inland toward the mountains. Bordered by lush palms, feathery pines, and spikey succulents, the trail begins to climb. When you see the hillside where huge boulders are arranged in lines and in clusters, you've arrived.

Above a wall of rocks, cliffs rise in the background, and the land abruptly drops off to the water. Pandanus trees and casuarinas rustle in the breeze while yellow and red flowers splatter the greenery. The view of the turquoise ocean, set off by white surf, is truly spectacular from here.

൭

Hanakapiai, Na Pali Coast, northwest shore.

Hikers reach this picturesque strand after trekking about two miles on the Kalalau Trail along the cliffs of Na Pali Coast. While it's a scenic place to relax, the currents can be treacherous, so stick to the sand. A freshwater stream adds to the beauty of the setting. However, sometimes during the winter, the beach vanishes at high tide.

Sports & Other Activities

Most accommodations will give you a hand in arranging activities such as catamaran cruises, winter whale watching trips, and Na Pali Coast tours, as well as tennis, golf, snorkeling, and scuba diving.

Biking

Cycling is particularly rewarding on this largely rural island. Mountain bikes can be rented at **Outfitters Kauai,** Tel. 742-7421, in Poipu, and the company will provide maps, helmets, water bottles, and other gear and information. If coasting is more your speed and your children are at least 12 years old, Outfitters Kauai hosts an enjoyable downhill ride. Beginning at 3,500 feet, you'll ride twelve miles of snaking road from the rim of breathtaking Waimea Canyon down to the shore. No need to worry about biking up, since you and your wheels are transported to the top by van. After having coffee and warm muffins, you hit the road. Bikes, helmets, and other safety gear are included. "No extra charge for brakes!" the guides joke. Along the way, guides pause at the most scenic spots to chat with bikers about the history, legends, and natural life of the area. Since it's all downhill, it's easy riding for most folks. However, if at any point the trip is too much for you, you can always travel the rest of the way in the van.

For more biking options, contact **Aloha Kauai Tours**, Tel. 245-6400 or 800/452-1113, www.alohakauaitours.com, or **Pedal and Paddle**, Tel. 826-9069, in Hanalei. Plan to spend $15 to $30 a day for rentals. Four-day and weekly rates are also available.

Fishing

Arrange ocean charters through **Sportfishing Kauai**, Koloa, Tel. 742-7013; **True Blue Kauai**, Lihue, Tel. 246-6333; or **Anini Fishing Charters**, Kilauea, Tel. 828-1285.

Golf

Serious golfers stay in Princeville on the verdant north shore. Made up of three 9-hole courses, the renowned **Princeville Makai Golf Course**, Tel. 826-3580 or 800/826-1105, was designed by Robert Trent Jones, Jr. Green fees range from about $125 for non-resort guests during prime time to $50 after 4pm. At the 18-hole **Princeville Prince Golf Course**, Tel. 826-5000 or 800/

826-1105, green fees range from about $175 during morning hours to $90 for nine holes.

If you're staying down south in the Poipu area, try the 9-hole **Kukuiolono Golf Course**, Tel. 332-9151 ($10 all day), or the 18-hole Robert Trent Jones, Jr., **Poipu Bay Golf Course**, Tel. 742-8711 or 800/858-6300, by the Hyatt (from $185 for non-guests or $125 for Hyatt guests before noon to $65 after 3pm). Another Robert Trent Jones, Jr., design, the 18-hole **Kiahuna Golf Course**, Tel. 742-9595 ($80 in the morning or $40 after 3pm), is also in Poipu.

Puakea Golf Course, Tel. 245-8756 (from $125 for 18 holes to $65 for 9 holes), is in the Lihue area. The 18-hole **Wailua Municipal Golf Course**, Tel. 241-6666 (from $45 on weekend mornings to $16 after 2pm on weekdays), in Wailua, is another good option.

Greens for Young Tigers

The two Jack Nicklaus-designed golf courses at the **Kauai Lagoons Golf Club**, Tel. 241-6000 or 800/634-6400 (from $170 or $120 for the public and $125 or $75 for Kauai Marriott guests to $90 or $55 for 9 holes), are near the Kauai Marriott in Lihue. Both of these courses offer junior rates for children age 17 and younger ($75 or $45).

Helicopter Tours

If your wallet is amenable and if you're traveling with older children, don't miss an opportunity to take a helicopter tour on Kauai. Prices begin at about $135 per person for a 45-minute flight covering the whole island. While Waimea Canyon, Hanalei Valley, and Kalalau Valley can all be seen from lookout points on land and the cliffs of Na Pali Coast can be seen by boat, there's nothing like getting an aerial view of these spectacles. And unless you're a hiker, a bird, or in a low-flying plane, the only way to see lush Mt. Waialeale Crater is by helicopter. Flights take off from both Princeville and Lihue Airport. Some companies provide complimentary ground transportation from hotels to take-off points.

Try **Heli USA**, Tel. 826-6591 or 866/936-1234, **Island Helicopters**, Tel. 245-8588 or 800/829-5999, or **Ohana Helicopter Tours**, Tel. 245-3996 or 800/222-6989.

Hiking

Some 45 miles of Hawaii's most rewarding and extensive hiking trails crisscross 4,435-acre **Kokee State Park**, beginning at around 3,000 feet. Before setting out on any trail, call the **Kokee Natural History Museum**, Tel. 808/335-9975, for a weather update, after 8am. When you arrive, be sure to stop at the museum for trail maps and information about current trail conditions. Trails range from comfortable strolls to challenging treks. For instance, the trail to scenic Waipoo Falls is not long, while more extensive, more rugged routes will take you through dense eucalyptus-studded forest to a cluster of California redwoods. Some families with teenagers enjoy a half or full day of hiking here. All kinds of rare birds and plants flourish in this region. Defying gravity, goats perch precariously at the nearly vertical edges of Waimea Canyon. Delicious *lilikoi* (passion fruit), blackberries, and local Methley plums grow wild. Vistas take in the imposing cliffs of Na Pali Coast, beaches, jungled valleys, and even a swamp.

The Kukui Trail is the only hiking path that goes into **Waimea Canyon**. Some three miles long, it is well marked and well maintained. Of course, it's all downhill (about 90 minutes), then all uphill (about three hours), so you'll have to pace yourself carefully. The trailhead is along the road up to Waimea Canyon Lookout, after the western and eastern roads have met. Other trails lead to waterfalls, swimming holes, or deep into the forest, where you can find a stand of California redwood trees. Nude bathers are not an uncommon sight in the pool below Waipoo Falls No. 1. A favorite spot for relaxation and a picnic is stunning Waipoo Falls No. 2, which overlooks the canyon.

Families with younger children should consider trying the two mile hike along the **Puu Ka Ohelo-Berry Flat Trails**. In addition to California redwoods, you'll pass Australian eucalyptus, Japanese Sugi pines, and other striking trees. Look out for Methley plums and vines laden with ripe *lilikoi*. Banana poka is a favorite snack for Kokee's wild pigs.

Old Wood & Feathers

Kokee State Park's misty forests were once a prime source of lustrous **koa wood**, which was cut into surfboards, canoes, paddles, and weapons. Ancient Hawaiians also came here armed with nets and poles smeared with a glueli1ke substance. They caught the most brilliantly colored birds, plucked their feathers, then released the animals. The plumes were fashioned into ceremonial helmets, robes, and leis to be worn by the alii. Today you can still hear Kokee's moa (wild fowl) conversing loudly with each other. The ancestors of these chickens arrived in Hawaii by canoe with the early Polynesian settlers. Kauai is one of the only parts of the state where these birds still thrive.

Horseback Riding

In the gorgeous Princeville area in the north, **Princeville Ranch Stables**, Tel. 826-6777, conducts trail rides along sea cliffs high above the churning Pacific, through wide open fields, and in Hanalei Valley, with its patchwork of farm plots. The 4-hour Waterfall Picnic Ride ($110 per person, including a gourmet picnic lunch) features a short but steep hike (you'll have to use a rope to get down and up a 10 foot drop) to the 70-foot Kalahiwa Falls, where you'll swim. The ride is about an hour each way, with the rest of the time for picnicking and swimming. The Anini Bluff & Beach Ride ($100 for 3 hours) is another fun excursion.

For families with younger children and slimmer wallets, the 1.5-hour Hanalei Valley Country Ride ($60) is also wonderful. During the ride along the ridge line through fields of ginger, hip-high ferns, and purple-blue wildflowers, you'll have gorgeous, sweeping views of Hanalei Valley, far below. The entire ridge line is a conservation area. At the beginning and end of the trail, you might spot your dream house among the luxurious homes on the other side of the road. During the summer, make reservations at least a week in advance, especially for the picnic ride. The size of groups is anywhere from two to eight people year-round.

Another good company is **Silver Falls Ranch**, Tel. 828-6718, near Kilauea; during the two-hour waterfall picnic ride ($105, age 7 or older), you'll even have a chance to swim in a secluded natural pool. **CJM Country Stables**, Tel. 742-6096, near the Hyatt Regency Kauai in Poipu, leads 2-hour hidden beach rides ($75); 3-hour beach and breakfast rides ($85); and 3 + hour swim-beach-picnic rides ($95). Children must be at least age 7 and able to ride and control the horses by themselves.

Kayaking

One of the most exhilarating activities in Kauai is paddling a kayak along the tranquil Hanalei River, through a wildlife refuge. With hulking mountains in the distance, you'll glide beneath canopies of trees and past taro fields and all kinds of birds, including rare red-headed boobies. Bright yellow hau blossoms float on the water. Being chased by bass, tiny white fish suddenly jump out of the water from time to time. The river is extremely peaceful, since no motorized craft are allowed. The paddling is easy, with plenty of time to simply float and enjoy the scenery.

Contact **Kayak Kauai**, Hanalei, Tel. 826-9844, 800/437-3507, www.kayakkauai.com, which runs a 3-hour guided kayak and snorkel trip through the Hanalei River National Wildlife Refuge ($60 per person). The padded seat cushions make for an especially comfortable trip. When you reach the beach by the Princeville hotel for snorkeling, by the point where the river pours into the ocean, guides show you how to prevent your mask from fogging. You simply rub the inside of the glass with the broken leaves of the morning glory plants growing in the sand. If you have older children, be sure to try **surf kayaking** here. You'll paddle out into the open ocean, beyond the breakers, then catch a wave to ride back to shore. Talk about moving fast! You might spot a sea turtle or two between waves.

For a combination of kayaking, hiking, wagon ride, waterfall swimming, and picnicking, book the Kipu Falls Safari ($130 for adults; $100 for children age 3 to 14) with **Outfitters Kauai**, Tel. 742-9667 or www.outfitterskauai.com. This full-day trip begins with a paddle down the Hulei'a Stream, edged by lush banks, followed by a brief hike up to a valley studded with waterfalls and swimming holes. Although the stream is fed by rain-drenched Mt. Waialeale, its average depth is only four feet and it is no more than ten feet at its deepest. It meanders through densely jungled Hulei'a National Wildlife Refuge, where the opening scenes of Raiders of the Lost Ark were filmed.

Mynah birds screech and egrets perch amid the tangle of mangroves along the shore. Fiery red ginger, monkeypod, and mango trees, hibiscus, and elephant ear plants also border this 18-mile waterway, only three miles of which are navigable. Some parts of the stream swirl around boulders. Try a zip line (attached to a harness, you'll go flying through the forest). Pulled by a tractor, you'll take a covered wagon ride to the Kipu Falls trailhead, then hike down to the picnic area at the edge of the cascade. A twin-hulled powered Hawaiian canoe takes you back down the river.

Scuba Diving

Children as young as age 10 can take an introductory scuba diving course or even get certified. Since Kauai is the oldest of Hawaii's main islands, the coral below its waters has had more time to build colonies on top of colonies. Thus, its reefs are some of the state's most complex and scenic. Most of Kauai's best diving is along the southern, protected coast. Many good south shore dive sites are just 10 to 30 minutes away from Port Allen and Kukuiula Harbor.

Koloa Landing is a good place for new divers to test the waters. The reef here at this old boat landing slowly descends to 25 feet. Old bottles and fittings from 18th and 19th century whaling ships and trading vessels can be found on the ocean floor. Underwater explorers will also see parts of the old train track that once ran between Koloa Landing and the area's sugar mill. All kinds of fish swarm around, including butterfly fish and blue-striped snapper. Divers get a kick out of feeding the moray eels here.

To arrange dives or to take scuba classes, try **Sea Sport Divers**, Tel. 742-9303, in the Poipu area, or **Dive Kauai**, Tel. 822-0452, in Kapaa. Dives begin at about $100. Certification classes start around $425 for one person or $375 for two or more. One-day introductory courses start at about $135, including the pool session and two-tank boat dive.

Snorkeling

Many accommodations rent snorkel gear or help guests arrange snorkeling cruises. Most of the Na Pali boat or raft cruises include snorkeling. Sea turtles and dolphins are often spotted in this area. During most of the winter, when the water is rough along the north shore, the majority of cruises are conducted along other coasts. Try **Captain Zodiac Raft Expeditions**, in Hanalei, Tel. 826-9371; children must be age 5 or older, but these rides may be too bumpy for young children. **Kauai Kayak Outbound**, in Hanalei, Tel. 826-9844, offers a three-hour kayak trip that includes about 30 or 40 minutes of paddling plus time for snorkeling and playing on the beach. You can also rent gear or arrange boat trips through your accommodation. Also try **Aloha Kauai Tours**, Tel. 245-6400 or 800/452-1113, www.alohakauaitours.com.

Surfing

The best surfing is along the north shore during the winter and in the Poipu area in the summer. To rent boards or to arrange lessons, try **Nuku Moi Surfing School**, Tel. 742-8019, at Brennecke's Beach in Poipu. They say they have taught kids as young as three years old, "as long as they can swim." In the Kapaa area, consider **Kauai Water Ski, Surf & Kayak**, Tel. 822-3574. You may also make arrangements through your accommodation.

Tennis

Kauai has no shortage of tennis courts. In addition to scores of hotel courts, there are many public courts lit for night play. Some resorts charge guests a small fee to play, while others offer free tennis.

Windsurfing

Anyone age 5 and older can take windsurfing lessons with **Windsurf Kauai**, Tel. 828-6838, at Anini Beach. On the north shore just before Princeville, this three-mile sandy stretch is protected by reefs, so it's excellent for novice windsurfers, snorkelers, and swimmers. Many hotels can also arrange windsurfing lessons or board rental.

Working Out & Spas

If you're staying in the Princeville area, you'll find it convenient to use the extensive spa and fitness center at the entrance to the **Prince Golf Course** for a daily fee. The exercise room and class studio have one of the world's most spectacular views. You'll be so dazzled by the rolling green swards of the golf course and the verdant mountains that you won't even realize you're breaking a sweat. This is also the place for exceptional toe-to-earlobe massages among other delicious body treatments.

The **Hyatt Regency Kauai Resort & Spa** has another snazzy exercise room and a health spa, where the facials and massages are fabulous. Consider scheduling a private exercise session with a personal trainer while the kids are at the children's program.

I'm Hungry!

Kauai may not be famous for its culinary expertise, but it has enough good restaurants to keep most vacationers—and residents—satisfied. They run the gamut from roadside to gourmet settings. Note that some serve dinner only. Dress is casual at all but a couple of places.

Many restaurants offer crayons, paper, and children's menus. The usual suspects for the young crowd are chicken tenders, fish and chips, grilled cheese, and pasta. Some places offer kids international fare such as teriyaki chicken, miniature pizzas, and cheese quesadillas. Restaurants that don't have mini menus are generally amenable to serving children's portions.

Price ranges at each restaurant below are for *most* dinner entrees; for instance, lobster and prime rib may cost more and sandwiches may be less.

Mini Yum!

Snack time on Kauai can lead to all kinds of delicious mini adventures. When you're tooling around up north, be sure to stop at roadside **Hanalei Taro & Juice Co**. Here versatile taro root is turned into delicious hi-calcium fresh-fruit smoothies in flavors including banana, pineapple, strawberry, coconut, mango, papaya, and guava. My favorite treat here, though, is the taro butter mochi, a scrumptious dessert (somewhere between cake and pudding) made of taro, coconut milk, butter, and sugar.

Also in Hanalei, try **Hanalei Mixed Plate**, a roadside stand with a few tables in the Ching Young Village shopping strip. Among the most popular plate lunches here are the mahi mahi sandwich, teriyaki chicken, grilled ahi, Kalua pork sandwich, and fresh vegetable stir-fry.

Created by Walter Lappert to combat the idleness he found in retirement, **Lappert's Ice Cream** is manufactured near Hanapepe. You can buy some at the stand there, or at restaurants and stores around the island. Fresh local fruits are incorporated into this smooth, rich treat, such as *lilikoi* (passion fruit), guava, coconut, papaya, mango, pineapple, and lichee.

Sold at **Taro Ko Chips**, a tiny Mom-and-Pop factory in a former home in Hanapepe, crisp sliced and fried taro is a refreshing alternative to potato chips. Tiny purple threads decorate each delicious chip, sprinkled with garlic salt. This snack is made from the same root that when mashed and fermented becomes poi. But unlike the ancient Hawaiian staple, these chips win over the uninitiated with one bite.

Another winner is locally produced **Kukui Nut Guava Jam**. Hanapepe's **Kauai Kookie** is also a good stop. For mouth-watering pastries and breads, try **Kilauea Bakery** in Kilauea.

The West & South

TIDEPOOLS, Hyatt Regency Kauai, Poipu. Tel. 742-1234. Dinner only. Reservations recommended. Dinner entrees: $27 to $38. Credit cards accepted.

Plants spill over the rafters in the large circular bar where diners wait to be seated. Various dining areas are scattered in this series of thatched roof hales (shelters) at the edge of a lagoon. Some tables have the open-air nooks overhanging the water all to themselves. The specialties of the house include fish, which comes blackened, sautéed, grilled, or baked. You might try macadamia nut crusted mahi mahi or steamed Hawaiian snapper with ginger, cilantro, scallions, soy, and sesame oil. Meat eaters can choose between filet mignon and prime rib. If you can't decide between land and sea, try one of the combination meat and seafood entrees, such as filet mignon and Alaskan king crab. On the children's menu, you'll find chicken tenders, fish and chips, grilled cheese, and pasta.

DONDERO'S, Hyatt Regency Kauai, Poipu. Tel. 742-1234. Dinner only. Reservations recommended. Dinner entrees: $27 to $38. Credit cards accepted.

At this excellent Italian restaurant, decorative tiles and wine bottles adorn walls, and colorful jars of antipasto are on display. The soft fresh bread that accompanies meals is dipped in a wonderfully seasoned tomato and onion sauce. The wine list is outstanding. Among the pasta, my favorites are the roasted red bell pepper gnocchi with sautéed lobster and the spaghettini alla pescatora. The midwest lamb chops with warm potato salad, marinated chicken breast with a spicy diablo sauce, and the delicately seasoned veal scaloppini are beautifully prepared and presented. Come before dark for a view of the palms, gardens, and the sea. Pasta and mini pizzas are on the children's menu.

KEOKI'S PARADISE, Poipu Shopping Village, 2360 Kiahuna Plantation Drive, Poipu. Tel. 742-7534 Reservations recommended. Dinner entrees: $18 to $27. Credit cards accepted.

A lagoon, fringed with lush vegetation and complete with lava rocks and waterfalls, meanders between the tables in this very popular open-air restaurant. Dishes on the menu include several different types of fish prepared in a choice of ways (from teriyaki to baked with orange-ginger sauce), pork ribs glazed with plum sauce, and shrimp with macadamia nut pesto. Whet your appetite with a tangy lilikoi (passion fruit) margarita, a frozen mai tai, or a frothy pina colada. While the dining room is often filled with families, the thatched roof bar, which serves pupus and other snacks, draws a friendly crowd of young singles.

For dessert, few pass up the hula pie (macadamia nut ice cream on an Oreo cookie crust, topped with chocolate sauce, whipped cream, and macadamia nuts). The live music (several nights a week, plus Sunday afternoons) adds to the pleasant atmosphere. Expect to find Koloa ribs, teriyaki chicken, burgers, and pasta on the children's menu.

BRENNECKE'S BEACH BROILER, Poipu. Tel. 742-7588. Reservations recommended. Dinner entrees: $12 to $30. Credit cards accepted.

Diners may watch the chef in action at this popular restaurant overlooking the water. Tables on the second floor have the best view of the shore. Distinctively flavored kiawe-grilled ahi and seafood, such as Alaskan King Crab, are house specialties but they also do a fine job with prime ribs and steak, as well as the more mundane burgers and pizza. Kids seem to enjoy the burgers, chicken tenders, cheese quesadillas, and spaghetti. Some patrons have noted that the food here is uneven, but the view of the Pacific is always excellent.

ROY'S POIPU BAR & GRILL, Poipu Shopping Village, 2360 Kiahuna Plantation Drive, Poipu. Tel. 742-5000. Dinner entrees: $15 to $29. Credit cards accepted.

After making a name for himself on Oahu and Maui, Roy Yamaguchi opened this dining spot in 1994. With a hefty selection of daily specials, the creative European-Asian-Pacific menu is always changing. Expect to find dishes like seared opakapaka (snapper) with black bean sauce, dumplings stuffed with smoked duck, crispy lemongrass chicken with Thai red curry, ravioli of summer vegetables with green peppercorn sauce, and grilled shrimp with mushrooms and risotto. The children's menu includes some imaginative dishes as well as old standards.

CASA DI AMICI, 2301 Nalo Road, Poipu. Tel. 742-1555. Reservations required. Dinner entrees: $16 to $28. Credit cards accepted.

Along with views of the ocean, Casa di Amici serves some delicious Italian food with an international twist. You might find pasta with walnuts in a Romano cheese cream sauce or glazed salmon with grilled tiger prawns and jalapeño refried black beans. Children's portions are available.

WAIMEA BREWING CO., 9400 Kaumualii Highway, Waimea (adjacent to Waimea Plantation Cottages). Tel. 338-9733. Dinner entrees: $15 to $30. Credit cards accepted.

Open for lunch and dinner, this brewery serves some good "handcrafted" ales, along with wine and a full bar. Several nights a week, live music, sometimes played by a group of renowned Hawaiian musicians, entertains patrons. The Jawaiian Chicken (chicken breast made with spicy jerk seasoning and served with Caribbean rice and peas) is reminiscent of Hawaii's love of Jamaican reggae music. Ale-battered fish and chips is another good choice. My favorite is the furikaki-crusted ahi, which is pan-seared tuna coated with seaweed and served with sticky rice. Children gravitate toward the burgers, tacos, pasta, and chicken dishes.

KOKEE LODGE, Kokee State Park. Tel. 335-6061. Open for lunch only. $5 to $10. Credit cards accepted.

Nestled in thick wilderness 3,600 feet above Kauai's tropical coast, this rustic mountain lodge serves salads, soups, sandwiches, and other home-style favorites. Your midday meal might include Portuguese red bean soup, chili and cornbread, or smoked barbecued beef.

GREEN GARDEN, Hanapepe. Tel. 335-5422. Dinner only. Reservations recommended. Closed Tuesdays. $13 to $18. Credit cards accepted.

Many locals recommend this family-oriented dining spot for its steak, fish, and shrimp. The emphasis is on homestyle Chinese and American cooking. Soup and the salad bar come with each meal. The name is a perfect description of the restaurant—all the potted and hanging orchids and other plants and flowers give diners the feeling that they are outdoors. Children like the fish, shrimp, and chicken teriyaki, the fried chicken "wing dings," the breaded mahi, the pork chops, and the burgers.

BRICK OVEN PIZZA, 2-2555 Kaumualii Highway, Kalaheo. Tel. 332-8561. Open 11am to 10pm. Closed Mondays. Inexpensive. Credit cards accepted.

Many residents consider this the best place to come for pizza on Kauai.

Lihue Area

BARBECUE INN, 2982 Kress, off Rice Street, Lihue. Tel. 245-2921. Dinner entrees: $10 to $25. Closed Sundays.

For decades, this restaurant has won the praise of locals who have recommended it highly for its varied plate lunches and other home-style dishes. The family owners pride themselves on baking their own breads and pies daily. Even the gourmet fish and lobster dishes have homestyle touches, and at moderate prices. If crab-stuffed mahi mahi is on the menu, try it. For children, choices include burgers and fries, grilled cheese, teriyaki chicken, and spaghetti.

HANAMAULU CAFE, TEA HOUSE, AND SUSHI BAR, Highway 56, Hanamaulu, just north of Lihue. Tel. 245-3225. Closed Mondays. Open Tuesday through Friday for lunch, and Tuesday through Sunday for dinner. Reservations recommended. Entrees: $8 to $18. Credit cards accepted.

You can choose between Japanese and Chinese food at this attractive indoor/outdoor teahouse set off with a pond and landscaped gardens. While there's a sushi bar, some Japanese selections are cooked on an open grill. Cantonese entrees include sweet and sour spareribs, crab claws, and chop suey. The restaurant is known for its Chinese fried chicken plate lunches and its Japanese plate lunches with teriyaki beef, chicken, or fish, and miso soup. For dessert, try the deep-fried custard rolled in powdered sugar and sesame seeds.

HAMURA SAIMIN, 2956 Kress, off Rice Street, Lihue. Tel. 245-3271. Open Monday to Saturday 10am to midnight; Sunday 10am to 9pm. Entrees: $4 to $7.

People are often standing in line for the swivel stools at the low counters in this local favorite that looks as though it hasn't changed since the 1960s.

If you're not patient enough to eat in, take-out is available. The heaping bowls of delicious saimin are filled with homemade noodles. Other popular items are barbecued beef or chicken, udon, wonton, and fried noodles. For dessert, treat yourself to a slice of *lilikoi* (passionfruit) chiffon pie or buy a whole pie to take back to your condo. Watch the chefs in action in the open kitchen.

The East Coast

A PACIFIC CAFE, 4-831 Kuhio Highway, Kauai Village, Kapaa. Tel. 822-0013. Dinner only. Reservations recommended. Dinner entrees: $22 to $28. Credit cards accepted.

Woks and a wood-burning grill add a special flavor to the Pacific Rim dishes served at this restaurant. Framed photos and paintings (for sale) adorn the walls of the bright, cheerful dining room. The grill is in full view, and chefs' hats constantly bob up and down behind the pick-up counter. To help you decide what to have, take a peek at other people's orders before waiters whisk them away. Consider the award-winning signature dish: wok-charred mahi-mahi.

Each day, there's a new array of selections, all prepared and presented with an artistic eye for color, texture, and surprise. To start, you might find Thai Caesar salad with wonton chips, sautéed crab cakes with papaya basil sauce, or sizzling squid salad with sesame lime dressing. Then perhaps you'll choose among seared Australian salmon with orange ginger sauce, sirloin steak with lemon grass peanut crust and citrus sauce, and potato and tofu lasagna with ginger scallion pesto. Children enjoy the pasta, grilled chicken, spaghetti, and grilled mahi. Leave room for one of the delicious desserts.

COCONUTS ISLAND STYLE GRILL & BAR, 4-919 Kuhio Highway, Kapaa. Tel. 823-8777. Dinner only. Reservations recommend. Dinner entrees: $12 to $26. Credit cards accepted. Closed Sundays.

Split bamboo mats decorating the ceiling and banana-leaf menu covers set the tone for this tropical restaurant full of pleasant surprises. Bread is served with hummus. The delicious lobster bisque is unusually spicy. Candied pecans add a nice touch to the salad of organic Kapaa garden greens and gorgonzola cheese. Grouper might come flavored with strawberries. Even the tempura-dipped ono (a fish) with ginger-wasabi, stir-fried rice, and veggies is somehow lighter and tastier than at other restaurants.

For dessert, you can't go wrong with the crème brulee mixed with tropical fruits, the chocolate volcano cake (warm chocolate cake with coffee sauce), or pineapple upside down cake. Although this restaurant is dimly lit and there is no children's menu, high chairs are available and the youngest diners enjoy dishes such as the chicken pot pie, spaghetti, and macaroni and cheese.

PAPAYA'S, Village Shopping Center, Wailua. Tel. 823-0191. Open Monday to Saturday 9am to 8pm (café closes at 7pm). Closed Sundays. Inexpensive. Credit cards accepted.

We tried this restaurant, espresso bar, and bakery after several readers had written to me raving about it, and I found it as good as they said. Food here is prepared with all natural ingredients, without preservatives. Most of it is locally grown and raised. For breakfast, consider the tofu scramble, banana pancakes, frittata, or granola with fruit. For lunch or dinner, you might try the ginger udon noodles, the tempeh, tofu, or chicken burgers, the chili with cornbread, or the basmati rice with eggplant. The curries and vegetable lasagna also get high marks, as do the salads, pizza, and homemade chocolate cake. The garden burgers are just as delicious. If you're staying somewhere with a kitchen or a refrigerator, you may want to stop at the natural foods grocery section.

KOUNTRY KITCHEN, 1485 Kuhio Highway, Kapaa. Tel. 822-3511. Breakfast and lunch only (open 6am to 2pm). Lunch entrees: $6 to $8.

Locals pile in for breakfast. Friendly waiters serve large portions, such as the Polynesian omelet, stuffed with kim chee, Portuguese sausage, onions and cheese; or the Kountry Kitchen omelet, with hamburger or tuna, onions, peppers, tomatoes and cheese; both with cornbread. The lunch menu features burgers, from bleu cheese to mushroom, club sandwiches, grilled mahi-mahi, and you might find blueberry cobbler for dessert.

DUANE'S ONO-CHAR BURGER, Anahola. Tel. 822-9181. Entrees: $5 to $10. Credit cards accepted.

Not to be confused with Ono Family Restaurant in Kapaa, this is a roadside stand. "Ono" means delicious in Hawaiian, and these burgers are just that, according to many residents who rarely pass by without stopping to munch. This is a good lunch spot along the way to the north shore. If you'd prefer not to eat on the run, take a seat at one of the round tables in the shade of the royal poinciana trees. The house specialty is the avocado burger, which also comes piled with alfalfa sprouts, cheddar cheese and lettuce, and is smothered in teriyaki sauce.

The North

THE HANALEI DOLPHIN, Hanalei. Tel. 826-6113. Dinner entrees: $18 to $27. Credit cards accepted.

Grab an umbrella-shaded table at the river's edge, sit on the lanai, or dine inside with a view of the beautifully landscaped rock garden. Both lunch and dinner are served in this attractive setting. For lunch, consider a Cajun fish burger, a teriyaki chicken sandwich, or a tempeh veggie burger. For dinner, the stars of the steak and seafood menu include the charcoal broiled teriyaki shrimp, the scallops baked in wine and topped with mozzarella, and the king crab-filet mignon combination. For dessert, New York cheesecake is a good choice, along with banana-coconut-macadamia nut ice cream pie with an Oreo crust. A children's menu is available.

ZELO'S BEACH HOUSE CAFE, Hanalei. Tel. 826-9700. Dinner entrees: $12 to $25. Credit cards accepted.

This restaurant and grill is a good place to stop while you're touring the north shore, but it's often quite busy at lunch time. Consider an omelet; a hummus, Cajun chicken, or tuna wrap; a seafood quesadilla; a fish taco; or the soup and salad—maybe a bowl of seafood chowder and a salad of organic wild greens. For dinner, you might find crab-stuffed fish baked in lemon and ginger; fresh catch and prime rib; coconut shrimp; Hawaiian chicken (boneless breasts marinated in teriyaki sauce and grilled with fresh pineapple); sun-dried tomato pesto rigatoni; or burgers (veggie or beef). Room for dessert? The grasshopper pie (mint ice cream on an Oreo cookie crust, topped with fudge, whipped cream, and macadamia nuts) and the *lilikoi* (passion fruit) chiffon pie both move quickly.

TROPICAL TACO, Hanalei. Tel. 827-8226. Inexpensive. Closed Sundays.

Sure, it's called Tropical Taco, but it's the aroma of freshly baked cookies that draws many patrons into this casual roadside dining spot. I dare you and the kids to eat only one just-out-of-the-oven chocolate-chip walnut cookie! But before you do, order a taco, burrito, or tostado with beef, chili, vegetables, or—the hands-down favorite—fish.

PAU HANA PIZZA & KILAUEA BAKERY, Kong Lung Center Garden Courtyard, Kilauea Road and Keneke Street, Kilauea. Tel. 828-2020. Open daily. Bakery hours: 6:30am to 9pm. Pizza hours: 11am to 9pm. Inexpensive.

Try this cafe for soup, salad, pizza, and fresh baked goods. You'll have a choice of whole wheat or traditional crust. While cheese and tomato pies are certainly available, these pizzas can also be far from ordinary. Toppings include anchovies, tiger prawns, house smoked ono (wahoo), barbecue chicken, smoked ham, roasted onions and red peppers, seasoned eggplant, sun-dried tomato pesto, and pineapple. Among the assorted cheeses are goat, feta, gorgonzola, and grated parmesan. At the bakery, the sourdough breads are popular, along with the cinnamon buns, croissants, and sesame, garlic, and chili pepper breadsticks.

Which One is My Bed?

Where you stay on Kauai may depend on how much time you have and what you plan to do. You can see the whole island comfortably in a few days from a single home base. However, some families enjoy the dramatic contrast of dividing their vacation between an accommodation in the drier south and one in the more flourishing north.

Poipu, along the southeast coast, is the island's driest resort area. The beaches are excellent here, especially during the winter when most of those along the north coast are too rough for swimming. During the summer, Poipu's shores are great for surfing, both body and board. This area is close to Lihue, the capital, and attractions such as Kilohana Plantation, Grove Farm Homestead, Waimea Canyon, Kokee State Park, and golf.

Because of rocky shores or strong currents, many east coast beaches are never safe for swimming. Along this shore, hotels and condos in Wailua and Kapaa are near golf, restaurants, and lots of shopping. Also nearby are sights including ancient heiau (temples), both Opaekaa and Wailua waterfalls, Wailua River, and Fern Grotto.

In the north, where refreshing showers aren't unusual, Hanalei and Princeville attract serious golfers to various courses. Lovers of verdant tranquility are also drawn to this region. As gorgeous as they are to look at, the waters off many of the beaches along this coast should be avoided during the winter. Attractions in this area include river and ocean kayaking, dramatic hiking trails, impressive Na Pali cliffs, stunning valleys covered with taro patches, the distinctive peaks known as "Bali Hai," wet and dry caves, and excellent arts and crafts shops (in Hanalei).

Kauai's hotels with formal children's programs are the Hyatt Regency Kauai, the Sheraton Kauai, and Kiahuna Plantation, which take kids from 3 to 12 years old; and the Kauai Marriott and the Princeville Resort, which take children ages 5 to 12.

Home Sweet Home on Kauai

On Kauai, staying in vacation homes puts visitors in some of the prettiest parts of the island, usually in quiet residential communities. Note that most rates for condos and private homes are based on a minimum three-night to one-week stay, so nightly rates may be higher for shorter stays or lower for longer visits. For information about condos and vacation home rentals in addition to those I describe, contact the following:
• Gloria's Vacation Rentals, Tel. 800/684-5133 or 808/742-2850, www.gloriasvacationrentals.com
• Hanalei North Shore Properties, Tel. 800/488-3336
• Kauai Vacation Rentals, Tel. 800/367-5025, www.kauaivacationrentals.com

Poipu

WHALERS COVE, 2640 Puuholo Road, Koloa, HI 96756. Tel. 808/742-7571 or 800/225-2683, www.whalers-cove.com. 39 units. Rates begin at $480 (two-bedroom). Major credit cards.

Although this attractive condo complex is on a rocky shore, it's a great place for winter whale watching and the beach is only a five-minute drive away. It is close to a fine snorkeling/scuba diving cove. Facilities include a heated oceanfront swimming pool.

All suites have two bedrooms and two baths, but some units are larger than others. Some units have whirlpool baths. Cooled by ceiling fans instead of air conditioning, these modern apartments have TVs, high ceilings, huge walk-in closets, cushiony carpets, and rich brown koa molding and doors. In most master baths, there's a whirlpool tub, some with a view of the Pacific, along with two free-standing sinks. Patios are large and shaded by palms. Kitchens are decked out with microwave ovens, dishwashers, and washers/dryers. The 18-hole Poipu Bay and Kiahuna golf courses are nearby, as are tennis courts and other Poipu attractions. The hosts are always happy to direct vacationers to family-friendly activities around the island.

HYATT REGENCY KAUAI RESORT & SPA, 1571 Poipu Road, Koloa, HI 96756. Tel. 808/742-1234 or 800/233-1234, www.hyatt.com. 602 rooms. Rates begin at $425. Major credit cards.

Where sugarcane fields once sprawled, this lavishly landscaped hotel is built into a hill that slopes gently toward the ocean. Long a prime local surfing spot, the water here can be dangerous for swimming. However, with the Hyatt's heated saltwater lagoons at the edge of the Pacific and its elaborate swimming pools terraced down the hillside, guests hardly notice. Complete with waterfalls, the main pool winds under bridges, past flourishing greenery and boulders draped with bougainvillea.

It's great that the hotel sprawls horizontally instead of vertically. But this means you may have a very long walk between your beautifully appointed room and the elegant lobby, gourmet restaurants, pools, and beach. So make sure you haven't forgotten anything when you leave your room! (Note that some rooms face the parking lot, golf course, and mountains.)

The Hyatt takes three-year-olds (as long as they are potty trained) into their children's program, which goes up to age 12. Our daughter thoroughly enjoyed the arts and crafts, swimming, lei-making, story time, and other activities. Parents are content that their children are being well-supervised and -entertained while they check out the 18-hole Robert Trent Jones, Jr., golf course, the tennis courts, and the extensive health spa (with a lap pool in a sunny courtyard, open-air whirlpools, and massage rooms with private lanais), or just cool out by the pool. If there are enough children staying here, the program runs year-round.

Many families enjoy the contemporary Hawaiian music and hula performances each evening on the ocean-view terrace. Each week, authentic hula halau (schools) entertain guests as well, and Hawaiian old-timers have been enlisted to teach visitors (both adults and children) traditional arts such as making leis, quilts, and Niihau necklaces (stringing rare, extremely valuable shells from Hawaii's "Forbidden Island," once off-limits to most non-Hawaiians). The hotel's library, where you can hear live jazz every night, is a pleasant place to relax and flip through the many books on Hawaiiana.

KIAHUNA PLANTATION, 2253 Poipu Road, Koloa, HI 96756. Tel. 808/742-6411 or 800/688-7444, www.outrigger.com. 333 units. Rates begin at $225. Major credit cards.

Wake up to the sound of birds and roosters at this pleasant resort with a rural feel. Our children love running wild across the sprawling lawns, and during the summer and other school holidays, the resort offers a children's program. Set amid 35 acres of landscaped grounds, beachfront cottages and low-rise buildings contain one- and two-bedroom apartments. With lanais and high ceilings, these home-like condos are decorated with tropical furniture, ceramic floors, and wall-to-wall carpeting. The small kitchenettes are equipped with microwaves, stoves, refrigerators with icemakers, dishwashers, and even wine glasses. Note that there are no elevators, so if your unit is on the third floor, pack lightly! Your apartment won't have air-conditioning, but cross-breezes seem to do the trick.

Wander through exquisite Moir Gardens, with colorful flowering plants, trees, bushes, lily pads in ponds, and over 100 varieties of cacti from all over the world. The original plantation manager's house is where you'll find the restaurant. Here the wraparound lanai and garden view make it especially inviting.

A variety of water sports may be arranged at the beach. Guests are welcome to use the nearby tennis courts and the garden swimming pool at the neighboring Sheraton Kauai Resort. Note, however, that you should consider taking a picnic lunch to the pool at the Sheraton. You can charge lunch here to your room at Kiahuna Plantation. But you have to order your meal by phone from the pool area and sometimes wait for 30 minutes for it to arrive.

POIPU KAPILI, 2221 Kapili Road, Koloa, HI 96756. Tel. 808/742-6449 or 800/443-7714, www.poipukapili.com. 45 units. Rates begin at $210. Major credit cards.

Across the road from the water, these sprawling low-rise buildings with balconies are set amid artfully landscaped grounds. Some of the greenery has a practical use: Guests are encouraged to pick their favorite seasonings from the herb garden. All of the spacious one- and two-bedroom apartments and penthouse units have high ceilings, ceiling fans, and louvered wooden sliding doors leading to lanais. (There's no AC, but it's not missed.) Microwave- and dishwasher-equipped kitchens with stools at their counters open onto tremendous living/dining rooms. A tub is in one bath while the other has a stall shower. At this small, quiet accommodation, a swimming pool and tennis courts are on the premises and good beaches are within walking distance. When you're in the mood for more action, head to the nearby Sheraton.

SHERATON KAUAI RESORT, 2440 Hoonani Road, Poipu Beach, HI 96756. Tel. 808/742-1661 or 800/782-9488. www.sheraton-kauai.com. 414 rooms. Rates begin at $200. Major credit cards.

You'll want to dive right into the water as soon as you see the wonderful view from the check-in area of the Sheraton's oceanfront section. In various low-rise buildings near the beach or gardens, the spacious guest rooms come complete with everything from *yukatas* (Japanese robes) to Sony Play

Stations. Guests may hit the massage and fitness center, two swimming pools (with toddler wading pools), tennis courts, and shops, all set amid tropical foliage and koi ponds. Scuba lessons are free for adults and teenagers, and boogie boards and snorkel gear are available for rent.

This resort is particularly family-friendly, with connecting guest rooms, in-room refrigerators, coin-operated washers and dryers, and children's discounts. Parents who need a break can drop off the little ones (aged 5 to 12) at the children's center.

Ask for a table near the windows at Shells, the main restaurant, which offers panoramic views of the ocean along with the fish, pork, beef, lamb, and pasta. Be sure to dine here for the weekly seafood buffet. Other dining spots, in a variety of indoor and outdoor settings, include Naniwa, featuring Japanese cuisine and views of a koi pond. The Point is the perfect place for light lunches and suppers, sunset-watching, pupus, and after-dinner drinks with live music.

KOLOA LANDING COTTAGES, 2704-B Hoonani Road, Koloa, HI 96756. Tel. 808/742-1470 or 800/779-8773, www.koloa-landing.com. 8 units. Rates begin at $145 (two-bedroom unit).

This small accommodation appeals to vacationers looking to escape the crowds. It offers one- and two-bedroom cottages, with full kitchens, exposed beam ceilings, and cable TV. Accommodations in the main house include two bedrooms and two baths. Tradewinds stand in for AC. Fruit trees on the grounds provide kids with delicious snacks. Beaches are a stroll away, and various restaurants are also nearby. The owners give guests as much—or as little—personal attention as they need. A laundry room is on the premises. Note that a one-time clean-up fee (about $100) is added to the rates.

NIHI KAI VILLAS, 1870 Ho'one Road, Koloa, HI 96756, Tel. 808/742-1412, 808/ 742-2000, 800/325-5701, or 800/742-1412, www.grantham-resorts.com. 70 units. Rates begin at $140.

A short walk from Brennecke's Beach (popular among body surfers) and Poipu Beach Park (with its shallow toddler-size natural pool), these spacious, individually furnished apartments are a hit with families. Whether you choose a one-, two-, or three-bedroom unit, you'll find at least two lanais, a fully-equipped kitchen, cable TV, VCR, CD player, and washer/dryer. Views take in the ocean and gardens. Most vacationers don't mind the lack of AC (ceiling fans cool things off just fine) and housekeeping service, especially when you consider Nihi Kai Villas' appealing facilities: adult and children's oceanfront swimming pools, two tennis courts (complimentary to guests), a paddle-tennis court, and a barbecue area.

WAIKOMO STREAM VILLAS, 2721 Poipu Road, Koloa, HI 96756, Tel. 808/742-7220, 808/742-2000, 800/325-5701, or 800/742-1412, www.grantham-resorts.com. 60 units. Rates begin at $105.

Trying to stretch those dollars? Consider booking a one- or two-bedroom apartment at this pleasant condo set amid tropical gardens. From some units, you can even see the ocean in the distance. Swimming pools, for both children and adults, a complimentary tennis court, and barbecue grills keep guests happily occupied on the premises. Kids love following the stream that winds throughout the resort, which is next door to the Robert Trent Jones 18-hole Kiahuna Golf Course. A 10-minute stroll along the coast will take you to the beach at the Sheraton, and "Baby Beach," with its sheltered lagoon, is even closer. For all kinds of water sports, Poipu Beach Park and Brennecke's Beach are about a five-minute drive away.

While there is no housekeeping service or air-conditioning, the huge, comfortable apartments do come with tiled lanais, koa wood and teak accents inside, plus cable TV, VCR, CD player, and washer/dryer. In the split-level two-bedroom units with vaulted ceilings, the second bedroom (with its own full bathroom) overlooks the living room and dining room downstairs.

Waimea

WAIMEA PLANTATION COTTAGES, Kaumualii Highway, Waimea, HI 96796. Tel. 808/338-1625 or 800/9-WAIMEA, www.waimea-plantation.com, 58 units. Rates begin at $250 (two-bedroom cottage). Major credit cards.

Away from south shore crowds, this secluded accommodation is an excellent place to unwind. Waimea Plantation Cottages feels exactly like the kind of environment people come to Kauai for. Dating from 1910 to 1930, these homey cottages, some of which are on the beach, were once the homes of sugar plantation workers. Set amid a beautiful palm grove, they now have one to five bedrooms, full kitchens, cable TV, VCR, telephones, and cassettes or CD players. Most units are not air conditioned, but ceiling fans and ocean breezes do the job. Because of the size of units, this is a good choice for large families.

All cottages are on the ocean side of the road, but some are closer to the water than others. The sand is dark on this tranquil beach and the water is murky due to silt from the river that runs into the ocean. However, there's a pool on the grounds, and a swimming beach is about a mile west of here, in Kekaha. **Waimea Brewing Company,** a pub and restaurant, is on the premises and other dining spots are not far. Limited shopping is nearby in the town of Waimea. Horseback riding and other types of recreation can easily be arranged.

Planning a family reunion or traveling with friends? Ask about the hotel's 6-bedroom house in Hanalei Bay, on Kauai's north shore. (For this house, there's a 7-night minimum stay.)

KOKEE LODGE, Waimea Canyon Drive, Kokee State Park, Box 819, Waimea, HI 96796. 12 cabins. Tel. 808/335-6061. Rates begin at $50 (two-bedroom cabin). Major credit cards.

Nature-loving families will appreciate these simple cabins high in the mountains of Kokee State Park. Three-thousand-six-hundred feet above sea level, they are halfway between spectacular Waimea Canyon and Kalalau Lookout. Wild fowl roam the grounds. The cool misty air in these thick woods is sweet with the smell of eucalyptus and pine. Here on a tropical island, blankets and wood-burning stoves get much use (wood is available at an additional cost). Each of the studio and two-bedroom cabins (sleeping from three to six people) contains a refrigerator, gas or electric stove, cooking and eating utensils, beds, blankets, pillows, linens, and a hot shower. The cabins that are paneled in aromatic cedar are far nicer than the other units.

Hikers enjoy picking wild plums (in season, during the first week of July) and fishing for rainbow trout in streams (August; freshwater fishing licenses are required). In the main building, the restaurant serves light lunches daily. A gift shop and the petite **Kokee Natural History Museum** next door are also worth some time. The Lodge is 40 miles from Lihue Airport, at least a 90-minute drive. The last 15 miles are along a steep, curvaceous, narrow road.

Lihue Area

KAUAI MARRIOTT RESORT & BEACH CLUB, Kalapaki Beach, Lihue, HI 96766. Tel. 808/245-5050 or 800/220-2925, www.marriotthotels.com. 464 rooms. Rates begin at $260. Major credit cards.

Part hotel, part time-share, this sprawling resort is a handsome vacation playground with 51 acres of bright gardens. While the children's program takes kids ages 5 to 12, there are also activities such as arts and crafts designed for children as young as age 2, accompanied by parents.

The attractive guest rooms differ in size and view. In addition to regular hotel rooms, the one-bedroom villas comfortably sleep four. Vacationers splash in the huge swimming pool, rimmed by waterfalls and five whirlpools, or relax at the beach. You can also go kayaking, windsurfing, snorkeling, scuba diving, sailing, and fishing. There is a fitness center and four restaurants, from casual to elegant. Two 18-hole championship golf courses, both designed by Jack Nicklaus, and tennis courts are within walking distance at 800/acre Kauai Lagoons.

THE BANYAN HARBOR RESORT, 3411 Wilcox Road, Lihue, HI 96766. Tel. 808/245-7333 or 800/422-6926, www.vacation-kauai.com. 148 units. Rates begin at $155 (two-bedroom). Major credit cards.

A reader from Ventura, California, wrote to me with high praise for this condominium on Kalapaki Bay (across from the Kauai Marriott Resort & Beach Club). The individually decorated ocean- or garden view one- and two-bedroom apartments are a serious bargain, especially if you factor in the pool, barbecue area, tennis court, shuffleboard courts, washer/dryer in each unit, and the proximity of the beach. Golf at a nearby course is easily arranged. The grounds may be rather undistinguished, but the economical rate may be a deciding factor. Children enjoy the weekly hula and lei-making classes.

Kilauea

KILAUEA LAKESIDE ESTATE, Tel. 310-379-7842 (in California), www.kauaihoneymoon.com. Rates begin at $595 a night for up to six adults, plus children.

If you're in the market for a true fantasy vacation, this flourishing five-acre peninsula hits the spot. In your own private three-bedroom, three-bathroom house surrounded by botanical gardens, you can have all the perks of a luxury resort—except with total privacy, with the exclusive use of a 20-acre freshwater lake, and (when shared with friends or extended family) without the high price tag.

The lake is perfect for swimming, kayaking, canoeing, rowing, and fishing. Staff members can teach kids to angle for the plentiful bass and catfish and a chef can clean and prepare the fish they catch for dinner. Children get a kick out of the little island in the middle of the lake, with its tree house, diving platform, and rope for swinging into the water. Want to take hula or surfing lessons? In the mood for a lomilomi massage? Ready for a guided kayak tour in the open ocean? Owner Steve Hunt is happy to design your vacation any way you like.

Around the grounds, children can pick everything from bananas, mangoes, and papayas to lilikoi (passionfruit) and scores of other tropical fruits. Orchids, heliconia, and plumeria are among the 150 varieties of flowers that splash the property with intense color. Both children and adults can practice their swings at the one-hole golf course and miniature putting green. (Clubs are provided.) Walk along the stream, search for petroglyphs (ancient rock carvings), explore the tropical rainforest, find the waterfall, or simply cool out in a hammock.

Across the road, you can be the first to make footprints along the ten miles of secluded beaches, where sandcastles are the only type of buildings allowed. Bird lovers will be pleased to know that this hideaway is adjacent to the Kilauea Point Wildlife Refuge. The shops, restaurants, and other attractions of Princeville resort and the towns of Kilauea and Kapaa are also nearby.

Up to six adults (plus children on single beds and futons) can sleep in the main house at Kilauea Lakeside Estate. Amenities of this spacious, sunny home include cable TV (including a big-screen TV in the living room), CD-player, VCR, a bathtub large enough for two, an outdoor hot shower, a gas barbecue grill, and a washer/dryer. Planning a family reunion? You can also rent additional cottages.

Princeville & Hanalei

The beaches along this coast can be too rough for swimming during the winter, but they calm down during the summer.

PRINCEVILLE RESORT, P.O.Box 3069, Princeville, HI 96722. Tel. 808/826-9644 or 800/826-4400, www.princeville.com. 252 rooms. Rates begin at $475. Major credit cards.

This resort is terraced into a cliff above the beach. As you drive into the porte cochere, you'll feel as though you're driving right into the huge lobby, which is behind a tall wall of glass sliding doors. Inside, the two- or three-story windows dazzle with fabulous views of Hanalei Bay and the jagged Bali Hai mountains. Sunshine pouring in through skylights in the ceiling glints off Italian marble. (The only problem is that the floors can be quite slippery when it rains.) Antiques catch the eye, such as the 18th-century Flemish tapestry of children playing. One fireplace is near the entrance and another is found in the living room, where the lobby bar is. Here travelers relax in hefty couches and chairs while absorbing the view or listening to nightly live music. The ambience is one of quiet elegance.

The spacious swimming pool area sports a swim-up bar, three half-moon-shaped Jacuzzis, one of the hotel's three restaurants, and a children's pool. (The children's program takes kids from age 5 to 12.) A fitness center is near the pool. Connecting guestrooms are available. Some are graced with imported antiques, whirlpool bathtubs, VCRs and lanais. All rooms also have snazzy marble baths with double sinks accented with gold-plated fixtures. Transportation to the Princeville golf courses, extensive health spa, tennis courts, and shops is complimentary.

HANALEI BAY RESORT, 5380 Honiki Road, Princeville, HI 96722. Tel. 808/826-6522 or 800/827-4427, www.hanaleibaykauai.com. 280 rooms. Rates begin at $190. Major credit cards.

Banana trees, palms and other tropical foliage flourish throughout the extensive grounds of this clifftop condominium-hotel. In addition to Bali Hai Restaurant, which serves Pacific Rim cuisine, there's Happy Talk Lounge, eight tennis courts, adult and children's swimming pools, and a huge whirlpool on the premises. Transportation is provided around the property and to or from the beach (about a five-minute walk away) and golf course. Guest quarters are quite spacious. Hotel rooms are available as well as studios (with kitchenettes) and one-, two- and three-bedroom suites. Lanais come with absorbing views. The top-floor units of these low-rise buildings have lofts. Hotel rooms share coin-operated laundry facilities while suites have their own laundry and ice machines.

Chapter 13

MOLOKAI WITH KIDS

Although Molokai is the closest neighbor island to Oahu, it couldn't possibly be more different. Lying about 25 miles across Kaiwi Channel, it is considered by many to be the most Hawaiian member of the archipelago. This is in part because Molokai is home to more descendants of the original inhabitants of the island chain than anywhere else in the state. But this "authentic" perception is also due to the rural island's sleepy pace, the friendliness of its people, and its historic sights, such as ancient fishponds, crumbling *heiau* (temples), and legend-laden valleys.

Molokai has a smattering of hotels, condominiums, and vacation rental homes, but residents have little use for the concept of tourism. No buildings rise higher than three stories, and traffic lights and shopping malls are nonexistent. Kaunakakai (COW-nah-kah-KIE), the only real town, consists of one main street lined with weathered, single-story shops. Visitors are happily absorbed into the gentle life of the island, where people often stop what they are doing to watch the sun set. Molokai draws nature-loving families, those who thrive on hiking, horseback riding, and kayaking, or vacationers simply looking to kick back.

Just eight miles across the Pacific, the high rises of Maui's Kaanapali Beach resort seem to be in another world. Part of Maui County, Molokai is Hawaii's fifth largest island. Only Lanai, eight miles to the south, is less developed. A long, narrow strip of land some 261 square miles in size, Molokai was formed by two main volcanoes. Maunaloa stands 1,381 feet tall in the parched and prairie-like west while 4,970-foot Kamakou soars in the flourishing east.

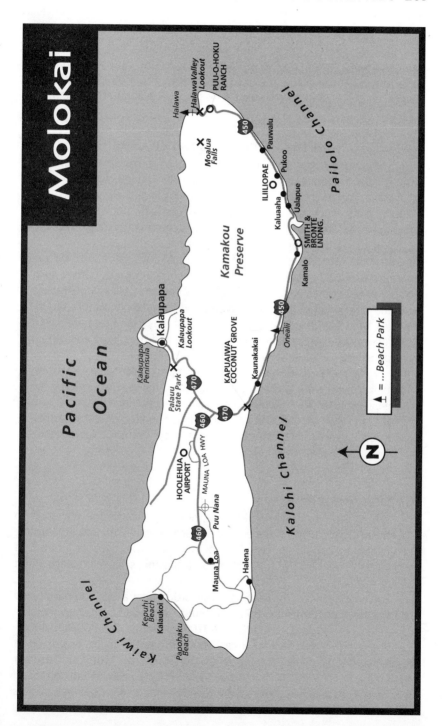

Also lush, the north shore is treated to some 245 inches of annual rainfall, which has created magnificent ravines. Clouds cling to multi-hued mountainsides. Where the elements have cracked the earth apart, gashes of red dirt peer through the green. At the bottom of a 1,600-foot cliff, huge, pancake-flat Kalaupapa Peninsula seems to be a geologic afterthought.

Let the Games (and Dance) Begin

As soon as you arrive, ask hotel staff or other residents if there are any special events taking place on Molokai during your stay. For instance, if you are here on the third Saturday in January, you and your kids might enjoy the annual **Makahiki festival**. Once lasting from October to February, this season of peace was a respite from the frequent warfare among ancient Hawaiians.

In the abbreviated revival celebrated on Molokai since 1981, visitors can watch local children compete in traditional Hawaiian games, such as ulu maika (lawn bowling), 'o'o ihe (spear hurling), kukini (foot races), pohaku ho'oikaika (lifting or throwing a weighty rock), hukihuki (tug-of-war), uma (hand-wrestling while standing), haka moa (arm wrestling within a circle while standing on one leg), and moa pahe'e (sliding a wooden dart across the grass through two sticks).

Hula is said to have been born on the slopes of Maunaloa, in western Molokai, where the goddess Laka learned to dance. Held in May, the annual **Molokai Ka Hula Piko Festival** commemorates this birth, with local handicrafts and food in addition to music and dance performances. For details about other Molokai happenings, visit www.molokaievents.com.

Getting Around

Driving is pure pleasure in Molokai, not only because the scenery is so spectacular (particularly in the east), but because you'll run into little traffic. Just watch out for mongooses, fond of dashing across the road in front of moving vehicles. It's difficult to get lost on this island, since main roads aren't plentiful.

For renting wheels (the best way to get around), try a local company called **Island Kine Auto Rental,** Tel. 866/527-7368 or 808/553-5242, www.molokai-car-rental.com, **Budget,** Tel. 800/527-0700, or **Dollar,** Tel. 800/800-4000.

If you don't plan to rent a car, you can arrange to be picked up at Hoolehua Airport, near the center of the island, by **Molokai Outdoor Activities,** Tel 877/553-4477 or 808/553-4477. By the way, in addition to taxi service, this company arranges kayaking and biking excursions as well as tours of the island.

For an hour and 45 minute ferry ride to a neighboring island, board the **Maui** or **Molokai Princess**, Tel. 866/307-6524, running between Kaunakakai Harbor and Lahaina. Stroll through the picturesque streets of Maui's old whaling port, now packed with shops, restaurants, and historical sights. Roundtrip fare is about $85 for adults, $43 for children ages 4 to 12, and free for kids age three and younger. (Note that the water can be rough at times, so this may not be the best bet for those who get seasick.)

Top Sunset-Watching Spots
1. Kapuaiwa Coconut Grove
2. Kaunakakai Pier
3. the Ninth Fairway at Kaluakoi Golf Course

At the end of the day, join Molokaians talking story in beach chairs, with coolers at hand, while taking in the spectacular light show.

Where Are We Going Now?
Sights & Adventures
KAPUAIWA COCONUT GROVE, just west of Kaunakakai, along the main road.

In the mid-1800s, these neat rows of coconut palms were planted (and nicknamed) for Prince Lot, a Molokai resident who went on to become King Kamehameha V. This is one of Hawaii's few remaining royal coconut groves.

CHURCH ROW, across the street from Kapuaiwa Coconut Grove, just west of Kaunakakai.

A handful of late 19th century houses of worship stand along this picturesque stretch. The simple architecture of these churches reflects the plain lifestyles of Hawaii's early missionaries.

PURDY'S MACADAMIA NUT FARM, Hoolehua, near the airport, Tel. 567-6601, Web site: www.molokai.com/eatnuts.

A family-run business since 1980, this macadamia nut grove was acquired by the Purdy family through the Hawaiian Homestead Act, which gave people of Hawaiian ancestry opportunities to return to the land. While touring the farm, which sells natural, hand-picked macadamia nuts (raw or roasted) along with mac-nut honey, you'll learn some mac-facts: For instance, it takes about seven years for a macadamia tree to bear fruit and the first of these trees came to Hawaii in 1882 from the rain forests of Queensland, Australia.

PALA'AU STATE PARK, off Route 470, north coast, central Molokai.

Picnic tables, bathrooms, camping facilities, and awesome views from a 1,000-foot elevation make this park a favorite among visitors. Children (and

Early Outsourcing

During the 1920s, Dole and Del Monte leased sections of Molokai, and pineapple plantations flourished at the hands of Japanese and Filipino immigrant workers. The plantation towns of **Maunaloa** and **Kualapuu** were born. Then in the 1970s, the pineapple industry began to die on Molokai, ironically, because owners had found that doing business in places such as the Philippines was far more profitable than having Filipinos and others work in Hawaii. Tourism and diversified agriculture have replaced pineapple as the island's economic base.

Before pineapple flourished in West Molokai, some 64,000 of these acres were owned by King Kamehameha V during the late 1800s. Isolated in the west, Maunaloa has come back to life since the current landowner, a working cattle ranch, built **The Lodge & Beach Village at Molokai Ranch**. Here vacationers may stay in solar-powered canvas bungalows on platform decks or in regular hotel rooms.

adults) love walking barefoot through the ironwood forest on a carpet of pine needles along a trail that leads to Kauleonanahoa. More commonly known as **Phallic Rock**, this huge stone points skyward. It has been shaped by the elements—and with a little help from human hands, no doubt. In the old days, women who hadn't been successful in becoming pregnant would sit on the rock in an attempt to awaken their fertility.

Another trail leads to **Kalaupapa Lookout**, which takes in the peninsula (officially named Makanalua), which looks like a huge tongue protruding from the bottom of the 1,664-foot sea cliffs. This isolated peninsula is where people with Hansen's Disease (leprosy) were once banished. Here's the story:

The tragedy and triumph that made **Kalaupapa Peninsula** famous began after the arrival of foreigners in Hawaii. Since the indigenous population had been without contact with outsiders for so many centuries, they had no natural immunities to the communicable diseases of other peoples. When Westerners arrived, bringing their new illnesses, Hawaiians were unable to combat these alien germs. Within a century after the arrival of Caucasians in 1778, the population had shrunk from some 300,000 to a mere 50,000.

Hawaii's first known case of Hansen's Disease (leprosy) occurred in 1835. The frightfully disfiguring affliction was so contagious that King Kamehameha V, thinking first and foremost of protecting the larger general population, began banishing the victims to Molokai's isolated Makanalua Peninsula (a.k.a. Kalaupapa). Like the walls of a fortress, the sheer cliffs that rise up from this large flat tongue of land quashed any notion of escape. So did the rough water that hurls itself against the glossy black lava rocks on all three sides of the peninsula. Treated like criminals, the exiles were not even provided with building materials or other supplies. They were forced to live out in the blazing sun by day or in the chilly air at night. Some found shelter under trees or in caves. Others fashioned makeshift driftwood huts.

When 33-year-old **Father Damien Joseph de Veuster**, a Catholic priest from Belgium, arrived in Kalaupapa in 1873, he planned to stay only a few months. But within two days he decided to remain indefinitely. He turned **St. Philomena** chapel into a hospital until a permanent one could be built. He himself slept under a tree until every other resident had shelter. This tireless self-sacrificing man built another church and served as a doctor, farmer, and gravedigger.

In 1889, Father Damien himself died of Hansen's Disease. In April 1989, on the 100th anniversary of his death, a week-long tribute to this revered priest took place in Hawaii. Today, leprosy can be treated with sulfone antibiotics. While these miraculous drugs were introduced to Kalaupapa in 1946, the isolation laws were not abolished until 1969. Although most victims of the ailment have left the peninsula, some have chosen to remain, having known no other lifestyle since they were either born here or brought as young children.

MOLOKAI MULE RIDE, Pala'au State Park, north shore, central Molokai, Tel. 567-6088 or 800/567-7550, www.muleride.com. Monday through Saturday, 7:50am to 3:15pm. Make reservations at least two weeks in advance. All riders must be at least 16 years of age and physically fit, and must weigh no more than 225 pounds. Cost: $150. (Packages including round-trip airfare available from Maui or Oahu.)

I've taken this mule ride along the narrow, zigzag trail down the 1,600-foot cliff to Kalaupapa Peninsula several times, and it remains the most memorable, moving part of my visits to Molokai. Completed in 1887, the trail is just over three miles long. (Participants are asked to bring rain gear since the clouds are often dripping up here. As riders descend, the weather usually dries up quickly, so the trip isn't called off unless a downpour at the top is extremely heavy.)

On automatic pilot, the sure-footed mules safely navigate the trail's 26 switchbacks. (The first time I rode a mule, I was very surprised to discover how much smoother it is than riding a horse.) With sheer drop-offs on one side, the cliff walls are festooned with clinging ferns and unusual flowers on the other. Look for clusters of air plants, whose tubular sprouts resemble the intact, empty skins of grapes. Tree branches form umbrellas. When you reach the pancake flat peninsula that seemed many miles down from above, you'll come out along a shore covered with charcoal rocks and boulders that give way to a black sand beach. If it's the right time of year (winter), you might spot whales. With the mountains in the distance, you'll look back at the cliff and be amazed that you were "topside," as residents say, not long before.

After tying up the mules, you'll climb into a van for a tour conducted by one of the last remaining residents of the community where people with Hansen's Disease (leprosy) were exiled before antibiotics were discovered to treat the illness. Sights include St. Philomena Church, which once served as a hospital; medical facilities; houses; graveyards; a bookstore in a former Buddhist temple; and the memorial to Blessed Father Damien, the 19th century Belgian priest who made such a difference in the lives of ailing residents until he himself contracted the disease and died. Cameras are welcome, but photos of residents are not allowed. Sightseers are served a (very light) picnic lunch before returning on mule-back (or leaving on foot, if they have arranged to do so).

Scenic Drives

Take a drive east of Kaunakakai and you'll treat yourselves to some of the island's best scenery, both natural and human-made. Plan to spend the good part of a day, especially if you want to have time for leisurely swimming and picnicking. (But don't wander off onto hiking trails without clear directions, maps, or an authorized guide, since much of the area is private property.)

Kaloko'eli Fishpond is among a mere handful of ponds that remain out of more than 60 that once bordered the southern shore. Many of them were constructed during the 13th century. These rocky walls enclosed fish so that they could be fattened up while protected from all but human predators. When they were plump enough, they were netted for the *alii*. You'll see some beautiful homes in this area. If you drive up to Kawela Plantation, a residential development, you'll have a great view of the fish pond down below.

On the *makai* (ocean) side of the road at Kamalo, watch closely for the **Smith and Bronte Monument** that honors Ernest Smith and Emory Bronte. On their way from California to Honolulu, the pair survived the crash landing of the world's first transpacific flight in 1927. Nearby is **St. Joseph's Catholic Church**, built in 1876 by Blessed Father Damien, famous for his selfless work with victims of Hansen's Disease (leprosy) who had been banished to Kalaupapa Peninsula. He served as pastor to the rest of the island as well. A few miles farther down the road, he also built **Our Lady of Seven Sorrows**, which stands behind a tall wooden cross planted in the spacious lawn. In the background looms majestic Mt. Kamakou, Molokai's tallest mountain. From the waterfront, you can gaze across to Maui and Lanai.

Along Highway 450 at mile marker 15, just east of Kamalo on the *mauka* (mountain) side of the road, a trail leads to **Ili'ili'opa'e Heiau**. Constructed during the sixteenth century, this sprawling temple is the second largest in the state. It once spread over more than five acres. Honoring Hawaii's highest gods, its four terraces were 150 feet wide and 50 feet tall. The rocks used to build it were lugged all the way from the Wailau Valley, separated from this shore by a mountain. Human sacrifices were performed at this heiau.

Near **Wavecrest** condominium, the vegetation is extremely lush, and craggy mountains soar on the left. The road narrows and the greenery becomes increasingly thick, with banana trees and palms along the coast in the Pukoo area. More trees appear, each one taller than the last, with vines clothing the entire length of their trunks.

There is good swimming as well as camping at sandy **Waialua Beach**. Nearby you might come to a self-service stand piled with fresh fruit—simply leave your money in a box. Once you see **Murphy's Beach**, you'll begin climbing uphill on a narrow, winding road through **Pu'u O Hoku Ranch**. From here you'll have spectacular views of the rocky shoreline, crashing waves, and endless greenery, including tall stands of bamboo. At **Rock Point**, a fishing and surfing area, rugged outcroppings stand like huge anthills along the coast. Soon the eye takes in rolling hills and verdant open land.

Finally, you reach dramatic **Halawa Valley Overlook**. Historians believe this valley is Molokai's oldest settlement, dating back to about A.D. 650. Few people have lived here since the massive tidal wave swept through in 1946, destroying both homes and crops. Just before the road begins to dip into the valley, the grove of kukui nut trees stands in memory of Lanikaula, the beloved *kahuna* (high priest). This is the most sacred part of the whole island. The wide stream that once fed the valley's farms meanders through the lush greenery before pouring into the ocean. This shore was once a favorite surfing spot among *alii* (chiefs).

Beaches

Molokai's best beaches lie along the west coast, with views of Oahu in the distance. However, during the winter, when waves grow their tallest, on this coast it's best to stick to dry land. The narrow south shore beaches that run past visitor accommodations in the Kaunakakai area aren't especially attractive, but their waters remain more placid year round. Here are Molokai's most appealing sandy stretches:

Kepuhi Beach, Kaluakoi Resort.
There's a constant breeze at this half-mile stretch of white sand that individual Kaluakoi Resort guests often have to themselves. Be careful during the winter when waves are the roughest.

Papohaku Beach, Kaluakoi Resort, West Molokai.
One hundred yards wide, three miles long, and enclosed by rugged lava flows, this is Hawaii's most expansive white sand beach. Wells were once dug for the fresh water that gets trapped in the rocky outcroppings in back of the sand. Picnic facilities, barbecues, showers, and restrooms are provided. Tent camping is permitted amid the palms and kiawe trees on the spacious lawn that backs the sand.

Pohakuloa Beach, about 1.5 miles past Papohaku Beach, West Molokai. This tranquil cove is especially popular on weekends, particularly among families. However, on Molokai, there is no such thing as a crowded beach. Swimming is excellent most of the year. An outdoor shower is on the grounds.

Po'olau Beach, about a half-mile past the Kaluakoi Resort.

Locals sometimes fish from surfboards off this inviting white shore. The waves are often good for surfing. A pleasant setting for camping out, this beach has a view that reaches all the way to Kaneohe, 35 miles away on Oahu, when the sky is clear.

Onealii Beach Park, off Highway 450 on the south shore, near Hotel Molokai.

While cooling off in calm waters, you'll gaze across to the islands of Lanai and Maui. Although the shore is narrow here, this is the most appealing of the south shore beaches, where nature has been stingy with the sand. Tree-shaded picnic tables, outdoor showers, and restrooms make this a good choice if you're staying in the area. Impromptu concerts, beach parties, and other frivolity often take place here.

Halawa Beach Park, at the eastern end of Highway 450.

At the far eastern end of the island, this dark sand beach is a bonus after the spectacular snaking drive through this lush region. This crescent was once favored by Hawaiian royalty for surfing. Don't go near the water during the winter, when currents are extremely dangerous. However, during the summer, swimming is usually fine. Even when you're not swimming, the setting is wonderful, so take advantage of the picnic facilities. Outdoor showers mean you don't have to feel gritty during the return drive.

Sports & Other Activities

With its sporting goods store and wide selection of Molokai T-shirts, **Molokai Fish & Dive** in Kaunakakai, Tel. 553-5926, www.molokaifishanddive.com, has become a convenient place to book all kinds of island action. From sport fishing, winter whale watching trips, and scuba (for certified divers) to cultural hikes, mountain biking, and cowboy roundups, this is the hook-up.

Although many activities are designed for families to do together, this company also offers **Keiki Adventure Days**, when children ages 5 to 12 can attend half-day ($40) or full-day ($80) supervised programs on their own. While you have some time to yourselves, the kids can learn how to make shell necklaces, string leis, and hula dance, explore tide pools, or go kayaking and mountain biking. You'll need to provide drinks, snacks, and lunch. And don't forget their bathing suits, sunscreen, water shoes, and a change of clothes.

·For a foray into lei making, the whole family can take the two-hour class and **Plumeria Farm Tour** (adults: $25; children: $12). Walk through the fragrant orchard, learn how to pick the best blossoms, then sew your own leis. Be sure to bring our own drinks, along with sunscreen and cash (since you may be tempted to buy additional leis—which you can keep fresh for days in plastic bags in the refrigerator, by the way).

Here are some other Molokai Fish & Dive offerings:

·**Biking.** Children age 10 or older can join you on the easy 6- to 8-mile guided downhill mountain bike ride ($40), during which you lose 1,100 feet elevation on the descent. Don't worry about peddling back uphill—you can return to the base camp by van. Younger children can ride on a carriage pulled behind a parent's bike. If you'd rather explore on your own, Molokai Fish & Dive will help with bike rentals.

·**Horseback Riding.** Has your child always dreamed of being a cowboy (or cowgirl)? **The Paniolo Roundup** is his (or her) chance. Learning how to approach, hold, and sort cattle, and participating in penning races, children age 10 and older (and adults) get a real kick out of training to be paniolos (Hawaiian cowboys). They also compete with each other in obstacle courses. Looking for something a bit tamer? Then go for the **Kaupoa Beach Trail Ride.** Both are $80 for 90 minutes to 2 hours, and long pants and covered shoes are required.

·**Ocean Kayaking.** Glide through tropical mangroves, learn how to throw ancient Hawaiian fishnets, and explore Samoan crab ponds during the guided **Palaau Reef** paddle ($85, including lunch and beverages). You'll also have a chance to snorkel at the reef, and maybe even swim with turtles. Be sure to try surf kayaking on the waves. While the whole excursion lasts for six hours, you'll spend part of the time being towed back to the starting point so you don't have to paddle against the wind and currents. If you prefer to strike out on your own, Molokai Fish & Dive will provide you with a cell phone, just in case, while you spend four hours kayaking and snorkeling around **Kamalo Reef** ($40, without lunch or beverages). To ride alone, children must be at least age 12. Otherwise, they can ride with you.

Golf

Residents say that you'll find the nine-hole **Ironwood Hills Golf Course,** Tel. 567-6000, at Kalae, in central Molokai to be the most laid-back golf course in the state of Hawaii. Originally built for executives of Del Monte, it sits some 1200 feet upcountry, with stately trees, cool breezes, and wonderful views. Here, you don't have to dress the part, act the part, or even pretend to be a golfer. Carts are available and if there isn't anyone at the club house when you get there, the course is on an honor system. Just pay your $14 greens fee (and $14 cart fee) when you finish.

In dry West Molokai, the **Kaluakoi Golf Club**, Tel. 552-0255, overlooks Oahu across the Kaiwi Channel. Rentals of clubs, shoes, and pull carts are available at this 18-hole course, where the greens fee is about $40 and carts run around $25.

Kite-Flying

When someone on Molokai tells you to "go fly a kite," don't take it as an insult. You are being directed to **The Big Wind Kite Factory**, Tel. 552-2364, www.molokai.com/kites, in Maunaloa town, in the west. Run by former comedy writer Jonathan Socher, this shop sells an amazing array of colorful high-quality nylon kites and windsocks, most handmade on the premises. From hula girls and endangered animals to multi-string controllable kites, no two are exactly alike. You can even order a custom-designed kite or windsock. Prices range from about $16 to more than $500! (You can easily pack what you buy or have it shipped home.) Watch the craftspeople in action in the factory. Then take a free kite-flying lesson in the park next door.

Farm Fresh

For bananas, mangoes, papayas, and other local fruits and vegetables, stop at **Bill's Farm**, in Molokai Agricultural Park, Hoolehua, near the airport. **Kumu Farms**, in Kualapuu, central Molokai, sells fresh herbs and specialty sauces along with its papaya. Nearby, **Plantation Store Coffees of Hawaii** is the place to go for 100% Molokai grown coffee and homemade jams and jellies, plus arts and crafts. More handicrafts, fruits, vegetables, and herbs are on hand at the **Kaunakakai Farm & Craft Market** every Saturday morning across from the library in town.

I'm Hungry!

If you're into unpretentious restaurants that serve as local social centers, and enjoy home-style food from a variety of ethnic backgrounds, then Molokai is your island. Saimin (a hearty local noodle soup), poi and plate lunches, Filipino stews, Chinese chicken with cashew nuts, Korean ribs, New York strip steak—it's all here. The smallest and least expensive places line Ala Malama Street in Kaunakakai. For instance, while some call **Oviedo's Lunch Counter** a "greasy spoon," others can't get enough of the adobos (stews), made with turkey, beef, pig's feet, or mongo beans. Dessert here might be rocky road or mint chocolate chip ice cream.

At nearby **Kanemitsu Bakery and Coffee Shop**, choose among raisin nut, cheese, onion cheese, brown wheat, and mildly sweet Molokai breads. For the widest selection, be sure to arrive early. Hundreds of loaves are baked here each day, but they are often sold out within an hour and a half of the bakery's 5:30am opening! The delicious Mexican butternut, sesame, and macadamia nut cookies are also baked fresh daily.

Along with pizza, **Molokai Pizza Café**, on Kaunakakai Place in town, serves burgers, sandwiches, and pasta. On your way to the beach or to explore the island? Consider stopping for takeout at **Molokai Drive Inn** on Kamoi Street in town. The saimin and the mahi-mahi sandwiches are good. Another popular choice for picnic provisions is **Outpost Natural Foods**, a deli on Makaena Place.

When you're ready to do your own cooking, you'll find **grocery stores** in Maunaloa, Kualapuu, Kaunakakai, and at the mile 16 marker in East Molokai.

For sit-down restaurant meals with atmosphere, here are your best bets:
MAUNALOA ROOM, Molokai Ranch Lodge, Maunaloa, West Molokai, Tel. 660-2725. Breakfast, lunch, and dinner. Moderate to Expensive.

This is the most upscale dining spot on Molokai—but remember, most restaurants on this island are very low key. Along with your steak, seafood, and other basics, you'll be treated to expansive views of prairie-like West Molokai.

HOTEL MOLOKAI, Kamiloloa, Kaunakakai, Tel. 553-5347. Open daily for breakfast, lunch, and dinner. Inexpensive to Moderate.

At this al fresco oceanside dining room, dinner often comes with entertainment, perhaps a singer strumming an ukulele or a hula dancer, but the sunset is usually the star of the show. While the steak and prime rib can be pretty ordinary, the coconut shrimp has a loyal following. Kids may enjoy the virgin versions of the imaginative tropical drinks.

KAMUELA'S COOKHOUSE, Highway 470 and Uwao Street, Kualapuu, near the airport, central Molokai. Tel. 808/567-9655. Open daily, 7am to 8pm. Inexpensive.

A handsome weathered wooden building trimmed with lush vegetation houses this local favorite. Island artwork decorates the cozy dining room. Patrons gravitate toward the chicken katsu, mahi-mahi sandwiches, and saimin. Burgers, salads, and stir-fried or teriyaki beef or chicken are also served. For many, the highlight of a meal here is a slice of macadamia nut or chocolate macadamia nut pie. (If your accommodation has a refrigerator, you might be tempted to buy a whole pie to take with you.) Arrive early for dinner. The menu sometimes shrinks near closing time.

Which One is My Bed?

The island's main hotel (actually a lodge and bungalows for soft camping) is tucked away in arid West Molokai, along with condos, a golf course, and some of the best beaches. More small accommodations are scattered across the island, becoming fewer and farther between as you head toward the flourishing east. Crowds on Molokai just don't exist, so no matter what part of the island you park your bags, you'll *really* be able to get away.

For information about vacation home rentals (especially in East Molokai), contact **Swenson's Real Estate,** Tel. 808/553-8334 or 800/367-2984, www.molokai-vacation-rental.com, or **Dunbar Beachfront Cottages,** Tel. 800/673-0520 or 808/558-8153.

Note that most rates for condos and private homes are based on a minimum three-night to one-week stay, so nightly rates may be higher for shorter stays or lower for longer visits.

West Molokai

THE LODGE & BEACH VILLAGE AT MOLOKAI RANCH, 100 Maunaloa Highway, Maunaloa, Molokai, HI 96770, Tel. 808/552-2741 or 888/627-8082, www.molokai-ranch.com. Lodge rooms begin at $300 (22 rooms). Beach Village bungalows begin at $195 (40 two-bedroom bungalows). Children under age 12 stay free with parents. Major credit cards.

Real estate in parched West Molokai has gone through many transformations over the years, from royal land to pineapple plantations to East African wildlife safari land. Many of today's visitors come because they like the *idea* of camping out more than actually camping out. So they book a solar-powered (and dimly lit) two-bedroom canvas bungalow here at the Beach Village, which is popular among families with children.

Set amid palm trees and built on platforms, all units are close to double-crescent white-sand Kaupo Beach. They come with either a queen-size bed in one room and twins in the other or a queen in each. Bathrooms (with sink, composting toilet, shower, and amenities) are open air. Solar energy gives you hot running water and ceiling fans. You won't find a refrigerator in your room, but the cooler will come in handy. From the decks of some bungalows, you can spot humpback whales during winter months and spinner dolphins year-round. Throughout the grounds, hammocks—perfect spots for sunset-watching—provide respites from ocean kayaking, horseback riding, archery, mountain biking, and hiking along sea cliffs. Breakfast, lunch, and dinner buffets are served al fresco in an oceanfront pavilion.

For Molokai's version of fine dining, head to the Maunaloa Room, at the Lodge, eight miles away and linked to the Beach Village by an hourly shuttle. In the quiet town of Maunaloa, perched 1200 feet above the sea, the Lodge offers panoramic views of the countryside and the Pacific. Guests chat in the living room by the two-story stone fireplace, check in with the office in the den (with computer and wireless internet access), work out at the fitness center, and swim in the heated outdoor pool. Rooms come with elegant touches you might expect at a luxury resort, such as claw-foot bathtubs, separate rain-simulated showers, pedestal sinks, bathrobes, and wet bars, along with cable

TV, clock radios, refrigerators, high-speed data ports, and irons and ironing boards.

Thinking about visiting Maui also? Ask about the two-island package that includes four nights at **Napili Kai Beach Resort**, one of my absolute favorite places in all of Hawaii.

KE NANI KAI RESORT, Kaluakoi Resort, P.O. Box 289, Maunaloa, HI 96770. Tel. 808/552-2761 or 800/535-0085, www.marcresorts.com. 120 rooms. Rates begin at $180 for a one-bedroom unit. Major credit cards.

This condominium has a pleasant residential feel. One- and two-bedroom units each have a fully-equipped kitchen and washer/dryer. Pleasant rooms open onto lanais. The two-story townhouses overlook colorful gardens and the par 72 oceanfront Kaluakoi golf course. Tennis courts, a swimming pool, a whirlpool, and barbecues are among the other facilities. The beach, which can be seen from some rooms, is about a five-minute walk away. Housekeeping service is provided every three days. Ceiling fans and natural breezes cool apartments instead of air-conditioning.

The office is open from 8am to 4pm, so if you'll be checking in or out before or after hours, be sure to make arrangements beforehand to pick up your key or finalize your departure.

KALUAKOI VILLAS, 1131 Kaluakoi Road, Maunaloa, HI 96770. Tel. 808/552-2721 or 800/367-5004, www.castleresorts.com, 72 units. Rates begin at $145 per unit. Major credit cards.

Choose where you want to stay from an array of ocean-side villas, suites, and studios at this condo neighboring the Kaluakoi Golf course. Some units have wonderful full ocean views while others have partial water views. They all come with lanais, TV/VCRs, kitchenettes with microwaves, daily housekeeping service, and other home-style conveniences. Ceiling fans stand in for air-conditioning. You won't find telephones in units, but messages are relayed to guests from the office or manager. Unlike many condos, where the decor varies from unit to unit according to the owners, these are standardized, and attractively furnished. Vacationing families often get to know each other around the communal barbecue grill.

Central Molokai

HOTEL MOLOKAI, Tel. 808/553-5347 or 800/535-0085, www.hotelmolokai.com. Rates begin at $140. Major credit cards.

The old-style Polynesian-inspired architecture sets beachfront Hotel Molokai apart from the island's other places to stay. While most rooms are small, some (with kitchenettes, a king-size bed, and twin beds) will comfortably accommodate a family of four. The most Hawaiian of Molokai's hotels and condos, Hotel Molokai boasts a friendly staff and a scenic oceanfront restaurant with evening entertainment. Whale watching (during the winter) and snorkeling are good here.

Chapter 14

LANAI WITH KIDS

With excellent golf courses and an exceptional beachfront hotel with a supervised children's program, Lanai is a great choice for families looking for a low-key vacation far from the crowds. Swimming, snorkeling, and fishing are good off Hulopoe Beach (where the island's only oceanfront hotel is located), with its broad stretch of white sand and rugged chocolate-colored cliffs.

During a visit when rustic, 11-room Hotel Lanai was the only game in town, I got into a conversation with a man while I was wandering around the village known as Lanai City. We talked about the impending tripling of hotels on the island. He had mixed feelings, he said. He was glad that people would have more employment opportunities than just picking pineapple, but he was concerned that the small-town flavor of the island would be lost. "Now I guess I'll have to start locking my door," he told me.

When I mentioned that I would be leaving the next day, he insisted on driving me to the airport. And sure enough, there he was the following afternoon, jumping out of his pickup truck to help me with my bags. The Lodge at Koele, the second hotel, opened in the spring of 1990 and the Manele Bay welcomed its first guests in 1991. Now with far more visitors on the island, residents can't be expected to keep up that man's brand of hospitality toward every stranger. However, so much of the openness and generosity that has been Lanai's trademark remains.

Getting Around

There is no public transportation on Lanai. However, if you are guests at Manele Bay, Koele Lodge, or Hotel Lanai, you are welcome to use the

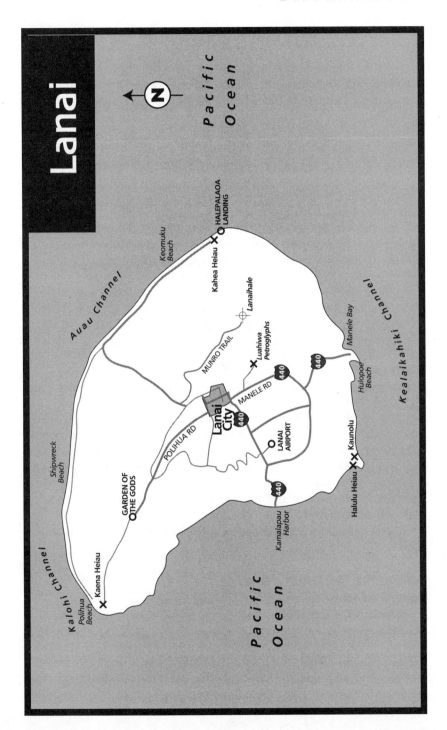

The Way It Was

Habitation came hard to this island. The early Polynesian settlers believed that demons lived here. For five centuries after they had first colonized other parts of Hawaii, they left Lanai alone. In one story, the rebellious son of the king of Maui uprooted some prized breadfruit trees, just to annoy his father. To punish his son, the king sent him to spend a night on uninhabited Lanai. Everyone knew that the evil spirits had always seen to it that no one could survive here until dawn.

The king told his son that if he somehow managed to escape Lanai's wicked forces, he should let the people of Maui know by building a fire that they could see from across the water. An expert in his craft of trickery, the young man fooled the demons into thinking he was in one place when he was really in another, hiding from them throughout the night. To top it off, he sneaked up on a group of these spirits, who had had too much to drink during one of their dances on Mt. Lanaihale, and set them afire.

The king and his entourage saw the blaze and came to collect the son. Shocked by his masterful survival skills, Maui's ruler decided to let the young man help settle Lanai.

complimentary shuttle bus that runs regularly among the three hotels. The shuttle also links the hotels to the airport.

To see anything beyond town, Hulopoe Beach, and the hotels, you'll need to rent a four-wheel drive vehicle and hit the red-dirt roads. Before you set out, make sure you have very clear directions. Although the island is a mere 13 miles wide and 18 miles long, it is easy to get lost driving through the endless fields and the desert-like expanses strewn with rocks and tufts of hearty brush. While searching for one sight or another, you might suddenly discover that you've been going in circles.

The island's only car rental agency is **Dollar Rent a Car**, Tel. 800/533-7808.

Where Are We Going Now?
Sights & Adventures
GARDEN OF THE GODS.

Here in Kanepu'u in northern Lanai, this jumble of golden brown boulders is set against the ocean gleaming in the distance. As the light changes, so do the various hues of the strangely shaped rocks, which cast even stranger shadows. The most dramatic time of day to come is the early morning or late afternoon. On your way, you'll ride through the pumpkin colored, desert-like landscape. The red canyons that open to the Pacific are gorgeous. The wind, by the way, can be amazingly strong in this area.

A LOOK AT THE PAST.

Bits and pieces of old Hawaii are scattered throughout Lanai. Just south of Lanai City, a dirt road leads to **Luahiwa Petroglyphs**, extensive hillside rock carvings of stick figure people, animals, and boats that were probably etched sometime between 1500 and 1700. Near the southern coast, temple sites and more petroglyphs can be seen at **Kaunolu**, while **Kaleina a Kaheekili**, an awesome cliff, was once used as a testing ground of prowess among warriors who leaped off the edge. Crumbling fishing shrines and foundations of old canoe houses remain in the Manele Bay area.

THE "CITY."

Manele Bay hotel guests may take the shuttle into town. Hardly a city despite its name, Lanai City is a trim plantation town of symmetrical cross-hatch streets. It was built to house the people who worked the island's pineapple fields that once dominated the island. Neat gardens ablaze with electric-green banana trees and purple, orange, and red bougainvillea adjoin the small wooden homes. A tranquil park sprawls near the collection of small shops. The town is so informal that the first Hawaiian Bank is located in a private house! Since this upland village is nowhere near the beach and tall triangular Cook Island pines pierce cool, misty air, it's easy to forget that it's on a tropical island.

Beaches

Although there aren't many beaches on Lanai, those that exist are extremely picturesque. The swimming is best at **Hulopoe**, on the south shore, overlooked by the Manele Bay hotel. Here you might see spinner dolphins spiraling out of the water. When **whales** are around (December through

A Sweet Idea

It took more than two decades after the rest of Hawaii had been introduced to foreigners for the first outsider to settle on Lanai. In 1802, Wu Tsin arrived from China with plans to grow sugarcane. But he found the island's dry climate uncooperative.

In 1917, the Baldwins, a wealthy *haole* family from Maui, bought the island of Lanai. No one could get off the ground with sugarcane crops. Some explained that this failure was divine payback since Kahea Heiau had been desecrated in order to build a railroad for transporting the cane. Then, in 1922, Jim Dole had other sweet thoughts. What about a major pineapple plantation? The Baldwins sold the island to him for $1.1 million, and Hawaii's pineapple industry was born.

☙

April), it's not unusual for them to breach right offshore or for one to give birth in the bay.

The first time I came to this beach, when there was only a single 11-room hotel on the island, there was one other person here. This was a weekday, and when I returned on a weekend, the beach was "packed"—with two local families having a barbecue and playing ukuleles. However, despite the added tourism, this is still a wonderful beach and the island's most attractive. Walk or drive up a rocky road (to the left if you're facing the water), and you may see people fishing off the coffee-colored lava cliffs.

Around the point, the striking **monolith**, Pu'upehe, just offshore, is also known as Sweetheart Rock. In front of this huge chocolate chunk, you'll see a cozy cove with even whiter sand than Hulopoe Bay. Hulopoe is the only beach that you can get to on a paved road. You'll need to rent a four-wheel-drive vehicle to visit the others.

With its rust-colored sand and dramatic churning waves, **Kaiolohia Bay**—more commonly called **Shipwreck Beach**—is best for adults who are very strong swimmers. When the water is at its calmest, snorkeling can be fun here along the northeastern shore. You might see some people fishing for lobster. As long as they stick to the sand, kids will enjoy collecting shells. The shore faces Molokai and Maui, whose cloud-ringed heights make for some awesome scenery. Out in the water, you'll see a large rusted ship that was salvaged, later towed, and then became mired here. This coast is very windy, resulting in some strangely shaped boulders along the coast.

You'll reach this beach after twisting and turning down a long paved road with wonderful views of pine trees against a background of the Pacific, Molokai, and Maui. Then you'll turn left onto a tree-shaded road, with branches forming a roof overhead. A few private houses line this road.

Sports & Other Activities

Through your hotel, or directly through **Trilogy Lana'i Ocean Sports**, Tel. 888/MAUI-800, www.visitlanai.com, you can arrange guided **kayak** trips (kids are half price when sharing a kayak with an adult), **snorkeling** excursions, **scuba** trips (for anyone age 12 or older), **catamaran rides**, and even guided **hikes**.

Golf

Although people have described the nine-hole **Cavendish Golf Course**, adjacent to the upland Lodge at Koele, as "very average," you can't beat the price: it's free. But there are no carts and you'll need to take your own clubs. Serious golfers head to the **Experience at Koele**, an 18-hole Greg Norman/ Ted Robinson course near the Lodge, and the 18-hole oceanfront Jack Nicklaus signature beauty, the **Challenge at Manele**, at the Manele Bay hotel, on the south shore. Wild turkeys and other island birds inhabit the lushly landscaped Experience at Koele, loved for its waterfalls. Overlooking the island of Maui, the Manele course sits above rocky cliffs. Bill Gates tied the knot on the 17th hole (the signature hole at Manele), which has become a favorite spot for weddings.

Hiking

Hikers should try the Cook Island pine-lined 8.8 mile **Munro Trail**, which winds up to Lanaihale. From this spot, you'll have a sweeping view of the island, including a dramatic canyon, as well as much of the rest of the state. This difficult hike can take a full day. Older children may enjoy hiking part of the eight miles that connect Shipwreck and Polihua beaches on the windy north shore.

Horseback Riding

Make arrangements through the **Lodge at Koele**, Tel. 565-4000.

Tennis

Check out the courts at the **Lodge at Koele**, Tel. 565-4000, and the **Manele Bay Hotel**, Tel. 565-2000.

Working Out & Spas

For relaxing massages, facials, and other pampering, or to sweat your way to a better body, visit the fitness center at the **Lodge at Koele**, Tel. 565-4000, or the snazzy **Manele Bay hotel** spa, Tel. 565-7700. Spring for an al fresco massage to the sound of the waves, or try a hot rocks massage, or an herbal wrap.

I'm Hungry!

Apart from the upscale dining rooms at the **Lodge at Koele**, Tel. 565-4580 and the **Manele Bay hotel**, Tel. 565-2290, eating out is a low-key affair on Lanai. In town, there are a couple of unassuming breakfast and lunch spots, along with Hotel Lanai, which serves delicious dinners.

All good places to take young children (and to mingle with residents), **Blue Ginger** serves burgers, fries, and fish and chips; **Canoe's Lanai** offers chicken plates along with its burgers; **Café 565** has pizza, subs, and local "plate lunches" on its menu; and **Pele's Other Garden** is a deli known for its sandwiches, soups, salads, pasta, and pizza.

For a special night out, try **Henry Clay's Rotisserie**, Tel. 565-7211, at Hotel Lanai, which serves dinner only. The fireplace at one end of the room takes the chill off cool winter evenings. Expect to find hearty Cajun-inspired dishes, such as Louisiana-style pork ribs, corn bread, Grandma's crab gumbo, and creamy clam chowder. Both the daily fresh catch and the hand-rolled pizza are yummy. More than a few patrons have called the rotisserie chicken here "amazing." Entrees run between $18 and $30. (If your kids need child-size portions, let your server know.)

Which One is My Bed?

MANELE BAY HOTEL, P.O. Box 310, Lanai City, HI 96763. Hulopoe Beach, south shore. Tel. 808/565-7700 or 800/321-4666, www.islandoflanai.com. 250 rooms. Rates begin at $400.

At Lanai's first (and only) luxury beach resort, the lobby (on the third floor of the terraced building) is for admiring, strolling, mingling—not for mundane activities such as checking in. Arriving guests are escorted to their elegant rooms. Along the way they pass murals depicting the plight of the son of the king of Maui who was banished to Lanai to rid it of evil spirits; Oriental rugs; antiques and reproductions; striking sculpture, statues and vases; and Chinese, Hawaiian, and Japanese gardens where lily pads float on ponds.

Some guest rooms overlook the ocean while others gaze out to the flower-filled courtyards and pool. All have lanais and can be cooled by either ceiling fans or air conditioning. The dazzling marble baths come with double sinks and glass-enclosed stall showers in addition to tubs. Video tapes for the VCRs are complimentary.

Two whirlpools sit at the edge of the swimming pool on the broad patio off the lower lobby lounge. Tennis courts, a fitness center, and a health spa help keep vacationers in shape. Jack Nicklaus designed the island's third golf course for the resort, a challenging oceanfront 18-holer. Water sports include scuba diving, snorkeling, and sailing.

Kids age 5 to 12 may take part in the full-day or half-day supervised children's program. Twice a week, this camp also runs in the evening (from 5pm to 10pm) and includes dinner. Parents wanting some alone time on other nights may arrange for a babysitter, through the hotel, who is trained in CPR and first aid.

HOTEL LANAI, P.O. Box 520, Lanai City, HI 96763. Tel. 808/565-7211, 800/262-9912, or 800/795-7211,www.hotellanai.com. 11 rooms. Cottage: $180, plus $10 for a child age 8 or older, including continental breakfast.

Built in 1923 for guests and executives of the Dole Plantation (which once blanketed this island with pineapple fields), this wooden country lodge has lots of character. Rooms in the main building are small, but the adjacent one-room cottage can accommodate two adults in a queen size bed and a child on a fold-up futon.

From the front lanai of the main building, there's a great view of the sun setting between the pine trees. Island residents often gather in the small bar area or on the spacious back lanai after work for drinks and conversation, or in the casual dining room, where dinner is served.

INDEX

Things Change!

Phone numbers, prices, addresses, quality of food, etc, all change. If you come across any new information, we'd appreciate hearing from you. No item is too small! Drop us an email note at: Jopenroad@aol.com, or write us at:

Hawaii with Kids
Open Road Publishing, P.O. Box 284
Cold Spring Harbor, NY 11724

Travel Notes

Travel Notes

Open Road Publishing

U.S.

America's Best Cheap Sleeps, $14.95
America's Most Charming Towns &
   Villages, $16.95
Arizona Guide, $16.95
Boston Guide, $13.95
California Wine Country Guide, $12.95
Colorado Guide, $16.95
Hawaii Guide, $18.95
Hawaii with Kids, $14.95
Las Vegas Guide, $15.95
Las Vegas With Kids, $14.95
National Parks With Kids, $14.95
New Mexico Guide, $16.95
San Francisco Guide, $16.95
Southern California Guide, $18.95
Spa Guide, $14.95
Texas Guide, $16.95
Utah Guide, $16.95
Vermont Guide, $16.95
Walt Disney World Guide, $14.95

Middle East/Africa

Egypt Guide, $17.95
Kenya Guide, $18.95

Eating & Drinking on the Open Road

Eating & Drinking in Paris, $9.95
Eating & Drinking in Italy, $9.95
Eating & Drinking in Spain, $9.95
Eating & Drinking in Latin America, $9.95

Latin America & Caribbean

Bahamas Guide, $13.95
Belize Guide, $16.95
Bermuda Guide, $14.95
Caribbean Guide, $21.95
Caribbean With Kids, $14.95
Central America Guide, $21.95
Chile Guide, $18.95
Costa Rica Guide, $17.95
Ecuador & Galapagos Islands Guide, $17.95
Guatemala Guide, $18.95
Honduras Guide, $16.95

Europe

Czech & Slovak Republics Guide, $18.95
Greek Islands Guide, $16.95
Holland Guide, $17.95
Ireland Guide, $18.95
Italy Guide, $21.95
Italy With Kids, $14.95
London Made Easy, $9.95
Moscow Guide, $16.95
Paris Made Easy, $9.95
Paris with Kids, $14.95
Prague Guide, $14.95
Rome Guide, $14.95
Scotland Guide, $17.95
Spain Guide, $18.95
Turkey Guide, $19.95

Asia

China Guide, $21.95
Japan Guide, $21.95
Philippines Guide, $18.95
Tahiti & French Polynesia Guide, $19.95
Tokyo Guide, $13.95
Thailand Guide, $18.95

For US orders, include $5.00 for postage and handling for the first book ordered; for each additional book, add $1.00. Orders outside US, inquire first about shipping charges (money order payable in US dollars on US banks only for overseas shipments). Send to:
Open Road Publishing, PO Box 284, Cold Spring Harbor, NY 11724